**This book is dedicated to the memory and work of the late**

# Ellis Skolfield

1927 - 2015

"If I have seen further, it is by standing on the shoulders of giants"
**Sir Isaac Newton**

# PROPHECY SHOCK

**Every timeline decoded.**

**Every prophecy connected.**

**The real story finally revealed.**

ASHLEY CHURCH

**NEWTON HOUSE**

Published by Newton House

# Contents

## Foreword:

# A challenge to everything we think we know about prophecy

If you grew up watching classic westerns, you'll be familiar with **Monument Valley** on the Utah / Arizona border. You may not know it by that name, but it's the backdrop to dozens of movies and features a vast horizon broken by huge red, sheer-sided, flat topped, stone monoliths rising abruptly from the desert floor – perhaps with a lone rider in the foreground; and the sun sinking slowly behind a mesa.

That mental picture shapes the way that we view and romanticise the Old West, and it isn't random. It has been *taught* to you.

Acclaimed movie Director John Ford, who made Monument Valley iconic, didn't do so by accident. He used that location to **create an America in the imagination**. He took one striking landscape and let it stand in for an entire era. And it worked so well that it didn't matter that it wasn't true.

The real setting for the cattle towns, gunfights and hard life of the frontier lay largely on the Great Plains and eastern Rockies and looked nothing like Monument Valley – in fact most of the "Old West" was defined by flat plains, few landmarks, and vast, endless miles.

But Ford's image of the West endured and was so regularly repeated by those who came after him that it became *more real than the reality* and the power of that image has become so pervasive that it has framed the way that we've pictured the Old West ever since. We believe it - not because we're foolish, but because the image is so compelling that it *feels* true.

In a very real sense, that's exactly what has happened to the Churches view of Bible prophecy. Over generations, Christians have inherited a prophetic "landscape" that feels just like the real thing. We've absorbed a set of assumptions, a cast of characters, and a storyline that seems obvious simply because it's everywhere - preached, charted, published, and repeated.

Like the Old West of the movies, it has become the default background against which we interpret everything.

But it's based on a fiction. Just like the Old West, the prophecies of the Bible are set in different locations to those that we've been led to believe. And it's not just the locations that are different. Those prophecies are also about different events, set in a different time – and, most importantly, most of them are about a different people: **the Jews**.

This news will be a bombshell to many: people who believe that most of the prophecies in the Books of Daniel and Revelation are about Christians and about events that will unfold in the near future. To be fair, many of these will be people who also love and pray for the Jews.

People who support Israel publicly. People who admire Jewish resilience and feel genuine affection for the land and its story.

But love and understanding are not the same thing. You can love the Old West and still believe that it looked like Monument Valley. You can love Israel and still carry a prophetic framework that, without meaning to, **pushes Israel off-centre stage from its own story** – and turns the Jewish people into supporting actors in what is treated as mainly the Churches end-times drama.

That doesn't make us dishonest. It just makes us human. We inherit pictures. We keep them because they're familiar. And if the picture is compelling, comfortable and widely taught, it becomes very difficult to notice when the landscape doesn't actually match the map.

### A warning before you proceed

For this reason, *Prophecy Shock* won't be for everyone. This book doesn't just rearrange a few ideas – it challenges everything that we think we know about prophecy – and there are many who will be unable to take that journey because the familiar appeal of old beliefs will be too strong.

Those who do make their way through this book will be confronted by revelations that strip away decades, even centuries, of assumption, forcing them to re-examine what they've been taught - not with speculation, not with opinions - but by returning to the actual words of scripture, read in context, measured against history, and tested for truth. As such, *Prophecy Shock* is written for those who are prepared to accept that **they have been reading the prophetic story against the wrong background.**

In the pages ahead you'll discover that:

- The prophecies in Daniel and Revelation are **clear, precise, and anchored in real history** – and many of them have **already been fulfilled** - mostly in plain sight of the world.

- Prophecy isn't a dusty checklist of tomorrow's headlines. It is the unfolding story of God's plan, **already in motion**, but we've been trained not to see it.

- **The Jewish people** - not the Church - are the central subject of most bible prophecy.

- Almost all *time-defined* prophecy is told through the lens of **the City of Jerusalem** and the empires and ideologies which have controlled it over the past 2,500+ years.

- **Antisemitism**, that persistent and irrational hatred of the Jews, is no random accident. It was predicted in detail, is woven into the prophetic story and will intensify until Christ Himself intervenes.

- Most of the confusion surrounding prophecy comes not from God's Word but from our habit of ignoring context, flattening symbols, or assuming the Church is the focus when, mostly, it isn't. **Interpretations that merely "fit" the apparent clues are not enough** – true prophetic solutions must be measurable, testable, and anchored in verifiable history.

**My Challenge to you**

If you are willing to set aside assumptions, traditions, and second-hand explanations in order to see prophecy through fresh eyes - **this book is the red pill**. But it's not the kind of book that you can just pick bits from at random. Its impact lies in seeing how multiple solutions all weave together into one comprehensive picture – which means that you can't just read a few chapters here and there. If you want to understand what prophecy really means, you'll need to put the time in.

So let's make a pact. If you afford me the courtesy of your time and attention and read this book in the order in which it was written – I promise to transform your understanding of some of the best known prophecies in the Bible using plain language and easily accessible ideas. I'll show you how to read them in a way that is logical, scriptural, and testable – a way which clears away the fog of tradition and replaces it with clarity - **and by the time we get to the end of this book you will understand exactly what those prophecies mean.**

That process of clarity starts with the structure of this book, itself. It looks big (it *is* big - around 500 pages) but it's very easy to read and it's broken up into **9 easy to understand sections**:

- Section 1 **Explains why modern prophecy teaching is so confused**

- Section 2 **Re-centres prophecy on Israel and Jerusalem**

**These first two sections establish the core foundations of the book.**

- Section 3, **Is where we start solving these prophecies** using easy-to-understand math to reveal a completely new meaning for the Visions in the Book of Daniel.

- Section 4 **Explains why we haven't been able to understand the Book of Revelation** – until now.

- Section 5 **Identifies 'the beast'** and explains why it was able to hide in plain sight for so long.

- Section 6 **Explains the prophetic roots of antisemitism** and connects prophecy with what's happening to the Jews right now.

- Section 7 **Describes the final judgment of God's enemies** and identifies "Babylon the great."

- Section 8 **Tests our solutions in Daniel and Revelation against other famous prophecies in the Bible**

- Section 9 **Draws the full prophetic picture together** and explains what this means for you.

Each of these Sections is further divided into a series of Chapters that make the ideas being presented easy to understand – and once we get to Section 3, we'll start solving each individual prophecy, with an introduction, an explanation, and a solution for each.

And running through all of this, placed strategically throughout the book according to relevance and impact, are standalone Chapters covering **the Ten Principles of Israelism**. These are the framework of the core ideas behind this book.

---

So – what will you do? **Will you take the red pill** and have your eyes opened to the reality of prophecy as God intended it to be understood. Or will you stay in the familiar comfort of inherited interpretations and continue believing what you've always believed.

If you choose to take it - if you open your heart and mind to the possibility that prophecy is clearer, sharper, and more urgent than you've been told - **you will never see the Bible, or the times we're living in, in the same way again.**

Section One

# CONFUSION IN THE HOUSE OF GOD

1

# Are you being deceived?

***Rethinking the most popular end times narratives***

Imagine this: You've watched *The Matrix, The Sixth Sense*, or *The Thirteenth Floor*. You remember that moment - the one where everything flips, when the protagonist suddenly realizes that the world they've trusted isn't real. That what they thought was solid ground was actually a carefully layered illusion.

**What if you're in that moment right now?**

What if the way that you've been taught to think about bible prophecy - the timelines, the symbols, the big events - has lulled you into a false sense of security? What if it's not just a little wrong - but almost entirely inverted? Not because someone lied to you - but because well-meaning people promoted ideas that were already misaligned - layer upon layer, decade after decade - until today's prophetic worldview has become something that the earliest Christians would barely recognize.

Christ Himself warned us about this, in advance. In Matthew 24:4 the disciples asked Jesus what signs would mark His return and the end of the age and He responded by saying:

> *"Take heed that no man deceives you. For many shall come in my name, saying, I am Christ; and shall deceive many."*

This passage is usually interpreted as a warning about a handful of false messiahs or deceptive leaders who would set out to deceive – but what if the meaning is broader?

The Greek word used here - **Christos** - means "anointed" and while that term is most commonly applied to Jesus, it's also a term that, in a broader theological sense, can refer to those who claim to speak in His authority.

Read this way, the warning in Matthew 24 can be understood as:

*"Take heed that no one deceives you. For many shall come in my name, saying, **'I speak for Christ'**; and shall deceive many."*

So the warning is **not only** about people claiming to *be* Christ – it is also about people claiming to **speak for Him**. In other words, Jesus' warning includes both false messiahs **and** false representatives who trade on His name and authority.

This hits much closer to home. It suggests that the deception that Christ warned us about doesn't just come from outside the Church - it also comes from within it - and that the biggest risk to the faith comes from Christians themselves (or those who claim to be Christian).

And while the purpose of the Lord's warning was to alert us to deception in all of its various forms – it's fitting that He should have raised it in the context of a discussion about prophecy.

Prophecy is a topic about which many of us speak with bold assurance of our position - but how many of us are aware of the consequences of repeating prophetic error?

In Revelation 22, Jesus gives us a stern warning about this:

*"If anyone adds anything to [this prophecy], God will add to that person the plagues... And if anyone takes words away... God will take away that person's share in the tree of life."* ***(Revelation 22:18–19)***

That's not hyperbole. It's a blunt warning against promoting error and an echo of a similar message in the Book of Deuteronomy:

> *"If what a prophet proclaims... does not take place or come true, that is a message the Lord has not spoken."* ***(Deuteronomy 18:21–22)***

That's very clear. If it doesn't happen as predicted, it wasn't from God - and this has serious implications for popular prophecy teachings. If the things we're telling people don't match what scripture actually teaches - then we fail the biblical test.

That should ring alarm bells because, when we boldly express our opinions about where we're at in the prophetic countdown right now we're making **prophetic statements** - and if those statements don't come true, scripture calls them **false prophecy** - no matter how well intentioned we might be - and *we are inviting, upon ourselves, the consequences outlined in those scriptures.*

Jesus knew that we'd be vulnerable to this kind of deception - especially from within the faith community - and the irony is that those who are most affected by misleading beliefs about prophecy are often the most sincere and committed prophecy students!

If that sounds confronting, it's because it should be. Prophecy is a statement of God's truth - so when we speak confidently about what He is about to do we are making claims about His words and actions. Scripture does not treat that lightly.

But how do we tell the difference between faithful interpretation and well-meaning error? If sincere, Bible-believing Christians can repeat prophetic ideas without ever stopping to test whether they actually match the text or the outcomes of history, then good intentions are not enough. What's needed is not more excitement, more charts, or more confident voices - but a better method. A way of reading prophecy that is disciplined, testable, and anchored in what the Bible itself says prophecy is meant to do: point to real events, in real history, concerning real people.

That's the problem this book is written to address. Not to attack faith, but to strengthen it. Not to replace Scripture, but to take it seriously enough to test the stories that we've built around it.

Over the next few pages I'll summarise the way in which this book does that. I'll outline the core framework that *Prophecy Shock* is built on – including the assumptions that are challenged, the methods that are used, and the themes that run through the entire work.

Once you've read it, the rest of the book will feel less like wandering into a maze and more like taking a guided tour over ground that you already understand.

## The core themes of *Prophecy Shock*

### 1. Accurate prophecy solutions can be measured

Every generation thinks that it's living in "prophetic times" – ours is no different. Blood moons, microchips, pandemics, globalism, wars - everyone has a theory that seems to 'fit' the prophetic clues - and most of them contradict each other. The result is confusion, fatigue, and a quiet sense that bible prophecy is either impossible to understand or better left alone.

But prophecy wasn't written to confuse anyone. If a solution is correct it won't merely fit the clues - it will be measurable, testable, and anchored in verifiable history. If prophecy solutions can't be counted, confirmed, and clearly matched to real events, they are not solutions at all.

### 2. Time-defined prophecy describes real events

Whenever the Bible gives us specific time periods - 1,260 days, 2,300 evenings and mornings, "time, times and half a time," 42 months, and so on – they're there for a reason.

- They describe **real stretches of time** that can be counted.
- they land on **real events** that match what the text describes.

These aren't vague symbols or flexible metaphors - they're fixed spans of **real** time – and to interpret them, we will keep coming back to the same core questions:

1. **What's being predicted?**
2. **Who is the prophecy addressed to?**
3. **Who is the prophecy about?**
4. **When does the prophecy start?**
5. **How long will the prophecy last?**
6. **When does the prophecy end?**

These six questions will keep turning up throughout the book, and if the interpretation doesn't answer them and land on a clear, historically verifiable event - then it's wrong. No matter how popular it is. No matter who teaches it.

**3. The Book of Revelation is structured as Seven-Visions**

Revelation is **not** one continuous story. It is **explicitly structured as a series of seven visions.** Four of these tell the story of the same broad span of history from different angles – three are about events which are yet future. The book itself signals the breaks and restarts between these visions, and the internal resets only make sense if you recognise that John is being shown distinct visions, not one unbroken film. Once you read Revelation according to its own structure as seven visions, rather than forcing it into a single linear timeline, the apparent contradictions disappear. It becomes **coherent and readable**, and its prophecies slot into the same historical framework as the Book of Daniel and the actual history of Israel and Jerusalem.

**4. Israel is the central story of prophecy**

If there's one theme this book keeps coming back to, it's this:

***Most prophecy is about the Jews, not the Church.***

The Church is part of God's plan - but it is not the subject of Old Testament prophecy – and much of the New Testament's prophetic material is also anchored in Israel's story.

This means that the modern State of Israel is not a prophetic curiosity; it's central to the fulfilment of long-running promises – **many of which have already been fulfilled**.

When you put Israel back where the Bible puts Israel - at the centre of the prophetic story - the puzzle pieces start to click together.

**5. Every Beast ruled Jerusalem**

Every beast in Daniel and Revelation was a real empire that directly ruled Jerusalem. There are no exceptions.

The beasts don't describe a speculative future superpower or a last days leader. They describe actual empires. Actual rule. Actual Jerusalem.

In the pages ahead we'll lay out the full list of beasts and show how each one appears in Daniel and Revelation.

For now, all you need to see is the pattern: from Babylon through to the Islamic Caliphates and the compromised "Christian" powers - the beasts are the real-world regimes that have each, at one time, controlled Jerusalem and oppressed the Jewish people.

**6. The point is not prediction - it's verification**

This is critical. *Time-defined* Prophecy hasn't been provided so that Christians can forecast the future or "guess the next date." It's about **authenticating the message.** When predicted events occur, in the predicted sequence, at the predicted times, **they confirm the reliability of the text and the Author.**

**7. The past matters – but there's more ahead**

This book will argue that all of the major prophecies that come with time-clues – the ones you can put a start date and an end date on – are now behind us. Those countdowns have already landed on real events in Jewish history and in the story of Jerusalem.

So we're not "waiting for a Beast to rise" or "waiting for prophecy to kick in." We are living **after** the fulfilment of most of the major prophetic arcs.

The long exile is over. The Jewish people are back, Jerusalem is restored, and the great conflict of the Beasts has played out exactly as foretold.

But even though the precise countdowns have ended – there's still plenty more to come:

- the final stages of God's dealings with Israel and the nations,
- the return of Christ,
- and the ultimate hope that Scripture holds out beyond history as we know it.

*Prophecy Shock* is not about guessing dates for those events or drawing new charts for the "next crisis." Instead, it shows you where we are on the timeline **right now** – after the fulfilment of the major time-defined prophecies – and then clears away the confusion about how the remaining, open-ended prophecies fit into that bigger picture.

Once you know which parts of the prophetic story are already complete, you will stop chasing every news headline as a "sign" and start seeing the future promises against the solid backdrop of what God has already done. The clocks have mostly finished ticking – but the Author hasn't completed the story yet.

2

# Why I wrote this book

***From Premillennial confusion to prophetic clarity***

The process which led me to write this book took more than a decade – and it certainly wasn't based on a desire to court controversy.

I'm from New Zealand. We're not a confrontational people. Mostly, we keep our heads down and mind our own business – so for most of the first 20 of my 40+ years as a Christian I saw my passion for understanding bible prophecy as a personal pursuit and I treated my findings as a source of personal edification – not as the basis upon which to challenge others.

Over that time I was happy to accept the teachings of the acknowledged experts and, for me, those experts were the great U.S. prophecy teachers of the era. Hal Lindsay, Chuck Missler, Dave Hunt and others. These men were giants of prophecy interpretation and people whose views I respected and followed.

Hal Lindsey's *The Late Great Planet Earth* was the first prophecy book that I read soon after becoming a Christian in the mid-80s, and it ignited something in me. I became a passionate cheerleader for the school of prophecy interpretation known as *Premillennialism* and devoured everything I could find about prophecy. I talked about it to anyone who would listen, I used it as a witnessing tool and I believed that I was helping people by showing them "what was coming."

Premillennialism gave me comfort, purpose, excitement and a strong sense of certainty about the way things were going to play out.

But as the years went on, something started to bother me. The longer I studied, the more I saw gaps that no one wanted to talk about.

I could see places where verses were being skipped, or explained away, or reinterpreted to make them fit the story we all liked. This wasn't the result of deception – just the act of sincere people smoothing over contradictions because admitting those contradictions would shake the whole system.

But for a long time I did what New Zealanders – 'Kiwis' – do. I assumed that the problem was with me. I told myself, "These people are experts. They know better than I do". After all, who was I to question popular teaching, far less replace it.

But the discomfort never really went away and I started searching for answers in obedience to Paul's instructions in **1 Thessalonians 5:20–21** - *"Do not despise prophecies, but test everything; hold fast to what is good."*

I took this, not only as an instruction to study prophecy – but to 'test' what I was being told to ensure that it lined up with scripture and what God actually said, in prophecy.

That decision was a huge milestone in my faith and - if you're reading this - I'm guessing that it will resonate with you too. You know that prophecy matters, but you have questions about some of the details and you're not satisfied with it being treated as a form of entertainment anymore.

For me, that hunt ran quietly in the background of my life for years until it finally led me to the work of Ellis Skolfield in the early 2000s.

Skolfield - a Bible teacher to whom the world owes an enormous debt - had walked a path that looked very like my own. He started in Premillennialism, believed the standard model, and promoted it to others. And then he hit the same wall I was hitting: too many places where the text and the popular interpretation *just didn't match*.

But instead of forcing the Bible to fit the system, Skolfield made a radical decision: he let the prophecy speak for itself. No tradition. No presupposition. Just: what does it say, and how does it line up with the recorded history.

What he uncovered was extraordinary.

Starting with the words of the Prophet Daniel, Skolfield showed that the prophecies are not vague guesses about some far-off future. They are specific, time-defined, and historically anchored, and they line up with real events that have actually happened - especially in the history of Israel. In doing so, he laid out a framework that was completely at odds with what I had been defending for decades.

His discoveries were revolutionary – but I didn't just accept his claims at face value. I'd previously been burned by interpretations that looked good but didn't stand close scrutiny – so I tested what he said. And when I say I tested it I mean I treated his claims like evidence: I clarified the data, confirmed the start points, checked the history and did my best to break the math. And when it held up, I couldn't ignore it.

That changed me – and I thought it would change others too. I expected those insights to explode through the Christian world and correct the confusion. I honestly thought, "Well, that settles it. This will spread on its own. I don't need to do anything. Other people will run with this."

It didn't happen.

Skolfield died in 2015 without his ideas ever really coming to significant attention and, as I watched, what little attention they had attracted slowly started to disappear. Few people were aware of them – and nobody seemed willing to carry them forward.

So, around 2018, I stepped up - reluctantly.

My reluctance didn't come from a lack of confidence in my ability to articulate the message. Even back then I was starting to become known for my analysis of Israel, Jewish history, and Middle Eastern geopolitics and I already had a significant audience for these views.

But I wasn't part of the American prophecy industry. Nor was I a seminary professor or a published televangelist – so I didn't fit the stereotype of someone who writes on these matters.

Additionally, I had a picture in my head of what a prophecy scholar should look like - and I wasn't it. My life has not been a picture-perfect example of exemplary Christian living - and too often I have let my selfishness and my ego outrun the God that I said I believed in – so I was concerned that my character didn't meet the standard a reader should expect of someone who talks about prophecy.

But the conviction to act wouldn't leave me. I knew that, if this material disappeared, the confusion would just keep recycling, and believers would keep getting versions of prophecy that sound exciting but fall apart under scrutiny.

So I decided to write a book.

At first I thought I could communicate all of this through fiction. During the COVID lockdown in 2020, I finished *The Book of Dan* - a novel built around these prophetic claims. But when I finished it, I knew that it wasn't enough. By then, my own understanding had gone far beyond what I had first learned from Skolfield. The framework had widened. The timelines had become clearer. Pieces that used to feel mystical now sat on top of specific dates and events in Jewish history. And, most importantly, the theme underlying it all had become obvious to me. I was no longer just telling an interesting story - I was holding something that the Church desperately needed to know: that prophecy is measurable, anchored, and that much of it is already fulfilled in ways that most of us have never been shown.

Storytelling wasn't the problem. Clarity was the problem.

And so, *Prophecy Shock* was born.

**The path less travelled**

This book is here for one reason: to lay out that framework so that you can see it for yourself.

I am not asking you to take anything that I say at face value. I haven't 'had a dream' or been the recipient of a special revelation. I've just followed the numbers and the evidence in scripture and I'm asking you to consider what's in this book and do the same:

- Read the prophetic text the way it's actually written.
- Line it up with real history.
- Watch what happens when you stop forcing the Bible to say what we were all told it "had" to say.

Following that process changed my life. It pulled me out of years of sincere confusion and took me down a path less travelled – a way of understanding prophecy which is at odds with most of what we have been told – but which, ultimately ends up somewhere far more stable and far more honest.

My hope - and the only reason I'm doing this - is that it will do the same for you.

3

# What's your prophetic worldview?

***The Four Schools of Prophecy Interpretation***

Since it was first translated into English in the $16^{th}$ century, the Bible has outsold any other book in history.

Some of that popularity comes from its role as a source of wisdom and its guidance on how to live and how to treat others – and within its pages, there's an answer to nearly every life situation you'll ever face.

But this hardly scratches the surface relative to its primary role as the blueprint by which we can understand the purpose of this life and the guidebook on how to make it, safely, into the next one.

In this respect, no other writing comes close to having the transformative power of the Bible because no other writing can offer direct access to the central character of history and the source of that transformation: **Yeshua, the Mashiach/Messiah** (or, as He is known in popular tradition, Jesus Christ).

### The Prophetic Puzzle

But there is also another layer of insight provided by the Bible - its ability to allow us to look into the future so as to know what is yet to come: Prophecy.

Put simply, Prophecy is Gods way of providing us with advance warning of events and trends before they happen – and the bible is teeming with it. It appears in many forms, employs symbolism and metaphor, and contains just enough ambiguity to give rise to different schools of interpretation.

And contrary to modern perceptions of the study of prophecy being a bit 'fringe' – it has actually been the pursuit of some of the greatest minds in history. Isaac Newton devoted more writing to biblical prophecy than to physics. Johannes Kepler, Francis Bacon, and other founders of modern science treated it as part of the search for order and truth.

Statesmen and political thinkers were no less engaged. John Adams studied Revelation closely. Abraham Lincoln framed national catastrophe in providential and near-prophetic terms. Winston Churchill viewed the modern Middle East, and the return of the Jews to their land, through a consciously biblical lens. Major historians such as Arnold Toynbee saw biblical prophecy as a framework for understanding the rise and collapse of civilisations. Writers including John Milton and Leo Tolstoy wrestled deeply with its moral and historical implications.

In other words, prophecy was once a mainstream intellectual pursuit and, as a result, hundreds of approaches to the interpretation of prophecy have developed over the centuries – however, these can be broadly summarised into just four main schools:

1. **Premillennialism**
   Proposes that Christ will return to Earth, soon, to rule the nations for 1,000 years – and that His return will be **before** that reign commences (in fact, it will be the event which kicks it off). This is the most commonly held evangelical prophecy view today.[1]

---

1. Premillennialism - especially in its Dispensational form - has dominated evangelical thinking since the late 1800s, thanks largely to the *Scofield Reference Bible* (1909). It's the foundation behind the *Left Behind* series and other "end-times" pop theology.

2. **Postmillennialism**
   Proposes that Christ will return only **after** the 1,000 years are over and the world has been prepared for Him (under Christian influence). Some/most versions of this view claim that the 1,000 years are already underway.

3. **Amillennialism**
   Sees the 1,000 years as largely symbolic (some versions accept that some parts may be literal).

4. **Historicism**
   Proposes that prophecy has unfolded progressively through history, and that many events once considered "future" have already been fulfilled in Christian history, with an emphasis on the European history of the Church.[2]

**What's your prophetic view?**
Which of these best represents what *you* mostly believe about prophecy?

Take a moment and see how you score by choosing the options that best reflect your beliefs. If you're unsure – don't worry – just choose option E and we'll explain it all as we make our way through the book:

2. Historicism was the default view of the Reformers. Martin Luther, John Calvin, and many others believed prophecy was unfolding progressively through Church history. It fell out of favour in the modern era. If you want a classic (though dated) explanation, try *Horae Apocalypticae* by E.B. Elliott (first published in 1844, and not for the faint of heart).

1. **What is the "Millennium" in Revelation 20?**
   a) A literal 1,000-year reign of Christ on Earth after His return
   b) A long era of gospel expansion before His return
   c) A symbolic description of Christ's present heavenly reign
   d) History unfolding in church-and-political history
   e) I'm not sure

2. **When will Christ physically return?**
   a) Before the Millennium to inaugurate His earthly kingdom
   b) After the world has been largely transformed by the gospel
   c) At the close of history (no earthly Millennium required)
   d) After all specific historic events have been completed
   e) I'm not sure

3. **What role does the Church play in end-time events?**
   a) A faithful remnant enduring persecution until Christ returns
   b) A primary agent in ushering in global gospel transformation
   c) A witness in a fallen world - neither conquering nor conquered
   d) A central institution through which prophecies unfold
   e) I'm not sure

4. **How do you read the Book of Revelation?**
   a) It's primarily about the future
   b) It's a blueprint of Christ's victory and the Churches mission
   c) It's a symbolic panorama of the entire Church age
   d) It's a chronological outline of church-and-state history
   e) I'm not sure

5. **Prophetic numbers like "1,260 days" represent...**
   a) Literal days in a future tribulation
   b) Symbolic numbers conveying theological truths
   c) Figurative language not tied to calendar time
   d) Prophetic years already counted
   e) I'm not sure

6. **What happens to evil in the end times?**
   a) It intensifies until Christ decisively defeats it
   b) It diminishes as the gospel permeates society
   c) It persists but is already spiritually defeated
   d) It peaks in recurring historical cycles and regimes
   e) I'm not sure

7. **How do you interpret the Antichrist figure(s)?**
   a) As a future individual who will deceive the world
   b) As a spirit of rebellion that will wane as the gospel advances
   c) As a recurring symbol of opposition - many antichrists, not one
   d) As a succession of historic figures or institutions opposing God's people
   e) I'm not sure

8. **How do you understand the 70 Weeks prophecy of Daniel 9?**
   a) Mostly future, with a final "week" culminating in the Antichrist
   b) Fulfilled in Christ and the early Church, enabling world redemption
   c) Largely symbolic of God's redemptive plan rather than literal years
   d) Completed in historical events
   e) I'm not sure

9. **What is the Mark of the Beast in Revelation 13?**
   a) A future, literal mark enabling economic control by the Antichrist
   b) A symbolic sign of allegiance to worldly powers that will fade over time
   c) A spiritual metaphor for rejecting Christ, present in every age
   d) A historic practice tied to specific political-religious systems
   e) I'm not sure

**10. What is the Primary message of bible prophecy?**

a) Hope in Christ's imminent return to a world in decline
b) Confidence that the gospel will ultimately renew society
c) Assurance that Christ already reigns and evil's end is certain
d) Clarity that history is unfolding on a precise prophetic schedule
e) I'm not sure

**Tally your letters to determine your worldview**

**Scoring Guide**

1) **Mostly A's?** You're probably Premillennial - like many modern evangelicals. This is the dominant interpretation in popular books and media. A helpful introduction is *Things to Come* by Dwight Pentecost (Zondervan, 1958), still a staple in Premillennial circles.

2) **Mostly B's?** You likely favour Postmillennialism - a more optimistic view than Premillennialism where the world improves through Christian influence before Christ returns. This was once widely held, especially during the revivalist and missionary movements of the 18th and 19th centuries.

3) If you landed **mostly on C**, that's Amillennialism - a symbolic interpretation in which the "millennium" is the present Church age, and Christ reigns spiritually, not physically. This is the majority view of Roman Catholic and Eastern Orthodox Churches as well as many mainline Protestant churches. Augustine of Hippo was one of its earliest advocates.

4) A **mostly D** score means you're drawn to Historicism - the idea that prophecy unfolds throughout Church history. This view was common among the Protestant Reformers and early

Adventists. A dense but rewarding resource is *The Approaching End of the Age* by H. Grattan Guinness (1878).

5) If you circled **a lot of E's**, you're in a good place: open, cautious, and ready to explore with fresh eyes.

Whichever of these positions best describes you – they're all widely held prophecy views within the Christian community, worldwide.

But there's a problem. If God gave prophecy to be understood, these models of interpretation can't all be correct. At best, only one can be 'right', and at worst, they're all wrong.

So how can we know? Is there a measure by which to judge prophecy and determine whether it meets Gods standard?

There is – and it's the subject of the next chapter.

4

# Testing prophecy

***4 biblical warnings to separate God's truth from man's tradition***

In 2 Peter 19, the apostle tells us that his faith is grounded in firsthand experience - but that even this is surpassed by what he calls "**a more sure word of prophecy**."

He compares prophecy to a light shining in a dark place "until the day dawns," and makes the extraordinary claim that he trusts prophecy even more than the evidence of his own eyes.

## Confusion inside the Church...

But if prophecy is so certain, why is the Church flooded with conflicting interpretations? Why do some believers see signs in every headline while others spiritualize everything away? If the Bible is so reliable - why can't Christians agree on what it means?

Is it the result of differences in interpretation? Human error? Ego? The corruption of scripture by Church Traditions?

The answer to all of these is 'yes' – and many more.

Jesus, Himself, warned us that this would happen over 2,000 years ago. In fact, much of His teaching assumes that we would get prophecy wrong and that much of this confusion would come from inside the Church.

## ...and outside the Church

But it would be a mistake to believe that *all* of the confusion about prophecy comes from within. As predicted, Christian faith has fallen away over the past 200 years – with that decline accelerating over the past few decades – and in its place has arisen an aggressive atheism which seeks to undermine every tenet of belief in the God of the Bible.

In scholarly circles this view is represented by the field of **Higher Criticism** – which began, in the 1700s, as a method by which to better understand scripture – but has evolved into a fully secular movement which now rejects the existence of a **supernatural** origin to the Bible and treats the Bible no differently to any other historical document.

That may sound reasonable - but it strips prophecy of its most important distinctive: **inspiration**. If scripture isn't inspired - accurate prophecies can't be miraculous - so they are treated as literature or even **fraud**. Later dates are then assigned to such texts so that the "predictions" can be reclassified as after-the-fact commentary. That usually requires denying that the traditional author was a real historical person tied to the original date. And once those late dates are assumed, the supposed lack of evidence for the author in the **new, invented timeframe** is then cited as proof that the Author didn't actually exist.

This is **circular reasoning** and it is why some scholars end up ascribing **patently absurd dates** to certain biblical books. Not because the evidence compels them, but because their starting assumption forbids the miraculous.

This book rejects that loop. If you exclude the miraculous, you will neutralise the key claim that prophecy makes of itself – that it is inspired by God and that it 'sees the end from the beginning'.

Instead, *Prophecy Shock* lets the text speak on its own terms and tests its claims against verifiable history – not the assumptions and prejudices of men living thousands of years after the fact.

The chapters ahead will unpack these errors and offer a new model - one grounded in scripture, **numerically testable**, aligned with well-known dates in history, and consistent from start to finish.

Fortunately, God also gave us multiple tools by which to test prophecy. Here are four of them, in the form of warnings:

## Warning 1: Prophecy was sealed until the time of the end

*"The words are rolled up and sealed **until the time of the end.**"*
***Daniel 12:10*** [3]

Daniel 12:10 tells us that Daniel's prophecies weren't meant to be understood until a certain point in history - what the Bible calls "the time of the end". As you'll see as we get further into this book, the Key events which unlock this time of the end are the rebirth of Israel in 1948 and the recapture of Jerusalem in 1967.

This means that any system of interpretation that was developed prior to these events, no matter how devout its originators, is almost certain to be incorrect.

## Warning 2: No private interpretation allowed

*"No prophecy of the scripture is of any private interpretation."*
***2 Peter 1:20***

These warnings are not symbolic – they are literal. God's Word interprets itself. Prophecy interpretation isn't a contest of opinions – it is a study of facts and we are instructed not to build doctrines from outside sources - whether theological systems, academic scholarship, visions, or traditions. If an interpretation can't be directly and explicitly drawn from Scripture, it doesn't belong in our understanding of prophecy. Period.

## Warning 3: The Day of the Lord will come like a thief

*"The day of the Lord will come as a thief in the night..."*
***2 Peter 3:10***

---

[3] The idea that prophecy was "sealed until the time of the end" is unique to Daniel 12 and is interpreted differently depending on your theological background. Some scholars argue that this "unsealing" began in the time of Christ (e.g. John Walvoord, *Daniel: The Key to Prophetic Revelation*), while others - like Ellis Skolfield - believe it points specifically to modern events like the rebirth of Israel. If that's a new idea for you, keep reading. This book will unpack it in depth.

Scripture consistently teaches that Jesus will return suddenly and without warning and that His return will mark the end of the current age. This return is not allegorical - it is literal and appears **consistently and repeatedly** throughout the Bible. Any theory that spiritualises this event or requires a checklist of things that must happen first contradicts this.

If your prophecy model allows you to hit the snooze button, it's not biblical.

### Warning 4: If it doesn't come true, it isn't from God

> *"If what a prophet proclaims... does not take place or come true, that is a message the Lord has not spoken."*
> ***Deuteronomy 18:22***

If a system repeatedly makes predictions that don't happen, it fails. No exceptions. God doesn't deal in vague guesses. Failed prophecy isn't just disappointing - it disqualifies the system behind it.

---

These certainly aren't the only tests against false prophecy in the Bible - but they're more than sufficient for our purposes. They form a biblical firewall around our understanding of prophecy and protect us from error, sensationalism, and spiritual deception.

But how do the four schools of prophecy interpretation stack up against these simple tests? Is there one that stands out – or do they all fail under the weight of scriptural scrutiny?

We're going to examine that question throughout this book – starting with the most popular school of prophecy interpretation in the world today: Premillennialism.

5

# Exploring Premillennialism

***A popular theory built on scripture - and speculation***

If you completed the quiz in chapter 3, there is a strong chance that your answers aligned with Premillennialism – putting you in the theological mainstream of modern evangelical Christianity.

However, if you identified with one of the other options, or if you only have a hazy sense of what Premillennialism actually is, this chapter will help you to understand the belief system that now dominates popular Christian thinking about the future.

In simple terms, Premillennialism teaches that the world is moving toward a final period of global upheaval, after which Jesus will return to intervene in history, rule the world for a literal thousand years, and then bring about the final judgement and the creation of a new heaven and new earth.

This expectation is drawn primarily from a literal reading of Revelation 20 and this belief, on its own, is not complicated.

What *is* complicated is what has grown out of it.

**A comprehensive prophetic ecosystem**

Over time, Premillennialism has expanded from a belief about the timing of Christ's return into a complete storyline about how history is supposed to end. Wars, political leaders, economic systems, the fate of Israel, and the experience of Christians in the last days have all become woven into a single prophetic framework which now functions as the default lens through which world events are interpreted.

This did not happen by accident – in fact, Premillennialism emerged as a response to a problem that the Church, itself, created:

**Antisemitism in the early Church**

In the earliest years of the Church, Christianity was still unmistakably Jewish. The apostles preached in synagogues, the festivals were observed, and the hope of Israel's restoration remained central. But after the destruction of Jerusalem in AD 70, and again after the Bar Kokhba revolt in AD 135, attitudes shifted. Many believers concluded that these disasters were evidence that God had rejected the Jews.

Over the following centuries, influential voices drove this home: **Justin Martyr** argued that the Church had replaced Israel as God's chosen people and was now the "true Israel," **Origen** reinterpreted Israel's promises in spiritual terms so that they applied to Christians instead. **Augustine** reframed the thousand year reign of Revelation as a metaphor for the Church age.

This way of thinking - later called **supersessionism** or "replacement theology" - became the standard view of the Catholic, and later the Protestant, churches. Even during the Reformation, men like Luther and Calvin, who had thrown out papal authority, still retained Augustine's view of the Jews because the assumption that God was finished with Israel was so deeply ingrained that nobody questioned it.

But there was a problem: history did not cooperate with this theology. The Jewish people did not disappear. Jewish identity did not dissolve into Christianity. The Jews not only survived – they spread to every corner of the world and the old assumption that Israel had no further place in God's purposes became increasingly difficult to maintain.

## Dispensationalism and the shape of modern Premillennialism

Enter John Nelson Darby of the Plymouth Brethren movement. In the 1830s, Darby rejected replacement theology and argued that God still had a distinct prophetic destiny for Israel. To make sense of this, he developed **dispensationalism:** the idea that God works through different historical eras and that Israel and the Church are two distinct peoples with different roles in God's plan. Darby's ideas spread rapidly across the former British Empire and the United States, especially through Bible conferences, preaching networks, and later popular study Bibles.

But this solution came at a cost. By putting Israel and the Church on two separate prophetic tracks, dispensationalism ended up putting the Church at the centre of prophecy, with Israel's redemption pushed into the future. In trying to rescue Israel from theological oblivion, Darby also accelerated the Churches tendency to read prophecy as being primarily about itself.

That paradox - Israel defended in theory but sidelined in practice - continues to shape modern premillennial thought. This history explains why contemporary prophecy teaching is such a hybrid: with much of Protestant Christendom fiercely defending Israel while still interpreting most current events through a church-centric lens.

In practice, this meant that the prophecies of Daniel and Revelation were increasingly appropriated by Christianity and read as forecasts of future global events affecting the Church. As such, they have come to be treated less as windows into God's dealings with His covenant people, and more as coded predictions about the Churches future trials, enemies, and ultimate deliverance.

## The Premillennial Checklist

Once prophecy was treated this way, it naturally began to demand identifiable future villains, identifiable crises, identifiable political structures, and identifiable technologies. Over time, that system hardened into a series of key expectations that form the backbone of popular Premillennial teaching:

**The Tribulation**

Most Premillennial models anticipate a future period of extreme global turmoil known as the Tribulation, marked by war, famine, disease, disaster, and widespread persecution of Christians.

**The Antichrist**

Within this scenario, a powerful world leader known as the Antichrist rises to prominence, initially promising stability before revealing himself as a tyrant demanding absolute loyalty.

**The mark of the beast**

In most versions the Antichrist typically enforces this loyalty through something called the Mark of the Beast - a literal system of identification tied to economic participation and often linked, in modern teaching, to emerging technologies and cashless systems.

**A rebuilt temple**

Many Premillennial teachers also expect a future rebuilding of the Jewish Temple in Jerusalem, which becomes the setting for the Abomination of Desolation - the moment when the Antichrist openly claims divine status.

**A global order**

Alongside this, there is an expectation of a dominant global political structure in the last days, sometimes imagined as a revived Roman sphere of influence, sometimes as a resurgent Islamic caliphate. In each case, this empire is seen as the platform through which the final world ruler comes to power.

## Premillennialism in the White House

These ideas dominate evangelical Christian thinking – but the influence of Premillennialism is not just confined to pulpits and prophecy conferences. Over the past fifty years, Presidents Reagan, Bush senior, Bush junior, and Trump have all strongly and publicly aligned themselves with Premillennial ideas, particularly in relation to Israel and the Middle East. Indeed, this alignment has been so obvious that, in 2023, the documentary *Praying for Armageddon* explored how evangelical end times beliefs have shaped segments of American political culture. Although hostile in tone, the film correctly identified the extent to which prophecy expectations have migrated from theology into policy thinking.

**The default view?**

For millions of Christians, Premillennialism now feels like simple biblical realism. It presents itself not as one interpretive tradition among many, but as the plain meaning of Scripture.

**But what if it's not? What if the Premillennial interpretation of prophecy is wrong?**

What would we do if we found that the interpretations we've adopted are based, not on a correct understanding of prophecy, but on **decades of accumulated error?**

That's what we'll begin to test next.

6

# Did we misread the signs?

***What prophecy doesn't say - despite what millions believe***

As we can see, Premillennialism is built on an elaborate framework of beliefs - all broadly centred on the idea that God is currently dealing with Christians in the last days and that there are a series of events which must soon take place in order to complete His prophetic outline.

This is an appealing narrative – one that I was fully immersed in for almost 20 years - but how does it stack up against the four tests that we identified earlier? Sadly, not well:

1. **Does Premillennialism add to (or subtract from) Scripture?**
   Yes it does. Premillennialism introduces details and ideas that aren't in the biblical text [4] and omits or downplays those that contradict its timeline. Many examples of this will be provided throughout this book.

2. **Does Premillennialism produce false prophecies?**
   As we will see as we progress through this book, much of what Premillennialism has predicted has either failed to happen or keeps being pushed back into a smaller and smaller window within which it must take place. This matters

[4] Many of these additions - like a pre-tribulation rapture or a rebuilt temple - are based on interpretations that require complex theological scaffolding. These weren't part of historic Christian eschatology and were largely absent before the 19th century.

because scripture tells us that repeated false prophecy disqualifies both the messenger and the message.

3. **Does Premillennialism undermine 'Imminency'?**
   By requiring a checklist of events before Jesus returns, some schools of Premillennialism dull the urgency of being 'ready' and multiple New Testament warnings to "stay awake"

4. **Was Premillennialism developed prior to 'the time of the end'?**
   Throughout this book I will demonstrate that 'the time of the end' began in 1948. The ideas which shape modern Premillennialism were first being developed around 100 years prior to this – violating Daniel 12:10 and failing our last test.

### What does this mean for prophecy?

But if Premillennialism is wrong - what does that mean for Christians who are trying to make sense of the last days? Is there a way to understand what's happening?

There is - and it's the basis of the message of the rest of this book.

The framework developed in *Prophecy Shock* shows that the major prophetic events in Daniel - and much of Revelation - have already been fulfilled. We are living *after* those events and now await the final one: the return of Christ. The prophetic events that God set in train over 2,500 years ago were never about things that would happen to Christians in the last days - they were (almost all) about the Jews.

By restoring Daniel and Revelation to their intended historical and biblical contexts - without inherited assumptions - we'll expose long-standing interpretive errors that have shaped modern expectations.

This will be hard for some to accept. A consensus model with guarded "core beliefs" has grown over decades, narrowing what can be questioned and often ostracizing those who test it.

That dynamic looks more like the defence of entrenched secular theories than the Berean posture of Acts 17:11. But I get it; I once embraced the Premillennial system for its clarity, timelines, vivid events, and urgency. Letting it go can feel like losing hope. I understand. I've been there.

But this book isn't about dismantling your hope. It's about grounding it in something deeper, more consistent, and more faithful to the Bible and to history. Approached prayerfully, it will reinforce your faith and demonstrate that a prophecy framework which is better and more scripturally based has been hiding in plain sight.

But if most prophecy isn't about the Church, who *is* it about?

That's the subject of the next section of this book.

---

**Note:**

There is a full summary comparison of the differences between Premillennialism and the findings of this book in Appendix B at the end of *Prophecy Shock.*

## Section Two

# INTRODUCING ISRAELISM

# Preview

***Prophecy begins with Israel - and ends with Israel too***

The first section of this book examined the confusion surrounding Bible prophecy. In this next section, we shift from critique to construction - introducing a new interpretive model built on a simple yet overlooked truth:

**Most bible prophecy is about the Jews - not the Church.**

This section introduces **Israelism** - a prophecy framework rooted in the idea that all Old Testament prophecy (and quite a bit of New Testament prophecy) speaks to, and about, **Israel**.

Israelism asserts that, while Christians are certainly beneficiaries of God's redemptive plan, they are **not the central subject of prophetic fulfilment**.

In this section you will explore:

- Why Christianity is, at its core, **a Jewish faith**, and how this reality reframes our reading of scripture.

- The **historical and biblical blindness** of Replacement Theology - and how it has distorted both scripture and Church doctrine.

- The prophetic importance of **Israel's rebirth in 1948**, not just politically, but also biblically.

- A new framework for interpreting prophecy - **Israelism** - based entirely on **scripture, history, and logic**.

- The beginning of a clear, evidence-based unravelling of prophecy that **requires no speculation** - only careful observation (and a bit of simple math).

By the end of this section, you'll see that we are not waiting for prophecy to unfold - we are living in its final stages. And the keys to unlocking it all have been hiding in plain sight all along: **the City of Jerusalem and the Jewish people**.

---

**Note:**
**Israelism should not be confused with "Israelology"** – a form of dispensationalism, proposed by Arnold Fruchtenbaum. The two share some superficial similarities but they are fundamentally different in their conclusions as will become clear as you make your way through this book. (For a direct comparison of both see Appendix B at the end of this book)

7

# Who was Jesus sent to?

***Before the Church: Why Old Testament Prophecy belongs to Israel***

Have you ever wondered why the Bible is split into an "Old" and a "New" Testament?

Some argue that this division reflects a change in God's focus - from His covenant with Israel to a new era centred on the Church. But if that's true, **why are the Gospels in the "New" Testament** when Jesus' ministry was, by His own words, **exclusively to the Jews**:

> *"A Canaanite woman from that vicinity came to him, crying out, "Lord, Son of David, have mercy on me! My daughter is demon-possessed and suffering terribly. Jesus did not answer a word. So his disciples came to him and urged him, "Send her away, for she keeps crying out after us. He answered,* ***"I was sent only to the lost sheep of Israel." (Matthew 15:22-24)***

Though He subsequently helps this woman, and while there are several instances of Him interacting directly with gentiles, this encounter makes clear that **His early mission was first and foremost to the Jewish people.** Only after His resurrection does He instruct His followers to "go into all the world and make disciples of **all** men."

So what changed? Did He turn His back on the Jews?

Not at all!

## Paul's Clarification: A Grafted Plan [5]

This is all explained in the Book of Romans where Paul tells Gentile believers that:

- Salvation through faith in Christ was originally intended for the Jews (the root) - but that they rejected Him

- The Jewish rejection of Christ brought salvation to the Gentiles - but a time will come when the full number of gentiles to be saved, is complete

- After which **all of Israel will be saved**

## The Gospels: a Jewish message?

None of this happened by accident, of course. God foresaw it all and it was all laid out in scripture in advance – but it has significant implications for our understanding of prophecy. If, up until the end of the Gospels, God was dealing with the Jews – what does that mean in respect of our understanding of the role of prophecy in the 'Old' Testament?

> [17] *"Do not think that I have come to abolish the Law or the Prophets; I have not come to abolish them but to fulfil them.* [18] *For truly I tell you, until heaven and earth disappear, not the smallest letter, not the least stroke of a pen, will by any means disappear from the Law until everything is accomplished.* ***(Matthew 5:17-18)***

Don't miss what is being said here. In this scripture, which was delivered during the Sermon on the Mount, Yeshua tells us that **the Law and the prophets were a message to the Jews** and that they will be fulfilled.

---

5 Romans 11 forms the foundation of what's often called **"olive tree theology"** - where Israel is the root, and Gentile believers are grafted in. Messianic Jewish theologian David H. Stern offers excellent commentary on this in his *Jewish New Testament Commentary* (1992), showing how the early Church understood its continuity with Jewish covenantal identity.

**Reframing Prophecy**

Once you understand this - that the **Old Testament is about Gods dealings with the Jews** - it follows naturally that **Old Testament prophecy is also about the Jews** - not modern Christians [6].

This will have significance to our study, particularly the Book of Daniel which is clearly about the Jewish people and their future - and schools of prophecy interpretation which apply its visions to the Church, ignore the book's actual focus.

**But aren't there some parts of the OT that speak about non-Jews?**

Yes, there are - but the primary audience being written *to* is always the Jews. These messages were spoken through Israel's prophets and recorded for Israel's hearing to show Gods people how He would ultimately deal with other nations. They show Israel that her God rules over all peoples and will, one day, hold everyone accountable.

The Old Testament messages to the nations are part of Israel's story, not a new audience replacing her - and failure to understand this has led millions into confusion.

But is there a way to interpret prophecy that honours its Jewish roots while properly placing the Church within God's redemptive plan?

There is - and that's what the rest of this book is about.

---

6 Most scholars agree that the Book of Daniel was written to and about the Jewish people, specifically addressing their exile, restoration, and future. The attempt to apply Daniel's prophecies to modern Church events is a hallmark of Dispensationalism and speculative prophetic models, as discussed in Tremper Longman's *Daniel* (NIVAC series, 1999).

8

# What is Israelism?

***Reclaiming the Jewish Heart of Prophecy***

The remainder of this book introduces another way to interpret Bible prophecy. It isn't Premillennialism, Postmillennialism, Amillennialism or Historicism (although it carries echoes of all of these).

It's **Israelism**.

**Israelism is not a 'new' school of prophecy interpretation.** Rather, it is the discovery of a set of principles that have been right there, in scripture, all along. As such, Israelism simply **restores the original meaning set by the text itself** - its geography, its subjects, its timelines, its structure, and its historical anchors.

**Where did Israelism come from?**

Israelism gradually evolved from my encounter with Ellis Skolfield's work in the early 2000s. His discoveries were astonishing - but his model lacked a consistent framework for testing prophetic solutions.

So I began to search for **clear, scriptural criteria** - consistent standards that could be used to evaluate prophetic interpretations.

What emerged was a set of 'core principles' - hidden in plain sight within Scripture – placed there by God to help us to uncover truth and avoid error.

**The Core Principles of Israelism:**

1. **Prophecy is centred on the Jews and Jerusalem** - which means that all of Daniel and most of Revelation are about Israel - not the Church.

2. **Prophecy is anchored in real history**. 2,300 evenings and mornings, 42 months, 1,260 days, 1,290 days and many more – they're all exact *time-defined* testable periods pointing to real events that can be independently verified.

3. **Both books are structured around visions, not chapters**. This structure reorders the way in which we interpret timing and themes.

4. **All time-defined prophecy can be solved with Six Basic Questions**, which will be detailed later.

5. **The beasts in prophecy are the powers that have ruled over Jerusalem**, not individual Antichrist figures [7]

6. **The fulfilment of prophecy is designed to reveal God's foreknowledge after the fact**, bringing Him glory - not laying out a timeline for us to predict.

7. **Time-defined Prophecy is centred on a single significant event**, dividing Daniel and Revelation into "before and after" periods counted toward that fixed year in history.

8. **Prophecy covers 2,500+ years of history**, culminating in events which took place in the 20th century.

---

[7] This approach departs sharply from the view that prophetic "beasts" represent future individuals (e.g. the Antichrist). It aligns more closely with the interpretation of scholars like E.B. Elliott (*Horae Apocalypticae*) and Isaac Newton (*Observations on the Prophecies of Daniel and the Apocalypse of St. John*), who also interpreted beasts as kingdoms or empires in history.

9. **Prophecy prioritizes scriptural timing over academic opinion**. If God gives a detail, it's correct - even if it contradicts secular consensus.

10. **Prophecy confirms that we're now in the time of the end**.

Each of these principles will be unpacked in detail throughout this book and, together, they provide a toolkit not just for reading *Prophecy Shock*, but also for launching your own study into God's prophetic Word - free of speculation, free of tradition, and anchored in Scripture.

It's my passionate hope that, once you embrace this approach, **you'll uncover even more hidden truth** - not by chasing headlines or theories, but by letting the Bible interpret itself.

But why is the idea that prophecy is (almost) all about the Jews so radical and so threatening to other schools of interpretation?

We'll explore that next.

9

# Who are the Jews, to God?

***What if the Church has been reading someone else's mail?***

This book was nearly ready for publication in late 2023. But everything changed on the morning of October 7, when the terrorist group Hamas launched a brutal attack on Israel - an assault so horrific, so targeted, that it shook the world and exposed something deeper: **the true prophetic significance of Israel in the last days.**

The atrocities were savage - mass killings, rapes, kidnappings - and yet the months that followed saw something equally disturbing: **global condemnation of Israel** rather than the terrorists who initiated the violence[8].

Antisemitism surged worldwide [9], protests erupted in Western cities, and university campuses turned hostile toward Jews.

But what was even more concerning was the way that Christians responded to these events. While there was certainly strong support for Israel and the Jews among many Christian communities – others simply accepted the propaganda being served up by global media. Particularly alarmingly – some 'Christian' organisations went even further and advocated for Government action against Israel and

---

[8] Major Western cities, including London, Paris, and New York, saw mass protests where slogans like "from the river to the sea" were widely used. Numerous universities in the U.S. and UK issued controversial or delayed statements, sparking accusations of institutional antisemitism. See reporting by *The Atlantic*, *Wall Street Journal*, and the ADL's post-October 7 analysis.

[9] According to the Anti-Defamation League (ADL), antisemitic incidents increased by over 400% globally in the weeks following the attack. This included vandalism, assault, and open calls for violence.

support for the very terrorists who had initiated the October 7 massacre.

It was this reaction - not just the attack - that delayed this book's release pending a significant rewrite to more clearly reflect what I had long feared: **that many Christians are radically off-course in how they understand Bible prophecy** [10] and the role of the Jews.

In the pages ahead we're going to learn that **prophecy is overwhelmingly focused on the fate of the Jewish people** and while the events of October 7 aren't explicitly mentioned in those prophecies, **the world's response to them was clearly anticipated in Scripture.**

Israel is mentioned over 2,500 times in the Old Testament and while God does sometimes express anger toward it - it's always in the context of correction, not abandonment. Scripture consistently reaffirms His intention to restore and bless His people.

And here's a spoiler - Gods protective hand is very firmly back on the Jewish people in the 21st century and the consequences of trying to harm them should act as an ominous warning to us all:

*"Whoever touches you touches the apple of His eye."* ***(Zechariah 2:8)***

Despite this, there are still many 'Christians' who openly defy the repeated messages in which God instructs us to support His people:

## The error of Replacement Theology [11]

As I noted earlier, some claim that Israel has been cast aside, and that biblical references to "Israel" should now be read as "the Church" or are figurative references to Christians. This idea, which had its

---

10 Surveys by Pew Research and Lifeway over the past decade have shown widespread confusion among Christians regarding Israel's theological role. Many hold a mix of Premillennial, Amillennial, and Replacement views without clearly distinguishing between them. This lack of clarity impacts both theology and political attitudes.

11 Replacement Theology has a long and complex history. It gained institutional traction after the early church began distancing itself from its Jewish roots, especially following the Bar Kokhba revolt (135 AD). It later became embedded in Catholic and Protestant teaching. Scholars like Michael Brown (*Our Hands Are Stained With Blood*) and Arnold Fruchtenbaum (*Israelology*) have detailed how this doctrine has contributed to centuries of antisemitism and scriptural distortion.

origins in the writings of some early Church leaders and later became embedded in much of Catholic and Protestant theology, is known as Replacement Theology and asserts that the Church has replaced the Jews in God's redemptive plan - an assumption that continues to influence many modern interpretations of biblical prophecy. But even within this framework, opinions vary. Some suggest Israel that may eventually be restored while others deny it any spiritual significance at all.

This isn't just a theological misstep - it's dangerous. It rewrites scripture, undermines prophecy, and has fuelled antisemitism for centuries.

As such, *Prophecy Shock* rejects Replacement Theology. To distort biblical references to Israel is to add to and take away from God's Word, violating the very principles outlined earlier in this book.

### Understanding the Jews

But if prophecy is really about the Jews – *who are the Jews?*

What's the difference between a Jew and an Israeli? Is it about ethnicity, nationality, religion - or something else? Sadly, despite their central role in both Testaments, **many Christians know little about the Jewish people** [12] and this lack of knowledge has led to racism and blatant stereotypes.

So to fully understand the Jews, let's go right back to the beginning of Jewish history to understand where they came from and how they came to play such a central role in the 21st century.

---

12 In a 2018 Lifeway Research study, 41% of evangelical Christians couldn't name Abraham as the father of the Jewish people, and most lacked a basic grasp of Jewish holidays, culture, or biblical history. This lack of awareness contributes to theological error and, in some cases, latent prejudice.

# 10

# A short history of the Jews

***The story of God's chosen people - and why it still matters***

In chapter 11 in the Old Testament Book of Genesis we're introduced to a man named Terah who lived in a city called Ur in the Chaldean province of Babylonia in what is now the southern part of modern-day Iraq.

Terah was a direct descendant of Shem, one of the sons of Noah and the man from whom we get the word 'Semitic'.

There is debate over when Terah lived and, indeed, debate over the precise timing of the events of the following 650+ years but for the purposes of this book I have adopted the timings of British Archaeologist *David Rohl* who has done an outstanding job of dating early Israeli history and its relationship to the rest of the Middle East.

But back to Terah. We know that he had three sons - Nahor, Haran and Abram - and it is Abram (or, as we know him, Abraham) who became the 'father' of the people we know, today, as the Jews.

## Jacob becomes Israel

I'd recommend a full study of Abraham, his wife Sarah, and their lineage - but for the purposes of this book we'll just focus on the fact that Abraham moved to the land of Canaan, that his son, Isaac, became next in the line of succession - and that Isaacs son, Jacob, followed after him.

Jacob is significant because his name was changed, by God, to 'Israel' ('God prevails') and this also became the name of Canaan in which he and his twelve sons lived. Those sons also became the patriarchs of the 'twelve tribes', one of which was **Yehūdāh** (pronounced *yeh-hoo-DAH*) from which we get the anglicised name 'Judah' from which we get the word 'Jew'. But more on that later.

**Joseph and Egypt**

Another of Jacobs sons, Joseph, was favoured by his father. If you've seen the Stage Musical 'Joseph and his Amazing Technicolour Dreamcoat' [13] you know the story and have a basic understanding of how this favouritism caused conflict between Joseph and his brothers. This jealousy eventually spilled over and resulted in his brothers selling him to Ishmaelite traders and telling Jacob that he had been killed by a wild animal.

Instead, Joseph was taken to Egypt and sold to a wealthy dignitary named Potiphar, before ending up in prison for a crime that he didn't commit. Eventually he came to the attention of the Pharoah as a result of interpreting a dream for one of his fellow cellmates who had subsequently ended up in Pharaoh's service.

Joseph was called to appear before Pharoah who had also had a troubling dream, in which seven fat cows and seven lean cows came up out of the Nile.

Joseph successfully interpreted the dream as a warning of seven bountiful years, followed by seven years of famine - and, as a result, was placed in a position of great authority over Egypt in order to prepare the nation for these events.

Several years later Joseph was reunited with his father and brothers who all moved to Egypt, along with their families, where they lived out their days in honour and comfort. However over time the Israelites, who had remained a distinct group within Egypt, were progressively marginalised and, four centuries later, they had become slaves to the Egyptian people.

[13] The musical, by Andrew Lloyd Webber and Tim Rice, is a retelling of the Genesis story of Joseph. While dramatized, it's surprisingly faithful to the core biblical events from Genesis 37–50.

## Moses and the Exodus

This led to the emergence of Moses, an Israelite who had been adopted by Pharaoh's sister after she found him, as a baby, floating down the Nile in a reed ark in which he had been placed by his Hebrew family.

Moses became a favourite of Pharoah and was treated as a son. However, after an incident in which he killed an Egyptian official for mistreating an Israelite slave, he fled to Midian (on the Northwest Arabian Peninsula) where he encountered God and where he spent forty years learning His ways.

After this, he returned to Egypt, where a new Pharoah was on the throne, and he demanded that this new Pharoah release the Israelites and allow them to leave Egypt.

Pharoah refused, and God responded by sending a series of plagues - the last of which killed the firstborn child of every Egyptian. The firstborn children of the Israelites were protected from this by the spreading 'the blood of a sacrificial lamb' over their doorways - an act which caused the Angel of Death to 'pass over' those houses. This is the genesis of the event which is still celebrated today as 'Passover' and which clearly portends the redemptive role of Christ, the sacrificial Lamb of God [14].

As a result of this final plague, Pharoah relented and allowed the Israelites to leave - however, after they had left, he changed his mind and pursued them to the Red Sea.

This set up the scene for one of the great miracles of the Bible - the parting of the Red Sea to allow the Israelites to cross. After this, the sea closed back over, drowning the Egyptian army which was in pursuit.

You would think that such an awesome event would forever indenture the Israelites to the power of their God - but it didn't, and they quickly fell into idol worship, causing God to curse them to

[14] This typological view is a common Christian interpretation found in texts like *Jesus in the Feasts of Israel* by Richard Booker, which explores how Old Testament festivals foreshadow the Messiah.

wander in the desert for forty years until the adults of that generation had died out.

### Joshua and the Judges

Toward the end of the forty years a new hero, Joshua, emerged to succeed Moses. Joshua was responsible for leading the reconquest of Canaan and the re-establishment of the twelve tribes in their former homeland, each in different areas of the land.

Following Joshua's death, and for several hundred years after, the nation was ruled over by a succession of 'Judges' who served in a kind of non-hereditary leadership role which was as much military as it was legal [15].

### Kings and Division

After the period of the **Judges**, the people of Israel asked for a king. God gave them **Saul**, then **David**, who first established **Jerusalem** as the capital of the Hebrew nation. David was followed by his son, **Solomon**, who built the first Temple.

After Solomon's death, the kingdom split into Israel (north) and Judah (south).

The history of these separate nations is colourful and turbulent, and the story of their various kings is a repeated tale of corruption, idol worship and repentance - but their chequered relationship ended, in 722BC, when the northern Kingdom of Israel was conquered by the Assyrians.

It's important to note that both Judah and Israel lasted for several hundred years and that, over that time, members of all tribes moved around - so, by the 8th century BC, Judah (from which we derive the word 'Jew' [16]) was a melting pot of all of the descendants

---

[15] The Book of Judges describes this transitional period from tribal confederacy to monarchy. Key figures include Deborah, Gideon, and Samson. Historians such as Israel Finkelstein have studied this era archaeologically in *The Bible Unearthed*.

[16] The idea that the ten "lost tribes" were absorbed into Judah has scholarly support. Jewish historian Simon Schama affirms this in his book *The Story of the Jews* (2013), noting Judah became the de facto heir to all Israelite identity after the Assyrian exile.

of Jacob - not just descendants of Judah. Additionally, remnants of the inhabitants of Israel almost certainly fled into neighbouring Judah at the time of the Assyrian invasion and were absorbed into the population of that nation.

As such, the term 'Jew' can be regarded as a generic description referring to Israelites from all of the twelve tribes. This has remained the case up until modern times and while there is a fringe view that the ten so-called 'lost tribes' of Israel migrated to eastern Europe or can be found amongst the Europeans, Americans, Canadians, Australians and New Zealanders of today - such a view defies scripture and logic as all of the tribes now exist under the general banner of the 'Jewish' people and are not 'lost'.

### The Babylonian Exile and Return

Meanwhile, the southern state of Judah lasted for a little over one hundred more years until it was conquered by the Babylonians. Even then, the Babylonian King Nebuchadnezzar allowed the Jews to continue to nominally rule themselves and placed Zedekiah on the throne as his proxy in 597BC.

This arrangement continued for several years, until Zedekiah allied himself with the Egyptians. This act enraged Nebuchadnezzar and led to the siege of Jerusalem in 589BC, ultimately leading to the total conquest of the Jews.

Over this time many Jews were exiled to Babylon in waves between 606 and 580 BC. Prophets like **Daniel and Ezekiel** were among these exiles, but after the **Persians** conquered Babylon in 539 BC, the Jews were allowed to return and rebuild.

### The Birth of Yeshua

Although back in their land, they remained under foreign rule - first by the Persians, then the Greeks, and eventually the Romans, who governed through provincial rulers and, later, Herod the Great, a non-Jewish "king."

Shortly before his death, Herod ordered the **Massacre of the Innocents,** an obscene act, recorded in the second chapter of the Gospel of Matthew. It took the form of an order to slaughter all male Jewish boys under two years of age and was designed to eliminate Yeshua, who Herod saw as a rival to his throne.

Herod was first alerted to the birth of Christ through the visit of a group of Magi 'from the east' who were 'led by a star'. Putting aside the romanticism of this story, the Magi were initiates of a Babylonian/Persian Mystery School that the Prophet Daniel had presided over five centuries earlier, and they were almost certainly acting on a star alignment which they had first been taught to watch for, hundreds of years earlier.

However, Joseph, the adoptive father of Yeshua, was warned of Herod's plot and escaped to Egypt with his family, where they stayed until Herod died, before returning to Judea and settling in Nazareth in the north of the country. There the family remained until Yeshua began his ministry - culminating in His role as the focus of the defining event of human history. Indeed, until recently, Yeshua was the very basis upon which we measured time, which was divided between BC (Before Christ) and AD (Annos Domini - 'in the year of our Lord').

Yeshua's message of Grace and redemption, which was offered to all who would accept it took, first the Middle East, and then Europe, by storm and, over the following centuries, transformed previously pagan societies into a belief in one God - the God of the Jews.

Over time, in recognition of this new faith, additional writings were discovered and added to the original scriptural canon, and by 200 AD, we saw the first compilation of a collection of writings which looked broadly similar to what we now know as the New Testament.

### Jewish Dispersal and Early Persecution

Meanwhile, the Jews had continued to live in Judea and even staged several revolts against the ruling Romans - but after the Bar Kokhba revolt in AD 135 they were expelled from Jerusalem and the city was refounded as the pagan Roman colony Aelia Capitolina. This severed Jewish residence there for centuries with Jewish access remaining heavily restricted under both Roman and Byzantine rule until the city passed from Byzantine Christian control to the Muslim Rashidun Caliphate in AD 637.

This change resulted in a period of harmony between the Muslims and the Jews - but starting in, or around, 688 under the orders of Caliph Abd al-Malak, construction of the building that we now know as the **Dome of the Rock** began on the Temple Mount in Jerusalem and was built over the next 3 or 4 years.

For Jews, this act was an overwhelming desecration of their most holy site which irrevocably changed the previously tolerant relationship between the Muslims and the Jews. It also led to a very large numbers of Jews 'taking flight' and abandoning Jerusalem to avoid growing persecution - first to Eastern Europe in the 6th century and, by the 7th century, through large scale migration to Western Europe as well.

**Christian Persecution of the Jews**

Sadly, these migrations were accompanied by antisemitism in the nations to which the Jews went - most of it fuelled by racist beliefs that were developing, and even encouraged, within Christianity. These included the widely held belief that the Jews were responsible for the death of Jesus.

These persecutions increased over the centuries and became widespread during the Crusades when a number of Jewish communities in France and the Rhineland were massacred. By the 12th century, we also saw the emergence of the 'blood libel' in which Jews were falsely accused of murdering Christian children in order to use their blood for ritual sacrifices [17].

---

[17] The first major case was in Norwich, England in 1144. This lie spread across Europe and was used to justify pogroms. The term is still used today to describe conspiratorial antisemitism.

From 1215, following the Fourth Lateran Council[5], Jews were ordered to wear distinctive clothing or symbols in a chilling precursor of a similar order which would be enacted seven hundred years later [18] - and by the late 13th century Jews were being increasingly expelled, in their entirety, from locations across Western Europe including Germany, England, France and also Spain and Portugal where they were given an ultimatum: convert to Christianity or leave the country.

By the 14th century Jews were being blamed for the Black Death which devastated Europe and many Jewish communities were destroyed in an hysterical wave of violence between 1348 and 1350. In Strasbourg alone, two thousand Jews were burnt to death before the plague had even reached the city. In Germany, around 300 Jewish communities were destroyed over this same period of time.

As antisemitism grew, an increasing burden of restrictions were placed on the Jews in many countries, and they were also excluded from many occupations because of fear of competition with local populations. They were also prohibited from owning land and their places of residence were often limited to specific areas known as 'ghettos'.

## The Protestant Reformation

The 16th Century saw a titanic change in the Christian faith with the rise of the Protestant Reformation which fundamentally reshaped Christianity. Protestantism returned the focus of the faith to personal responsibility and the pre-eminence of *sola scriptura* - the belief that scripture, alone, took precedence over the manmade traditions, roles, heresies and titles of the Catholic Church.

But any hope that this might lead to an easier lot for the Jews was quickly dashed. In his shocking book 'On the Jews and their Lies', Protestant Reformer Martin Luther proposed that Jews should have

---

[18] Canon 68 of the Fourth Lateran Council required Jews to wear identifying badges. This policy later inspired Nazi Germany's yellow star law. For further context, see Paul Johnson's *A History of the Jews*.

their synagogues and schools burnt down, be banned from Christian homes, have their holy writings taken away, be banned from preaching, be offered no protection on highways, and be put to work in manual roles [19].

Unsurprisingly, this ongoing tide of relentless antisemitism fuelled resentment and defiance in the Jews, and, by the late 19th century, nationalist movements were starting to form. Chief among these was the movement known as 'Zionism', founded by Hungarian Jew Theodor Herzl [20], which advocated strong support for a Jewish homeland centred in the ancient lands of Judah and Israel. This must have seemed a forlorn hope, at the time, as these lands were under the control of the Islamic Ottoman empire and the chances of that power returning them to the Jews were effectively zero.

However, just 17 years after the First Zionist Congress was held, the world was plunged into the first world war - a conflict which reshaped Europe and ended with Palestine (as Israel was known, at the time), and most of the Middle East, coming under the control of the British and the French.

### The Balfour Declaration

Even before the war was over, the British had already made known their support for the formation of a 'national home for the Jewish people', in Palestine which, even then, had a significant Jewish population. The 1917 'Balfour Declaration' [21] – a public statement contained in a letter from British Foreign Secretary Arthur Balfour to Lord Rothschild, a leader of the British Jewish community - made this support official and was widely covered in media at the time.

---

[19] Luther's 1543 treatise *On the Jews and Their Lies* is deeply antisemitic and a stain on the Reformation legacy. Scholars have acknowledged its disturbing influence on later German antisemitism, including the Nazi regime.

[20] Herzl's *Der Judenstaat* (1896) launched the modern Zionist movement, calling for a Jewish homeland in response to rising European antisemitism. He chaired the First Zionist Congress in Basel, Switzerland, in 1897.

[21] This was a letter from UK Foreign Secretary Arthur Balfour to Lord Rothschild. It was later incorporated into the League of Nations Mandate for Palestine, laying groundwork for Israel's re-establishment. See *Palestine and the Balfour Declaration* by Jonathan Schneer.

This development looked extremely promising for the creation of a Jewish state, particularly when the British and French took formal control of parts of the Levant and divided the area up under the Syke Picot agreement and the granting of a formal Mandate, by the League of Nations, in 1922.

Sadly however, the initial promise of the declaration became increasingly watered down over the next 10 years and, despite American support of Jewish statehood, the proposal became mired in the politics of the region and the victim of British horse trading with Middle Eastern states with different agendas.

This dragged on for over a decade until it was eventually overshadowed by the greatest threat to the Jewish people in a history that spanned back thousands of years.

**The Holocaust**

In 1933, newly appointed German Chancellor Adolf Hitler set about enacting a series of racist reforms which were designed to isolate Jews from civil German society. These included the construction of concentration camps for the detention of political opponents and the confiscation of the property of Jews.

Six years later Hitler annexed Austria and invaded Czechoslovakia and Poland - the last of these leading to a declaration of war by Britain and its allies. However, Germany continued to act with impunity and, by 1940, had occupied most of Europe, rounding up Jews as it moved from country to country.

1.3 million Jews were murdered in mass shootings and pogroms in the summer of 1941 alone and, by 1942, Germany had formalised a policy to determine the fate of all Jews in Europe. The 'Final Solution' authorised the elimination of Jewish populations and led to the mass deportation of Jews, from ghettos across Europe, to Extermination Camps where they were gassed, worked or beaten to death, or killed by disease, starvation, cold, medical experiments, or during death marches. This slaughter continued until the eventual defeat of the

Nazis and the close of World War 2 in May 1945, by which time over 6 million Jews had been murdered [22].

**From Holocaust to homeland**

After millennia of persecution - including one of the worst genocides in human history - you might have expected the Jewish people to fade into silence. Instead, within just a few years of the Holocaust, **two prophetic milestones** reshaped modern history:

**1948: A Nation Reborn**

Following the Holocaust, the world turned its focus to the Middle East and, in 1947, after Britain announced plans to end its rule of the Holy land, the newly formed United Nations proposed partitioning the land into two states[1]: one Jewish, one Arab. The proposed borders were imperfect, offering the Jews limited access to some key sites of historic and religious importance - but the Jewish leadership accepted regardless, grateful to reclaim part of their homeland after 2,500 years.

On **November 29, 1947**, the UN voted to support the plan. **33 nations approved**, with 13 opposing and 10 abstaining [23].

Not surprisingly, Arab nations rejected the plan entirely and when Israel declared independence on May 14, 1948, five Arab armies attacked that same night [24], vowing to wipe it off the map.

Instead, Israel survived, securing victory in what became known as the War of Independence - though at great cost: 1% of the

[22] This figure is supported by records from Yad Vashem, the United States Holocaust Memorial Museum, and Nazi documentation. Notable scholarly treatments include *Ordinary Men* by Christopher Browning and *The Destruction of the European Jews* by Raul Hilberg.

[23] This refers to *UN General Assembly Resolution 181*, passed on November 29, 1947, which recommended the partition of Mandatory Palestine into independent Arab and Jewish states. The full text and vote count are available on the UN website and in most major histories of the Middle East.

[24] On May 15, 1948, armies from Egypt, Jordan, Syria, Iraq, and Lebanon invaded Israel. This marked the beginning of the 1948 Arab-Israeli War. The events are documented in *1948: A History of the First Arab-Israeli War* by Benny Morris.

population was killed. 700,000 Arabs became refugees [25] - many leaving at the urging of Arab leaders - but those who remained in Israel were granted full citizenship. Meanwhile, 800,000 Jews were expelled from Arab countries, many of whom also found refuge in Israel.

In 1949, Israel joined the United Nations and emerged as a democratic state - with full rights for all citizens. But the story didn't end there.

**1967: Jerusalem Reunited**

Tensions simmered for years, flaring in 1956 when Egypt blocked Israeli shipping routes. A UN force was deployed to keep the peace, but in 1967, Egypt's Nasser again closed the Straits of Tiran and demanded UN withdrawal. War was inevitable.

On June 5, 1967, Israel launched a pre-emptive strike on Egyptian airfields, igniting the Six-Day War. It quickly spread. Syria shelled from the north and, despite Israeli warnings to stay out of the conflict, Jordan attacked from the east.

In response, Israeli forces advanced toward the Old City of Jerusalem, then controlled by Jordan - and on June 7, General Mordechai Gur radioed history [26]:

*"The Temple Mount is in our hands. I repeat, the Temple Mount is in our hands!"*

Shortly after, Chief Chaplain Shlomo Goren blew the Shofar at the Western Wall[6]. That same day, Défense Minister Moshe Dayan declared:

---

25 The displacement of Arabs during the 1948 war is widely documented, though causes are debated. See *The Birth of the Palestinian Refugee Problem* by Benny Morris. Jewish expulsion figures are supported by records from the World Jewish Congress and Jewish advocacy groups such as JIMENA. The number is also affirmed by historian Edwin Black in *The Farhud*. This quote is well documented and widely quoted. Gur's announcement is part of Israeli national memory and is preserved in IDF transcripts and archival recordings.

26 A famous image and moment from June 7, 1967. It is featured in documentaries, newsreels, and Oren's *Six Days of War*. Goren later became Chief Rabbi of Israel.

*"We have returned to the holiest of our holy places, never to part from it again."*

Over the following days, more than 200,000 Jews visited the Western Wall. Yet tensions resurfaced and, seeking peace, Prime Minister Levi Eshkol handed administrative access to the Temple Mount over to the Islamic Waqf [27], a decision still debated today due to the spiritual and political complexities that followed.

Still, for the first time in 2,500 years, both Jerusalem and the ancient homeland were back in Jewish hands [28] - exactly as God had promised [29].

From exile to Holocaust, from independence to restoration, the story of Israel is the story of prophecy fulfilled. The events of 1948 and 1967 are not only geopolitical miracles - but they are also theological milestones and, as the next chapters will show, God's redemptive timeline runs *through* Israel - not around it.

---

27 A famous image and moment from June 7, 1967. It is featured in documentaries, newsreels, and Oren's *Six Days of War*. Goren later became Chief Rabbi of Israel.

28 This refers to sovereignty over the city and land, not necessarily continuous Jewish presence. Historian Martin Gilbert's *Jerusalem: A History* explores the city's turbulent past and its centrality in Jewish history.

29 The status of Jerusalem remains one of the most contentious issues in international politics. UN resolutions, multiple peace talks, and widespread diplomatic debate centre on this city. For an overview, see *Jerusalem: A Biography* by Simon Sebag Montefiore.

11

# The immovable rock

***A people preserved by prophecy, restored by promise***

Only the most hardened sceptic could fail to be moved by the story of the Jewish people. Great Empires like the Hittites, Sumerians, Assyrians, Phoenicians, Aztecs, and many more have come and gone: - taking their languages, customs, and religions with them.

But the **Jews remain**.

Despite centuries of exile, oppression, and genocide, they not only survived but they also preserved their national and religious identity. And now, after being dispersed from their homeland for over 1,200 years, they've returned - speaking the ancient language of Hebrew and rebuilding a nation from the dust [30].

Their very existence in the modern world is nothing short of a miracle - and more than that, it's **a fulfilment of prophecy**.

> *"I myself will gather the remnant of my flock out of all the countries where I have driven them... and bring them back to their pasture."* ***(Jeremiah 23:3–4)***

---

[30] Modern Hebrew was revived by Eliezer Ben-Yehuda in the late 19th and early 20th centuries. His work is detailed in *Tongue of the Prophets* by Robert St. John. The cultural and linguistic revival of Hebrew is considered one of the most successful in human history.

*"Surely I will take the children of Israel from among the nations... and bring them into their own land." **(Ezekiel 37:21–22)***

These aren't poetic metaphors. They are precise descriptions of what is happening right now. Israel isn't just back - it's back **exactly as foretold**: in the land, as one people, with Jerusalem at the centre. These prophecies are being fulfilled **in our time**, with stunning clarity [31].

Yet many Christians remain unaware of the pinpoint accuracy of these prophecies. Worse still, some try to **recast them as metaphors for the Church** [32], ignoring the reality of what has taken place in Israel since 1948.

### Modern Israel

Israel, today, is home to just over ten million people. About three-quarters of these people are Jews, drawn from Jewish communities that once lived across Europe, the Middle East, Africa, and the former Soviet Union. Around one-fifth of Israelis are Arab citizens - mostly Muslim, with significant Christian and Druze minorities - and the remainder belong to smaller ethnic and religious groups. The result is a nation of remarkable diversity, where people whose families once lived thousands of miles apart now share a single national identity.

Politically, Israel operates as a parliamentary democracy in which *all* citizens of voting age, vote. Its national legislature, the Knesset, consists of 120 elected members chosen through proportional representation. Governments are formed through coalitions, often representing a wide range of political and cultural perspectives. The prime minister serves as head of government,

---

31 While interpretations vary, many historians and political scholars - religious and secular alike - acknowledge the extraordinary alignment between biblical prophecy and 20th-century Jewish history. For example, see *The Case for Israel* by Alan Dershowitz or *The Everlasting Hatred* by Hal Lindsey (noting theological bias).

32 This refers to doctrines aligned with *Replacement Theology*. The debate over whether Old Testament promises to Israel apply to the Church is explored in *Has the Church Replaced Israel?* by Michael J. Vlach and *Israel Matters* by Gerald McDermott.

while a separate president - largely a ceremonial role - serves as head of state. Elections are frequent, political debate is vigorous, and the country maintains an independent judiciary, a free press, and the democratic institutions typical of modern Western democracies.

Economically, Israel has undergone one of the most remarkable transformations of any nation in the modern era. When the state was established in 1948 it was poor, largely agricultural, and absorbing hundreds of thousands of refugees. Today its economy produces well over half a trillion US dollars in annual output and ranks among the most technologically advanced in the world.

Israel has more startup companies per capita than almost any nation on earth - so many that it has earned the nickname "the Start-Up Nation." It spends a higher proportion of its national income on research and development than any other country, and its universities and research institutes have produced dozens of Nobel Prize laureates.

Despite this, agriculture remains an important part of the national story. In the early decades of the state, pioneering collective communities known as kibbutzim helped transform swamps and desert landscapes into productive farmland. Those early agricultural experiments produced techniques that are now used worldwide. Israel's drip-irrigation systems, greenhouse farming, and desert agriculture technologies are exported globally. Even today, citrus fruits - especially the famous Jaffa oranges - remain an iconic symbol of Israel's agricultural heritage.

Perhaps the most surprising statistic of all concerns water. Despite being located in a largely arid region, Israel now produces a majority of its drinking water through large-scale desalination plants and recycles nearly ninety percent of its wastewater for agriculture - the highest rate in the world.

Security has also shaped the country's development. Israel maintains one of the most capable militaries anywhere in the world. The Israel Defense Forces consist of ground forces, an advanced air force, and a naval component, supported by universal military service for most young Israelis. In terms of technological sophistication and readiness, Israel consistently ranks among the leading military powers globally.

Yet the entire country is geographically tiny - roughly the size of New Jersey – and from north to south it can be crossed in a just few hours by car.

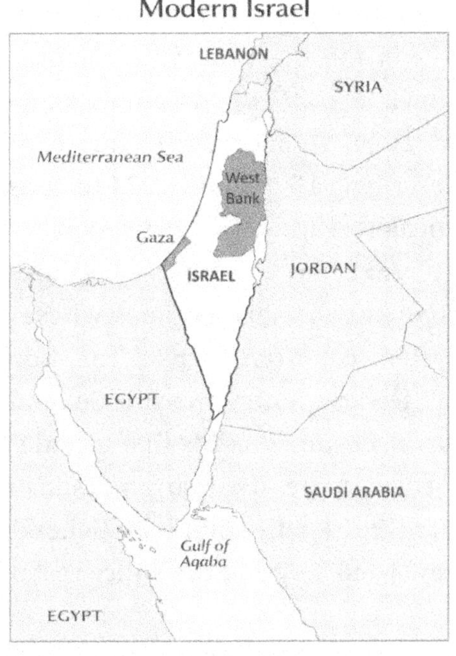


Its modern borders are significantly smaller than the territory associated with the united kingdom ruled by King Solomon during the biblical period and described as extending "from the Euphrates to the land of the Philistines and to the border of Egypt" in 1 Kings 4:21. Yet within this smaller space a remarkable nation has emerged and in less than a century Israel has become a thriving democracy, a technological powerhouse, a military force of global significance, and a society built from the return of a people who were scattered across the world for nearly two thousand years.

But it's Israel's impact on international politics which most concerns us, in this book:

> *"On that day... I will make Jerusalem an immovable rock for all the nations. All who try to move it will injure themselves."* ***(Zechariah 12:3)***

Zechariah predicted that Israel would not just become controversial, but that it would become disproportionately controversial – a prediction which has proven hauntingly accurate 2,500 years later. Israel is not a vast empire. It is not a superpower. It is a tiny nation, yet it commands a level of international attention that bears no rational relationship to its size.

The argument is not that Israel is above criticism. No nation is. The argument is that Israel is treated as though it alone stands at the centre of the world's moral disorder.

In the UN General Assembly, the pattern has become almost ritual. In 2023, the Assembly adopted 13 Israel-related resolutions. In 2024, it adopted 16 more, with the U.S. State Department describing 15 of those 2024 texts as *one-sided and biased*. That is not normal scrutiny. That is fixation.

And the imbalance becomes even starker when Israel is contrasted against regimes whose brutality is real. In the same UN system, countries such as Iran, North Korea, Syria, Myanmar attract far fewer country-specific General Assembly condemnations than Israel, despite records that include mass imprisonment, state terror, torture, aggressive war and industrial-scale repression. One widely cited 2024 tally found 17 General Assembly resolutions aimed at Israel and only 7 at the entire rest of the world combined.

The pattern is unmistakable: Israel is not merely criticised; it is singled out. The resolutions do not prove that Israel is the world's worst offender. They prove that Israel has become the world's default defendant.

That institutional obsession is even clearer in the UN Human Rights Council, where Israel remains the only country with its own permanent agenda item - Item 7. Britain itself, hardly a reflexive defender of every Israeli policy, called this "systematic institutional bias" and said the Council's disproportionate focus on Israel damaged its credibility. That is an extraordinary admission, because it comes not from a pro-Israel pressure group but from a Western government explaining its own vote. In other words, even states that criticise Israel have recognised that the machinery of international condemnation has become structurally warped. When one nation alone is placed on permanent trial, the issue is no longer justice. It is prejudice dressed up as process.

That is why the phrase "immovable rock" feels so unnervingly precise. The world cannot leave Israel alone. It keeps returning to it, debating it, denouncing it, pressuring it, isolating it, and trying to force it into retreat.

Since the Hamas atrocities launched from Gaza on 7 October 2023 - atrocities that included the deliberate murder of civilians, hostage-taking, and sexual violence - the campaign to delegitimise Israel has only intensified. Gaza and the West Bank, the two territories most closely bound to the unfinished legacy of the 1948 war and its aftermath, remain the focal point of an international obsession that is far more about destroying Israel than gaining territory,

This is exactly what Zechariah said would happen: Jerusalem would become a weight the nations could not resist trying to lift, even though every attempt to move it would only wound the hands that tried.

We'll address the reasons for this obsession later in the book – but, for now, how does the restoration of Israel relate to the critique of Premillennialism? Why does Israel's re-emergence expose flaws in that interpretive system?

That's where we will go next, as we begin to lay out the foundations of Israelism. These stand-alone Chapters are spread throughout the rest of the book, usually in proximity to chapters which rely on their content – and always with a grey wash and headlined ***The Principles of Israelism*** to set them apart from the rest of the book:

12

## THE PRINCIPLES OF ISRAELISM

# It's all about the Jews

Over the last few chapters, we've traced the extraordinary survival of the Jewish people - through exile, persecution, dispersion, and repeated attempts at annihilation. But what does that have to do with prophecy?

Quite a lot, because the Book of Daniel isn't just ancient history. It is a prophetic timeline of Jewish destiny, mostly told through the lens of their ancient Capital, Jerusalem.

Spanning more than 2,500 years, from the 6th century BC to the 20th century AD, Daniel's visions chart the fate of Israel with breathtaking precision. He foresaw the rise and fall of global empires, the invasions that would scatter his people, the persecutions that would nearly destroy them, and ultimately, their restoration to their homeland.

This matters, because Daniel's book is also claimed as the prophetic foundation of Premillennialism. And here lies the collision: the two interpretations cannot coexist. If Daniel's visions are about the Jews, then they are not about the Church. And that contradiction exposes a fatal flaw in much of modern prophecy teaching.

Ask yourself which is more plausible? That God would use a Jewish prophet, living in exile in Babylon in the 6th century BC, to write a sweeping forecast of his people's fate across two and a half millennia? Or that He would skip past all of that to outline the plight of an as-yet unborn group of (mostly) non-Jews (Christians) living thousands of years in the future?

The answer is self-evident, and once you recognize that **Daniel was writing about his own people**, the implications are staggering.

**Key Conclusions**

- The Jewish identity is rooted not merely in ancestry and religion - but in a divine calling that has shaped the very course of world history.
- Despite relentless displacement, persecution, and attempts at annihilation, the Jewish people have survived with unparalleled resilience and cultural continuity.
- Their survival across millennia - barred from their homeland for much of that time - defies all historical precedent and underscores the uniqueness of their covenantal role.
- The story of the Jews is not only about survival but about purpose. Their enduring presence continues to challenge, confront, and shape humanity's understanding of faith, justice, and destiny.
- And holding this story together is Jerusalem – the City of God – the key piece which makes all other prophecies make sense.

This book will demonstrate that Daniel not only foresaw **key events in modern Jewish history**, but that he pinpointed the exact years in which they would occur. Yet for more than half a century, these revelations have been buried beneath layers of alternative interpretations - interpretations that have distracted us, pointing prophecy toward the wrong people at the wrong time.

**Prophecy hasn't failed** us - we've simply been reading it through the wrong lens.

13

# Who are the Jews today?

***Defining Jewish identity: birth, belief, and belonging***

So is Jewishness defined by ethnicity, a common culture or a shared religion (Judaism)? The answer is, all three – kind of.

**Born Jewish**

For most of history, Jewishness has been inherited. According to traditional Jewish law (*halakha*), a person is Jewish if their mother is Jewish. This matrilineal principle goes back to ancient rabbinic rulings and remains the standard in Orthodox and Conservative Judaism. If both parents are Jewish, the matter is simple: the child is unquestionably Jewish.

That said, not all streams of Judaism agree. Reform Judaism and some other modern movements accept either parent - mother or father - provided the child is raised with a Jewish identity. Meanwhile, the Karaite community, a smaller group within Jewry, passes Jewishness through the father rather than the mother.

But here is the key: **once you are born Jewish, you remain Jewish**, regardless of personal belief or practice. A Jew who no longer follows Judaism - whether becoming secular, atheist, or embracing other philosophies - is still considered Jewish. Culture, faith, and identity may drift, but heritage remains fixed.

**Converted Jewish**

A second form of Jewish identity is through **conversion**. A non-Jew who formally embraces Judaism through the recognized process of study, ritual, and commitment is regarded as fully Jewish, both culturally and legally, as though born into the people.

Conversion might suggest that Judaism is purely a religion, but Jewish identity goes further. Even if a convert later abandons the faith or ceases religious practice, Judaism still considers that person Jewish. They may be seen as estranged or even apostate, but their Jewishness remains. In this sense, Judaism holds membership to be permanent - whether entered by birth or by choice.

The children of converted Jews are also considered Jewish provided they were born after the mother converted.

**Jewish vs. Israeli**

It is also important to note the difference between **being Jewish** and **being Israeli**. The two overlap, but they are not the same. A Jew can be born in New York, Paris, or Auckland and remain fully Jewish without ever setting foot in Israel.

Conversely, not all Israelis are Jewish. Of Israel's roughly ten million citizens, nearly **two million are Arabs**, most of them Muslim or Christian. They are Israeli by nationality, but not Jewish by heritage or religion.

This distinction matters:

Judaism is both a people and a faith, stretching back thousands of years and preserved across the world.

Israel is a modern nation-state, restored in 1948, which serves as the homeland of the Jewish people but also includes other ethnic and religious communities.

# 14

THE PRINCIPLES OF ISRAELISM

## Why this book is different to all other books on prophecy

Earlier in this book, we explored the confusion that surrounds the interpretation of Bible prophecy. We saw that sincere, knowledgeable, Bible-believing Christians can arrive at very different conclusions about what prophecy means and how it should be understood.

That confusion is not accidental. It exists because most systems of prophecy interpretation rely on what I have, somewhat tongue-in-cheek, dubbed ***"best fitism."***

*Best fitism* is the process by which an interpretation is considered valid when it appears to fit the prophetic clues better than competing explanations.

Each major school of prophecy - premillennialism, postmillennialism, amillennialism, and historicism - ultimately builds its case on a form of *best fitism*. Each presents a framework that seems to align with the biblical text, and each argues that its alignment is more convincing than the alternatives.

But there is an obvious problem with that approach.

If prophecy is open to multiple "best fits," then the final outcome is not clarity, but competition. The result is what we see today:

centuries of disagreement, competing charts, conflicting timelines, and no consistent way to determine which interpretation is actually correct.

In other words, *best fitism* does not solve prophecy. It perpetuates confusion because the competing solutions are based on opinions, not facts.

## Different Types of Prophecy

So can this problem be resolved? Is there a way to be *sure* about the meaning of any particular prophecy?

There is.

When we use the word "prophecy," we are actually describing the many different ways in which God demonstrates that He knows the end from the beginning – but not all prophetic passages function in the same way.

Some are **conditional prophecies**, where the outcome depends on human response: if people change, one result follows; if they do not, another outcome unfolds. Others are **unconditional prophecies**, which announce what will happen regardless of human action.

There are also prophecies that identify specific individuals, lineages, victories, or periods of rule, as well as **restoration promises** which describe return, renewal, peace, and the re-establishment of God's presence after judgment.

In each of these cases, the meaning of the prophecy is largely defined by the conditions surrounding it. The context, the people involved, and the nature of the event itself provide the framework for understanding what is being described. As a result, these prophecies are generally recognised through their fulfilment in real events, rather than solved through precise calculation. They are interpreted by **what happens**, not by **when it happens**.

However, there is another category of prophecy which operates very differently.

**The Nature of Time-Defined Prophecy**

Throughout Scripture, we are also given prophecies that include **specific measurements of time**. These *time-defined prophecies* include tantalising specific number references and are the prophecies of:

- *Time, times and half a time* - ***Daniel 7***
- *Time, times and half a time* - ***Daniel 12***
- *2,300 evenings and mornings* - ***Daniel 8:13–14***
- *1,290 days* - ***Daniel 12:11***
- *1,335 days* - ***Daniel 12:12***
- *42 months* - ***Revelation 11:1–2***
- *1,260 days (the Two Witnesses)* - ***Revelation 11:3–4***
- *Three and a half days* - ***Revelation 11:9–10***
- *Five months* - ***Revelation 9:5, 9:10***
- *1,260 days (the Woman in the Wilderness)* - ***Revelation 12:6***
- *Time, times and half a time* - ***Revelation 12:14***
- *42 months (the Beast's authority)* - ***Revelation 13:5***
- *69 weeks (sevens)* - ***Daniel 9:24–26***
- *70th seven* - ***Daniel 9:27***
- *390 + 40 days* - ***Ezekiel 4:4–6***

These are not symbolic placeholders or flexible estimates. They are precise durations This changes everything because once a prophecy includes a measurable period of time, it moves out of the realm of *best fitism* and into the realm of verification.

These prophecies appear, mainly, in the Books of Daniel and Revelation – and they are not casual, nor are they background details.

Some prophecy books devote themselves entirely to just one of them; others address a number of them.

*Prophecy Shock* solves ***all*** of them.

**How they have been treated**

For centuries, interpreters have been divided on how to handle them:

- **Premillennialism** has *appropriated* them, using them as the basis of its own end-times timeline - often rearranged or spiritualized into a futuristic seven-year tribulation framework.

- **Others,** uncomfortable with the apparent mismatch between numbers and history - have simply *spiritualized them away entirely,* treating them as symbolic expressions of "persecution," "opposition," or "a long period of time."

The result is confusion, misapplication, or dismissal. But what's been missed is the most straightforward and faithful explanation: that these numbers are exactly what they appear to be - time spans given by God to pinpoint prophetic fulfilment.

**The real meaning of *time-defined* prophecies**

Far from being vague symbols or speculative tools, these *time-defined prophecies* are **exact markers**, placed deliberately by God to show the precise unfolding of His plan. They are not elastic, nor are they metaphorical - and they're not "about the Church age" in some abstract sense. They are countdowns and calendars, tied to real-world events.

And here's the critical point: **they are Jewish, not Christian, in focus.**

- ***Every** time-defined prophecy* in Daniel finds its fulfilment in the history of Israel, from Babylon through to the modern rebirth of the Jewish state.

- Revelation, too - often wrongly read as being entirely about the Church - contains time spans and prophecies that point again and again to Jewish history and destiny.

These numbers are not an invitation to speculation about rapture timetables or church revivals. They are God's way of proving His faithfulness to His covenant people, Israel.

**Our approach to prophecy in this book**

This book is different to all other books on prophecy because it bases its solutions on the numbers and details provided by God – not opinion. As such, it approaches prophecy as follows:

- **The primary focus will be on time-defined prophecies** in the Books of Daniel and Revelation because they yield checkable dates and concrete outcomes.

- These time-defined prophecies must be **measurable and anchored in real history.**

- The prophecies will be presented as **coherent visions and integrated messages** - not isolated riddles or chapter fragments.

- **One rulebook:** Every time-defined prophecy will be tested by the **same Six Basic Questions** so that results are consistent and falsifiable.

- **Visible arithmetic:** A close 'fit' is not enough. We will show the year counts plainly so that you can **verify the math** for yourself with clear rules, transparent math, and outcomes you can **check, challenge, or confirm**.

Following this consistent approach, ***every one*** of these prophecies will be solved and tied to a definable span of history, measured in years, and culminating in modern events like the rebirth of Israel in 1948 or the recapture of Jerusalem in 1967.

**On prophetic start dates and historical uncertainty**

One last - but important - point before we begin testing Daniel's prophecies against specific historical timelines:

Throughout the rest of this book, we will identify specific years - start and end dates - for each prophecy we examine. In some cases, those dates are widely agreed. In others, the exact starting point is debated. This is not unusual. Archaeology and historical chronology is often refined as new evidence emerges.

For example, Machu Picchu was long dated to the mid to late 15th century based on Spanish records and traditional reconstructions. That view stood for generations. Yet in 2021, radiocarbon analysis showed the site was in use by around AD 1420 - decades earlier than assumed. The past hadn't changed; only our understanding of it. That is how history works.

The point is simple: if well-established dates from relatively recent history can be revised, it should not trouble us when dates from deep antiquity are debated.

Where start dates are broadly accepted, we will say so. Where there is legitimate debate, we will acknowledge it. In those cases, dates will be selected based on the strongest biblical and historical alignment. Scripture takes priority; history informs but does not override.

If that raises concerns about accuracy, it shouldn't. The strength of this framework does not depend on any single solution. It depends on coherence. A valid solution will consistently align across multiple prophecies, timelines, and historical events. These aren't weak interpretations that require constant adjustment – they are strong ones that repeatedly land on the same outcomes.

Prophecy is not proven by forcing certainty at the beginning, but by recognising consistency at the end.

### The Backbone of Prophecy

If time-defined prophecies are measurable and testable, then they are not open-ended:

They each have one correct solution – not multiple interpretations or 'major', 'minor' or 'dual' fulfilments

They are not waiting for a future interpretation.

They are not the subject of *opinion*.

They are not defined by the interpretation that *best fits*.

They resolve.

They are completed timelines that land on real points in history.

They are **the backbone of prophecy**.

They prove that God's Word is exact and they demonstrate that He knew and declared the milestones of Jewish history long before they happened. They establish Israel as the prophetic centre of gravity - not the US, Rome, the papacy, or the Church.

To ignore or misread these time spans is to miss the very mechanism that God gave us for unlocking prophecy. To grasp them is to see the Scriptures vindicated, Jewish history illuminated, and God's faithfulness confirmed beyond doubt.

But before we unpack the visions themselves, we need to meet the man who wrote many of them - and discover why Daniel is far more important than most Christians have ever imagined.

## Section Three

# THE PROPHECIES OF DANIEL

# Preview

***The Prophecies of Daniel: The Blueprint for the Last Days***

The first two sections of this book have laid the foundation for what comes next: a complete re-evaluation of Daniel's prophecies - not as abstract allegories or end-times riddles for the Church, but as precise, historically anchored messages about **Israel and the Jewish people**.

This next section is where the fulfilment framework of Israelism comes alive, bringing logic and clarity to texts long considered symbolic or speculative.

You'll come away from this section with a renewed sense of awe - not just at the content of Daniel's visions, but at the God who authored them with such flawless precision.

You'll also discover that the **Book of Daniel is not about Christians at all**. Instead, it's a detailed, time-coded map of Jewish history - written in advance, fulfilled exactly, and impacting directly on the times in which we live.

Over twelve chapters and seven visions, Daniel outlines a prophetic timeline stretching from the Babylonian exile in the 6th century BC to the miraculous rebirth of the State of Israel in the 20th century.

These visions aren't vague symbols to be loosely interpreted - they are made up of specific, datable, and testable prophecies, and they align with real events that have already taken place.

You'll learn:

- How applying **Six Basic Questions** to each prophecy consistently reveals clear meaning.

- Why terms like *"Time, Times and Half a Time"*, *"2,300 evenings and mornings"*, and *"1,335 days"* are not poetic metaphors - but **precise, datable time periods**.

- That the "beasts" that Daniel sees are not mythical figures or future tyrants - they are the **empires that historically ruled Jerusalem**.

- Why every one of these visions centres on **Jerusalem, the Temple, and the fate of the Jewish people**

- How Daniel's prophecies align with major real-world events and places - **from Babylon to the liberation of Jerusalem in 1967**.

This is where the speculative gives way to the scriptural - where timelines replace theories, and history confirms what Daniel saw.

If you've ever wanted clarity on what Bible prophecy really says - and doesn't say - this is where the fog begins to lift.

15

# Who was Daniel?

***The man behind the Visions***

Despite his massive influence on Christian prophecy interpretations, surprisingly little is known about **Daniel the man**. What we do know comes largely from his own writings and reveals a figure of deep faith, unwavering integrity, and prophetic purpose.

Daniel was born in Jerusalem in the late 7th century BC [33], during the time of a growing threat from the Babylonian Empire. As a young man, he was exiled to Babylon[2], where he quickly rose to high political office under King Nebuchadnezzar II [34] - serving at the highest levels of power in a foreign empire.

It was during this time that Daniel began receiving the visions that would eventually form the basis of one of the most significant prophetic books in the Bible: **The Book of Daniel**.

Though we don't know when or where Daniel died, Chapter 9 of his Book suggests that he lived into his eighties or nineties, having witnessed the full seventy years of Babylonian captivity.

---

[33] This dating aligns with traditional biblical chronology, placing Daniel's early life during the reign of King Jehoiakim (circa 609–598 BC). His exile is associated with the first Babylonian deportation around 604 BC, documented in 2 Kings 24 and affirmed in standard biblical reference works like *The Zondervan Illustrated Bible Dictionary*.

[34] Nebuchadnezzar II ruled Babylon from 606–562 BC and is credited with multiple deportations of Jews to Babylon, corroborated by both biblical sources (Daniel 1:1–2) and Babylonian chronicles, such as the *Babylonian Chronicle Tablets*, now housed in the British Museum.

Some modern scholars claim that Daniel never existed [35] - that he was a symbolic figure, or a literary construct used to communicate spiritual truths and, shockingly, even some Christians have accepted this. But these claims are not based on historical evidence. Instead, they are the product of an unwillingness to accept that Daniel could have so accurately predicted events which happened long after his death [36] and a determination to find another explanation by placing the writer of his prophecies hundreds of years after his time.

In essence, critics reject Daniel because he was right about what would happen in the centuries following his death - a remarkable case of circular reasoning. These objections say less about Daniel, and more about a worldview that cannot accept the supernatural precision of God's word [37].

**If you haven't read the Book of Daniel recently (or ever), now is the time to do so.** It will take about an hour and will provide invaluable context for what follows.

Once you've read it, return to these pages - and together, we'll begin to uncover what Daniel's visions really reveal.

---

[35] Daniel's ascent within the Babylonian and later Persian governments is well recorded in the Book of Daniel itself (e.g., chapters 2, 5, and 6). While secular sources don't mention Daniel by name, such silence is not unusual in ancient administrative records, which often omitted foreign or non-royal figures.

[36] This critical view, often associated with the *Maccabean dating theory*, argues that the Book of Daniel was written around 165 BC during the Seleucid oppression. Key proponents include scholars from the 19th-century German *Higher Criticism* tradition. See *Introduction to the Old Testament* by Raymond E. Brown for a mainstream overview of this debate.

[37] The detailed prophecies in Daniel - particularly in chapters 8 and 11 - align so closely with the rise of Persia, Greece, and Antiochus Epiphanes that critics argue they must have been written *after* the events occurred. For a defense of the traditional dating, see *Daniel in the Critics' Den* by Josh McDowell and *The Prophet Daniel* by Edward J. Young.

16

THE PRINCIPLES OF ISRAELISM

# Visions, not Chapters

Have you ever considered how easy it is to find specific scriptures, quickly? That's due to the familiar **chapter and verse system** that was first introduced in the **13th century** by English Cardinal **Stephen Langton**, who added chapter divisions. Two centuries later, **Robert Estienne**, a French printer, added verse numbers.

These tools made Bible study more efficient - but also introduced new problems. While helpful for reference, chapter and verse divisions have led to the 'cherry-picking' of isolated texts - plucking verses out of context to support arguments rather than interpreting them within the full narrative. This has fuelled theology that often deviates from the original meaning and strips scripture of its context and coherence.

This becomes especially problematic in books like Daniel and Revelation and constitutes one of the most overlooked but critical keys to understanding prophecy: the structure of the biblical text itself.

Take Daniel, for example. His book wasn't originally written as chapters, but as **seven distinct visions** and the final vision spans **three chapters** - yet modern interpretations often separate these chapters, breaking apart what was meant to be read as one message.

The issue is even more pronounced in Revelation, where every vision is divided by artificial chapter breaks. These disruptions fracture the prophetic flow and have led to skewed understandings.

But the Bible was never intended to be read as a collection of disconnected statements. It was written as a series of complete, structured messages - each with a beginning, a development, and a conclusion. When those structures are broken, interpretation becomes guesswork. Once a vision is split apart, it becomes possible to assign meanings to fragments that were never meant to stand alone.

When you restore the structure, much of that confusion disappears. In this book, we'll return to the original prophecies - **vision by vision** - reconnecting the threads that chapter divisions have obscured. By doing so, we'll uncover deeper meanings and prophetic truths that have long been hidden in plain sight.

As we begin examining Daniel's prophecies, this structural shift will prove critical. What once seemed cryptic will begin to make sense - because we'll finally be reading the text the way it was written.

17

# What's in Daniel's Book?

***The Prophet's Seven Visions and what they reveal***

We tend to think of the Book of Daniel as a book of Prophecy - and it is - but it also recounts events which took place during Daniel's lifetime.

It is structured into twelve chapters and, in the original text, switched between two languages: Hebrew through until chapter 2:4, then Aramaic (the common Babylonian language), before reverting back to Hebrew in chapter 7:8. Here's an overview of the key focus of each chapter:

**Chapter 1 – Biographical**

Written around 605 BC, this chapter introduces Daniel and his three Hebrew companions, who were taken to Babylon during the early part of the exile. This chapter tells us that, despite immense pressure to conform, they remain faithful to their Jewish customs.

**Chapter 2 - Vision: The control of Jerusalem**

Daniel successfully interprets King Nebuchadnezzar's dream about a multi-metal statue, symbolizing successive kingdoms which controlled Jerusalem. This feat earns him high political status.

**Chapter 3 – Biographical**

Daniel's friends are thrown into a fiery furnace for refusing to worship Babylonian gods. They survive unscathed - causing Nebuchadnezzar to honor their God.

**Chapter 4 - Vision: The King's Madness**

This vision, written or dictated by Nebuchadnezzar himself, describes his rise, descent into madness, and eventual repentance. It's fulfilled exactly, showcasing God's sovereignty.

**Chapter 5 - Vision: The Writing on the Wall**

A disembodied hand writes "MENE, MENE, TEKEL, UPHARSIN" on the palace wall[2], and the king calls for Daniel who interprets it as divine judgment. That very night, in 539 BC, the city falls to the Medo-Persians.

**Chapter 6 – Biographical**

Under the new rulership of the Medo-Persian ruler, Darius, Daniel is thrown into a lions' den yet emerges unharmed. This leads Darius, like Nebuchadnezzar before him, to acknowledge the power of Daniel's God.

**Chapter 7 – Vision: The restoration of the Holy Land**

Written in 552 BC, this dream parallels Nebuchadnezzar's dream of a statue - but features beasts, not metals – and this time there are only four. The terrifying fourth beast persecutes "the saints" until a time, times, and half a time.

**Chapter 8 - Vision: The reconsecration of the Sanctuary**

Written in 549 BC, this vision spans the time from the Medo-Persian empire's defeat by Greece to a "fierce-looking king." It predicts the sanctuary's defiling / desecration and eventual reconsecration after 2,300 "evenings and mornings."

**Chapter 9 - Vision: Seventy Sevens**

Written in 539 BC, this vision is delivered by the Angel Gabriel in response to Daniel's prayer. Though the 70-year exile nears its end, Daniel is told that Israel's full restoration will take "seventy sevens," divided into 69 sevens and 1 seven.

**Chapters 10–12 - Vision: Israel's Long Future**

Written in 533 BC, this is Daniel's most detailed prophecy. It outlines a sweeping historical timeline - from Babylon to a self-exalting final king and a time of trouble ending in resurrection and reward.

**Seven Visions, One Theme**

So now we can see that Daniel's book comprises three biographical accounts and seven prophetic visions – and if we look more closely at those Visions we will also find that they don't appear in the chronological order in which they took place.

For example the Vision of 'the Writing on the Wall' which appears in Chapter 5 of Daniel's book, took place in 539BC - the same year as the Vision of 'Seventy Sevens' which appears in Chapter 9. When corrected to appear in the correct chronological order in which they were written (first to last), Daniel's Visions look like this:

| *Year* | *Vision* |
|---|---|
| **605 BC** | **Vision 1: The control of Jerusalem** |
| **Unknown** | **Vision 2: The Kings madness** |
| **552 BC** | **Vision 3: The restoration of the Holy Land** |
| **549 BC** | **Vision 4: The reconsecration of the sanctuary** |
| **539 BC** | **Vision 5: Seventy sevens** |
| **539 BC** | **Vision 6: The Writing on the wall** |
| **533 BC** | **Vision 7: Israel's long future** |

Or, they can be presented visually, like this::

| 1st Vision | 2nd Vision | 3rd Vision | 4th Vision | 5th Vision | 6th Vision | 7th Vision |
|---|---|---|---|---|---|---|
| **The control of Jerusalem** | **The Kings madness** | **The restoration of the Holy land** | **The consecration of the sanctuary** | **The Seventy Sevens** | **The Writing on the Wall** | **Israels long future** |
| *Dan Ch 2* | *Dan Ch 4* | *Dan Ch 7* | *Dan Ch 8* | *Dan Ch 9* | *Dan Ch 5* | *Dan Ch 10-12* |

This chronological ordering isn't essential to understanding what Daniel wrote – but we have used it throughout this book because it makes his prophecies, and the structure of the visions within which they exist, easier to understand.

It also helps us to better understand the placement of ***time-defined prophecies*** throughout Daniel's book. These are the prophecies which contain an explicit reference to a specific number or numbers and they are the prophecies on which we will be focusing most of our attention because they hold the key to pinpointing exact years of fulfilment.

But which Visions contain time-defined prophecies and which don't? Let's have a look:

**Daniel's time-defined prophecies**

| | |
|---|---|
| *Vision 1*<br>**The control of Jerusalem** | *Contains*<br>- No time-defined prophecies |
| *Vision 2*<br>**The Kings madness** | *Contains*<br>- The prophecy of Seven times |
| *Vision 3*<br>**The restoration of the holy land** | *Contains*<br>- The prophecy of time, times and half a time |
| *Vision 4*<br>**The reconsecration of the sanctuary** | *Contains*<br>- The prophecy of 2,300 evenings and mornings |
| *Vision 5*<br>**The Seventy Sevens** | *Contains*<br>- The prophecy of 69 sevens<br>- The prophecy of the 70th seven |

| *Vision 6* | *Contains* |
|---|---|
| **The Writing on the wall** | - No time-defined prophecies |

| *Vision 7* | *Contains* |
|---|---|
| **Israels long future** | - The prophecy of time, times and half a time (again)<br>- The prophecy of 1,290 days<br>- The prophecy of 1,335 days |

Each of these *time-defined* prophecies relates to the theme of the overall vision in which it appears. For example, the prophecy of 2,300 evenings and mornings is directly linked to the overall Vision of the Reconsecration of the Sanctuary. These links will become much clearer as we address each prophecy.

**Our initial focus**

Visions 1 and 6 contain no time-defined prophecies and Vision 2 was fulfilled within Daniel's lifetime – leaving us with the time-defined prophecies which appear in Visions 3, 4, 5 and 7.

Of these, we will be covering the prophecies of the Sixty Nine Sevens and the Seventieth Seven which appear in Vision 5, later in this book - which means that our focus, for now, is on identifying the solutions to the five time defined prophecies which appear in Visions 3, 4 and 7. These are:

- Both prophecies of time, times and half a time
- The prophecy of 2,300 evenings and mornings
- The prophecy of 1,290 days
- The prophecy of 1,335 days

Each of these will be the subject of its own chapter in this section of the book.

**Quick reference**

At the beginning of each of those chapters I will also include a simple graphic to enable you to quickly identify which Vision we're reviewing:

| 1st Vision | 2nd Vision | 3rd Vision | 4th Vision | 5th Vision | 6th Vision | 7th Vision |
|---|---|---|---|---|---|---|
| **The control of Jerusalem** | **The Kings madness** | **The restoration of the Holy land** | **The consecration of the sanctuary** | **The Seventy Sevens** | **The writing on the wall** | **Israels long future** |
| *Dan Ch 2* | *Dan Ch 4* | *Dan Ch 7* | *Dan Ch 8* | *Dan Ch 9* | *Dan Ch 5* | *Dan Ch 10-12* |

(In this sample we would be reviewing a prophecy which appeared in the 4th Vision – the only one which isn't greyed out)

---

But who are these prophecies about? Are they about the future of the Jewish people, from Daniel's perspective and as Daniel himself confirms they are - or are they about the fate of Christians in the last days, as others claim?

The answer to that question will shape our entire understanding of prophecy - but how can we know, with certainty?

That question is answered in the next chapter.

# 18

## THE PRINCIPLES OF ISRAELISM

# 6 Questions that solve all time-defined prophecy

As I mentioned in the opening to this book, my understanding of prophecy was radically reshaped by the writings of Ellis Skolfield, which I first read in the early 2000s.

Skolfield's interpretations of Daniel's prophecies revealed remarkable coherence and stunning truths and provided a picture of the last days which was completely at odds with other prophetic views.

But there was something missing - a standardised methodology that I could apply to all prophecies to ensure that their solutions were logical, repeatable and in line with scripture.

Eventually I found that methodology - not as a flash of divine inspiration, but through reference to the logic puzzles I had loved since childhood.

If you've never seen one, they're usually structured as a series of clues with a grid that you complete as you solve the clues. Each puzzle normally provides the first few answers to get you started, but after that you have to apply logic to work out the rest.

Here's a very simplified version of what one of these looks like:

1. Kirsty did not win on Monday or Wednesday.
2. Renee did not win on Tuesday or Wednesday.

| | MONDAY | TUESDAY | WEDNESDAY |
|---|---|---|---|
| KIRSTY | | | |
| MAC | | | |
| RENEE | | | |

In this example, we know that Kirsty must have won on Tuesday and that Renee must have won on Monday – - meaning that Mac won on Wednesday. Of course most logic problems are considerably more complex and multi layered with clues stretching over several grids, forcing the solver to keep coming back to the same clues repeatedly in order to solve the puzzle.

In this way, you can use the grid itself to work out some of the other solutions and, as you fill in more and more of the answers, the overall solution becomes more obvious.

The prophecies in the Book of Daniel prophecies operate in much the same way – but unlike a Logic Puzzle where the questions are different every time you start a new puzzle - the questions being asked of Daniel's prophecies are always the same.

**The Six Basic Questions**

Once I had the basic structure, it was relatively easy to develop the six questions that solved all of Daniel's prophecies:

1. **What's being predicted?**
   First and foremost – what does the prophecy actually *tell us* it's about – right from the words of scripture? This may seem obvious – but many interpretations actually ignore it!

2. **Who is the prophecy addressed to?**
   Daniel consistently *tells* us who each prophecy is for - and it's never Christians.

3. **Who is the prophecy about?**
   The recipient isn't always the subject of the prophecy. Understanding this difference prevents serious interpretive errors.

4. **When does the prophecy start?**
   Start dates are clearly embedded in Daniel's writing and ignoring them has led to wildly inaccurate interpretations.

5. **How long will the prophecy last?**
   Time-defined periods like *time, times and half a time*, *2,300 evenings and mornings*, and *1,290 and 1,335 days* are all explicit. They're not vague or symbolic - they're clues.

6. **When does the prophecy end?**
   With the start time and duration established, the end point becomes clear. There's no need for speculation or trying to "fit" world events to match prophecy - God has already given us the answer.

To make this even easier to grasp, I've developed a visual template that you'll see throughout this book.

This template is an easy way to review the answers to each of the six questions applied to each prophecy - and how those answers fit together to reveal the full solution.

| **The Name of the Prophecy**<br>Scripture reference | | | |
|---|---|---|---|
| **What's being predicted?** | | | |
| **Question** | **Clue from Scripture** | **Math** | **Solution** |
| **Who is the prophecy addressed to?** | | | |
| **Who is the prophecy about?** | | | |
| **What year does the prophecy start?** | | | |
| **How long will the prophecy last?** | | | |
| **What year does the prophecy end?** | | | |

As you can see, there are three columns to be completed for five of the six basic questions - one in which the actual wording from the biblical text provides the clue, one in which the math identified by these clues is completed, and one in which the solution is provided.

**Why This Matters**

These six questions form more than a method - they represent a total rethinking of Bible prophecy which strips away speculation and assumptions and focuses on what can be empirically proven.

This approach produces radically different outcomes to what you may have seen in the past and challenges long-held views - but it does so with clarity, accuracy, and above all, *scriptural integrity.* Rather than wrestling to *interpret* events into the Bible, it lets the Bible interpret itself.

And like the logic puzzles of my youth, the more clues you place, the clearer the full picture becomes.

---

**One last thing before we start solving prophecies**

I've gone to a lot of effort to make the math in the solutions that lie ahead as accessible and easy to understand as possible – but there may still be places where you find your eyes glazing over trying to understand some of the numbers (because numbers aren't everyone's thing).

If this happens, give yourself permission to fast forward to *the Solution at a Glance* page at the end of each chapter. This will give you a precise summary of the chapter without getting bogged down in the math detail – enabling you to experience the full impact of the book without getting tied up in calculations.

Remember – the real value of *Prophecy Shock* is in the overall pattern and consistency of design that will become more obvious as you read – not in understanding the inner workings of any particular prophecy solution.

And so, with that introduction behind us - let's start with our first time-defined prophecy - the reference to **time, times and half a time** which appears in Vision 7 in Chapter 12 of the Book of Daniel.

19

# The Scattering Ended

## The Prophecy of Time, Times and Half a Time

which appears in **Daniel 12:7** in the

| 1st Vision | 2nd Vision | 3rd Vision | 4th Vision | 5th Vision | 6th Vision | 7th Vision |
|---|---|---|---|---|---|---|
| **The control of Jerusalem** | **The Kings madness** | **The restoration of the Holy land** | **The consecration of the sanctuary** | **The Seventy Sevens** | **The writing on the wall** | **Israels long future** |
| *Dan Ch 2* | *Dan Ch 4* | *Dan Ch 7* | *Dan Ch 8* | *Dan Ch 9* | *Dan Ch 5* | *Dan Ch 10-12* |

We're going to start our journey with a prophecy which appears within the last Vision that Daniel ever recorded – the cryptic prophecy of *"time, times, and half a time"*.

Yes, I understand that beginning with Daniel's last (and longest) Vision might seem counter-intuitive - but this particular Vision serves as an excellent summary of Daniel's entire book and it also provides a great introduction to the way that the *Six Basic Questions* work.

### The Vision in Summary

Vision 7 spans Chapters 10 to 12 of Daniel and I would ***strongly*** recommend that you read those chapters, first, so that you will understand the context within which the prophecy appears.

At the time of writing it, Daniel would have been somewhere between 78 and 85 years old – so when he tells us, in **Chapter Ten** of his book that the Vision begins near the Tigris River (about 25 miles / 35 kms east of Babylon) we can picture him there, as an old man.

In the early part of the Vision Daniel meets a heavenly figure after which he falls into a deep sleep. An angel then wakes him from this sleep and tells him that he is "highly esteemed" and that he is going to be shown what will happen to his people.

In **Chapter Eleven**, the angel outlines an extensive history of the rise and fall of empires, starting with Persia and Greece and ending with a "king who exalts himself."

Then we get to **Chapter Twelve** where Daniel asks the Angel how long it will be before all of these things (the things outlined in Chapters Ten and Eleven) are fulfilled and is told that his people are going to endure a time of 'great trouble' which will last for:

> *"...a time, times, and half a time; and when he shall have accomplished to scatter the power of the holy people, all these things shall be finished."* ***(Daniel 12:7)***

This is our key verse. It answers the question that Daniel asked, summarises the entirety of the vision which has preceded it and clearly outlines a prophetic duration (time, times and half a time), a target group (the Holy People), and a milestone to mark its conclusion (the end of the 'scattering' of those people).

But how long is **time, times and half a time**? Many people reading this will understand it as a reference to three-and-a-half years because that's how it is interpreted by Premillennialism – but that definition comes from tradition, not strict interpretation.

In fact, the Book of Daniel never actually defines the term. Daniel wrote his book in two different languages - Aramaic and Hebrew – and neither gives an exact definition. In Daniel 12, written in Hebrew, the word 'time' is translated from the word *môʿēd*, which means an *appointed time or season* - something fixed or scheduled by God. This word tells us that a moment has been set, but not how long it lasts.

In Daniel 7, the same phrase - "time, times, and half a time" – appears, written in Aramaic and there the word translated as "time" is *iddān* and describes a *period or span of time*, but again, without naming a specific unit.

So, neither word defines a set time period and in both cases their length is subjective and determined by the context. We also see this in Daniel 4, where King Nebuchadnezzar goes mad and loses his mind for "seven times" (*iddāns*). This is often understood as seven years - but this time length is determined by the outcome, not the other way around.

As such, when God tells us, in Daniel 12:7, that 'time, times and half a time' will pass before the scattering of the holy people will be over – this can be reasonably read to mean that we won't know how long this time period is until *after the prophecy has been fulfilled*. This doesn't mean the prophecy is unknowable - only that its meaning must be established by fulfilment rather than assumed by tradition.

But how can we know when the prophecy is fulfilled if we don't know the length of the units of time we're being referred to?

### Solving the prophecy with the Six Basic Questions

Fortunately, this question is resolved through the application of Six Basic Questions which are common to all *time-defined* prophecies. When these questions are applied to each prophecy they will tell us what's being predicted, who the prophecy is about, when it starts, how long it runs, what period of time we're working with, and how we will know it's fulfilled.

When we apply these questions we're going to learn that this entire vision reveals God's prophetic plan for the Jewish people - beginning during the time of the Babylonian empire and culminating in events which took place in the 20th century.

I understand that this is a big claim – so let's remind ourselves of what the prophecy says by recalling the Angels answer to Daniel when he asks how long it will be before 'all of these things' (the things in the vision) are fulfilled.

He is told that his people are going to endure a time of 'great trouble' which will last for:

> *"...a time, times, and half a time; and when he shall have accomplished to scatter the power of the holy people, all these things shall be finished."* ***(Daniel 12:7)***

**1. What's being predicted?**

Based on the three chapters in the overall vision we can see that this is a summary of the long history of a group called the 'holy people' and that it predicts that their 'scattering' will come to an end after 'time, times and half a time'.

**2. Who was the prophecy addressed to?**

Identifying who the prophecy was addressed to is actually very easy. We're told who the vision was given to right there in the first line of chapter 10:

> *"In the third year of Cyrus king of Persia a message was revealed to Daniel."* ***(Daniel 10:1)***

So the prophecy is addressed to **Daniel** (a Jew) and we have our answer to Question 2.

**3. Who was the prophecy about?**

We don't need to guess who the prophecy is about because the scripture tells us plainly:

> *"There will be a time of distress such as has not happened from the beginning of nations until then. But at that time* ***your people*** *- everyone whose name is found written in the book - will be delivered.* ***(Daniel 12:1)***

The Vision tells us, three times (once in chapter 10 and twice in chapter 12) that the prophecy is about **Daniel's people - the Jews.**

There is no ambiguity here. **Daniel's people weren't Christians - they were Jews** living over 500 years before Christ.

Armed with this information, we can complete the first three solutions to the six basic questions - a process you will become very familiar with in the pages ahead.

| **What's being predicted?** | *That the 'scattering' of a group called the 'holy people' will come to an end after 'time, times and half a time'* | | |
|---|---|---|---|
| **Question** | **Clue from Scripture** | **Math** | **Solution** |
| **Who is the prophecy addressed to?** | *"...a message was revealed to Daniel" (Daniel 10:1)* | | The prophecy is addressed to Daniel |
| **Who is the prophecy about?** | *"...your people..." (Daniel 12:1)* | | The prophecy is about the Jews |

So we've answered the first, second and third questions, using information that is right there in the text of the prophecy and, already, we can see that the basic premise of the Premillennial interpretation of the prophecy – that it is about Christians in the last days - is in error. But we need to continue and see what else we can uncover by answering the fourth of the Six Basic Questions:

### 4. When does the prophecy start?

To answer this, we need to return to the prophecy itself and see whether it gives us a clue about *when* the timeline begins.

It does - and you've already seen it - right at the opening of the vision in Daniel 10:

*"In the third year of Cyrus king of Persia..."* ***(Daniel 10:1)***

The Medo-Persians conquered the Babylonian Empire, including Jerusalem, in 539 BC and some sources suggest that Cyrus immediately became King of Babylon at that point - but Daniel himself tells us that this was *not* the case. In chapter 6 of his book, Daniel states clearly that it was **Darius the Mede,** not Cyrus, who took control of Babylon in 539 BC (see the 6th chapter of the Book of Daniel and Chapter 27 of *Prophecy Shock* for a detailed discussion).

So when *did* Cyrus take the throne?

As we noted in Chapter 14 of *Prophecy Shock*, some historical dates are debated, and this is one of them – so there are several contender years for Cyrus's ascension. These range from 538 BC to 536 BC and, for the purposes of this book, we've adopted the year which best matches the other details of the prophecy - **536 BC**.

Three years after this is **533 BC**.

| Question | Clue from Scripture | Math | Solution |
|---|---|---|---|
| **What year does the prophecy start?** | *"In the third year of Cyrus, King of Persia" (Daniel 10:1)* | *–533* | The prophecy begins in 533 BC |

**5. How long will the prophecy last?**

Earlier in this chapter we explained that neither of the two words defined as meaning 'time' in the Book of Daniel (*môʿēd* and *iddān*) imply a specific period. In both cases, the length of 'time' being measured is subjective and is determined by the context. So we're looking for **a period of time that started in 533BC** and ended...

*"...when He shall have accomplished to scatter the power of the Holy People..." **(Daniel 12:7)***

But looking for a prophetic fulfilment which meets those two criteria would be like looking for a needle in a haystack – right?

Well actually, no. There aren't *that* many units of time to check: days, weeks, months, and years.

We know that the prophecy is measured over a very long period of time because Daniel was told that it defined the fulfilment of "all these things" in a vision that spanned many empires and culminated in the resolved fate of his people – but how long are we talking?

Since Daniel doesn't define it we look to other books of scripture for an answer. This is standard bible hermeneutics (the rules and methods we use to figure out what a text actually means) – and takes us to a curious passage in the New Testament in 2 Peter 3:8 where we're told that:

> *"...one day is with the Lord as a thousand years, and a thousand years as one day."*

This scripture is generally understood to be telling us that God, Who is infinite, is not bound by time and reminds us that, what appear as extremely long passages of time to us, are trivial to God.

But it also has an application to Daniel 12:7. We've already identified that 'time' could refer to a year, a month, a week, or **a day**, depending on context – and this passage is telling us that, **to God, a day is as a thousand years**.

Remember, Daniel's book doesn't specifically define the meaning of *môʿēd*, or *iddān* – in fact, these words suggest that we won't know how long the prophecy lasts until it is fulfilled. So 2 Peter 3:8 isn't a direct interpretation – rather, it's telling us that God can speak of time on a scale that dwarfs ours – so it's not unreasonable to conjecture that the subjective term 'time' might equal one thousand years.

But what about the multiplier? Premillennialism proposes that 'time' should be read as one and 'times' should be read as two more. But the script doesn't demand this – it's just an interpretation.

An alternative reading of the phrase is that it is simply repeating the first 'time' - much like an auctioneer when he or she says, "going once, going twice," – to mean once, then once more.

Read this way, the phrase equals 2.5 times, not 3.5 – giving us:

| | |
|---|---|
| Time | = 1,000 |
| Times | = 1,000 more |
| Half a time | = 500 |
| | **= 2,500 years** |

Is this number significant? Let's find out.

6. **When does the prophecy end?**
   The vision tells us that the prophecy will be fulfilled:

   *"...when he shall have accomplished to scatter the power of the holy people"*

   So we're looking for a fulfilment year that satisfies that description - and the process for finding it is simple. We just add the number of years in the prophecy (2,500) to the year in which it begins (533BC) and we should have our answer:

-533 → + 2,500 → = **1967**

And there it is. The prophecy ends in **1967** - the year in which the Jews reclaimed Jerusalem during the Six-Day War, ending over 2,500 years of mostly foreign control over their historic Capital and finally bringing to a close the **Diaspora** (scattering) which saw them separated from their ancestral Capital.

So let's review all of our answers to the six questions:

| **The Prophecy of Time, Times and half a Time**<br>Daniel 12:7 | | | |
|---|---|---|---|
| **What's being predicted?** | *That the 'scattering' of a group called the 'holy people' will come to an end after 'time, times and half a time'* | | |
| **Question** | **Clue from Scripture** | **Math** | **Solution** |
| **Who is the prophecy addressed to?** | *"...a message was revealed to Daniel" (Daniel 10:1)* | | The prophecy is addressed to Daniel |
| **Who is the prophecy about?** | *"...your people..." (Daniel 12:1)* | | The prophecy is about the Jews |
| **What year does the prophecy start?** | *"In the third year of Cyrus, King of Persia" (Daniel 10:1)* | *–533* | The prophecy begins in 533 BC |
| **How long will the prophecy last?** | *"It shall be for time, times and half a time..." (Daniel 12:7)* | *plus 2,500* | The prophecy will last for 2,500 years |
| **What year does the prophecy end?** | *"...When He shall have accomplished to scatter the power of the Holy People..." (Daniel 12:7)* | ***equals 1,967*** | **The prophecy ends in 1967** |

So this isn't a prophecy about Christians in the last days – it's Gods declaration that His people, the Jews (the Holy People), were about to enter a long period of punishment – but that He would eventually restore them to their ancient Capital, 2,500 years into the far future, in 1967.

In the Book of Daniel, God provided us with a specific year from which to start the count - 533BC (the year in which Daniel recorded the prophecy) - and it has been hiding in plain sight for 2,500 years waiting for the events, themselves, to take place before we could confirm that year and understand what the prophecy really means.

But who is the 'He' referred to in the prophecy? If the people in focus are the Jews, then the identity of 'He' is obvious and scripture gives us the answer: It's **God Himself.** If that surprises you, it shouldn't, because it's consistent with the overwhelming warning of the Old Testament.

> *"I myself will gather the remnant of my flock out of **all** the countries where **I have driven them**..." **(Jeremiah 23:3)***

God repeatedly told the Jews that, if they continued to disobey His commandments, His patience would eventually run out and He would punish them – but He also told them that this punishment would be limited, after which He would regather them to their own land.

**Being sensitive to scripture**

So now we can see that Daniel's Chapter 12 prophecy of **time, times and half a time** is about a period of 2,500 years during which the Jews lost control of their Holy City, Jerusalem.

But if you know your Israeli history, you will know that the Jews regained control of Israel in 1948, not 1967. Does this invalidate the solution?

Not at all. Instead, it provides an early and important lesson in being sensitive to the precision of wording in scripture.

The phrase - 'the scattering of the *holy people'* – tells us that we're talking about the Jews in respect of their relationship to God - a relationship which is centred on the site of the former Temples which had stood on the Temple Mount in Jerusalem - a return to which has been the fond hope of Jews for thousands of years.

This matters because, even though the Jews were back in control of Israel in 1948, they couldn't truly regard their scattering as over until they had reclaimed that important piece of real estate in 1967.

Only when Jerusalem was back in Israeli hands could the scattering of *the holy people* be said to be finally over.

But what about the historic significance of 1948? Is that also addressed in prophecy?

We'll address that question shortly – but first let's review our first prophecy summary:

*The solution at a glance*

# Time, times and half a time: The Scattering Ended

***Scripture:*** *Daniel 12:7*

1. **What's being predicted?**
   That the 'scattering' of a group called the **'holy people'** will come to an end after 'time, times and half a time'

2. **Who is being spoken to?**
   **Daniel**. A Jewish man in exile.

3. **Who is the prophecy about?**
   The angel says it three times: "your people." Daniel's people. That means **the Jews**, not the Church.

4. **When does it start?**
   The third year of King Cyrus of Persia - **533 BC**.

5. **How long does it last?**
   "Time" = 1,000 years, "Times" = 1,000 more, "Half a time" = 500 - **Total = 2,500 years**

6. **When does it end - and what happens?**
   "When the power of the holy people is no longer scattered." 533 BC + 2,500 years = **1967 AD**

## 20

### THE PRINCIPLES OF ISRAELISM

# The 'beasts' are powers that controlled Jerusalem

If you're familiar with Premillennial theology you'll know that the idea of an "antichrist" who rises up to control the world, in the last days, is a core expectation of that school of prophecy interpretation.

This belief is built on a fundamental misunderstanding of scripture which we will progressively address as we make our way through this book – particularly the belief that the "antichrist" and some of the "beasts" described in the Books of Daniel and Revelation are interchangeable terms for the same thing. Indeed, this connection is so strong that many Premillennial prophecy writers simply refer to their last-days antichrist as "**the Beast**."

Sadly, this simple error has done enormous damage to our understanding of prophecy. It has blinded many Christians to the true meaning of the term *beast* - and, more importantly, to the true focus of bible prophecy itself.

Here's the key: while individual kings may have been on the throne during prophetic milestones, we will find that the beasts never describe individuals. They always describe kingdoms and powers – and always in their role as occupiers of Jerusalem. That's the thread that ties it all together.

From Daniel's empires to Revelation's timelines, prophecy tracks the succession of foreign rulers who trample the holy city, because Jerusalem - not the wider world - is the fixed point of God's prophetic focus.

This is why so many past attempts to interpret prophecy have failed. Interpreters in the West have tried to read Daniel and Revelation through the lens of their own European or American history - or as an account of the rise and fall of the "greatest" empires of the age. But the empires highlighted in the prophecies of Daniel weren't necessarily the largest or most powerful on earth at the time they existed. What they have in common is that they all ruled Jerusalem.

Prophecy is not about the fate of the world's superpowers - it's about the fate of God's city. Every beast is a foreign power trampling Jerusalem. Every vision in the Book of Daniel turns our eyes back to the destiny of Israel – starting in the time of Daniel and ending in 1967.

This is the foundation stone on which all prophetic understanding rests: if your interpretation does not begin and end with Jerusalem, it will collapse. If your focus drifts to Rome, Europe, or America - or a charismatic leader in the last days - you've already missed the point. Prophecy isn't tracing the story of Western Christendom. It's tracing the story of Jerusalem.

As we make our way through this book and you're exposed to solution after solution - the simple truth of the centrality of Jerusalem will become obvious to you.

That's why the beasts matter, and that's why we will keep coming back to this theme. Bible prophecy is Israel's story, set in Jerusalem, unfolding on God's timetable.

Miss that - and you miss everything.

# The Nation Reborn

## The Prophecy of Time, Times and Half a Time

which appears in **Daniel 7:25** in the

| 1st Vision | 2nd Vision | 3rd Vision | 4th Vision | 5th Vision | 6th Vision | 7th Vision |
|---|---|---|---|---|---|---|
| **The control of Jerusalem** | **The Kings madness** | **The restoration of the Holy land** | **The consecration of the sanctuary** | **The Seventy Sevens** | **The writing on the wall** | **Israels long future** |
| *Dan Ch 2* | *Dan Ch 4* | *Dan Ch 7* | *Dan Ch 8* | *Dan Ch 9* | *Dan Ch 5* | *Dan Ch 10-12* |

As we've already highlighted, there is another appearance of the phrase *'time, times, and half a time'* in the Book of Daniel – this time in Chapter 7 where we find the 3rd Vision: *The Restoration of the Holy Land*. This was written about 16 years prior to the previous Vision making Daniel somewhere between 62 and 69 when he wrote it.

Let's review the specific prophecy:

.

*And he shall speak great words against the most High and shall wear out the saints of the most High and think to change times and laws: and they shall be given into his hand until a time and times and half a time.* ***(Daniel 7:25)***

So is this a repeat of the same prophecy that we've already solved? Or is it a different prophecy? And how does it relate to the theme of the overall Vision – *the restoration of the holy land?* Once again I encourage you to read the entire thing, first, so as to understand the context.

**The Vision**

Like the previous vision, this one also came to Daniel as a dream. But here, the prophecy is presented symbolically through four strange beasts rising from the sea.

> *"The first was like a lion, and had eagle's wings...*
> *The second, like a bear, raised on one side, with three ribs in its mouth...*
> *The third, like a leopard with four wings and four heads...*
> *Then a fourth beast, dreadful and terrifying, with iron teeth, ten horns, and a little horn speaking great things..."* ***(Daniel 7:4–8)***

Daniel asks the angel to clarify what these beasts represent and is given the following additional explanation:

> *"These great beasts... are four kings who shall arise from the earth. But the saints of the Most High shall receive the kingdom and possess it forever..."* ***(Daniel 7:17–18)***

Still confused, Daniel presses for even more detail about the fourth beast and is told that:

> *"It devoured and crushed its victims... and had ten horns. A little horn rose among them, uprooting three, and spoke arrogantly. This horn made war against the saints and was prevailing - until the Ancient of Days came..."* ***(Daniel 7:19–22)***

So the angel confirms that the fourth (ten horned) beast is also a kingdom, but explains that it is distinct from the others, and that it will trample the whole earth – and that yet *another* 'little horn' will rise up among these ten horns.

Most Premillennialists read this as a preview of a **future Antichrist** and a **global empire** that will appear and persecute Christians just before Christ returns. However, that interpretation reflects modern tradition - not what the text actually tells us.

To find out what the prophecy really means let's go back to the **Six Basic Questions**:

**1. What's being predicted?**

Summarised, the prophecy tells us that a succession of beasts, followed by a 'ten horned' beast and finally another 'little horn', will wear out 'the saints' until a '**time, times and half a time**'

**2. Who is the prophecy given to?**

Once again, we find that the vision is delivered *to* **Daniel**, through a dream:

> *In the first year of Belshazzar king of Babylon,* ***Daniel had a dream*** *and visions of his head upon his bed: then he wrote the dream and told the sum of the matters.* ***(Daniel 7:1)***

**3. Who is the prophecy about?**

Let's review the core prophecy:

> *"And he shall speak great words against the most High and shall wear out* ***the saints of the most High*** *and think to change times and laws: and they shall be given into his hand until a time and times and half a time".* ***(Daniel 7:25)***

Whereas Daniel was told that the prophecy in chapter 12 was about his own people (the Jews) - this one is about a group called 'the saints'.

But who are 'the saints'? Are they Christian martyrs or all Christian believers as many Protestants would have us believe? Or are they, instead, the 'Saints' of Catholicism, the Orthodox Church and some traditional protestant Churches which claim, to themselves, the right to use that word as a title and decide who it should be conferred upon? Or are they another group entirely? We don't yet know - so let's move to the next question.

**4. When does the prophecy start?**

In the previous solution, Daniel told us when the prophecy would start right there within the prophecy itself and he does the same thing here. In the first sentence of chapter 7 he tells us that he is writing in:

*'...the first year of Belshazzar, King of Babylon'.*

Not much is known about Belshazzar (not to be confused with Belteshazzar – the Babylonian name given to Daniel) but we do know that he was the son of Nabonidus, a nephew of Nebuchadnezzar who seized the Babylonian throne in 555BC following the three unstable reigns of sons of Nebuchadnezzar, following the death of their father in 562BC. There are mixed accounts of the reign of Nabonidus suggesting that he was a capable leader, but that he was unpopular with the Babylonian Court and that, after three years, he left the Kingdom in the hands of his son and went off to pursue other interests. The general consensus is that Belshazzar's reign commenced in either 553 or 552BC - either as King in his own right or as co-regent with his absent father. For reasons that will become more obvious later in this book, we'll adopt the 552BC date as our start year. So the answer to Question 4 is: **552 BC**.

**5. How long does the prophecy last?**

Let's assume, for now, that **time, times and half a time** means the same thing in this prophecy as it did in the previous prophecy: **2,500 years.**

**6. When does the prophecy end?**

Unlike the earlier prophecy, where we were told the circumstances by which the ending of the prophecy could be identified - this one simply tells us that the prophecy will be fulfilled once 2500 years have passed.

> *"...and they shall be given into his hand **until** a time and times and half a time". **(Daniel 7:25)***

But which year is identified? To find out, let's do the math by adding 2,500 years to 552BC:

-552 → + 2,500 → = **1948**

And there it is: adding 2,500 years to 552 BC takes us to **1948** - the year of the **rebirth of the modern State of Israel** which had been ordained by God *(the Ancient of Days)* 2,500 years previously.

This is not a theory. It's **testable history matched precisely to prophecy**. Just as predicted – control over the Jewish people was delivered into the hands of other empires (beasts). And it was written down - 2,500 years in advance.

This is an extraordinary discovery, confirming that the two prophecies of **time, time and half a time** correlate to the two most important events in modern Jewish history - 1948 (the year in which the state of Israel was born in one day) and 1967 (the year in which Israel recaptured Jerusalem).

The chances against *both* years being featured in this way, by accident, are astronomical.

**But who are the saints?** Logically there is only one group for whom 1948 is prophetically significant and who have existed for the entire period covered by the prophecy: **The Jews**.

So let's complete our template with what we now know:

| **The Prophecy of Time, Times and half a Time**<br>Daniel 7:25 | | | |
|---|---|---|---|
| **What's being predicted?** | *That a succession of beasts, followed by a 'ten horned' beast and finally another 'little horn', will 'wear out' the saints until a 'time, times and half a time'* | | |
| **Question** | **Clue from Scripture** | **Math** | **Solution** |
| **Who is the prophecy addressed to?** | *"...Daniel had a dream and visions" (Daniel 7.1)* | | **The prophecy is addressed to Daniel** |
| **Who is the prophecy about?** | *"...the saints of the Most High..." (Daniel 7.25)* | | **The prophecy is about the Jews** |
| **What year does the prophecy start?** | *"In the first year of Belshazzar, King of Babylon" (Daniel 7.1)* | ***-552*** | **The prophecy begins in 552BC** |
| **How long will the prophecy last?** | *"...they shall be given into his hand until a time, times and half a time..." (Daniel 7:25)* | ***plus 2,500*** | **The prophecy will last for 2,500 years** |
| **What year does the prophecy end?** | | ***equals 1,948*** | **The prophecy ends in 1948** |

So now we can see the real meaning of the prophecy of 'time, times and half a time' in the 7th Chapter of the Book of Daniel.

It isn't an outline of speculative events in the last days – **it's an exact prediction of the restoration of the Jewish people, to their own land, 2,500 years after Daniel recorded these words.**

**The 'little horn'**

But who are the 'beasts' described in this prophecy – and, in particular, who is the 'little horn' into whose hands the Jews were delivered in the closing years of the prophecy? We can have certainty that it isn't a last days Antichrist because whoever 'he' is, the prophecy tells us that his control ended in 1948.

So who controlled the destiny of the Jews in the period just prior to the re-establishment of Israel and does 'he' fit the description in the prophecy?

We'll answer that question – and identify all of the other beasts - later in the book.

But first – let's take a moment to reveal the real purpose of prophecy.

*The solution at a glance*

# Time, times and half a time (again)

# The Nation Reborn

***Scripture:*** *Daniel 7:25*

1. **What's predicted?**
   That a succession of beasts, followed by a 'ten horned' beast and finally a 'little horn', will 'wear out' the saints until the completion of a **'time, times and half a time**'

2. **Who is being spoken to?**
   **Daniel** - receiving a dream in the first year of Belshazzar.

3. **Who is the prophecy about?**
   "The saints" – but it's not the Church, it's **the Jews**, the only group for whom 1948 has prophetic significance across 2,500 years.

4. **When does it start?**
   In the first year of Belshazzar's reign - **552 BC**.

5. **How long does it last?**
   "Time" = 1,000 years, "Times" = 1,000 more, "Half a time" = 500 - **Total = 2,500 years**

6. **When does it end?**
   552BC + 2500 = **1948** - when the State of Israel is reborn.

This prophecy isn't about future Christians - it's about Jewish history and ends with **the rebirth of the nation of Israel.**

22



# The real purpose of prophecy

If God gave us prophecy so that we could know the future before it happens it hasn't worked out very well because we keep getting it wrong.

Down through the centuries, literally thousands of people have claimed to understand Gods prophetic message and hundreds of millions of words have been written outlining theories which ultimately end up on the scrapheap of error.

Despite this, the desire to be the first to reveal Gods message to the masses is as strong today as it has been at any time in Church history with a new book claiming to unravel the meaning of prophecy being published every week.

**A High-Profile Failure**

Take the case of American evangelist Harold Camping. In 1994, he predicted that Judgement Day would occur on September 6. When that failed, he tried again in 2011, claiming that Christ would return on May 21 and that the world would be destroyed by October 21.

His predictions were supported by a global media campaign, which only magnified the ridicule when they failed to materialize. The ensuing embarrassment extended beyond Camping, drawing Christianity itself into public mockery.

**Why wasn't God clearer?**

But why all the confusion? Why did God encode His prophecies in a way that was open to multiple interpretations? Why didn't He just spell out what He meant, clearly, in the plain text? If He wanted us to understand that 'time, times and half a time' meant 2,500 years (for example) – why not just say that instead of using mystical codes and esoteric clues?

I grappled with this question for years and was convinced that the solutions *were* easy to understand but that we were just looking in the wrong places.

I searched the Bible looking for a hidden key - a clue that would unlock these predictions just in time for our generation.

**A Voice from the Past**

But that perspective changed when I encountered the prophetic writings of English scientist Sir Isaac Newton.

Newton (1642–1727) is a towering figure in science. His work in calculus, optics, and gravity still underpins modern physics and the mathematician Joseph-Louis Lagrange once called him "the greatest genius who ever lived,". A 2005 Royal Society survey also ranked him first, even ahead of Einstein, in his all-time historical impact on science.

Yet Newton's greatest intellectual output was not scientific – it was biblical. He wrote over 1.3 million words on scriptural topics - three times more than on science – and his main prophetic focus was the Books of Daniel and Revelation.

His writings were compiled posthumously in *Observations upon the Prophecies of Daniel and the Apocalypse* and for decades, these views were largely ignored - until 1936 when his papers were purchased at a Sotheby's auction by famous economist John Maynard

Keynes, who revealed their full scope. Today, they're freely available online via Oxford University's Newton Project.

But it's what Newton discovered about Bible prophecy that's most profound. After years of study, hoping to crack the prophetic code, he wrote:

> **"The folly of interpreters has been to foretell times and things by prophecy, as if God designed to make them prophets. By this rashness they have not only exposed themselves but brought the prophecy also into contempt.**
>
> **The design of God was much otherwise. He gave the prophecies of the Old Testament, not to gratify men's curiosities by enabling them to foreknow things, but that after they were fulfilled, they might be interpreted by the event, and His own providence be then manifested thereby to the world.**
>
> **For the event of things predicted many ages before will then be a convincing argument that the world is governed by Providence".**
>
> **Sir Isaac Newton, (1642 - 1727)**

Newtons message is clear: God didn't give us prophecy to predict the future, but to recognize its fulfilment after the fact. Why? So that God, not men, would be glorified.

Newton couldn't have known the significance of this insight to the prophecies we've solved in this book because the events hadn't happened yet. But his conclusion echoes across centuries.

**An Analogy**

Imagine I handed you a sealed envelope and told you to open it only when your favourite sports team won a game by a specific score over a particular rival. Years pass. They win often, but never by that exact margin - until one day, they do.

You open the envelope and find, inside, an otherwise blank sheet of paper on which is inscribed that day's date.

That's what God has done with the prophecies in Daniel and Revelation. He embedded precise dates into prophecy - but they only make sense after the events occur. And instead of waiting a decade or two, these events were set in motion over 2,500 years ago - hidden in plain sight until they were fulfilled.

That's the true purpose of prophecy. Not to make celebrities of mortal men – but to demonstrate Gods divine providence and control over the Universe and everything in it.

We were never meant to use prophecy to predict times and dates – but rather, to recognise the fulfilment of those times and dates after they had happened so that the glory – *all of it* – would go to God.

23

# The Passover Clock

## The Prophecy of 2,300 Evenings and Mornings

which appears in **Daniel 8:13-14** in the

| 1st Vision | 2nd Vision | 3rd Vision | 4th Vision | 5th Vision | 6th Vision | 7th Vision |
|---|---|---|---|---|---|---|
| **The control of Jerusalem** | **The Kings madness** | **The restoration of the Holy land** | **The consecration of the sanctuary** | **The Seventy Sevens** | **The writing on the wall** | **Israels long future** |
| *Dan Ch 2* | *Dan Ch 4* | *Dan Ch 7* | *Dan Ch 8* | *Dan Ch 9* | *Dan Ch 5* | *Dan Ch 10-12* |

The first two riddles that we've reviewed, so far, point with uncanny precision to **1948 and 1967.**

But in Vision 4 the angel doesn't speak in "times" - he gives Daniel a different countdown measured in *"2,300 evenings and mornings."*

For generations, this puzzle seemed impenetrable and commentators argued, speculated, and moved on, unable to make sense of it. But once you recognize what "evenings and mornings" really mean in Israel's calendar - a hidden timer tied to the Passover itself - the mystery resolves itself.

If you haven't already read Chapter 8 of his book – here's a quick summary of what Daniel sees:

- He pictures himself several thousand miles away from Babylon in a city called Susa (which is now called 'Shushan' and is in modern day Iran)

- He sees a **ram with two horns** charging in multiple directions
- Then a **goat with a prominent horn** attacks and defeats the ram.
- The goat's horn then breaks and is replaced by four new horns.

Out of one of these emerges a **small horn**, which grows in power and throws truth to the ground, removing the **daily sacrifice** and profaning the **sanctuary**.

Then comes the key part of the prophecy. Daniel asks the Angel Gabriel:

> [13] *"How long will it take for the vision to be fulfilled - the vision concerning the daily sacrifice, the rebellion that causes desolation, the surrender of the sanctuary and the trampling underfoot of the LORD's people?"*
>
> [14] *He said to me, **"It will take 2,300 evenings and mornings; then the sanctuary will be reconsecrated." (Daniel 8:13-14)***

This last part of the prophecy leads us directly to **Question 5** of the Six Basic Questions: **How long does the prophecy last?**

The prophecy tells us that it will end after **2,300 evenings and mornings** - a reference to a "Passover night" that is extensively explained in Chapter 12 of the Book of Exodus. This highlights an annual event which is tied to lunar cycles and commemorates Gods protection of Israel's during Egypt's final plague. A spotless lamb is killed at twilight, eaten that night (with bitter herbs and unleavened bread), and anything that is left over must be burned by morning.

This event is commemorated only once every 365.24 days, a measurement of time which happens to exactly coincide with the length of a year in our modern era. So 2,300 of these Passover Nights

**equal 2,300 of our modern years** and we have our answer to Question 5. Now let's circle back to the other questions:

**Question 2: Who is the prophecy addressed to?**

The very first sentence of the vision makes this clear:

*"In the third year of King Belshazzar's reign, I, Daniel, had a vision.... "*

So, once again, the vision was delivered to **Daniel**.

**Question 3: Who is it about?**

In verse 12 of the vision, we see a reference to **the Lord's people**. This might be the Jews, once again, but there's not enough information to be sure yet - so we'll come back to it.

**Question 4: When does the prophecy start?**

In the two previous prophecies we found a start date right there within the prophecy itself - in fact, in both of those cases it was right at the beginning of each vision.

But that doesn't happen here. Although the prophecy tells us when Daniel is writing (in the third year of Belshazzar's reign – 549 BC) – adding 2,300 to -549 takes us to 1751, a year with no historical significance in history.

However, if we'd dug a little deeper into the two prophecies of 'time, times and half a time' we'd have found that both also gave us additional clues confirming when they started.

For example, in the prophecy of 'time, times and half a time' in chapter 7, in addition to telling us that he is writing in the 'first year of Belshazzar' (552BC), Daniel also tells us that he received the prophecy in a dream in which he saw 'four great beasts' and that the first was *'like a lion with the wings of an eagle'*. This confirmed that the Vision started during the time of the Babylonian Empire.

Likewise, in the prophecy of 'time, times and half a time' starting in chapter 10 he tells us that he is was *standing on the bank of the River Tigris* and the vision goes on to detail four kings that rise after Cyrus – confirming that the vision starts during the reign of Cyrus the Great (which started in 536 BC).

So note carefully what Daniel tells us in the second verse of the prophecy of 2,300 days:

> *"In my vision I saw myself in the citadel of Susa in the province of Elam..."* ***(Daniel 8:2)***

Susa (modern day Shushan, in Iran) was a major city at the time that Daniel was writing in 549 BC - but a little under 30 years later, in 521 BC, it also became a Capital of the Medo Persian Empire which conquered Babylon in 539 BC.

Daniel couldn't have known this, of course - he was simply recording what was in his dream - but take note of what he tells us next:

> *"I looked up, and there before me was a ram with two horns, standing beside the canal, and the horns were long. One of the horns was longer than the other but grew up later. I watched the ram as it charged toward the west and the north and the south. No animal could stand against it, and none could rescue from its power. It did as it pleased and became great."* ***(Daniel 8:3-4)***

Now that we know that Daniel saw himself in Susa this part of the prophecy makes perfect sense. The ram with 'two horns' was the Medo Persian empire which was an alliance of two empires in which the Persians were the younger, but more powerful, partner. Daniel is describing that combined empire as having absolute power - and this was certainly true of the Medo Persians for almost two hundred years until they were defeated by Alexander the Great in a series of battles which began in 334 BC.

With that knowledge in mind, take note of what Daniel tells us next:

*"...suddenly a goat with a prominent horn between its eyes came from the west, crossing the whole earth without touching the ground. [6] It came toward the two-horned ram I had seen standing beside the canal and charged at it in great rage. [7] I saw it attack the ram furiously, striking the ram and shattering its two horns. The ram was powerless to stand against it; the goat knocked it to the ground and trampled on it, and none could rescue the ram from its power"* ***(Daniel 8:5-7)***

This is a startlingly accurate description of the conquest of the Medo Persians by Alexander the Great - but what does it have to do with establishing a start year for the prophecy?

Note what the Angel Gabriel tells Daniel later in the vision:

*[19] He said: "I am going to tell you what will happen later in the time of wrath, because the vision concerns the appointed time of the end. 20 The two-horned ram that you saw represents the kings of Media and Persia.*

*[21] The shaggy goat is the king of Greece, and the large horn between its eyes is* ***the first king**. **(Daniel 8:19-21)***

Be careful not to miss this. Gabriel is giving Daniel a starting point for the prophecy of 2,300 years by telling him that the 'King of Greece' (Alexander) is **the 'first king'**.

The prophecy continues:

*[22] The four horns that replaced the one that was broken off represent four kingdoms that will emerge from his nation but will not have the same power.*

*[23] "In the latter part of their reign, when rebels have become completely wicked, a fierce-looking king, a master of intrigue, will arise. 24 He will become very strong, but not by his own power. He will cause astounding devastation and will succeed in whatever he does. He will destroy those who are mighty, the holy people.*

*[25] He will cause deceit to prosper, and he will consider himself superior. When they feel secure, he will destroy many and take his stand against the Prince of princes. Yet he will be destroyed, but not by human power.*

*[26] "The vision of the evenings and mornings that has been given you is true, but seal up the vision, for it concerns the distant future."* ***(Daniel 8:22-26)***

So Gabriel defines **the first king** (i.e., the start point of the prophecy) then goes on to provide an **end point** by telling Daniel that a 'master of intrigue' in the 'distant future' represents the last kingdom *in this prophecy*.

Understanding this makes the rest of the vision very clear. It's telling us that the vision starts with Alexander, whose kingdom will split into four separate kingdoms and that, in the distant future, a *fierce looking king* will come out of one of those kingdoms. But is this an accurate account of history?

It is. When Alexander died his four Generals fought between themselves until four new kingdoms emerged, just as the prophecy outlines. These were the kingdom of Cassander (circa 358-297 BC) which consisted of Macedonia, most of Greece, and parts of Thrace; the kingdom of Lysimachus (circa 361-281 BC) which included Lydia, Ionia, Phrygia, and other parts of present-day Turkey; the kingdom of Seleucus (later the Seleucid Empire) which comprised present-day Iran, Iraq, Syria, and parts of Central Asia; and the kingdom of Ptolemy I which included Egypt and neighbouring regions.

**When does the prophecy start?**

So now that we know that this vision starts from the time of the conquest of the Medo Persians by Alexander (the **first** King) – we need to determine when that took place.

Three battles in three different years define Alexanders defeat of the Medo Persians - the Battle of Granicus, which took place in 334BC in what is now north-west Turkey; the Battle of Issus, which took place in 333BC in Southern Turkey; and the Battle of Gaugamela which took place in 331BC in what is now Northern Iraq.

All three battles impacted on the conquest of the Medo Persians in different ways and represented a progressive march toward victory - but you'll note that, in the prophecy, the goat is described as striking the two horned ram 'suddenly'. There's no suggestion of an earlier battle or a progressive build up - so this is a description of Alexanders first victory – the defeat of the Medo Persians at the Battle of Granicus in 334BC.

So does this mean that 334BC - the year that 'the goat with the prominent horn' (Alexander) defeated the two horned ram (the Medes and the Persians) - is the starting year for the prophecy?

Not quite. This is another place where the precision of language once again comes to our aid.

The exact words of the prophecy were that "it will take 2,300 evenings and mornings; then the sanctuary will be reconsecrated". We've since learned that this unusual phrase refers to 'Passover Nights' so God is telling us that we're to count this period of time using the Passover as our reference.

In the Hebrew Calendar, the Passover is celebrated over several days starting with the first full moon in the Month of Nisan - usually around the 15th. This generally corresponds with April in our Gregorian Calander.

Why does this matter? Because the Battle of Granicus took place in June/July of 334BC, meaning the Passover Night for that year had already come and gone.

The next Passover Night took place in April 333BC so, if we're carefully following the instructions of the prophecy, **333BC is the year that we should count from**.

With that detail, we're now in a position to answer Question 1 and Question 6.

**Question 1: What's being predicted?**

We now know that the prophecy is predicting that 2,300 years will pass between the first Passover following the defeat of the Medo Persians by Alexander the Great and something called 'the reconsecration of the Sanctuary'.

**Question 6: When does it end and who is it about?**

Let's do the math:

-333 → + 2,300 → = **1967**

There it is again. **1967**. The same year that appeared in the prophecy that we reviewed, in chapter 12 of the Book of Daniel, and which coincides with the year in which the Israelis recaptured East Jerusalem, including the Old City, during the Six Day war.

So we can now identify 'the Sanctuary' as the site on which Solomon's Temple once stood on the temple mount because that's the site which was reclaimed in 1967 – which also means that we can now identify who the prophecy is about.

Once again, **it's the Jews** – the people for whom that ancient site has the greatest significance.

So let's put this new information into our template:

| **The Prophecy of 2,300 Evenings and Mornings**<br>Daniel 8:13-14 | | | |
|---|---|---|---|
| **What's being predicted?** | *That 2,300 years will pass between the first Passover following the defeat of the Medo Persians by Alexander the Great and 'the reconsecration of the Sanctuary'.* | | |
| **Question** | **Clue from Scripture** | **Math** | **Solution** |
| **Who is the prophecy addressed to?** | *"...I, Daniel, had a vision" (Daniel 8.1)* | | The prophecy is addressed to Daniel |
| **Who is the prophecy about?** | *"...the Lords people..." (Daniel 8.12)* | | The prophecy is about the Jews |
| **What year does the prophecy start?** | *The next Passover after the Battle of Granicus* | ***-333*** | The prophecy begins in 333 BC |
| **How long will the prophecy last?** | *"It will take 2,300 evenings and mornings...." (Daniel 8:14)* | ***plus 2,300*** | The prophecy will last for 2,300 years |
| **What year does the prophecy end?** | *"...then the Sanctuary will be reconsecrated" (Daniel 8:14)* | *equals 1,967* | **The prophecy ends in 1967** |

But what does the prophecy mean when it says that the sanctuary will be 'reconsecrated'? In simple terms, it means that it will be declared 'holy' - or, in this case, holy once again. As you'll recall from our chapter on recent Israeli history, that did, indeed, happen on the 7th of June 1967, when Israeli Défense Minister, **Moshe Dayan**, stood at the Western Wall and spoke these famous words:

*"This morning, the Israel Defence Forces liberated Jerusalem. We have united Jerusalem, the divided capital of Israel. We have*

*returned to the holiest of our holy places, never to part from it again".*

Although the Mount, including the site of the Temple, is currently under Muslim administration – this is by consent of the Israeli Government as Jerusalem is firmly under Israeli sovereignty. As such, it is back in Jewish hands, just as the prophecy said it would be.

Once again, we can see that these prophecies are not about the Christian Church in the last days and are not warnings of what lies just ahead for Christians. They are unequivocally about the Jewish people.

But what about the identity of the 'master of intrigue' described in this prophecy? We'll come back to him later in the book.

*The solution at a glance*

# 2,300 Evenings and Mornings: The Passover Clock

***Scripture:*** *Daniel 8:13-14*

1. **What's being predicted??**
   That 2,300 years will pass between the defeat of the Medo Persians by Alexander the Great and 'the reconsecration of the Sanctuary'.

2. **Who is being spoken to?**
   **Daniel** again.

3. **Who is it about?**
   "The Lord's people" = **the Jews**, for whom the sanctuary (the Temple Mount) is central to their identity.

4. **When does it start?**
   It begins **in 333 BC** with the first Passover after Alexanders defeat of the Medo-Persians at Granicus in 334 BC.

5. **How long does it last?**
   2,300 Passover nights = **2,300 years** in total. So: 333 BC + 2,300 years = 1967 AD

6. **When does it end?**
   When Israel recaptured the Temple Mount **in 1967**.

This prophecy isn't vague or symbolic - it's a precise 2,300-year timeline with a literal fulfilment: **Israel's recapture of the Temple Mount and reconsecration of the sanctuary in 1967.**

24

# Countdown to Abomination

## The Prophecy of 1,290 Days

which appears in **Daniel 12:11** in the

| 1st Vision | 2nd Vision | 3rd Vision | 4th Vision | 5th Vision | 6th Vision | 7th Vision |
|---|---|---|---|---|---|---|
| **The control of Jerusalem** | **The Kings madness** | **The restoration of the Holy land** | **The consecration of the sanctuary** | **The Seventy Sevens** | **The writing on the wall** | **Israels long future** |
| *Dan Ch 2* | *Dan Ch 4* | *Dan Ch 7* | *Dan Ch 8* | *Dan Ch 9* | *Dan Ch 5* | *Dan Ch 10-12* |

Earlier in this book, I acknowledged the extraordinary contribution of Ellis Skolfield, whose writings provided the conceptual foundation upon which *Prophecy Shock* has been built. Indeed, without Skolfield's original research, this book would not exist.

But while Skolfield's writings provided the initial scaffolding that made a project of this scope possible, this book should not be mistaken for replication. Over the past few years I have extended and expanded Skolfield's ideas – in most cases, substantially reworking them. I've clarified solutions, identified many new ones and have also developed a comprehensive interpretative framework along with clear criteria against which solutions can be independently tested.

As such, my work is unquestionably indebted to Skolfield's but is not defined by it.

I mention this because there are several areas in the book where I reach different conclusions to Skolfield – not as a criticism of his work but simply as an evolution of thinking based on the more stringent criteria that I have put in place. In each case I have identified a more consistent basis for my position in ways that strengthen the work without undermining Skolfield's overall message. I would like to think that Skolfield, himself, would have supported these changes – just as I hope that others will take my work and improve on it going forward.

But there is one prophecy – ***the prophecy of 1,290 days*** – where I have retained Skolfield's position in something close to its original form, even though I believe that there is a significant vulnerability in his argument. Let's explore his interpretation – along with my notes – before I explain where the weakness is and why I have left it in:

### The Prophecy

In Daniel chapter 12 we're told of a span of "1,290 days," beginning with "the abolition of the daily sacrifice" and ending in the rise of something called ***the abomination that causes desolation***.

This appears just after the prophecy of *time, times and half a time* which predicts "the end of the scattering of the holy people" and which was fulfilled when Israel recaptured Jerusalem in 1967 – and we pick up where Daniel is asking the angel for more clarification of the vision and is given two more prophecies. Here's the first of them:

> *"From the time that the daily sacrifice is abolished and the **abomination that causes desolation** is set up, there will be **1,290 days**." **(Daniel 12:11)***

Because this prophecy appears in Chapter 12 of Daniel's book we already know that it is addressed to **Daniel** and is about his people, **the Jews.** But what about the other questions in our template?

### How long is 1,290 days?

In the previous prophecies we were directed to relatively straightforward time periods: 2,500 years defined by 'time, times and half a time' and 2,300 years defined by annual Passovers.

But what are 'days'?

**Skolfield proposes that these should be read as years**, and I agree with him.

In **Numbers 13:34**, God tells Moses that the Israelites will wander in the Wilderness for forty years in punishment for complaining and for their lack of faith - one year for each of the *days* in which scouts had explored Canaan. Again, in Ezekiel 4:4-7, God gives Ezekiel a strange instruction to lie on one side for 40 'days', and then to lie for 390 days on the other - 430 in total - symbolising the number of years in which He was going to punish Israel and Judah.

This is known as the 'day/year principle' where 'days' are interpreted as 'years' – so 1,290 prophetic days could = **1,290 years**.

### How long is a year?

But if these days represent years – how many years are in view?

This may sound like a strange question – but we count today's years differently than they did in Daniel's time.

Our modern Gregorian years, which were introduced by Pope Gregory the 13th in the sixteenth century, are based on the time that it takes for the Earth to do a full circuit of the sun - 365.24 days. But at the time that Daniel and Ezekiel were writing their prophecies in the 6th century BC, a number of completely different calendars were in use throughout the Middle East - and some peoples even used multiple calendars depending on whether the purpose was trade, planting or religious. The trick is in identifying which one Daniel was using.

The civil calendar in use in Babylon during Daniel's time was the *lunisolar calendar* averaging about 354 days in a regular year – but we can have confidence that this was not the unit used by God to count prophetic years simply because its years constantly needed to be recalculated and it was far too unstable and inconsistent to support long-range prophetic timelines.

So what calendar would Daniel and Ezekiel have used instead?

### 360 Day years

The most likely candidate was the 360 day year calendar which was widely used by Mesopotamian cultures for mathematical and astronomical calculations at the time that Daniel and Ezekiel were writing. This 'Babylonian year' was an idealised time-measure - designed for tidy calculation rather than literal observation. It had developed out of Sumerian timekeeping and was based on the assumption that there were 12 months in every year, with 30 days in each month. If this is the year that Daniel was using - the process for converting his 1,290 'Days' (years) to our modern years is simple: we just divide a 360 day Babylonian year by a 365.24 day Gregorian year:

**360 / 365.24 = .9856532**

With this number we can now convert Babylonian years to our own years so that we can understand the length of time that Daniel was writing about.

**So - 1290 years x .9857 = 1271.55 of our years:**

If you've ever converted money from one currency to another – this is exactly the same process – except, here, we're dealing with time rather than currency. 1290 Babylonian years and 1271.55 Gregorian years are two different ways of describing *the same length of time* - we're just putting the number into a context that makes sense to us. On this clue, Skolfield and I are in agreement – so let's move on to the next question in our template.

**When does the prophecy start?**

The first *time-defined* prophecy in this vision – the prophecy of time, times and half a time – started in 533 BC. But we're given a new starting point for the prophecy of 1,290 days:

> ***"From the time that the daily sacrifice is abolished..." (Daniel 12:11)***

But when was that? History and scripture tell us that the daily sacrifice was a religious practice which had been established by Moses hundreds of years prior to Daniel's time. It involved sacrificing two one year old lambs, every day - one in the morning and one in the evening. This practice had taken place on the altar of Solomon's temple since its construction and it has been abolished a number of times throughout history, and then subsequently re-established. But which abolition is in view? There's a reference to one in the Old Testament Book of 2 Chronicles, and we also know that the Greek King Antiochus Epiphanes ended the sacrifices in 167BC.

**But Skolfield proposes a different year.** He notes that Jeremiah 52:30 tells us that told that "in the **23rd year** of Nebuchadnezzar" **745** Jews were deported from Jerusalem to Babylon as part of a total of **4,600** who were taken in a sweep that targeted what was left of Judah's elite: nobles, artisans, **and priests.** As such, Skolfield contends that **this marks the end of the sacrificial system**.

He then calculates the year when this happened by counting forward 23 years from the year that Nebuchadnezzar ascended the throne in 606 BC. I have made a small adjustment here because, if we're using Babylonian 360 day years we need to be consistent and apply them here too – so 23 Babylonian years converts to 22.67 of our years and, by simple math (-606 + 22.67) we arrive at **583.33 BC.**

It's at this point that I have a problem. Why? Because 583BC is not a recognised or historically verifiable year in which temple sacrifices were abolished and it feels 'forced'. While I understand Skolfield's explanation – that the exile of the Priestly class to Babylon would have meant the sacrifice in Jerusalem ended – it's a stretch to refer to that as 'an abolition' and I suspect observant readers will feel the same way.

To be clear – this does not necessarily mean that Skolfield is wrong - but it does mean that his solution rests on a speculative foundation.

### So why did I keep his solution in my book?

The answer to that question lies in where Skolfield's solution takes us. With 583 BC locked in as the start year, Skolfield then adds his previously resolved **1,271 years** to **583 BC** – and that takes us somewhere extraordinary:

# -583 → + 1,271 → = **688 AD**

### The Dome of the Rock

**688 AD** is not just any year – it is the year that construction began on Qubbat al-Sakhrah - the building that we now know as **the Islamic Dome of the Rock** on the Temple Mount in Jerusalem.

The Dome was completed in 691–692 AD and was Islam's first monumental sanctuary. It was commissioned by the Umayyad Caliph (ruler) **Abd al-Malik ibn Marwan** as a way to consolidate his power and establish both his political legitimacy and religious supremacy. His means of doing that was to build a dazzling sanctuary to a false god directly over the most contested ground in history – a site that was believed to be the ruins of the Jewish Temple and also the place from which Muhammad ascended into heaven during his 'Night Journey'. As such, the site was deliberately selected to mark this event while also insulting Jews and echoing Christian Byzantine architecture through the choice of an octagonal design.

The message was clear: Islam was positioning itself as the inheritor and conqueror of both Christianity and Judaism while, at the same time, desecrating Judaism's most holy place.

**Putting two and two together**

So Daniel's prophecy tells us that the 'setting up' of something called ***the abomination which causes desolation*** will mark the fulfilment of this prophecy – and Skolfield tells us that the year in which this fulfilment takes place is **688 AD – the year in which Islam began the construction of a dominant and imposing temple to a foreign God on Judaism's holiest site.**

Certainly, the construction of this building was devastating to the Jews. It brought to an end to any prospect of Jewish sacrifice on that site, making it 'desolate' and unusable for Jews for most of the following 1,250+ years. Indeed, to this day, over 1,300 years later, that same structure still dominates any postcard picture of Jerusalem.

**But is the Dome of the Rock the abomination of desolation?**

Over the pages ahead this book will demonstrate that it is. The year 688 AD will appear again and again in upcoming chapters and will assume huge significance within the broader interpretive framework that I am introducing.

However, I am not confident that I have made that point yet. Skolfield's solution is speculative, so you don't yet have sufficient context to judge whether this date represents a genuine structural centre of gravity in the prophetic material or whether it is merely a clever solution engineered to arrive at a particular year.

For now, I'm asking you to note this solution conceptually while recognising that the year 688 AD needs more support before it can be validated as the fulfilment year of this prophecy. (**Spoiler alert:** it can and will be).

| The Prophecy of 1,290 Days<br>Daniel 12:11-12 | | | |
|---|---|---|---|
| **What's being predicted?** | *That a period of 1,290 years will pass between the end of the daily sacrifice and the abomination of desolation being set up* | | |
| **Question** | **Clue from Scripture** | **Math** | **Solution** |
| **Who is the prophecy addressed to?** | *"...a message was revealed to Daniel" (Daniel 10.1)* | | **The prophecy is addressed to Daniel** |
| **Who is the prophecy about?** | *"...your people..." (Daniel 12.1)* | | **The prophecy is about the Jews** |
| **What year does the prophecy start?** | *"From the time that the daily sacrifice is abolished ..." (Daniel 12:11)* | ***-583*** | **The prophecy begins in 583BC** |
| **How long will the prophecy last?** | *1,290 Babylonian years (1,271 Gregorian years)* | ***plus 1,271*** | **The prophecy will last for 1,271 years** |
| **What year does the prophecy end?** | *Construction begins on the Dome of the Rock in Jerusalem* | ***equals 688*** | **The prophecy ends in 688 AD** |

So, for now, we're treating Skolfield's solution to *the prophecy of 1,290 days* with caution. But make no mistake: later chapters will prove that the Dome of the Rock **is** *the abomination of desolation* spoken of in Daniel.

We'll cover this in a lot more detail as we progress through the book.

*The solution at a glance*

# The 1,290 days: Countdown to Abomination

***Scripture:*** *Daniel 12:11-12*

1. **What's being predicted??**
   That **1,290 Babylonian years** will pass between the end of the daily sacrifice and the abomination of desolation being set up

2. **Who is being spoken to?**
   **Daniel** again.

3. **Who is the prophecy about?**
   "Your people." **The Jews**, not the Church..

4. **When does it start?**
   **583 BC**, when Nebuchadnezzar removed Jerusalem's remaining priests.

5. **How long does it last?**
   1,290 x 360 day Babylonian years ≈ **1,271** of our years.

6. **When does it end?**
   583 BC + 1,271 years = **688 AD**.

This prophecy points to **the construction of the Dome of the Rock in 688 AD, making the site of the Temple a 'desolate abomination' for the Jews.**

25

# The Mysterious Blessing

## The Prophecy of 1,335 Days

which appears in **Daniel 12:12** in the

| 1st Vision | 2nd Vision | 3rd Vision | 4th Vision | 5th Vision | 6th Vision | 7th Vision |
|---|---|---|---|---|---|---|
| **The control of Jerusalem** | **The Kings madness** | **The restoration of the Holy land** | **The consecration of the sanctuary** | **The Seventy Sevens** | **The writing on the wall** | **Israels long future** |
| *Dan Ch 2* | *Dan Ch 4* | *Dan Ch 7* | *Dan Ch 8* | *Dan Ch 9* | *Dan Ch 5* | *Dan Ch 10-12* |

The last of Daniel's prophecies adds a twist. It follows immediately after the prophecy of ***'1,290'*** days – but Instead of continuing with the theme of desolation, it dangles a promise: *"Blessed is the one who waits and reaches the end of the 1,335 days.* But why?

For centuries, the meaning was sealed. But when the countdown is traced, the answer becomes obvious.

Based on our first three solutions we found that Daniel's prophecies had end dates in the mid-twentieth century - aligning with the most significant years in modern Jewish history.

- In the two prophecies of *"time, times and half a time,"* God used two-and-a-half blocks of a thousand years - 2,500 years in total - leading us to 1948 and 1967.
- In the *"2,300 mornings and evenings"* prophecy, He used the Passover Night to indicate that these were 2,300 literal 365-day years - again pointing to 1967.

These prophecies not only harmonized, but also integrated with and reinforced one another, making their combined impact even more compelling than each individually.

But the prophecy of 1,290 days, which we've just reviewed, was different. In that prophecy God used *"days"* to connect us to the *"day-for-a-year"* principle in Ezekiel, showing that these were 360-day years that needed converting into modern terms. Based on Skolfield's solution, this pointed us to the seventh-century construction of a building on the Temple Mount – which is still standing over thirteen centuries later.

This different (and arguably more complex) basis of time measurement shouldn't surprise us. Daniel's prophecies were *sealed* and not meant to be understood until the last days. For example, the 2,500-year prophecies culminated in the very events that *triggered* those last days – which means that their meaning only became accessible once those events had occurred.

But the 1,290-year prophecy was fulfilled nearly 1,300 years before the last days began - so it stands to reason that God would embed the meaning of that prophecy in greater complexity, guarding it until the appointed time.

So what does this mean for the second part of the prophecy?

> *"Blessed is the one who waits for and reaches the end of the 1,335 days." **(Daniel 12:12)***

**Questions 1: What's being predicted?**

This time the prophecy doesn't actually give us a lot of information, upfront. We know that this is the last prophecy which appears in the Book of Daniel – but we're not told anything other than that those who reach '1,335 days' will be blessed.

As such we need to dig deeper into the five other questions to see if there is more information which will help us to understand what this prophecy means.

**Questions 2: Who is the prophecy addressed to?**

As a continuation of Daniel 12, this prophecy is also **addressed to Daniel.**

**Question 3: Who is it about?**

As a continuation of Daniel 12, this prophecy is also **about the Jews**.

**Question 4: When does the prophecy start?**

Because it continues on from the previous prophecy, and there are no additional instructions, we will assume that it also shares a common start date with that prophecy: **583 BC**.

**Questions 5 & 6: How long does the prophecy last, and when does it end?**

We can find out how long the prophecy lasts by using our 'Gregorian year convertor' (.9857) from the previous chapter:

**1335 x .9857 = 1315.91 of our modern years**

And what do we get if we add 1,315 years to 583 BC?

-583 → + 1,315 → = **732 AD**

And does 732 AD have any significance in Jewish history?
It certainly does.

**Questions 1: What's being predicted?**

We already know that Islam started in 613 and that, from 632, the Muslims had been engaged in large-scale military expansion throughout the Middle East and North Africa.

We also know that, for the most part, Jews had been able to worship and pray on the Temple Mount, when Jerusalem was under Muslim control – until the Dome of the Rock was constructed in 688.

However, from that time onward, the stark contrast of the two world views collided and the Jews were up against an increasingly implacable adversary which had its eyes on religious domination of the known world. Matthew 24 also vividly describes this time:

> *"When you see standing in the holy place 'the abomination that causes desolation,' spoken of through the prophet Daniel... then let those who are in Judea flee... For then there will be great distress, unequalled from the beginning of the world until now..."* ***(Matthew 24:15–22)***

We'll come back to Matthew's prophecy, later in the book - but, for now, let's go back to the 1335/1315 days in Daniel's prophecy.

History shows that both before, and after, the Dome was built many Jews fled Jerusalem – with many of them migrating into Eastern Europe in the 7th century and Western Europe in the 7th and 8th centuries. But even Europe wasn't safe for them. By 711, Muslims had conquered the Iberian Peninsula (modern day Spain and Portugal) and in **732**, Abdul Rahman Al Ghafiqi led a major assault on the Frankish (modern day French) cities of Tours and Poitiers.

Many scholars suggest that had this attack succeeded, the rest of Europe would have quickly fallen to Islamic control - but the Franks, led by Charlemagne's grandfather, Charles Martel ("The Hammer"), stopped the invasion at the **Battle of Tours** - despite being heavily outnumbered - preserving Europe from further conquest.

So now the prophecy makes perfect sense.

| The Prophecy of 1,335 Days<br>Daniel 12:12 | | | |
|---|---|---|---|
| **What's being predicted?** | *That those who reach the end of '1,335 days' will be blessed (safe from Muslim persecution and death)* | | |
| **Question** | **Clue from Scripture** | **Math** | **Solution** |
| **Who is the prophecy addressed to?** | *"...a message was revealed to Daniel" (Daniel 10.1)* | | **The prophecy is addressed to Daniel** |
| **Who is the prophecy about?** | *"...your people..." (Daniel 12.1)* | | **The prophecy is about the Jews** |
| **What year does the prophecy start?** | *"From the time that the daily sacrifice is abolished ..." (Daniel 12:11)* | ***-583*** | **The prophecy begins in 583BC** |
| **How long will the prophecy last?** | *1,335 Babylonian years* | ***plus 1,315*** | **The prophecy will last for 1,315 years** |
| **What year does the prophecy end?** | *Europe is secured against the Muslim onslaught at Tours* | ***equals 732*** | **The prophecy ends in 732 AD** |

In other words, the Jews who survived to **732 AD** had escaped the imminent threat of Islamic expansion. And that is exactly what history confirms. If Martel had failed, nowhere would have been safe for the Jews who had moved there. They would have been forcibly converted to Islam or killed, as was the practice under Muslim conquest at that time, and although the experiences of the Jews in 'Christian' Europe in the centuries which lay ahead were no bed of roses, either - at least, there, they were able to worship God.

**The Blessing**

So now we understand why those who made it to 'the 1,335 days' were 'blessed'. This prophecy lands us precisely on **732** - the year of the Battle of Tours in which a Muslim invasion of greater Europe was repelled and another existential threat to the Jews was avoided.

The second prophecy aligns perfectly with history:

*"Blessed is the one who waits for and reaches the end of the 1,335 days." **(Daniel 12:12)***

---

**Note**: Given the simplicity of this solution, I'm of the view that God placed it to act as a kind of 'watermark' by which to confirm that the prophecy of 1,290 days did, indeed, start in 583BC as proposed by Skolfield. By 'piggybacking' on the same clues to produce another historically sound solution, it gives us increasing confidence that Skolfield's reasoning and solution were correct.

*The solution at a glance*

# The 1,335 days:
# The Mysterious Blessing

***Scripture:*** *Daniel 12:12*

1. **What's being predicted??**
   That those who reach the end of '1,335 days' will be blessed (safe from Muslim persecution and death)

2. **Who is being spoken to?**
   Still **Daniel** - same vision, same recipient.

3. **Who is the prophecy about?**
   Daniel's people. **The Jews**. Not Christians, not the Church.

4. **When does it start?**
   **583 BC**, when the daily sacrifice ended.

5. **How long does it last?**
   1,335 Babylonian years ≈ **1,315** of our years

6. **When does it end?**
   583 BC + 1,315 years = **732 AD**.

This prophecy precisely predicts **the Battle of Tours in 732 in which Charles Martel halts the Muslim invasion into Europe – ensuring Jewish safety from Muslim persecution and death.**

# 26

summary

## The meaning of Daniel's Prophecies:

# From Exile to Redemption

As we walked through Daniel's time-defined prophecies we found that each of them aligned with significant events in Jewish history.

Now, stepping back, the scale of what we've seen becomes clear.

These prophecies aren't references to an Antichrist, a seven-year tribulation, or a persecution of Christians at the end of the world. They're a meticulously crafted love letter to the Jews. A countdown of specific events proving that God was never absent, never out of control, and never finished with His people.

Read on their own terms - and tested against history – an extraordinary picture of these prophecies emerges:

- They are all **addressed to Daniel**.
- They are all **about his people, the Jews**.
- They all **began more than two thousand years ago**.
- And they all **land precisely on milestones of Jewish history**.

This isn't just a new twist on old theories. It's a complete realignment of what these prophecies are, and who they are addressed to, as visualised in the graphic on the next page.

## The real meaning of the Prophecies in the Book of Daniel

**1,290 days** - Daniel 12:11
Started in 583 BC → 1,271 modern years → **688**
Construction starts on the Dome of Rock

**1,335 days** - Daniel 12:12
Started in 583 BC → 1,315 modern years → **732**
Muslims defeated in battle of Tours

**'Time, times and half a time'** - Daniel 7:25
Written in 552 BC → 2,500 years → **1948**
Israel is re-established

**2,300 Evenings and Mornings** - Daniel 8:13-14
Started in 333 BC → 2,300 modern years → **1967**
The Sanctuary is reconsecrated

**'Time, times and half a time'** - Daniel 12:7
Written in 533 BC → 2,500 years → **1967**
Jerusalem is liberated

Some readers might look at the historical fulfilments shown here and assume this framework is simply a form of *Historicism* – the school of Prophecy Interpretation that proposes that biblical prophecy unfolds progressively through history. But the two approaches are fundamentally different. Historicism has traditionally interpreted prophecy through the rise and fall of European powers and church–state institutions, reading Revelation largely as a coded history of Christendom. By contrast, the framework used in this book is anchored consistently in **Israel and the powers that physically ruled Jerusalem**, More importantly, Historicism places most prophetic fulfilment in the distant past, whereas Israelism shows that the decisive outcomes of Daniel's timelines landed **in the mid-20$^{th}$ century**, in events that still shape the world we inhabit right now. This is not just a retrospective theology of yesterday's empires, but a framework that insists that prophecy speaks directly into the present moment, because many of these prophecies have only just finished unfolding in history before our eyes.

Viewed in this way we can finally see the power of Daniel's message. He thought that his people were preparing for the end of seventy years of exile in Babylon – but, through his visions, God showed him that something far greater was in store:

- That the punishment of his people would last much longer, under successive foreign powers.
- That the site of the Temple would be desecrated.
- That his people would be scattered across many nations.
- But that redemption was certain and that the Jews would eventually return to the Holy Land, to Jerusalem, and to the Temple Mount.

What Daniel could not yet see - but we can see now - is just how precisely those promises unfolded. Independent prophecies, written decades apart, using different symbolic measures of time, yet all converging on exact dates in Jewish history. One lands on the seventh century and identifies the desecration of the Temple Mount. Another points to the halting of Islamic expansion into Europe. Three separate prophecies independently arrive at the most important dates in modern Jewish history - the rebirth of the Jewish nation in 1948 and the liberation of Jerusalem in 1967.

**The Jews at the centre of Prophecy**

The implications of these discoveries are profound. They restore the Jewish people to the position for which God has always intended them:

- the long centuries of dispersion were not abandonment.
- the loss of Jerusalem was not permanent.
- the return of the nation in 1948 and the recovery of the Old City in 1967 were not merely political outcomes, diplomatic accidents, or historical flukes

These things were all prophetic fulfilments written into Scripture more than two millennia earlier and Israel's modern rebirth is not an anomaly of history - it is the continuation of a plan, set in motion by God, that never stopped unfolding.

Daniel never lived to see Babylon fall, Persia rise, Greece fracture, Rome dominate, Islam conquer Jerusalem, or Israel return home. Yet every one of those turning points was already embedded in the visions that he recorded. What began with a series of dreams given to a young exile praying for the end of seventy years of captivity became a divine disclosure stretching across twenty-five centuries - culminating in the rebirth of a nation and the restoration of its capital.

Seen this way, prophecy stops functioning as a crystal ball and starts functioning as a signature. God did not give these timelines so that humans could boast about predicting the future - but so that, once fulfilled, His authorship of history would become unmistakable.

27

THE PRINCIPLES OF ISRAELISM

# God's Word always trumps academic consensus

When we reviewed the different prophetic interpretations earlier in this book we discussed the influence of the field of Higher Criticism and the role it has played in questioning the accuracy of Biblical writers through a process of circular reasoning which is mostly premised on the denial of the supernatural.

However, as we established in Chapter 16, Israelism begins the other way around - by letting Scripture define history rather than forcing Scripture to conform to academic consensus.

Understanding this is important because, as we make our way through this book we're going to come across dates and people which are the subject of academic debate - even amongst Christians.

**The Mystery of Darius the Mede**

An excellent example of this is **Darius the Mede** – a figure who features prominently in the book of Daniel but has puzzled historians for centuries.

Daniel introduces this character as the Medo Persian ruler who *"received the kingdom"* when Belshazzar was killed (Daniel 5:30–31), on the night of the fall of Babylon in 539 BC. He tells us that this man:

- Appointed governors to oversee the realm (Daniel 6:1).
- Issued laws and enforced them, including the infamous decree that landed Daniel in the lions' den.
- Was in power when Daniel prayed for Jerusalem's restoration (Daniel 9:1–2).

But when we turn to our current historical knowledge we find **no "Darius the Mede" listed among known Persian kings** in this period.

**How academics handle this**

Rather than investigate Darius as a genuine historical figure, most scholars simply gloss over him. They treat him as:

1. A fictional character - invented to bridge the gap between Babylon and Persian rule in the narrative;
2. Or a symbolic or literary device - representing the Medo-Persian takeover without being an actual individual.

These approaches all sidestep the question entirely and this explains why many historians have **Cyrus ruling Babylon from 539 BC** even though Daniel explicitly tells us that he did not and provides fulsome details of the man who did. As such we are faced with a clear decision – to accept Daniel (who was there) or to defer to the opinion of the modern academics.

**So who was Darius?**

The strongest candidate for that role is a man named **Gubaru (Gobryas) – a real character recorded in history.** Let's compare him to Daniel's description of Darius:

| | **Darius the Mede** (as recorded by Daniel) | **Gubaru** (Historical Records) |
|---|---|---|
| **Role in Babylon's fall** | *"Received the kingdom"* after Belshazzar's death in 539 BC (Dan 5:30); reorganised govt and appointed officials (Dan 6:1). | Took Babylon for Cyrus in 539 BC; immediately installed new officials and restructured admin. |
| **Political status** | Ruler of Babylon but not *King of Kings.* | Served as governor of Babylonia under Cyrus, |
| **Ethnic designation** | Called *"the Mede"* (Dan 9:1). | Likely Median by birth. |
| **Timing** | Governed between Babylon's fall in 539 BC and Cyrus's "first year". | Controlled Babylon from 539 BC until Cyrus assumed the kingship. |
| **Name: "Darius"** | This could be a title (*Dārayavahuš*, Old Persian for "upholder of the kingdom"). | May have received the honorific *Dārayavahuš* after the conquest. |
| **Biblical portrayal** | Real, active ruler who issued decrees. | Real, active ruler who had authority to issue decrees. |

It's possible, of course, that Gubaru was not Darius the Mede and that Daniel was describing another historical figure – however our point is to recognise that Daniel clearly describes such a person and that our academic approach should be to find him – not to whitewash him from history – particularly when there is also **strong evidence for a delay in the coronation of Cyrus**:

- The **Nabonidus Chronicle** records Babylon's fall in 539 BC and Gubaru's appointment as governor, but no coronation of Cyrus.

- The **Akitu festival** (Nisan, March/April) was when Babylonian coronations occurred but Cyrus arrived in October 539, too late for that year's festival, and political unrest or religious sensitivities could have pushed the ceremony back several years.

- A **gap in early Babylonian sources** shows some texts calling Cyrus "King of Babylon" only after a few years - pointing to a "two-phase" kingship: conquest first, ceremonial kingship later.

These discrepancies demonstrate that the dating of the kingship of Cyrus isn't the open-and-shut-case that some academics portray it to be. Nor is this situation unique in the annuls of biblical archaeology. Indeed, the study of ancient history (secular and Biblical) is littered with examples of people and places that 'did not exist' – only to be later discovered and quietly and retrospectively added to our bank of knowledge. (The City of Troy comes to mind as an obvious example among many).

As such, we need to be careful not to dismiss important Biblical dates and information simply because academics have not yet caught up with what the Prophets told us millennia ago,

Again and again, Scripture has preserved historical details that were either unknown, disputed, or dismissed by scholars for centuries - only for archaeology and primary records to later confirm what the Biblical writers had written - long before modern academia was in a position to verify it.

**The Hittites**

For a long time critics confidently asserted that the Bible exaggerated or even fabricated the existence of the Hittites. Outside of Scripture, there appeared to be no trace of them, and so they were written off as a minor or mythical people. Yet in the late nineteenth and early twentieth centuries, archaeologists uncovered an entire Hittite civilisation in Anatolia (Turkey) - complete with royal archives, international treaties, and evidence of a major imperial power that interacted with Egypt, Assyria, and Babylon. The Bible had been right all along; it was scholarship that was incomplete.

**King David**

For much of the twentieth century, a number of scholars argued that David was little more than a tribal chieftain, or perhaps a literary invention injected into Israel's past to legitimise later kings. However, that claim collapsed with the discovery of the Tel Dan Stele, which contains a reference to the "House of David" - clear evidence that David was recognised as the founder of a ruling dynasty. The Biblical account had preserved the political reality; archaeology merely caught up.

**Pontius Pilate**

Even figures central to the New Testament were not immune from this scepticism. Pontius Pilate was long treated by some as a convenient Gospel character whose historical footprint was suspiciously thin. That changed abruptly in 1961 with the discovery of a Roman inscription at Caesarea Maritima naming Pontius Pilate as prefect of Judea. Once again, the Bible had named a real man holding a real office at the right time and place - centuries before epigraphic evidence surfaced.

**King Cyrus**

Even Cyrus himself has been the subject of controversy. Scripture describes him as the ruler of Persia who permitted captive peoples to return home and restore their sanctuaries. But for a long time, this was dismissed as later Jewish embellishment. However, the discovery of the Cyrus Cylinder changed that conversation entirely. While it does not name Judah specifically, it confirms a broader Persian policy of repatriation and religious restoration, placing the Biblical account firmly within its authentic historical context.

**Belshazzar**

Perhaps most telling is the case of Belshazzar. For generations, critics pointed to Daniel 5 as an obvious error, noting that Belshazzar did not appear on standard lists of Babylonian kings. However, cuneiform records later revealed that Belshazzar was the son of Nabonidus and exercised royal authority during his father's absence - explaining both Daniel's portrayal of him as ruler and his inability to offer Daniel more than third place in the kingdom. What once appeared to be a mistake turned out to be an insight that only an insider would have known.

None of these examples eliminate debate – but they establish something far more fundamental to the method of Israelism: when Scripture speaks plainly about historical people, places, and events, it has repeatedly demonstrated itself to be a reliable witness - often centuries ahead of academic consensus.

This is why Israelism refuses to begin with modern assumptions about what *could* or *could not* have happened and instead starts where the Biblical authors themselves start. The question is not whether Scripture must be bent to fit prevailing scholarly models, but whether those models are complete enough to judge texts that have already proven their historical credibility time and again.

## Section Four

# INTRODUCING THE BOOK OF REVELATION

# Preview

***If Daniel reveals the plan, Revelation shows the execution.***

With most of Daniel's time-defined prophecies now decoded, we turn to the most symbol-heavy book in the entire Bible - **The Revelation of Jesus Christ**.

For many, Revelation is a chaotic whirlwind of beasts, bowls, trumpets, and catastrophes. But in this section, we cut through the confusion by applying the same framework that we used in Daniel: **consistent, contextual, history-anchored interpretation.**

Through this approach you'll learn that Revelation is not a single narrative, but a series of **seven distinct visions**, each with a specific purpose and audience. When properly understood, these visions not only complement the Book of Daniel - they *confirm* it.

In this section, you'll discover:

- How Revelation's visions map to **historic realities**, not speculative futures.
- Why understanding **vision structure and context** is critical to interpreting the book.
- The true identity and meaning of prophetic symbols such as the **Two Witnesses**, **the 42 months**, **the Beast**, and **the 144,000**.
- How themes like persecution, restoration, and antisemitism are **central, not peripheral** to the book.

Revelation is **not the script of an apocalyptic movie about future doom**, but a **cohesive, mostly completed message** of God's control over history - fulfilled, visible, and verifiable.

28

# Making sense of Revelation

***Finding order in apparent chaos***

I first read the Book of Revelation in my mid-teens in the late 1970s because I wanted to understand what it predicted for the future.

But instead of finding easy answers to my questions I felt like I'd entered Alice's Wonderland and was being swept up into a whirlwind of bizarre visions and constantly shifting settings.

Far from providing clarity, my early attempts at understanding left me confused and frustrated.

But why is this book so confusing? Afterall, the very name - *Revelation* - suggests its message should be *uncovered*, not concealed. In fact, Revelation 1:3 even promises a blessing to those who read it:

> *"Blessed is the one who reads aloud the words of this prophecy and blessed are those who hear it and take to heart what is written in it, because the time is near."*

To understand why a book that purports to be about 'revealing' mysteries is so hard to comprehend - let's review what we actually know about this enigmatic book.

First – and importantly – Revelation is in the New Testament. This means that it is not generally recognised as inspired, by Jews, and that it belongs to the part of scripture which was written by Christians and which records the life, resurrection and promise of

Christ and the Christian faith, Despite this, it draws heavily from other parts of the Bible - both Old and New Testaments. It contains 404 verses and over 800 Old Testament allusions - in fact the late Chuck Missler claimed that "everything in the Old Testament anticipates Revelation." In other words, you cannot understand Revelation without also understanding the scriptures that it references.

We know it was written by "John" - almost certainly the Apostle John, one of Yeshua's twelve disciples, who is wrote the Gospel of John. We also know it was written between AD 69 and 95, which would place John between about 60 and 90 years old at the time.

Revelation is a series of visions - dreams given to John - and while its Greek name *Apokalypsis* evokes dread, it simply means *unveiling*.

John wrote it while exiled on Patmos, a small island near Ephesus, where he had lived previously. This supports the traditional view that John the Apostle was the author.

**Who is the book about?**

In the Book of Daniel the prophecies were addressed *to* Daniel and were *about* the Jews. In Revelation, the opening verse tells us that it is Christ's revelation for His servants and in the first century that could only have meant **Christians**, (though they were not yet called by that name).

However, we will soon discover that although Revelation is written *to* Christians, it's not only *about* Christians. It covers multiple groups and also outlines the history of the Jews, Gentiles, and several major world powers.

**The Sevenfold Structure of Revelation**

If you've read Revelation you'll know that the number seven features prominently. Seven churches, seven trumpets, seven plagues, seven bowls, etc. But what is less obvious is that – like the Book of Daniel – it is also built around seven visions (a structure obscured by the 13th-century chapter breaks).

So, rather than one long vision, the visions and prophecies in the Book of Revelation actually look like this:

**THE SEVEN VISIONS IN THE BOOK OF REVELATION**

| 1st Vision | 2nd Vision | 3rd Vision | 4th Vision | 5th Vision | 6th Vision | 7th Vision |
|---|---|---|---|---|---|---|
| **The history of the Church** | **The trials of believers** | **The history of the gentiles** | **The origin of anti-semitism** | **The last plagues** | **The fall of Babylon** | **The reign of Christ** |
| *Rev Ch 1-3* | *Rev Ch 4-8.1* | *Rev Ch 8.2-11* | *Rev Ch 12-14* | *Rev Ch 15-16, 19-20* | *Rev Ch 17-18* | *Rev Ch 21-22* |

Each of these visions centre on Yeshua and end with His return - with the 7th one also detailing what follows that return.

But each vision is different. The first four present us with four different perspectives of the past 2,000 years of history. Each of these has a portion which is yet future - but all four devote most of their attention to events which have (now) been fulfilled:

**Vision 1. The History of the Church**

Chapters 1–3 present Yeshua dictating letters to seven real churches. These letters commend, correct, and warn. They also map the entire Church era across two millennia.

**Vision 2. The Trials of Believers**

Chapters 4 to 8:1 outline global events over 2,000 years, culminating in the salvation of Jews and Christians.

**Vision 3. The History of the Gentiles**

Chapters 8 to 11 describe natural disasters, supernatural signs, and a rising political power – ending with the end of the age.

**Vision 4. The Origin of Antisemitism**

Chapters 12–14 begin with a vision of Israel at the time of Christ's birth, then expose Satan's long-term strategy for eliminating the Jews.

### More sevens

You'll note that the pattern of sevens continues within the seven visions themselves. For example, the first vision is about seven Churches, the second is about seven seals and the third is about seven trumpets. This pattern is deliberate. It tells us where each vision starts and ends and gives us confidence that each of them is separate.

The remaining three visions deal with events that are still entirely in the future.

### Vision 5. The Last Plagues

Chapters 15–16 begin a long vision with seven plagues poured from bowls of judgment. It pauses for the fall of Babylon, then resumes in chapters 19–20 with the defeat of the Beast, the False Prophet, and Satan.

### Vision 6. The fall of Babylon

Chapters 17–18 identifies 'Babylon' in considerable detail and goes into more detail to describe her complete destruction and the fall of the beast that she rides.

### Vision 7. The 1,000-Year Reign of Christ and the New Creation

Chapters 21–22 detail final judgment, the new heaven and earth, and the destiny of the Bride of Christ.

I know it may be hard to accept that so much of Revelation has already been fulfilled. Many of us grew up believing it was entirely about Christians in the last days and this challenges that belief. But as you continue reading, the simplicity, accuracy and power of this interpretation will become clear.

29

# An Overview of
# The first Visions

which appear in the **Book of Revelation**

| 1st Vision | 2nd Vision | 3rd Vision | 4th Vision | 5th Vision | 6th Vision | 7th Vision |
|---|---|---|---|---|---|---|
| **The history of the Church** | **The trials of believers** | **The history of the gentiles** | **The origin of anti-semitism** | **The last plagues** | **The fall of Babylon** | **The reign of Christ** |
| *Rev Ch 1-3* | *Rev Ch 4-8.1* | *Rev Ch 8.2-11* | *Rev Ch 12-14* | *Rev Ch 15-16, 19-20* | *Rev Ch 17-18* | *Rev Ch 21-22* |

The first two visions in the Book of Revelation have two things in common:

1. They're both written *to* and *about* Christians
2. Neither of them contains time-defined prophecies that would allow us to identify specific years

Other than that, they're structured differently from each other and contain very different information:

- **The first Vision** takes the form of seven letters to seven churches, dictated by Yeshua Himself. These letters provide a remarkably accurate outline of 2,000+ years of the history of the institutional Church.

- **The second Vision** focuses on the challenges that will face individual believers. It presents these in the form of 'seals' that will be progressively opened and is concerned with reassuring readers that these things are all part of Gods bigger plan and do not, of themselves, mean that 'the end' has arrived.

As such, they are both more general in nature than the later, more specific Visions which contain time-defined prophecies – however, this does not mean that their content is of lesser value. Both Visions contain important information which will assist us when we address later Visions in this book.

Let's start with the first of them.

# 30

# The Mystery of the Church

## The Prophecies of the Seven Letters

which appear in **Revelation Chapters 2-3** in the

| 1st Vision | 2nd Vision | 3rd Vision | 4th Vision | 5th Vision | 6th Vision | 7th Vision |
|---|---|---|---|---|---|---|
| **The history of the Church** | **The trials of believers** | **The history of the gentiles** | **The origin of anti-semitism** | **The last plagues** | **The fall of Babylon** | **The reign of Christ** |
| *Rev Ch 1-3* | *Rev Ch 4-8.1* | *Rev Ch 8.2-11* | *Rev Ch 12-14* | *Rev Ch 15-16, 19-20* | *Rev Ch 17-18* | *Rev Ch 21-22* |

Before the seals, the trumpets, or the beasts, Revelation begins with a mystery: seven letters dictated by Christ Himself, sent to seven churches in Asia Minor. At first glance, these letters appear to be simple instructions for congregations in John's day. But beneath the surface, they read like messages sealed in time - a hidden history of the Church age, written in advance.

Beginning in chapter 2, after a formal introduction, Christ recites these seven letters to John, instructing him to write them down and send them to *the churches in Ephesus, Smyrna, Pergamum, Thyatira, Sardis, Philadelphia, and Laodicea.*

Who are these churches? Why are they mentioned, why are they in this order, and why do they feature in Revelation? Do they provide clues which would allow us to apply the Six Basic Questions? Let's find out.

**Who is the vision addressed to?**

As with the Book of Daniel, we must distinguish between who Revelation is written *to* and who it is *about*. Revelation tells us directly that it is:

> *"...a revelation from Jesus Christ, which God gave him to show his servants what must soon take place."* ***(Revelation 1:1)***

This is clear: the book is addressed to Christians - Christ's servants - as a warning of what's to come.

**Who is the vision about?**

The vision names seven churches, all located in Asia Minor (modern Turkey), and all active in John's time. The word "churches" here means assemblies or bodies of believers, not denominations or buildings in the sense that we understand that term. The first of these, Ephesus, was also the assembly to which Paul wrote the Epistle to the Ephesians. So we can say with confidence that this first vision is both addressed *to* and *about* Christians.

**When does the vision start?**

In Daniel, we had specific markers telling us when each prophecy began. Is there a similar marker here?

Apparently not. While we know that the Church of Ephesus, the first of the Churches listed, was established by Paul in the first century AD we don't know precisely when this happened. Nor do we have establishment years for each of the other churches[38] - so we can't establish a reliable start date for the vision.

But that doesn't mean that it has no prophetic value. When we review the seven letters we find that they all follow a similar (although not identical) structure. Three of the Churches are the

---

[38] (with one exception, which we outline in Chapter 64 of *Prophecy Shock*)

subject of both praise and correction. Two – Smyrna and Philadelphia – receive only praise. Sardis and Laodicea receive only criticism..

### The 'Church Age' view

There is a view that these Churches provide an outline of Church history. In this view, each Church defines a particular era and, based on the order in which the letters appear, there certainly seems to be some interesting congruence between scripture and this history:

- **Ephesus (AD 30–100):** Apostolic era
- **Smyrna (100–313):** Persecuted church (pre-Constantine)
- **Pergamum (313–590):** State church trajectory – Catholicism (post-Constantine)
- **Thyatira (590–1300s):** Medieval church
- **Sardis (1300–1517):** Stagnant era
- **Philadelphia (1517–1950s):** Reformation and Revival era
- **Laodicea (1950s–present):** Lukewarm modern church

However, these timelines are disputed and there is no universally accepted version (this one is my own) – so while they're a useful guide, they should not necessarily be regarded as having watertight scriptural authority.

Meanwhile, we can now see that there are four distinct theories offered to explain the purpose of these letters:

1. that they refer only to the specific churches being written to at that time.
2. that they describe common issues faced by all churches over 2,000 years.
3. that they're prophetic and that each church represents a different "age" in Church history, either sequentially or overlapping.
4. that they're layered – and that all of the above are true simultaneously.

This book supports the fourth view: that the vision outlines both Church history and universal challenges faced by churches throughout time.

This means that, while we can't apply the Six Basic Questions to this Vision in the way that we did in the Book of Daniel – the Vision *does* contain broad historical information that may be useful to us as we review the other visions in Revelation.

**What is the general message of the Vision:**

- That the vision has three levels of understanding:
  - *As a series of messages that are specific to the seven existing Churches to which it is addressed.*
  - *As a summary of common issues that will face all Churches throughout Church history.*
  - *As a prophecy of seven distinct Church ages (which may, or may not, have been overlapping).*

- That the role and nature of the true Church will change depending on time and location. Sometimes it will be under persecution, other times it will be integrated with society – even powerful.

- That the Church will never reach perfection – it will always suffer from errors in doctrine and practice – and sometimes these errors will be serious.

- That Yeshua is constantly calling on His people to repent of such errors and practices and is always willing to forgive these.

**Has the Vision been completely fulfilled?**

No. If we accept the 'Church age' theory we are currently living in the last of these ages – the Church of Laodicea – and this letter contains a prophecy of the Return of Christ, which has not yet happened.

It's particularly noteworthy that this Church is also the furthest from God and the most affected by apostasy. This passage – from the Book of Revelation – is directly aimed at Christians in the 21st century:

> *"I know what you do. I know that you are neither cold nor hot. And I wish that you were cold or hot. So I will spit you out of my mouth, because you are only lukewarm and not hot or cold. You say, `I am rich and have many things. I need nothing. You do not know that you are in trouble and need help. You are poor. You are blind. And you have no clothes to wear".*

Harsh words – and a significant cause for self-reflection as we review the other prophecies in this book.

31

# The trials of Believers

## The Prophecies of the Seven Sealed Scroll

which appear in **Revelation Chapters 4-8** in the

| 1st Vision | 2nd Vision | 3rd Vision | 4th Vision | 5th Vision | 6th Vision | 7th Vision |
|---|---|---|---|---|---|---|
| **The history of the Church** | **The trials of believers** | **The history of the gentiles** | **The origin of anti-semitism** | **The last plagues** | **The fall of Babylon** | **The reign of Christ** |
| *Rev Ch 1-3* | *Rev Ch 4-8.1* | *Rev Ch 8.2-11* | *Rev Ch 12-14* | *Rev Ch 15-16, 19-20* | *Rev Ch 17-18* | *Rev Ch 21-22* |

If the first vision was about the Church as a whole - the second vision lifts the curtain on what individual believers themselves would face. It begins with a mystery that has gripped readers for centuries: a scroll sealed seven times, which only *the Lion of the tribe of Judah* can open.

Each seal unlocks a force that has shaped history - conquest, war, famine, plague, persecution, cosmic upheaval – and Revelation makes clear that these are not just symbols of a distant future. They are the repeating trials of the faithful throughout the entire Church Age.

The Vision begins in Revelation Chapter 4 where John sees a door in heaven and is told, "Come up here":

> *"After this I looked, and there before me was a door standing open in heaven... At once I was in the Spirit, and there before me was a throne in heaven..."* ***(Revelation 4:1–2)***

The phrase *"in the Spirit"* confirms that this is a vision. The setting is the Throne Room of God. Though no time is given, we know it's before the end of the age because the four living creatures sing of Christ: *"who was, and is, and* ***is to come****."*

In chapter 5, John sees a scroll in God's hand, sealed with seven seals which only Christ - *the Lion of the tribe of Judah* - is found worthy to open. As He opens six of the seals, John witnesses the following:

1. A white horse whose rider holds a bow, is given a crown, and rides out as a conqueror.

2. A fiery red horse whose rider is given power to remove peace and incite violence.

3. A black horse with scales, referencing food scarcity - "a day's wages for wheat," with a warning not to damage oil and wine.

4. A pale horse named Death, followed by Hades, given power to kill by sword, famine, plague, and wild beasts.

These are known, in popular culture, as the "Four Horsemen of the Apocalypse," and are often assumed to describe end-time events.

5. Next, the fifth seal reveals the souls of martyred Christians under the altar. They ask when God will avenge their deaths and are told to wait until the full number of martyrs is complete.

6. The sixth seal reveals a great earthquake, a darkened sun, a blood-red moon, and stars falling from the sky. The heavens recede, mountains and islands are displaced, and people hide in terror at the coming wrath of Christ.

Before further destruction begins, four angels are told to hold back until 144,000 Jews - 12,000 from each tribe - are sealed. Then John sees a great multitude from every nation worshipping before the throne. These are described as *"those who have come out of the great tribulation."*

The seventh seal introduces half an hour of silence in heaven, concluding the vision.

### The key to understanding the Seals

So what does all of this mean? There are no clear time-defined clues here. Can we still know what the vision is about?

Yes. Helpfully, the same vision appears three times in the Gospels - in Matthew 24–25, Luke 21, and Mark 13. Each is Christ's response to the disciples' questions after He had predicted the destruction of the Temple in Jerusalem (an event that we will cover later in this book). They asked Him:

- *When will this happen?*
- *What will be the sign of your coming and of the end of the age?*

His response, in all three accounts, is a direct parallel to what John saw in Revelation. Let's review the account in Luke:

> *"Watch out that you are not deceived. For many will come in my name, claiming, 'I am he,' (or 'I represent Christ') and 'The time is near.' Do not follow them.* ***(False Christianity - this parallels the first seal)***
>
> *"When you hear of wars and uprisings, do not be frightened. These things must happen first, but the end will not come right away. 10 Then he said to them: "Nation will rise against nation, and kingdom against kingdom."* ***(War - this parallels the second seal)***

*"There will be great earthquakes, famines and pestilences in various places, and fearful events and great signs from heaven."* ***(Famine and plague - this parallels the third and fourth seals)***

*"They will seize and persecute you... put some of you to death..."* ***(Persecution of Christians - this parallels the fifth seal)***

The parallel continues a few verses later:

*"There will be signs in the sun, moon and stars. On the earth, nations will be in anguish and perplexity at the roaring and tossing of the sea. People will faint from terror, apprehensive of what is coming on the world, for the heavenly bodies will be shaken. At that time they will see the Son of Man coming in a cloud with power and great glory. When these things begin to take place, stand up and lift up your heads, because your redemption is drawing near."* ***(Signs in the heavens - this parallels the sixth seal) Luke 21:28-35***

And finally:

*"Be careful, or your hearts will be weighed down with carousing, drunkenness and the anxieties of life, and that day will close on you suddenly like a trap. For it will come on all those who live on the face of the whole earth. Be always on the watch, and pray that you may be able to escape all that is about to happen, and that you may be able to stand before the Son of Man."* ***(this highlights the main point of six of the seven visions in Revelation - the return of Christ) Luke 21:34-36***

So while we still don't have time-defined clues, these parallel accounts help us to fill in a lot more detail and we can see that the vision is not a narrow view of the end times but a sweeping overview of Christian experience throughout the Church Age.

And, like the first vision, we can also see that this one provides both a warning and reassurance - but on a more personal level. While the first vision spoke to the Church as an institution, this one speaks to individual believers and, with the benefit of 2,000 years, we can now see how accurately this vision describes Christian experience. Again, no specific dates are needed. This is a timeless overview of repeated events that many believers have encountered during the 2,000 years of the Church Age.

With that background let's see if we can provide a summary of the Vision:

| | |
|---|---|
| **Who is the Vision about?** | Individual believers within the Church |
| **What's the context?** | John, writing the Christians while imprisoned on the Island of Patmos. |

**What is the general message of the Vision:**
Whereas the first vision provided an overview of what would happen to the Church during the Church age - this vision is provided to give individual believers an insight into what they would face over that same period of time. The vision warns that:

- there's a long road ahead and much in store for believers – so not every crisis is a portend of the end (remember – this was written two thousand years ago)

- hardship is part of the Christian journey and many Christians (tens of millions) will endure suffering in this life based on the promise of the next

- Christians will face, and endure:
  - False Christianity
  - Ongoing wars and conflicts
  - Widespread famine
  - Deadly epidemics
  - Persecution and martyrdom

All of these happened, repeatedly, over the next two thousand years – just as predicted.

| | |
|---|---|
| **Has the Vision been completely fulfilled?** | No – the return of Christ, referred to in the 6th and 7th Seals, is yet future |

## Section Five

# THE HISTORY OF THE GENTILES

### AS FORETOLD IN THE BOOK OF REVELATION

32

# An Overview of the Third Vision:

# The history of the Gentiles

which appears in **Revelation Chapters 8-11** in the

| 1st Vision | 2nd Vision | 3rd Vision | 4th Vision | 5th Vision | 6th Vision | 7th Vision |
|---|---|---|---|---|---|---|
| **The history of the Church** | **The trials of believers** | **The history of the gentiles** | **The origin of anti-semitism** | **The last plagues** | **The fall of Babylon** | **The reign of Christ** |
| *Rev Ch 1-3* | *Rev Ch 4-8.1* | *Rev Ch 8.2-11* | *Rev Ch 12-14* | *Rev Ch 15-16, 19-20* | *Rev Ch 17-18* | *Rev Ch 21-22* |

The first two visions in the Book of Revelation were addressed to Christians and warned of things that would affect believers throughout the entire Church age. These were recurring patterns, shared by Christians in every century, so no specific years of fulfilment were provided in the Visions.

**But that's about to change.**

This next vision, spanning Revelation chapters 8 to 11, once again provides a panoramic overview of events. But this time it also contains **four time-defined prophecies** that can be tested against real, identifiable events in history.

What emerges is not a vague picture of a future apocalypse, but a **precise prophetic timeline.**

Here you'll see how Revelation's imagery falls into place, revealing events that can be measured, checked, and proven.

You'll learn:

- How the prophecy of **42 months** points to over 1,300 years of Gentile domination of Jerusalem.

- How the prophecy of **three and a half days** confirms the same timeline and lands on the very same year.

- How the **Two Witnesses** symbolise two communities which have been hiding in plain sight for centuries.

- And why the prophecy of **five months** takes us back to the worst year in recorded history.

- The highly visible structure/event that ties all of this together.

This is where Revelation's visions start reflecting events that we can verify. Together, they will confirm what Daniel has already showed us: that God writes His purposes into time with flawless precision.

The vision begins with an introduction to a new group of seven:

*"I saw the **seven angels** who stand before God, and **seven trumpets** were given to them." **(Revelation 8:2)***

Just as we found with the *seven letters* in the 1st vision and the *seven seals* in the 2nd vision, the use of *seven trumpets* alerts us to the fact that this is all one vision and the prophecy moves quickly into descriptions of what these trumpets bring:

- **First to fourth trumpets:** the sun, moon and sky darken leading to climactic instability; there is widespread burning and loss of vegetation across the land, marine life and sea-borne commerce are disrupted, and rivers and freshwater sources are poisoned.

- **Fifth**: A fallen star opens the Abyss, releasing locust-like creatures with power to torment but not kill people for five months. They have scorpion-like stingers and are led by someone called Abaddon (Hebrew) or Apollyon (Greek).

- **Sixth**: Four angels at the Euphrates are released to kill a third of mankind, leading 200 million mounted troops with lion-headed horses that spew fire, smoke, and sulphur.

Despite this devastation, we're told that the survivors of this onslaught refuse to repent of idolatry, murder, sorcery, immorality, and theft.

**The Interlude**

At this point in the vision we're waiting for the seventh trumpet to sound – but before that happens there is an interlude:

- John hears "seven thunders" but is told not to record what they say.

- He is given a scroll to eat and told to continue prophesying.

- He is then given a measuring rod to measure 'the temple' - but is told not to measure the outer court, which is given to the gentiles who will trample it for **42 months**.

- He is told that '**two witnesses**', described as "olive trees" and "lampstands," will prophesy for **1,260 days** in sackcloth.

- Then, a 'Beast from the abyss' attacks and kills these two witnesses, but after **three and a half days**, they rise, and God breathes life into them.

- A great earthquake follows, killing 7,000 people.

- Finally, the **seventh trumpet** sounds, announcing the return of Christ.

This is a lot to take in – but there is a coherent message in these dramatic images - and once you see it, you'll wonder how you ever missed it.

**Four Time-defined Prophecies**

This vision contains **four** time-defined prophecies:

1. **The prophecy of Five months** (Revelation 9)

2. **The prophecy of 42 months** (Revelation 11:1-2)

3. **The prophecy of 1,260 days** (Revelation 11:3-4)

4. **The prophecy of Three and a half days** (Revelation 11)

In the coming chapters, we'll see how each of these prophecies integrates with the others and with Daniel's prophecies – painting a picture of real events and historical dates that is both familiar and astonishing.

But once again, we won't begin at the start of the vision. Instead, we'll begin where the clues are clearest - in **chapter 11**, with the prophecy of **42 months**.

33

# The times of the gentiles

## The Prophecy of 42 Months

which appears in **Revelation 11:1-2** in the

| 1st Vision | 2nd Vision | 3rd Vision | 4th Vision | 5th Vision | 6th Vision | 7th Vision |
|---|---|---|---|---|---|---|
| **The history of the Church** | **The trials of believers** | **The history of the gentiles** | **The origin of anti-semitism** | **The last plagues** | **The fall of Babylon** | **The reign of Christ** |
| *Rev Ch 1-3* | *Rev Ch 4-8.1* | *Rev Ch 8.2-11* | *Rev Ch 12-14* | *Rev Ch 15-16, 19-20* | *Rev Ch 17-18* | *Rev Ch 21-22* |

In the Book of Revelation John introduces us to a prophecy in which he tells us that 'the nations will trample on the Holy City' for a period of **42 months.**

This prophecy is generally quoted as if it begins in Chapter 11 - but, because *The Vision of the History of the Gentiles* starts back in Chapter 8, and because there were no chapter breaks in the original text, we can now see that it actually starts one verse earlier, at the end of Chapter 10:

> *(John was told) "You must prophesy again about many peoples, nations, languages and kings."* ***(Revelation 10:11)***

> *"I was given a reed like a measuring rod and was told, 'Go and measure the temple of God and the altar, with its worshipers. But exclude the outer court... it has been given to the Gentiles. They will trample on the holy city for 42 months.'"* ***(Revelation 11:1–2)***

So John was being told, first, *who* he was prophesying about (*many peoples, nations, languages and kings)*, and then *what* the prophecy was about (*the temple of God and the altar*). Let's use our basic question template to see if we can shed light on what this all means:

**Question: Who is the audience for the prophecy**

In Revelation 1.1 we're told that the Revelation is:

> *...from Jesus Christ, which God gave him to show* ***his servants*** *what must soon take place.*

So John was writing to Christians.

**Question: What's being predicted?**

The meaning of the prophecy is straightforward. The references to the **Temple of God** and the **Holy City** tell us that it is about Jerusalem which: **will be 'trampled on by Gentiles** (the term that the bible uses to describe non-Jews) **from many nations for 42 months.**

**Question: But how long is 42 months?**

Premillennialism proposes that these 42 months represent a 3½-year period in the future on the basis that 3 x 12 months = 36 + 6 months = 42 months. But in the Book of Daniel, all of the prophecies hid references to very long periods of time (2,500 years, 2,300 years, 1,290 years and 1,335 years). Is the same true here, and if so, what length of time is covered by 42 months?

The 1,290 and 1,335 'days' in Daniel were references to 'years'. Since 'months' also contain days - could these days be years too? And, if so, how many 'days' are in 42 months?

At the time that John was writing, the Julian year was in use – a unit of time that was almost exactly the same length as our modern Gregorian year (365.24 Gregorian days per year vs 365.25 Julian days per year). And like our modern year, a Julian year was also made up of months of different lengths. This sounds complicated but it isn't really. We know how many days were in a Julian year (365.25) – so we just need to divide a Julian year by 12 to find the average number of days in a Julian month:

365.25 day Julian year divided by 12 months
**= 30.4375 days, on average, per month**

So we can now see that there are 30.4375 'days' in an average Julian month and it just remains to multiply these days by the 42 months in the prophecy:

30.4375 days x 42 months **= 1,278.3 days**

But what do we do with this? If these 'days' are years, as they were in the prophecies in the Book of Daniel, what time period do they apply to? Let's find out.

**Question: When does the prophecy start?**

When we were resolving prophecies in the Book of Daniel we generally began the process by trying to identify the year in which those prophecies *began* – but in the Book of Revelation we're going to do the opposite.

Here, we're going to find that the *end year* of each prophecy is usually easy to identify – and that the *start year* will be the puzzle to be solved (see Chapter 34 of *Prophecy Shock*).

This prophecy is a case in point. It tells us that there will be a time when the Holy City (Jerusalem) will be 'trampled down' by many different nations and it even tells us how long this will last – 42 months (1,278.3 years)

Not only has this already happened – but we know when it ended: **1967.** This was the year in which East Jerusalem and the Old City were liberated by the Jews, ending a period of over 1,250 years during which Jerusalem was 'trampled down' by many other nations.

So this isn't a future event – it's fulfilled history – and it aligns with Daniel's prophecy of "time, times and half a time" in chapter 12 of his book, which also ended in 1967 – *exactly* 2,500 years after it was recorded.

So - since we know when the prophecy ended – we can now see when it started by counting 1,278.3 years *backward* from 1967:

1967 → - 1,278.3 years → = **688.7**

And there it is again. **688 AD.**

As we learnt earlier, in *the prophecy of 1,290 days* in Daniel, 688 is marked out by God because it is the year in which the construction of the Dome of the Rock (**the abomination of desolation**) commenced on the Temple Mount in Jerusalem – and now we're being told that it was also the starting point for a 42 month period during which 'gentiles' would 'trample on' Jerusalem.

**The real link between Daniel and Revelation**

This is an extraordinary prophetic breakthrough! For the first time, Daniel and Revelation can be linked in concrete historical terms, with each solution reinforcing the other – and we can now confidently mark this prophecy as fulfilled. It's not about a future Gentile occupation of Jerusalem - it's about one that has already happened - and ended.

So let's put all of this into our template:

| **The Prophecy of 42 Months**<br>Revelation 10:11 – 11:1-2 | | | |
|---|---|---|---|
| **What's being predicted** | *That a period of 1,278.3 years will pass during which the Gentiles will trample on Jerusalem* | | |
| **Question** | **Clue from Scripture** | **Math** | **Solution** |
| **Who is the prophecy addressed to?** | *"...Jesus Christ ... to show His servants" (Revelation 1:1)* | | **The prophecy is addressed to Christians** |
| **Who is the prophecy about?** | *"...about many peoples, nations, languages and kings..." (Revelation 10:11)* | | **The prophecy is about the Gentiles** |
| **What year does the prophecy end?** | *When the "trampling on the Holy City..." ends* | ***1967*** | **The prophecy ends in 1967** |
| **How long will the prophecy last?** | *"... for 42 months..." (Revelation 11:1-2)* | ***minus 1,278.3*** | **The prophecy will last for 1,278.3 years** |
| **What year does the prophecy begin?** | *The first year of the construction of the Dome of the Rock* | ***equals 688.7*** | **The prophecy begins in 688 AD** |

**The 'times of the gentiles'**

But as amazing as this prophecy is – we're also going to find that it unlocks a slew of other prophecies in the Book of Revelation – and it also provides the key to understanding a dark warning from Yeshua, outlined in the Gospel of Luke:

> [20] *"When you see Jerusalem being surrounded by armies, you will know that its* ***desolation** **<u>is near</u>**. [21] *Then let those who are in Judea flee to the mountains, let those in the city get out, and let those in the country not enter the city.* [22] *For this is the time of punishment in fulfilment of all that has been written.* [23] *How dreadful it will be in those days for pregnant women and nursing mothers! There will be great distress in the land and wrath against this people.* [24] *They will fall by the sword and will be taken as prisoners to all the nations.* ***Jerusalem will be trampled on by the Gentiles until the times of the Gentiles are fulfilled". (Luke 21:20-24)***

Luke tells us two things here: that (1) the period during which Jerusalem is 'trampled on' (the period which encompasses the 1,278.3 'days') is called *the times of the gentiles* – and (2) that certain events will take place *just prior* to this.

Let's check that against history: In 614, the Persians briefly captured Jerusalem, from the Byzantines, and held it until 629. During this time they reversed a Roman/Byzantine ban on Jews living in the city which had been in place since the Bar Kokhba revolt of 135 AD. However, the respite was short-lived. In 629, the Byzantines reconquered Jerusalem and unleashed a terrible retribution: Jews were **slaughtered in large numbers,** expelled once again, or **taken prisoner, sold into slavery and scattered across the empire**.

Luke tells us that these events were a sign that ***the desolation was near***. Sure enough, just 59 years later, the construction of the Dome of the Rock (the abomination of desolation) commenced on the Temple Mount, **leaving the site 'desolate'** (unsuitable for Jewish worship) for over 1,278 years while Jerusalem – the Holy City – was trampled down by the Gentiles.

**So the prediction in the Book of Luke mirrors history precisely** and we can now see that the '42 months' and 'the times of the Gentiles' are the same thing. Not a prophecy of an uncertain future or a UN or Islamic invasion of Israel in the last days – but an exact description of the length of the historic 'trampling down' of Jerusalem by non-Jews which started in 688 and finally ended in 1967!

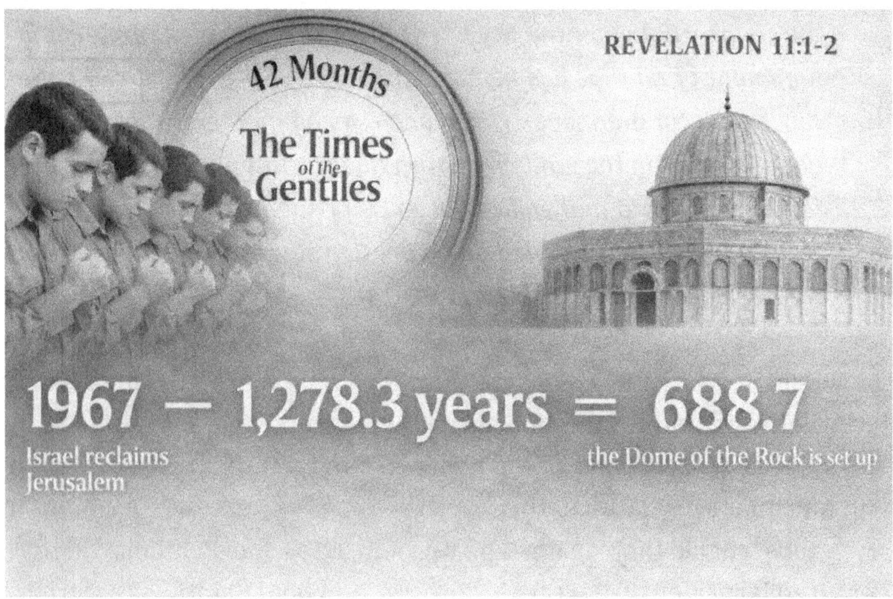


**What about the .7?**

The late Chuck Missler, and others, are known for prophecy solutions where the numbers after a decimal point have a meaning – usually narrowing down to a specific month or even day.

I'm not rejecting this approach but I don't think it's the case with this solution. 688.7 would suggest a date in late September of 688 and, as far as we know, that month holds no particular significance in history.

Instead, I'm of the view that God placed these sub-decimal numbers so that the discovered solutions would 'flick over' into the previous year when counting backward. If this solution had been a whole number (1278) it would have landed on 689 – a year which, while significant, would not have integrated with the other prophecies in Daniel and Revelation.

**An alternative path to the same solution**

I mentioned, earlier, that Premillennialism interprets 42 months as 3½-years on the basis that 3 x 12 months = 36 + 6 months = 42 months.

This is mathematically straightforward – but it forces us to find a solution which happens within a very short space of time – which is precisely why Premillennialism pushes the solution into a future fulfilment of a speculative last days event. (in other words, the Premillennial solution is someone's guess about what the prophecy *might* mean).

But something interesting happens when we add an additional step to the Premillennial formula by assuming that their 3.5 years, themselves, make up years of prophetic days:

3 x 12 months = 36 + 6 months = 42 months

42 months = 3.5 Years

**3.5 (Julian) years of days = 3.5 x 365.25 = 1278.3 years**

1967 → - 1,278.3 → = **688.7**

Using the Premillennial formula as a base, we still land on exactly the same year as we have already identified in this chapter – also confirming 688 AD as the solution. Different pathway. Same result.

---

**A reassurance on the math**

If you struggled with the math in this chapter – don't be concerned. The key takeaways are that:

- *The 42 months in the prophecy refer to a long period of time:* ***1,278.3 years***

- *Counted backward from* ***1967*** *– (the year that 'the trampling' ended and the Jews regained control of Jerusalem and the same year that we identified in one of the prophecies of 'time, times and half a time') - we land on* ***688 AD***

- ***688*** *is the same year in which construction of the Muslim Dome of the Rock (the abomination of desolation) began on the Temple Mount in Jerusalem and the same year that we identified in the prophecy of 1,290 days, in Daniel*

- ***This is an exact fulfilment of history***

But why did counting these years backward work? Was this solution a one off or have we just stumbled upon another Principle of Israelism?

We'll find out in the next chapter

*The solution at a glance*

# The 42 months
# The time of the Gentiles

***Scripture:*** *Revelation 11:1-2*

1. **What's being predicted??**
   That 'the Gentiles' would trample on Jerusalem for **1,278.3 years**.

2. **Who is being spoken to?**
   John, the apostle in exile, writing to **the early Church**.

3. **Who is the prophecy about?**
   Gentile nations - non-Jews - who would control Jerusalem.

4. **When does it end?**
   **1967 AD**: the year in which Israel retakes Jerusalem in the Six-Day War and Gentile trampling of Jerusalem ends.

5. **How long does it last?**
   42 average months of 30.43 days → **1,278.3 years**.

6. **When does it start?**
   1967 – 1,278.3 = **688.7 AD**

This prophecy tracks actual history - **from 1967 backward to 688** - not a future 3½-year crisis. It links directly to Daniel's prophecy in Daniel 12:11 and lands on the same pivotal year.

34

THE PRINCIPLES OF ISRAELISM

# Everything centres on 688 AD

All of the Schools of Prophecy Interpretation that we reviewed in the first section of *Prophecy Shock* agree that prophecy only moves in one direction – forward – based on scriptures like Isaiah 46:10 where God tells us that *"I make known the end from the beginning, from ancient time what is still to come".*

We understand this to mean that prophecy deals with the gap between 'now' and fulfilment and that this gap is always closing as more events are revealed.

But could this scripture also have a different meaning?

Could it also be telling us that God sometimes confirms a prophecy solution by reference back to the year in which the prophecy began?

In 1916, at just 13 years old, Slovakian Jew Michael Ber Weissmandl came across a commentary by 13th-century sage Rabbenu Bachya ben Asher of Saragossa, Spain. Bachya's notes outlined a phenomenon where words and phrases could be found in the Torah - the first five books of the Hebrew Bible - by skipping letters at evenly spaced intervals.

This concept lies at the heart of a modern school of interpretation known as **Equidistant Letter Sequencing (ELS)**.

ELS has earned a mixed reputation thanks to oversized claims and pop-culture "predictions," and critics - especially statisticians - have challenged some of the wilder versions of those claims.

But one particular example is hard to dismiss simply because it's so straightforward. It involves the Hebrew word **תורה (Torah)**, which was discovered to be encoded in four of the first five books of the Bible:

- In Genesis, if you start at the first tav (ת) and count by 49 letters (every 50th): you'll get ת–ו–ר–ה (Torah).

- The same 49-letter spacing in Exodus again yields Torah.

- In Numbers and Deuteronomy, the sequence reappears - but backwards.

- But Leviticus, the central book, breaks the pattern: count by sevens in that book and you will uncover the divine name יהוה (YHWH, Yahweh, or the name of God).

**TORAH → TORAH → YHWH ← HAROT ← HAROT**

So the word Torah ("law") points inward toward the Name of God from both sides - a neat, visual echo of the purpose of the Law.

To be clear, this book is not endorsing the claims of ELS, This example has been used, simply to make a point: **that God sometimes uses *direction* in prophecy**.

### The Rule of Direction in Prophecy

This principle – that **direction can be meaningful** – becomes especially obvious in the time-defined prophecies in **Daniel and**

**Revelation**. Daniel was shown what would unfold across centuries and his time periods count down from an origin point. But in Revelation, we will find that John was shown a set of visions that repeatedly look *back* across long stretches of history from the end of the age.

That difference in vantage point changes how these prophecies work and - as we solve the puzzles contained within both books - we will find that they all converge toward **a central year**.

That year is **688 AD**.

### Why 688 AD?

As we learnt in Chapter 24, 688 is not just any year – it is the year that construction started on **the Islamic Dome of the Rock** on the Temple Mount in Jerusalem – the structure that we now know to be **the abomination of desolation**.

The Dome was Islam's first monumental sanctuary and was constructed on what was believed to be the former site of the Temple as an affront to both Jews and Christians. For Jews, in particular, it was an abomination to God. It permanently closed off the site of the Jewish daily sacrifice and made that site desolate for Jewish worship for the next 1,250+ years.

### The Hinge Year

This extremely offensive character of the Dome is no accident. It identifies this structure as the central point of these prophecies for reasons that will become increasingly obvious as we make our way through this book – and in the pages ahead as we will learn that:

- **Time-defined prophecies in Daniel** are always counted ***forward***, toward 688, from their start year.

- **Time-defined prophecies in Revelation** always count ***backward***, from their fulfilment year (with one notable exception which we'll flag later).

- And **688 AD is the midpoint** - the anchor around which both directions turn.

Again and again the year 688 will appear – like a clock hand repeatedly swinging back to the same number on the dial. And when we recognise it for what it is, the compass point by which prophetic direction is set, prophecies that once seemed random suddenly harmonize. Daniel's timelines advance toward it; Revelation's visions repeatedly look back from beyond it.

This convergence is not imposed on the text - it emerges from the way that the prophecies themselves are structured.

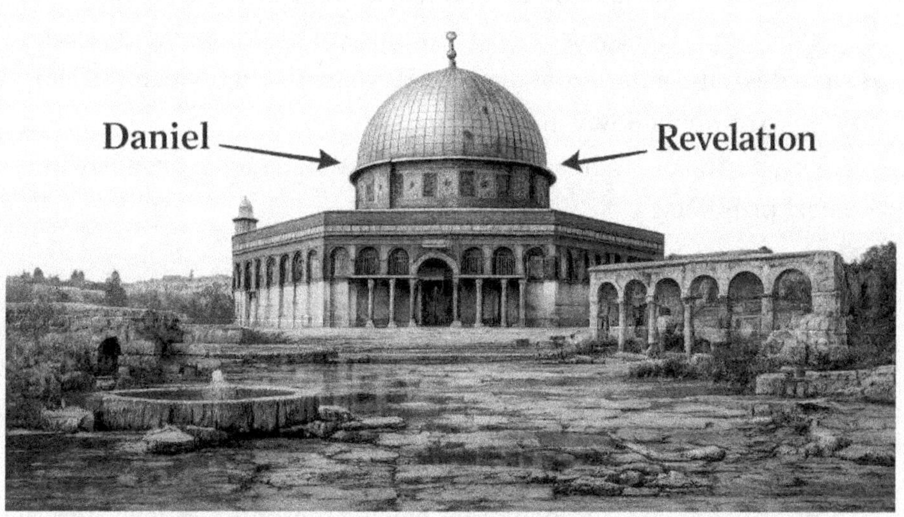

35

# A Case of Mistaken Identity

## The Prophecy of the Two Witnesses

which appears in **Revelation 11:3-4** in the

| 1st Vision | 2nd Vision | 3rd Vision | 4th Vision | 5th Vision | 6th Vision | 7th Vision |
|---|---|---|---|---|---|---|
| **The history of the Church** | **The trials of believers** | **The history of the gentiles** | **The origin of anti-semitism** | **The last plagues** | **The fall of Babylon** | **The reign of Christ** |
| *Rev Ch 1-3* | *Rev Ch 4-8.1* | *Rev Ch 8.2-11* | *Rev Ch 12-14* | *Rev Ch 15-16, 19-20* | *Rev Ch 17-18* | *Rev Ch 21-22* |

In the previous prophecy we learnt that the '42 months' of Revelation 11:1-2 were also a reference to *the times of the gentiles* and describe a period of over 1,278 years during which the Holy City was 'trampled down' by foreigners.

This period of 'exclusion' is key because it segues seamlessly into the next prophecy:

> *"I will appoint my two witnesses, and they will prophesy for 1,260 days, clothed in sackcloth. They are the two olive trees and the two lampstands, and they stand before the Lord of the earth."* ***(Revelation 11:3–4)***

Many prophecy commentators believe that this is a reference to two mysterious men - Moses and Elijah, Enoch and Elijah, or some other pair - who would suddenly appear at the time of the end and proclaim the gospel for 1,260 literal days. This interpretation is sometimes influenced by a passage, in the Book of Zechariah, where these same symbols are also mentioned:

*"I see a solid gold lampstand with a bowl at the top and seven lamps on it, with seven channels to the lamps. [3] Also there are two olive trees by it, one on the right of the bowl and the other on its left."* ***(Zechariah 4:2-3)***

*[11] Then I asked the angel ... "What are these two olive branches beside the two gold pipes that pour out golden oil?" [13] He replied ..."These are the two who are anointed to serve the Lord of all the earth."* ***(Zechariah 4:11-14)***

I can see how some interpreters might see these as people – but this is not what the prophecy means. These "two witnesses" aren't people, and they're not yet to come. They're two communities which have already been! They stood in plain sight for more than a thousand years, visible to the whole world, and speaking loudly through history.

I understand that this may be a significant challenge to what you've been taught – but bear with me as we use scripture to separate truth from error.

**Who – or what – were the witnesses?**

All of our solutions, so far, have been counted in years - which is a problem for those who see the Witnesses as people because nobody can live for 1,260 years.

But if the Witnesses weren't people - what were they. Let's remind ourselves of how scripture defines them:

*"..... They are the two olive trees and the two lampstands"*

So immediately we can see that the Witnesses are actually two pairings of two, symbolised by olive trees and lampstands. And what do these symbols represent? In the case of the lampstands we don't need to guess because the scripture tells us:

*"The seven lampstands are the seven churches."* ***(Revelation 1:20)***

**The two Witnesses**

There's nothing confusing or subjective about this. Revelation 1:20 very clearly tells us that the lampstands in Revelation 11:3-4 are Churches - and **Zechariah 4:2-3** tells us that these are the seven Churches of Revelation that we've already been introduced to in the Vision of the History of the Church (Revelation Chapter 1 – 3).

We first read about these seven Churches in Chapter 30 of *Prophecy Shock* where each of them was the subject of a 'letter', dictated by Yeshua, and addressed to groups of believers which had been established in various locations around the Near East. We found that, in addition to being an excellent summary of issues which affected all of these Churches (and still affect Churches today), these letters also provided us with a prophetic overview of the Church age, in chronological order.

But while we can be certain that these two Witnesses are Churches – we don't yet know *which* two of the seven Churches are in view - so let's turn our attention to the two remaining Witnesses – the two *olive trees.*

Throughout Scripture, fig trees often symbolise Israel as a nation, while *olive trees* reflect God's spiritual relationship with the Jews. So, if lampstands represent Churches, perhaps the olive trees represent the Jews? And if the lampstands represent Church eras – perhaps the two olive trees represent two Judaic eras?

There have been four such eras:

- **Biblical Judaism** (c. 1200 BC–AD 70) was centred on the Temple and sacrificial system, it ended with the Roman destruction of the Temple.

- **Hellenistic Judaism** (c. 332 BC–AD 70) was shaped by Greek culture following Alexander the Great's conquests and overlapped with the late Second Temple period.

- **Rabbinic Judaism** (from AD 70 to c. 1700) emerged after the Temple's destruction and was built around synagogues, study, and the Talmud.

- **Modern Judaism** (c. 1700–present) arose in the Enlightenment, diversified into Orthodox, Reform, and secular forms, and culminated politically in the establishment of the State of Israel in 1948.

But which two Judaic eras are in view? To find out, we need to know the period of time covered by the prophecy.

**How long does the prophecy last, and when does it start and end?**

We know that 1,260 days probably refers to 1,260 years – but when does this period start and end? Since the prophecy of the two Witnesses immediately follows the prophecy of 42-months, perhaps it also relates to the year of the commencement of construction of the Dome of the Rock in 688? Let's test that hypothesis:

688 → + 1,260 → = 1948

And suddenly we have another familiar year – **1948** - the year that Israel became a nation again! And because this solution can be counted both ways, from the start year or the end year, it still complies with our Revelation 'rule' in which solutions are counted *backward* from an identified end year:

1948 → - 1,260 → = **688**

Now the prophecy makes perfect sense.

In the previous prophecy the 'two witnesses' (Judaism and Christianity) were driven out of Jerusalem at the time of the commencement of construction of the Dome of the Rock in 688, and the Holy Land was 'trampled down' by foreign powers from that time.

But this new prophecy tells us that they didn't disappear – they 'prophesied' between 688 and 1948.

| **The Prophecy of the Two Witnesses**<br>Revelation 11:3-4 | | | |
|---|---|---|---|
| **What's being predicted?** | *That 'two witnesses' would 'prophesy' for the 1,260 'days' during which the Holy Land was controlled by foreign powers.* | | |
| **Question** | **Clue from Scripture** | **Math** | **Solution** |
| **Who is the prophecy addressed to?** | *"...Jesus Christ ... to show His servants" (Revelation 1:1)* | | **The prophecy is addressed to Christians** |
| **Who is the prophecy about?** | *"...many peoples, nations, languages and kings..." (Revelation 10:11)* | | **The prophecy is about the Gentiles** |
| **What year does the prophecy end?** | *"...and they will prophecy for 1,260 days" (Revelation 11:3-4)* | ***1948*** | **The prophecy ends in 1948** |
| **How long will the prophecy last?** | *"... 1,260 days..." (Revelation 11:3-4)* | ***minus 1,260*** | **The prophecy will last for 1,260 years** |
| **What year does the prophecy begin?** | *The first year of the construction of the Dome of the Rock* | ***equals 688*** | **The prophecy begins in 688AD** |

### The two Judaic witnesses

So this prophecy does more than identify the year of Israel's reestablishment. It also describes the condition of the Jewish people during the long period in which they were dispossessed from their land. It refers to them as 'witnesses' and tells us that they would prophesy for 1,260 days, clothed in sackcloth.

The use of the word 'prophesy' might confuse Christians who tend to view that term as referring to predicting the future – but to Jews, who see prophesying as being about declaring God's truth in the present - calling people back to faithfulness, justice, and covenant responsibility – it is a stunningly accurate description of what happened to them.

The years between 688 and 1948 coincide with the **Rabbinic and Modern eras in Judaism** – a period which saw a gradual rise in Jewish nationalism and observance, stemming from their collective grief at their separation from their homeland and eventually taking shape in a variety of nationalistic movements and initiatives. The **Zionist** movement, which held its first congress in 1897, wasn't the beginning of Jewish nationalism but simply the most visible sign of a movement which had been building for centuries. As such, the description of the Rabbinic and Modern eras of Judaism as 'Witnesses' is an extremely accurate accounting of their role over that time.

### The two Christian witnesses

But what about the other set of 'Witnesses'? The prophecy tells us that there were two 'lampstands' alerting us to the fact that they represent two of the seven Church eras.

Identifying these eras is a little trickier because, according to Revelation's 'seven church' pattern (see Chapter 30) there were actually three Church eras between 688 and 1948: **Thyatira, Sardis and Philadelphia.**

So which two of these were the two Christian witnesses?

The resolution lies in recognising that, in His letters, Christ only affirms two of these Churches as living, enduring lampstands capable of bearing witness. **Thyatira** represents the Medieval Church made up of the many different strands of Christian belief that challenged the dominance of the Catholic Church through many centuries, while **Philadelphia** represents the revived and outward-looking missionary Church that emerged later and carried the Gospel to the nations.

Together, these two lampstands describe a continuous Christian witness that not only survived exclusion, persecution, and political marginalisation, but steadily reshaped the world. Through the following centuries they pioneered universities, scripture preservation, exploration, translation, and global missions. Christianity became the primary engine for literacy, law, education, and moral thought across continents. By the modern era, the Gospel had been carried to virtually every inhabited region of the globe – fulfilling their mandate to bear witness to "the whole world".

By contrast, **Sardis** is uniquely described by Christ as having 'a name that lives, but is dead,' and is the only Church that receives no commendation at all - disqualifying it from functioning as a witnessing lampstand in the sense required by Revelation 1.

In this way, the prophecy spans three Church eras but identifies only two witnesses.

### Two Prophecies, One Story

So now the interrelationship between these first two prophecies in Revelation 11 becomes clear.

**The prophecy of the forty-two months explains *what happened to Jerusalem*** - how it was trampled by Gentile powers for over 1,278 years.

**The prophecy of the Two Witnesses then goes on to tell us *what happened to the Jews (and Christians) who were outside Jerusalem and the Holy Land over that time*.**

They did not disappear. Instead, both Jews and Christians went on the change the world. The Jewish people were scattered exactly as foretold but preserved their identity over centuries. Christians carried the Gospel outward, often at great cost, into every corner of the globe.

The very era during which both were constrained in the Holy Land became the era in which their presence and testimony spread globally.

The Two Witnesses prophecy does not describe a brief future calamity, but a long historical reality during which Jerusalem was 'trampled down' and God's witnesses survived in sackcloth - suffering, enduring, and testifying until the appointed time of restoration.

The forty-two months explain the loss of the city; the Two Witnesses explain the preservation of the people. Together, they tell one continuous story, not of extinction, but of faithful witness under pressure, culminating in return, revival, and renewal at the close of the prophetic timeline.

*The solution at a glance*

# The Two Witnesses:

# A Case of Mistaken Identity

***Scripture:*** *Revelation 11:3-4*

1. **What's being predicted??**
   That 'two witnesses' will 'prophesy' to the nations for 1,260 days.

2. **Who is being spoken to?**
   John, the apostle in exile, writing to **the early Church**.

3. **Who is the prophecy about?**
   The impact of Christianity and Judaism (the two witnesses) on **the Gentile nations**.

4. **When does it end?**
   **1948 AD**: Israel is reborn. Jews return to Israel in large numbers

5. **How long does it last?**
   **"1,260 days."** Prophetic days = years → 1,260 years.

6. **When does it start?**
   1948 – 1,260 = **688 AD**.

**The prophecy tracks real history - 1948 → 688**, not a future 3½-tribulation. It also dovetails, perfectly, with Daniel's 1,290-day timeline and the 42-month prophecy that we solved earlier..

36

# The Two-Phase Return

## The Prophecy of three and a half days

which appears in **Revelation 11:9-10** in the

| 1st Vision | 2nd Vision | 3rd Vision | 4th Vision | 5th Vision | 6th Vision | 7th Vision |
|---|---|---|---|---|---|---|
| **The history of the Church** | **The trials of believers** | **The history of the gentiles** | **The origin of anti-semitism** | **The last plagues** | **The fall of Babylon** | **The reign of Christ** |
| *Rev Ch 1-3* | *Rev Ch 4-8.1* | *Rev Ch 8.2-11* | *Rev Ch 12-14* | *Rev Ch 15-16, 19-20* | *Rev Ch 17-18* | *Rev Ch 21-22* |

We've now resolved the meaning of the first two prophecies in Revelation 11 and have seen that both are anchored to the year **688 - the year of the appearance of the Islamic Dome of the Rock:**

- **The prophecy of forty-two months explains *what happened to Jerusalem* and how it was trampled down by Gentile powers between 688 and 1967.**

- **The prophecy of the Two Witnesses tells us *what happened to Jews and Christians* over the 1,260 year period between 688 and 1948**.

But there's also a third *time-defined* prophecy in this vision. *The Prophecy of three and a half days*. Does this add to what we already know or deal with something completely different?

Let's review it.

*"If anyone tries to harm them* ***(the witnesses),*** *fire comes from their mouths and devours their enemies. This is how anyone who wants to harm them must die. They have power to shut up the heavens so that it will not rain during the time they are prophesying; and they have power to turn the waters into blood and to strike the earth with every kind of plague as often as they want."* ***(Revelation 11:5–6)***

*"Now when they have finished their testimony the beast that comes up from the Abyss will attack them and overpower and kill them. Their bodies will lie in the public square of the great city - which is figuratively called Sodom and Egypt - where also their Lord was crucified (i.e. Jerusalem).* ***(Revelation 11:7–8)***

So we can now see that these passages act as a summary of the two prophecies that we have just resolved in the last two chapters.

- The first (verses 5–6) deals with the international activity of the Two Witnesses, which ended in 1948 with the re-establishment of the State of Israel.

- The second (verses 7-11) refers to the occupation of Jerusalem ("the great city") between **688 and 1967** and describes the near absence of Christian and Jewish authority in the Holy Land over that time. In other words, Christianity and Judaism were 'dead' in Jerusalem and their houses of worship ("bodies lying in the public square") lay in ruins or were repurposed under Islamic rule.

This also makes sense of the next part of the vision:

*"For three and a half days* ***some from every people, tribe, language and nation*** *will gaze on their bodies and refuse them burial. The*

*inhabitants of the earth will gloat over them and will celebrate by sending each other gifts, because these two prophets had tormented those who live on the earth". **(Revelation 11:9-10)***

So a succession of Gentile powers (*some from every people, tribe, language and nation*) will 'gloat' over their control of Jerusalem and the near total absence of Jews and Christians from that city, for three and a half days. But how long is *three and a half days*?

This is the same term that we studied in the prophecy of 42 months. Note where it ends:

3.5 days = 3.5 (Julian) years of 365.25 days

3.5 x 365.25 = 1278.3 years

1967 → - 1,278.3 → = **688.7**

So this prophecy aligns, perfectly, with the earlier prophecy of 42 Months and identifies the same event (the commencement of construction of the Dome of the Rock) to the year.

But these passages also serve another important purpose: they remind us that the return of the Jewish people happened in two phases, not one. When we're told that *"the beast ... will attack, overpower and kill"* the witnesses we're being reminded that Israel failed to secure Jerusalem in 1948, and had to wait another 19 years before their national restoration was completed in 1967.

**The breath of life**

And just to make absolutely sure that we would understand this, God followed the prophecy up with this next passage:

*"But **after the three and a half days** (1,278.3 years) the breath of life from God entered them, and they stood on their feet, and great fear fell on those who saw them." **(Revelation 11:11)***

Again, this is what happened. The "breath of life" (literally, the Spirit of God) re-entered Jerusalem in 1967 when Israel finally reclaimed the city and Judaism and Christianity returned to their sacred ground.

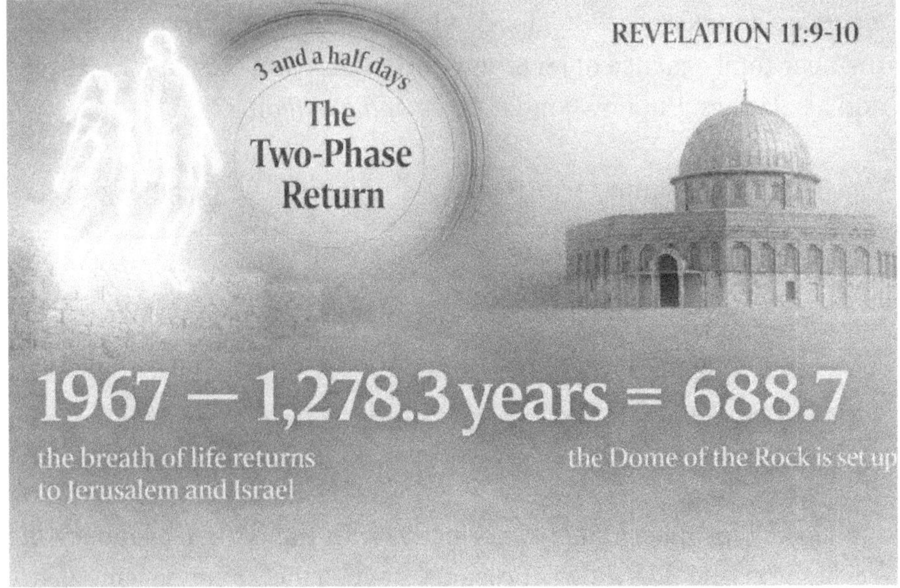


This fulfilment also mirrors Ezekiel's prophecy of dry bones coming to life:

> *"Then he said to me, "Prophesy to the breath; prophesy, son of man, and say to it, 'This is what the Sovereign Lord says: Come, breath, from the four winds and breathe into these slain, that they may live.'" So I prophesied as he commanded me,* ***and breath entered them; they came to life and stood up on their feet - a vast army.****"*
>
> ***(Ezekiel 37:9–10)***

So, *the Prophecy of three and a half days* summarises the two previous prophecies and encodes a hidden historical countdown centred on Israel and Jerusalem. The "death" of the witnesses marks the incomplete restoration (after 1,260 years) in 1948, while their revival marks the return of life to Jerusalem (after 1,278.3 years) 19 years later in 1967 – so the vision is built around the modern restoration of the Jewish people to their land ***and*** to their holy city.

### The Six Basic Questions?

You'll note that we managed to solve this entire prophecy without once referring to the Six Basic Questions – but let's fill in the template out so that we can see how this all fits together:

| **The Prophecy of the three and a half days**<br>Revelation 11:9-11 | | | |
|---|---|---|---|
| **What's being predicted?** | *That the re-establishment of Israel would happen in two phases: first, the Holy land, in 1948 – then the 'breath of life' would return to the Holy City, in 1967.* | | |
| **Question** | **Clue from Scripture** | **Math** | **Solution** |
| **Who is the prophecy addressed to?** | *"...Jesus Christ ... to show His servants" (Revelation 1:1)* | | **The prophecy is addressed to Christians** |
| **Who is the prophecy about?** | *"...about many peoples, nations, languages and kings..." (Revelation 10:11)* | | **The prophecy is about the Gentiles** |
| **What year does the prophecy end?** | *"...after the 3.5 days the breath of life entered them" (Revelation 11:11)* | ***1967*** | **The prophecy ends in 1967** |
| **How long will the prophecy last?** | *"For 3.5 days..." (Revelation 11:9)* | ***minus 1,278.3*** | **The prophecy will last for 1,278.3 years** |
| **What year does the prophecy begin?** | | ***equals 688.7*** | **The prophecy begins in 688 AD** |

*The solution at a glance*

## The three and a half days
## The Two-Phase Return

***Scripture:*** *Revelation 11:9-10*

1. **What's being predicted??**
   That the re-establishment of Israel would happen in two phases: first, the Holy land, in 1948 – then the 'breath of life' (the Spirit of God) would return to the Holy City, in 1967.

2. **Who is being spoken to?**
   John - writing to **believers**.

3. **Who is the prophecy about?**
   **The Gentiles** and their occupation of Jerusalem.

4. **When does it end?**
   **1967** – Israel's Six-Day War victory. 'Breath' returns - Jewish & Christian worship floods back into the old city,

5. **How long does it last?**
   "Three and a half days." 3.5 × 365.25 ≈ **1,278.3 years**.

6. **When does it start?**
   1967 – 1,278.3 ≈ **688.7 AD /** 1948 – 1,260 ≈ **688 AD**

The prophecy **lands on the same hinge years as the 42-month and 1,260-day prophecies** – further reinforcing a recurring historic theme and welding the prophecy to Daniel.

# 37

# The superficial appeal of the picture on the box

If you've ever tried to assemble a piece of furniture from a flatpack you'll know how frustrating it can be. The picture on the front is reassuring, the parts are neatly laid out, the instructions are short, and at first glance it all seems perfectly logical.

But then you start assembling it. One piece only fits if you turn it upside down. A screw seems to belong in two different places. Something lines up *almost* perfectly but not quite. Exasperated, you go back to the instructions, reinterpret a diagram, undo a step, and try again. Eventually, after a lot of cursing, it works - but only after improvisation, frustration, and a growing sense that that initial aura of simplicity was mostly an illusion.

We have the same experience with some traditional prophecy interpretations. Take the tidy Premillennial solution to the prophecies of **1,260 days**, **42 months**, and **"time, times, and half a time"** which are all interpreted as different ways of meaning the same thing: three and a half years. On the surface, that looks logical: the numbers appear to line up neatly, and it appears that God was merely repeating Himself in different formats.

But that perfect symmetry exists only in the imagination. It's easy to make the math in your interpretation work when you're describing something that hasn't happened yet – but it's important to remember that no premillennial theory has ever actually been fulfilled in the real world.

By contrast, the interpretations in *Prophecy Shock* - **42 months, 1,260 days and time, and times and half a time** – all point to real events that have already happened. The solutions aren't always pretty (eg, 1,278.3 years), but they're all based on the clues we're given in scripture and they all land on real historical dates and align with identifiable changes in the control of Jerusalem.

They require no redefinition, no backtracking, and no adjustments. Once assembled, the solution stands cleanly, applies to multiple prophecies, and does not need to be taken apart and rebuilt.

So the choice is not between complicated and simple interpretations. It is between numbers that look simple but can't be tested against any know solution vs numbers that are based on what the prophecies *actually tell us they mean* and which produce solutions that work exactly as intended, every time.

Time-defined Prophecy was given to function precisely in history. Not to look good on the box.

# 38

# The Forgotten Apocalypse

## The Prophecy of Five Months

which appears in **Revelation 9:5-6** and **9:10** in the

| 1st Vision | 2nd Vision | 3rd Vision | 4th Vision | 5th Vision | 6th Vision | 7th Vision |
|---|---|---|---|---|---|---|
| **The history of the Church** | **The trials of believers** | **The history of the gentiles** | **The origin of anti-semitism** | **The last plagues** | **The fall of Babylon** | **The reign of Christ** |
| *Rev Ch 1-3* | *Rev Ch 4-8.1* | *Rev Ch 8.2-11* | *Rev Ch 12-14* | *Rev Ch 15-16, 19-20* | *Rev Ch 17-18* | *Rev Ch 21-22* |

So now we can see the incredible symmetry of the three time-based prophecies in chapter 11 of the Book of Revelation. Rather than predicting a future 3.5 year 'tribulation' of Christians - we have discovered that they:

- provide an outline of a 1,278+ year period which was kicked off by the construction of a foreign structure on the Temple Mount in Jerusalem and during which Jerusalem was 'trampled down' by the Gentiles

- explain what happened to Jews (and Christians) over that time

- confirm that this period of Gentile control ended in 1948/67 and that Israel reemerged as a Jewish state, with Jerusalem as its capital – exemplified by the 'breath of life' returning to this ancient land

But these three prophecies actually appeared in the last part of the Vision of the History of the Gentiles and they all appear as part of a parenthetical period which takes place between the 6th and 7th trumpets in the vision.

So what takes place earlier in the vision and how does it tie into what we've already discovered? Let's review.

**The Seven Trumpets**

According to the Vision, the 1,278+ years during which Jerusalem is *trampled down* by the Gentiles are *preceded* by a series of cataclysmic events on an unimaginable scale and herald a succession of terrible calamities which strike those who dwell on the earth. These all take place, starting in Revelation Chapter 8, against a backdrop of seven trumpets which have traditionally been assumed to refer to the *last days* - but let's review what they actually predict:

- **the first four trumpets describe environmental devastation on a global scale:** the darkening of the sun, moon, and skies leading to climactic instability; widespread burning and loss of vegetation across the land, the disruption and death of marine life and sea-borne commerce, and the poisoning of rivers and freshwater sources.

- **the fifth trumpet** refers to 'a star' that had fallen from the sky to the earth' and tells us that this star is given 'the key to the shaft of the Abyss' - which it opens - and out of which come 'locusts' that are given power to harm 'those people who did not have the seal of God on their foreheads'.

These bizarre creatures are not allowed to kill these people - but they're given the power to torture and torment them for 'five months'.

- We're then introduced to **the sixth trumpet**, after which four angels who are bound at the river Euphrates are released to kill a third of mankind. We're also told that they command 200 million mounted troops. The heads of the horses of these troops are described as resembling the heads of lions, out of which came fire, smoke and sulphur. We're told that a third of mankind was killed by three plagues of fire, smoke and sulphur that came out of their mouths.

**What's being predicted?**

So what on earth does this all mean?

Earlier in this book I talked about the field of 'Higher Criticism' which reviews the authenticity of biblical documents and has created confusion about the authorship of the Old Testament. I explained that these challenges come, primarily, from a refusal, by some scholars, to accept that a Bible writer could provide an accurate and detailed account of history before that history happened.

But it isn't only Higher Criticism that rejects the miraculous. Within the space of less than two hundred years western society has gone from attributing most events to 'Gods will' to largely rejecting that the Christian and Judaic God plays any role in our lives.

The truth is somewhere in between these two extremes. We are, of course, the master of our own destinies (the very basis of free will) - but there is also, clearly, a reality beyond what we can see, which is populated by entities which influence and guide events.

These entities have been active throughout history and, despite the rationalisation of the 21$^{st}$ century, they continue to be active today - whether we choose to acknowledge their existence or not.

But recognising the role of these entities, in prophecy, is tricky. It's one thing to discover indisputable dates and events which confirm the evidence of our own eyes - but it's quite another to recognise the roles of 'angels' and 'demons' in recorded history. Unless, of course, we have dates to back those claims up. And we do.

The premise of this section of the book is that the entities described in this part of the Vision are demonic, that they are real, and that the events described have already happened in recorded history. If you find that hard to believe – hang on to your hat.

### When does the prophecy start?

But if these events happened prior to 688 AD, why don't we see evidence of them in history? Chapter 8 of Revelation reads more like the plot of a horror movie than an outline of real events and if something this climatically and environmentally significant has already taken place in the past – wouldn't it be recorded in historical accounts?

It would – and it is.

### The worst year in human history

In 2018, Harvard medieval historian Michael McCormick, coined the term "the worst year in human history" to describe **536 AD -** a year he highlighted as the bleakest time to be alive due to a mysterious atmospheric haze that darkened skies across large parts of Europe, the Middle East, and Asia. This drove sharp climate cooling, and set off crop failures, hunger, and wider social chaos. This misery was compounded in the following years by further climatic shocks and, soon after, by the **Justinian plague**.

McCormick's phrase is now broadly accepted as shorthand for an extreme series of climactic events in the mid-6th-century - kicked off by the eruption of a volcano – probably in Iceland. This volcano (and others which followed it) led to devastation on an unimaginable global scale and was followed by an ash cloud and a 'mysterious fog' so dense that it kept the northern hemisphere in near darkness for around 18 months.

Multiple witnesses across languages and nations recorded the same event. **Procopius** (in Constantinople) wrote that: "*a most dread portent took place. For the sun gave forth its light without brightness, like the moon, during this whole year...*" and added that from then on men were free of "*neither war nor pestilence.*" In Italy, **Cassiodorus** catalogues a dim, even "bluish" sun, **no noon shadows**, and "*a winter without storms, a spring without mildness, and a summer without heat,*" with fruit ruined and wine turned sour. **John of Ephesus** and **Michael the Syrian** report that the sun's darkness lasted **about eighteen months**, with only a few hours of weak daylight each day; "*the fruits did not ripen*."

But as bad as this sounds - things got much worse. After the initial volcanic eruptions, and as a result of the prolonged darkening that they caused, temperatures fell drastically. Europe, Asia and Africa entered one of the coldest decades in 2,300 years. China recorded summers that were marked by snow and crop failure. The **Nan Shi** (History of the Southern Dynasties) records **"yellow dust" falling like snow** in **536–537**, "filling scoops when picked up," an independent sign of extreme dryness and abnormal skies.

Two more massive eruptions followed in 540 and 547 AD but the effect of these events went well beyond just these few years. According to researchers, the reduced sunlight set off a series of cataclysmic events that took human civilization more than 100 years to recover from. These started with drought and famine, and were followed, in 541, by the Justinian Plague which hit Egypt before spreading to Europe and continuing, in wave after wave, for the next 150 years.

Modern researchers tie these reports to a sustained **Late Antique Little Ice Age** (~536–660), in which populations remained thin, harvests erratic, and states were fiscally weak throughout the **seventh century**.

In short: the documentary evidence from Greek, Latin, Syriac, Old Irish, and Chinese sources converges on a catastrophic crisis – and **by the time these events were over they had killed between 50 and 60 million people** – all at a time when the population of the entire world was only estimated to have been around 190 million.

But we're getting ahead of ourselves. How does all this relate to the Trumpet Judgements?

To answer that, let's revisit the wording of the first five Trumpet prophecies in chapter 8 of the Book of Revelation:

***Trumpet 1 - Rev 8:7***
*"Hail and fire, mixed with blood, were hurled to the earth... a third of the earth was burned up, a third of the trees... all green grass."*

***Trumpet 2 - Rev 8:8–9***
*"Something like a great mountain, burning with fire, was thrown into the sea... a third of the sea became blood, a third of the living creatures died, a third of the ships were destroyed."*

***Trumpet 3 - Rev 8:10–11***
*"A great star, burning like a torch, fell on a third of the rivers and on the springs... the name of the star is Wormwood... a third of the waters became bitter, and many people died from the waters."*

***Trumpet 4 - Rev 8:12***
*"A third of the sun was struck, a third of the moon, and a third of the stars, so that a third of them turned dark; a third of the day was without light, and a third of the night."*

***Trumpet 5 - Rev 9:1–2***
*"A star had fallen to the earth... he was given the key to the shaft of the Abyss. He opened the Abyss, and smoke rose like the smoke of a great furnace; the sun and the air were darkened by the smoke."*

Does this now sound familiar? Taken in context, this is a description of a major volcanic disaster, followed by the aftermath of that event. But is it describing the events of 536 - or are we just 'fitting prophecy to history'? That question is answered a few verses later where we're told that 'locusts' also rose from the Abyss and that:

***Revelation 9:5–6***

*"They were not allowed to kill them (people without the seal of God on their forehead), but to torment them for* ***five months*** *..."*

***Revelation 9:10***

*"They have tails with stingers like scorpions, and in their tails they have power to torment for* ***five months.****"*

**How long is five months?**

You may have already noticed that this is not the first time that we've considered the meaning of 'months' in Revelation. In fact, we encountered them in the later part of this same vision, in chapter 11, where we addressed the prophecy of '42 months'.

We learnt that those months were made up of Julian years (which average 30.43 days per month) and represented 1,278.3 years. When counted backward from 1967, this took us 688 - the year in which the Muslim Dome of the Rock appeared on the Temple Mount in Jerusalem.

So what happens if we also multiply these 5 months by 30.43 days and add those years to 536AD (the worst year in history)?

**5 months x 30.43 days**

**= 152.15 Julian years**

536AD + 152.15 years = **688.15 AD**

And there it is again. **The year 688.**

Suddenly the first four Trumpet judgements make perfect sense. They tell us that these judgements started with an eruption in 536 AD - kicking off cataclysmic events which took place between that year and 688. We're also told that these judgements were because mankind "did not stop worshiping demons, and idols of gold, silver, bronze, stone and wood - idols that cannot see or hear or walk. Nor did they repent of their murders, their magic arts, their sexual immorality or their thefts".

But as severe as these events were, we're also told that, initially, mankind was tortured, but not killed (ie, not almost completely wiped out, as it had been during the Flood).

This is not conjecture. The conditions described in the prophecy - crop failure, displacement, crowding, dust, and strained water – all lead to severe but non-lethal conditions. Aëtius of Amida (6th c.) writes extensively about eye disease; Paul of Aegina (7th c.) treats ophthalmia/trachoma, *psora* and pruritus (itching eruptions), and "herpes" eruptions – all conditions that thrive in the conditions described above and causing burning eyes, pain, abrasion and visual loss; relentless itching that wrecks sleep; belt-like, nerve-pain rashes - miserable, disabling, but generally non-lethal.

Add the Near Eastern profile of cutaneous leishmaniasis - sting-like onset and ulcers that linger for months – which were typically disfiguring rather than deadly. All of this strikes people, not fields or trees; and matches the text's emphasis on torment over killing - and it persisted across the exact span framed by 536–688.

This all happened at a time when Christianity was still mostly confined to parts of Europe and Asia Minor, so pagan worship was still the dominant religious influence throughout most of the planet, including large swathes of the Middle East and Europe itself. As such, most of mankind was, indeed, still 'worshiping demons, and idols of gold, silver, bronze, stone and wood' at this time.

So let's update our template with this new information:

| **The Prophecy of Five Months**<br>Revelation 9:5; 9:10 | | | |
|---|---|---|---|
| **What's being predicted?** | *That people would be tormented for 152 years (5 months) because they refused to stop worshiping demons, & idols of gold, silver, bronze, stone and wood* | | |
| **Question** | **Clue from Scripture** | **Math** | **Solution** |
| **Who is the prophecy addressed to?** | *"...Jesus Christ ... to show His servants" (Revelation 1:1)* | | **The prophecy is addressed to Christians** |
| **Who is the prophecy about?** | *"...about many peoples, nations, languages and kings..." (Revelation 10:11)* | | **The prophecy is about the Gentiles** |
| **What year does the prophecy start?** | *The worst year in human history* | ***536*** | **The prophecy begins in 536 AD** |
| **How long will the prophecy last?** | *"They had the power to torment people for 5 months...." (Revelation 9:10)* | ***plus 152*** | **The prophecy will last for 152 years** |
| **What year does the prophecy end?** | | ***equals 688*** | **The prophecy ends in 688 AD** |

You'll note that, for this prophecy, we're now pointing *toward* the year in which the prophecy ends. This is because this prophecy started in a year *prior* to 688 and so complies with our discovery that all prophecy in Revelation and Daniel counts time *toward* that year.

So we can now understand what this prophecy means – but let's continue with the vision. The sixth trumpet gives further details:

> [15] *"And the four angels who had been kept ready for this very hour and day and month and year were released to kill a third of*

*mankind. 16 The number of the mounted troops was twice ten thousand times ten thousand. I heard their number".* ***(Revelation 9:15-16)***

This makes clear that the locusts of the fifth trumpet and the mounted troops of the sixth trumpet are two different demonic judgements. The first are explicitly barred from killing and are responsible for prolonged torment (disease and misery). The second are explicitly authorised to kill and are responsible for the deaths of roughly a third of mankind. In history, these two layers of judgement overlap in the late antique crisis (536–688), but they represent different aspects of the same catastrophe – non-lethal affliction followed by lethal plague.

But what is being described in 9:15-16? There is no historical record of 'twice ten thousand times ten thousand' troops (two hundred million) ever being gathered anywhere in human history – so is there another way to view these 'troops'?

There is. The number two hundred million is within the range of estimates of the population of the entire world in the 6th and 7th century - and since the verse tells us that a third of mankind were going to be killed, and we already know that up to 60 million died over this time - we're dealing in numbers that are remarkably similar given the limitations of collecting such information during that period of history.

As such, is it possible that the two hundred million 'mounted troops' are demonic entities, released from 'the abyss' to torment mankind – enough of them for every person on earth? There would certainly be a sense of poetic irony in this since we're told that mankind was being punished for 'worshiping demons, and idols of gold, silver, bronze, stone and wood'.

**From conjecture to history**

We can now see that the Trumpet judgements are not about a final seven-year period – they're an outline of a series of cataclysmic events which started almost 1,500 years ago and which are recorded in history for anyone with the eyes to see them. They include several volcanic eruptions in Iceland in 536 and 540, major climatic changes as a result of these, the onset of the Justinian Plague which killed over 50 million, and the appearance of a mysterious figure who is simply identified as 'a star'.

The 5 months are a period of 152 years (five x 30.43 days) which start in 536 (the worst year in human history) and continue until the appearance of the Dome of the Rock in 688.

### The Star and the Abyss

But who was the 'star' that fell to earth in Revelation 8:10-11 and what was the nature of 'the abyss' that he was given a key to open in Revelation 9:1?

We'll find out more about both of these a little later in this book.

*The solution at a glance*

## The Five Months:
## The forgotten apocalypse

***Scripture:*** *Revelation 8:6 – 9:18*

1. **What's being predicted??**
   That people would be tormented for 152 years (5 months) because they refused to stop worshiping demons, & idols of gold, silver, bronze, stone and wood.

2. **Who is being spoken to?**
   John, writing to **the early Church**.

3. **Who is the prophecy about?**
   **The nations** - non-Jewish peoples, across the known world.

4. **When does it start?**
   **536 AD** - "the worst year in human history."

5. **How long does it last?**
   "Five months." Using the same length of an average month we used earlier (30.43 days): 5 × 30.43 = **152.15 years**.

6. **When does it end?**
   536 + 152 = **688 AD** - the year of construction of the Dome of the Rock launching centuries of Gentile control of Jerusalem.

The Trumpet Judgements aren't future - they were mostly fulfilled between **536 → 688 AD** and describe real disasters that wiped out around 1/3rd of humanity.

39

# The meaning of the Vision of the History of the Gentiles

which appears in the **Book of Revelation**

| 1st Vision | 2nd Vision | 3rd Vision | 4th Vision | 5th Vision | 6th Vision | 7th Vision |
|---|---|---|---|---|---|---|
| **The history of the Church** | **The trials of believers** | **The history of the gentiles** | **The origin of anti-semitism** | **The last plagues** | **The fall of Babylon** | **The reign of Christ** |
| *Rev Ch 1-3* | *Rev Ch 4-8.1* | *Rev Ch 8.2-11* | *Rev Ch 12-14* | *Rev Ch 15-16, 19-20* | *Rev Ch 17-18* | *Rev Ch 21-22* |

Earlier in *Prophecy Shock* we locked in solutions to most of the prophecies in the Book of Daniel and we found that these provided a countdown to historically significant years including **1948, and 1967** – the two most important years in modern Jewish history.

These years didn't just 'happen'. They were the result of millions of unrelated interactions by tens of millions of people over centuries – and, in many cases, their fulfilment was even influenced by events that were intended to conspire *against* Jewish interests. Yet they landed exactly where God said they would.

But none of this could have prepared us for what we then discovered in *the Vision of the History of the Gentiles (Chapters 8.2 to 11 of the Book of Revelation)*. Not only were the solutions to the time-defined prophecies in this vision *the same years* that we had previously identified in the prophecies in the Book of Daniel – but when we display these solutions together, all four prophecies converge on **one familiar year!**

## The meaning of the Prophecies in the Vision of the History of the Gentiles

| Prophecy | Event | Span | Result |
|---|---|---|---|
| **Five Months** - Revelation 9:5,9:10 | Started in 536 AD | 152 years | 688 AD |
| **42 Months** - Revelation 11:1-2 | Ended in 1967 | 1,278.3 years | 688.7 AD |
| **Two Witnesses** - Revelation 11:3-4 | Ended in 1948 | 1,260 years | 688 AD |
| **Three and a half days** - Revelation 11:9-10 | Ended in 1967 | 1,278.3 years | 688.7 AD |

This is remarkable. Whether the prophecy is counted forwards (as in the prophecy of Five Months) or backwards (as with the other three prophecies) the visual centre of gravity is the same. It hinges unambiguously on **688 AD** – the same year that we also identified in Daniel.

The message is clear. The construction of the Dome of the Rock on the Temple Mount in Jerusalem – ***the abomination of desolation*** – kicks off *the times of the Gentiles.*

**The storyline in one sweep**

**1. The Prelude - Five Months (536 → 688)**

The vision opens with the blowing of the first five of the seven trumpets: a world shaken by environmental disruption, civilisational upheaval, and divine judgement - not as an end-times montage, but as a measurable historical period. The forgotten apocalypse that sets the stage for Jerusalem's long displacement.

The five prophetic months resolve to 152 years, carrying us from **536 to 688** – functioning as a runway into the Gentile age and a watermark against which to confirm that 688 is, indeed, the year of focus in all four prophecies.

**2. One Era described three ways (688 → 1948 / 1967)**

Chapter 11 then presents three time-defined prophecies. These are not three different historical periods. They are three perspectives on the same Gentile era.

- **The 42 Months** describes what happens to Jerusalem itself: the Holy City trampled for **1,278+ years**, resolving in **1967**, when Jerusalem comes back under Jewish control.

- **The Two Witnesses (1,260 days / years)** describes what happens to God's witnesses during that same span: Judaism and Christianity – influencing the world until the restoration of Israel in **1948**.

- **The Three and a Half Days** re-expresses the same Jerusalem timeline as a compressed symbolic countdown, again resolving in **1967**, when "the breath of life" returns and the city stands restored.

These are not competing solutions. They are **one integrated prophetic map**.

- **536 → 688** - the prelude of judgement and destabilisation.
- **688 → 1948 / 1967** - the long Gentile era, told through the fate of Jerusalem and the endurance of the witnesses.
- **1948 and 1967** - the twin restoration milestones.

**What remains future**

The seventh trumpet hasn't yet been blown and still points beyond the fulfilled historical arc, to the final completion of God's purposes and the return of Christ. But the central claim of this vision is already clear: Revelation 8–11 is not a compressed, speculative end-times drama. It is a coherent, date-anchored history of the Gentile era - **with 688 as the hinge**, and **1948 and 1967 as the twin outcomes**.

**Convergence is the message**

Once again, these prophecies repeat the theme of the prophecies we've have already resolved in the Book of Daniel – focusing on the same key years – 688, 1948 and 1967 – with 688 as the hinge.

This is best exemplified in a mind map where the size of the year is weighted by the number of times it appears in solutions in the Book of Daniel, and in this Vision, and where the years are placed with the oldest year at the left, and the most recent years at the right. All are pointing to the midpoint of these prophecies – the appearance of the Dome of the Rock:

536 — **688** — 1948
1967

This is not a coincidence – this is God, demanding that we pay attention. The Vision of the History of the Gentiles is a coherent, panoramic prophecy, written in advance, and fulfilled in meticulous detail – proving, beyond doubt, that God never took His hand off Jerusalem.

## 40

### THE PRINCIPLES OF ISRAELISM

# Daniel and Revelation cover over 2,500 years of history

Peter warned us that belief in the return of Christ would be ridiculed in the last days:

> *"Above all, you must understand that in the last days scoffers will come, scoffing and following their own evil desires. They will say, 'Where is this 'coming' he promised? Ever since our ancestors died, everything goes on as it has since the beginning of creation.'"* ***(2 Peter 3:3–4)***

This is exactly what has happened. Two thousand years on, many dismiss both creation, and Christ's return, as myths.

The Church has tried to answer this by reminding the world of an **imminent second coming** that could happen *at any moment.*

The problem? This "any moment now" approach often comes packaged with a checklist of "signs" that, proponents claim, must occur in a compressed burst of years immediately *before* Christ appears – kind of like the opening night of a long-delayed stage play, endlessly postponed. These signs are mostly based on the prophecies in the Books of Daniel and Revelation.

We've seen this pattern again and again in:

- **Hal Lindsey's *The Late Great Planet Earth*** in the 1970s.
- **Edgar Whisenant's *88 Reasons Why the Rapture Will Be in 1988*.**
- The massively popular **Left Behind** series.

Each of these inferred that the end was right around the corner. Each failed.

But notice what Peter actually says. He doesn't describe God's plan as a short, frantic countdown of final fireworks. Instead, he reminds us that:

> *"With the Lord a day is like a thousand years, and a thousand years are like one day. The Lord is not slow in keeping his promise, as some understand slowness. Instead he is patient with you, not wanting anyone to perish, but everyone to come to repentance."* ***(2 Peter 3:8–9)***

That is not the voice of a man predicting a tidy seven-year finale. It is the voice of One pointing to a **long unfolding story** - a divine patience stretched out over centuries.

The great mistake of modern prophecy teaching has been to treat these prophecies as pointers to an "end-time drama" when, in reality, their visions cover a **sweep of more than 2,500 years.**

They are not merely predictions of the final generation but an **unfolding panorama of world empires and God's dealings with Israel across the ages.**

When interpreted correctly, these prophecies trace history with astonishing precision:

- From Babylon, Persia, Greece, and Rome…
- Through centuries of exile and scattering…

- To the climactic events of the modern era - including the Holocaust, the rebirth of Israel in 1948, and the recapture of Jerusalem in 1967.

This is prophecy at work: not crammed into a final week but stretched across millennia - its fingerprints visible in the turning points of nations.

And the return of Christ? It will not be heralded by a tidy sequence of "last days signs." It will arrive suddenly, like a thief in the night:

> *"But the day of the Lord will come like a thief. The heavens will disappear with a roar; the elements will be destroyed by fire, and the earth and everything done in it will be laid bare."* ***(2 Peter 3:10)***

No checklist. No countdown clock. Just suddenness. Unexpectedness.

The message is unmistakable: **history itself has been the stage on which prophecy has already unfolded.** We are not waiting for it to begin. We are living inside it.

And the return of Christ? That could happen today, tomorrow, next year, or long after our lifetimes are over. But He *will* return. And unlike the endless false countdowns, His coming will not be pencilled into a timetable of imaginary events. It will be the ultimate interruption - **unexpected, unmissable, and unstoppable.**

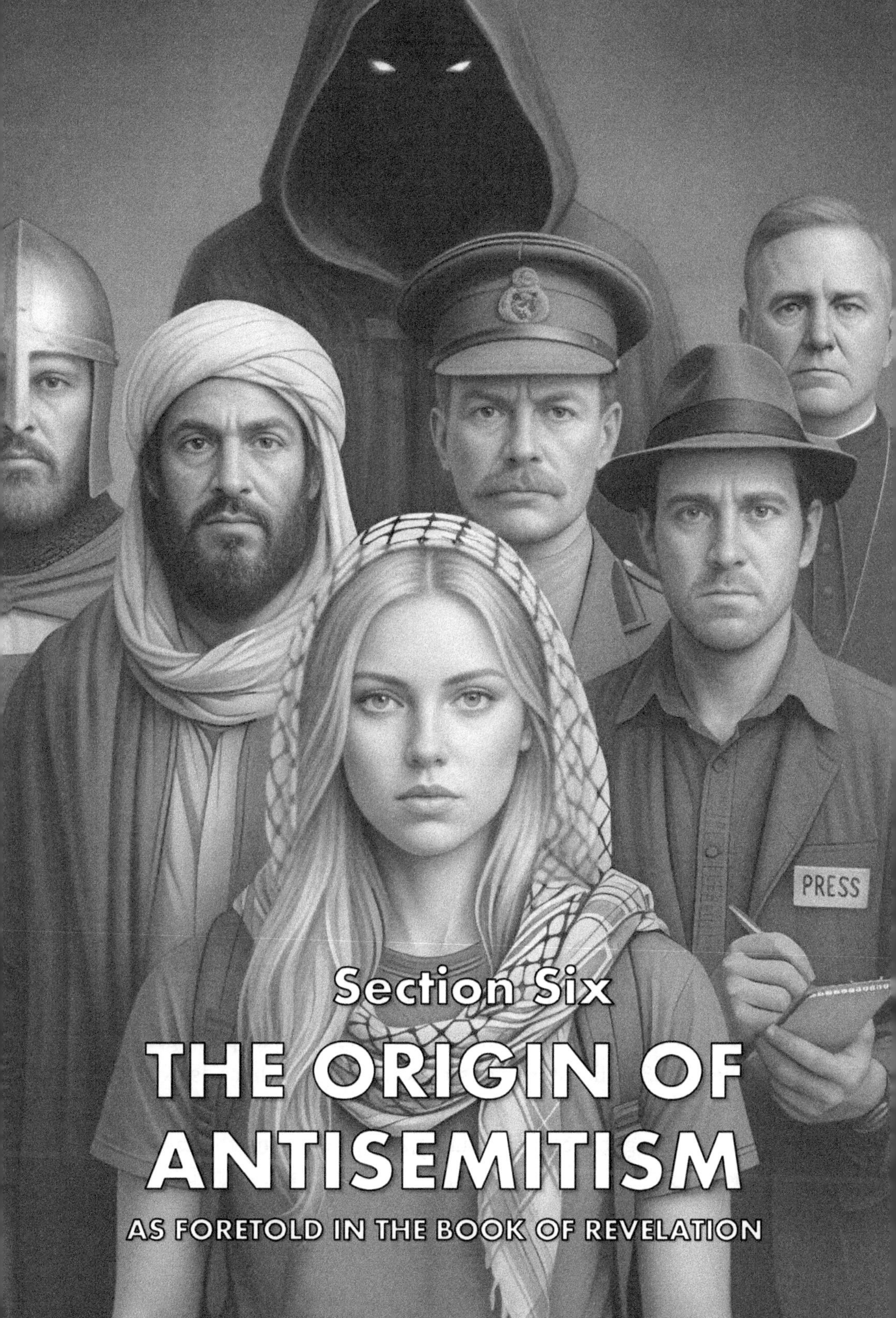


## Section Six

# THE ORIGIN OF ANTISEMITISM

### AS FORETOLD IN THE BOOK OF REVELATION

# 41

## An overview of the Vision of

# The origin of antisemitism

which appears in the **Book of Revelation**

| 1st Vision | 2nd Vision | 3rd Vision | 4th Vision | 5th Vision | 6th Vision | 7th Vision |
|---|---|---|---|---|---|---|
| **The history of the Church** | **The trials of believers** | **The history of the gentiles** | **The origin of anti-semitism** | **The last plagues** | **The fall of Babylon** | **The reign of Christ** |
| *Rev Ch 1-3* | *Rev Ch 4-8.1* | *Rev Ch 8.2-11* | *Rev Ch 12-14* | *Rev Ch 15-16, 19-20* | *Rev Ch 17-18* | *Rev Ch 21-22* |

Why is the history of mankind marked by such a burning hatred of the Jews? Why do successive generations reserve some of their most intense vitriol for a people that make up less than 0.01% of the world's population?

In Chapter 10 of *Prophecy Shock*, I outlined a few examples of this ongoing persecution over the past 2,000 years - but I could have filled a large book with such examples and would still have barely scratched the surface.

It is only around 80 years since this unique hatred reached its most infamous extreme: the systematic murder of six million Jews in the Nazi death camps. Yet we saw the same spirit on display again on 7 October 2023, when terrorists crossed into southern Israel and carried out atrocities beyond description - the rape of hundreds of women, the slaughter of more than 1,200 people, and the taking of 251 hostages.

Had the victims of those atrocities been from any other nation, the world's response would have been one of shock, grief, and overwhelming solidarity. Instead, within days, crowds marched in Western capitals chanting slogans against Israel, International agencies convened sham hearings to shift blame onto the victim and students occupied Ivy League campuses in the United States, reciting crude and racist chants as if they were moral slogans.

### Antisemitism – the hatred of Jews

Racism doesn't just affect the Jews, of course. It wounds many communities. scars nations, deforms cultures, and leaves generations carrying the weight of injustice.

But antisemitism is different. It doesn't only flare up over a border dispute or fade when a war ends. It isn't about the conflict of peoples of different skin colours (Jews cover the spectrum from light skinned to dark skinned). And it doesn't rise and fall with political tides. It is immune to reason, unshaken by time, and aimed always at one target: the Jewish people.

From the moment that the descendants of Abraham became a people, they have been marked. Empires came and went, but the accusations never stopped. Pharaoh enslaved them. Babylon exiled them. Rome scattered them. In Christian Europe, they were branded "Christ-killers," massacred in the Crusades, tortured in the Inquisition, and expelled from multiple countries over centuries. In medieval markets they were denied land and trades, forced into moneylending, and then condemned as greedy usurers - a necessity twisted into a vice.

In the 19th century, racial pseudoscience rebranded them as pollutants, paving the road to Nazi ideology, which industrialised their murder: six million lives, erased because they existed. In Tsarist Russia, they were accused of sparking revolution; in the Soviet Union, of capitalist conspiracy; in the West, of communist infiltration; in the Arab world, of imperialist collusion. The charges contradicted each other, but that didn't matter. The point was never truth. The point was hate - and hate adapts.

Today, antisemitism isn't a relic - it's a live wire humming through the 21st century, hotter and more dangerous than ever. It's wrapped in the pretence of justice but perpetuates the oldest *injustice*. It infects the media, where selective reporting and euphemisms smuggle ancient lies into modern headlines. It warps international bodies that single out Israel while ignoring bloody regimes. It stalks universities, where Jewish students face threats in lecture halls while administrators look away. It rides the celebrity microphone, where conspiracy theories are given the glow of legitimacy. And it multiplies online, where coded hate slips past casual eyes, amplified by algorithms until it becomes a torrent.

**The Zionist slur**

At the centre of it all is anti-Zionism - the most insidious slur of them all. Under the guise of political critique it attempts to strip Jews of the right to self-determination in their ancestral home. It takes a 3,000-year-old hope, fulfilled in 1948, and recasts it as apartheid, oppression, or colonial theft. By swapping "Jew" for "Zionist," it attempts to make the oldest hatred sound respectable while calling for the dismantling of the only nation where Jews can live as a majority and defend themselves.

This is not simply prejudice. It is a war - coordinated, global, and unrelenting. And it will not stop. Not with education. Not with legislation. Not with appeasement - because this hatred is not born of ignorance - it is born of rebellion. At its core it is spiritual – not rational – a demonic defiance of God's purposes and a rage against His people. The question is not whether antisemitism will rise, but whether we will have the courage to stand against it while there is still time.

**The Prophetic Perspective**

But if the Jews are God's chosen people, why has He allowed this hatred to continue? Some prophecy teachers claim that He has turned His back on them - but the Scriptures and the prophecies that we have already resolved in this book say otherwise. The Old Testament is full of God's promises to preserve Israel, even through discipline and exile. And as we have already seen, the Book of Daniel lays out specific time-defined prophecies which confirm that they are now back in their land – just as God promised they would be.

So what's going on? Why does the hatred of Jews continue?

The next section of Revelation – the fourth vision - picks this up and explains how it has played out in history. Spanning chapters 12 to 14 – it provides an extraordinary explanation of the origin of antisemitism and its role over the past 2,000 years. It reveals that this hatred is not merely human but driven by a spiritual adversary - the dragon of Revelation 12 - whose rage is directed at "the woman clothed with the sun" and "the rest of her offspring."

In the pages ahead, we will see why antisemitism cannot be reasoned with, why it isn't about the slogans used to justify it, and why it will not end until the Lord Himself returns.

This vision will also give us three more time-defined prophecies:

1. **Another 1,260 days (Revelation 12)**
2. **Another "time, times and half a time" (Revelation 12)**
3. **Another 42 months (Revelation 13)**

and five distinct prophetic figures:

- **A woman clothed with the sun**
- **A dragon**
- **A beast with many heads and horns**
- **Another beast, with two horns, speaking "like a lamb"**
- **144,000 Jews standing on Mount Zion**

How these fit together - and how they explain the unbroken history of antisemitism - is a story that has been hiding in plain sight for nearly two thousand years.

42

# The beginning of sorrows

## The Prophecy of the woman clothed with the sun

which appears in **Revelation 12:1-2** in the

| 1st Vision | 2nd Vision | 3rd Vision | 4th Vision | 5th Vision | 6th Vision | 7th Vision |
|---|---|---|---|---|---|---|
| **The history of the Church** | **The trials of believers** | **The history of the gentiles** | **The origin of anti-semitism** | **The last plagues** | **The fall of Babylon** | **The reign of Christ** |
| *Rev Ch 1-3* | *Rev Ch 4-8.1* | *Rev Ch 8.2-11* | *Rev Ch 12-14* | *Rev Ch 15-16, 19-20* | *Rev Ch 17-18* | *Rev Ch 21-22* |

While the previous Vision outlined *what* happened to the Jews during the period known as *the Times of the Gentiles* – this next Vision covers broadly the same events – but this time, explains *why* they happened. It tells this story through a series of distinct characters – starting with a 'woman' who we are introduced to in the very first sentence of Revelation 12:

> *12 "A great sign appeared in heaven: a woman clothed with the sun, with the moon under her feet and a crown of twelve stars on her head. 2 She was pregnant and cried out in pain as she was about to give birth".* ***(Revelation 12:1-2)***

We don't need to guess who this woman is because **Genesis 37** tells us:

> *... Joseph dreamed a dream, and he told it his brethren ... and said, Behold, ... the sun and the moon and the eleven stars made*

*obeisance to me ... and his father rebuked him, and said unto him, What is this dream that thou hast dreamed? Shall I and thy mother and thy brethren indeed come to bow down ourselves to thee ...* ***(Genesis 37:5-10)***

The response from Josephs father (Jacob) confirms that he recognized these symbols - the sun, moon, and the stars – as representing himself, his wife, and his sons - Israel's founding family. That's also confirmed earlier in Genesis 37, where God renamed Jacob "Israel". So, based on these scriptures, we can see that **the "woman" in Revelation 12 is a personification of Israel** and this is a prophecy about the Jews. The passage continues:

*"The dragon stood in front of the woman... so that it might devour her child... She gave birth to a son... who 'will rule all the nations with an iron sceptre.'... And her child was snatched up to God... The woman fled into the wilderness... for 1,260 days."* ***(Revelation 12:3–6)***

The male child destined to rule is Christ. He was born a Jew, in Israel, and He preached first to a Jewish audience. So the woman - Israel - gave birth to Christ.

But who is the dragon? Again, no guesswork is required:

*9 The great dragon was hurled down - that ancient serpent called the devil, or Satan, who leads the whole world astray. He was hurled to the earth, and his angels with him.* ***(Revelation 12:9)***

So the dragon is Satan. Let's recap:

- Israel gave birth to Christ.
- Satan tried to destroy Him (Herod's massacre of infants).
- Christ was crucified and returned to Heaven.
- The devil and his 'angels' were expelled from heaven
- The Jews fled into the wilderness

You may be surprised to read that the devil was cast down *after* the crucifixion. Many believe that he was cast out before the Fall of Adam and Eve, based on scriptures like Isaiah 14:12-14 and Ezekiel 28:12-18 - but while these passages explain *why* Satan fell, they don't explain *when*. We know that he still had free access to heaven in, at least, the time of Job (circa 1800 BC) - and there is no scripture, prior to the Book of Revelation, which specifically changes that status.

So it appears that Satan and many of his angels continued to transit freely between Heaven and Earth right up until the time that Christ returned to His Father's side in heaven. Only then was he cast down to earth permanently.

Let's see what happens after that:

*13 When the dragon saw that he had been hurled to the earth, he pursued the woman who had given birth to the male child. 14 The woman was given the two wings of a great eagle, so that she might fly to the place prepared for her in the wilderness, where she would be taken care of for a time, times and half a time, out of the serpent's reach.* ***(Revelation 12:13-14)***

**Two wilderness countdowns**

Note that the vision has now given us two descriptions of Israel in "the wilderness":

- In verse 6, the woman is in the wilderness for **1,260 days**.
- Here, in verse 12, she is in the wilderness for "**time, times and half a time**."

These are the first two *time-defined prophecies* in this Vision and, at first glance, they appear to be describing competing timelines – so we'll come back to them in more detail in Chapter 47.

For now, let's see what happens next in *the Vision of the Origin of Antisemitism*.

# 43

# Satan's Big Plan

## The Prophecy of the beast out of the sea

which appears in **Revelation 13:1-8** in the

| 1st Vision | 2nd Vision | 3rd Vision | 4th Vision | 5th Vision | 6th Vision | 7th Vision |
|---|---|---|---|---|---|---|
| **The history of the Church** | **The trials of believers** | **The history of the gentiles** | **The origin of anti-semitism** | **The last plagues** | **The fall of Babylon** | **The reign of Christ** |
| *Rev Ch 1-3* | *Rev Ch 4-8.1* | *Rev Ch 8.2-11* | *Rev Ch 12-14* | *Rev Ch 15-16, 19-20* | *Rev Ch 17-18* | *Rev Ch 21-22* |

We've now been introduced to five key events in this Vision:

- Israel has given birth to Christ.
- Satan has tried to destroy Him (Herod's massacre of infants).
- Christ has been crucified and returned to Heaven.
- The devil and his 'angels' have been expelled from heaven
- The Jews have fled into the wilderness

Let's review what happened next:

*[12] ...the devil ... is filled with fury, because he knows that his time is short ... he pursued the woman who had given birth to the male child. [14] The woman was given the two wings of a great eagle, so that*

*she might fly to the place prepared for her in the wilderness...* ***(Revelation 12:12-14)***

**What is "the wilderness"?**

Many interpreters have tried to identify the 'Wilderness' in this prophecy as a specific region or country based on their belief that it is a refuge for Christians in the last days. But as we will see when we get to the Chapter on the time-defined *Wilderness prophecies,* the wilderness is simply a generic term of sanctuary for Jews. It was the broad, scattered world into which the Jews fled and were driven over many centuries – Europe, North Africa, the Middle East, and beyond.

Wherever the Jews lived in dispersion, away from Jerusalem and the Temple Mount, they were in *the wilderness.*

This definition makes the next part of the prophecy easy to understand:

[15] *Then from his mouth the serpent spewed water like a river, to overtake the woman and sweep her away with the torrent.* ***(Revelation 12:15)***

So the devils next strategy was an attempt to fully assimilate the Jews into the nations to which they had escaped so that they would lose any sense of their national identity. If they didn't know who they were, they wouldn't yearn to return to their homeland.

This happened just as predicted. Over the following centuries, Christian and Muslim nations, in particular, put immense pressure on Jews to convert, under the threat of national expulsion or death.

But note the next verse. It tells us that even in the nations to which they migrated, the Jews remained under Gods protection:

[16] *But the earth helped the woman by opening its mouth and swallowing the river that the dragon had spewed out of his mouth.* ***(Revelation 12:15-16)***

History confirms that this is correct because we know that the Jews continued to maintain their unique identity and sense of their destiny, regardless of where they were in the world.

**But why was the devil "filled with fury"?**

The source of Satan's anger toward the Jews should come as no surprise to any Christian. He knows the scriptures inside out and he knows that they predict his ultimate demise – so he's been trying to stop that from happening for the past 2,000 years.

First, he tried to kill Jesus at birth. He failed.

Then, he helped to facilitate the crucifixion – not realising that it was an essential part of Gods plan.

After that, he turned to the Jews because he knew that they were the key to the completion of Christ's work. He knew that the scriptures predicted the Lords return to a Jewish controlled state in the Holy Land – with the Jewish people living and thriving there – so his efforts for most of the past two millennia have been to, first, get most of the Jews out of the holy land and then to stop them from ever coming back.

And how did he do that? Through one of the most audacious schemes in all of scripture:

**The beast coming up out of the sea**

> [13] *The dragon stood on the shore of the sea. And I saw a beast coming out of the sea. It had ten horns and seven heads, with ten crowns on its horns, and on each head a blasphemous name."* ***(Revelation 13:1)***

**A new beast?**

So now we see the dragon (Satan) standing on the shore and watching a *new beast* coming up out of the sea. This new beast has ten horns and seven heads, with *ten* crowns on its horns, whereas the entity in chapter 12 had ten horns, seven heads and *seven* crowns on its heads. So, this is not the same beast.

Let's read a bit more about this new beast:

*[2] The beast I saw resembled a leopard but had feet like those of a bear and a mouth like that of a lion. The dragon gave the beast his power and his throne and great authority.* ***(Revelation 13:2)***

*[4] People worshiped the dragon because he had given authority to the beast, and they also worshiped the beast and asked, "Who is like the beast? Who can wage war against it?"*

*[5] The beast was given a mouth to utter proud words and blasphemies and to exercise its authority for forty-two months. [6] It opened its mouth to blaspheme God, and to slander his name and his dwelling place and those who live in heaven. [7] It was given power to wage war against God's holy people and to conquer them.* ***(Revelation 13:4-7)***

**The enemy of Gods people**

The whole scene brings to mind the old black and white movie footage of Doctor Frankenstein breathing life into the monster that he had created in his own image, and you almost get the sense of the devil, in the guise of Frankenstein, exclaiming 'it's alive' as millions of volts course through it. But who, or what, is this beast?

We know that it:

- had ten horns
- and exercised its authority for forty-two months

We also know (from *the Vision of the History of the Gentiles*) that it 'came up out of the sea' at some stage in the 152 years following 536 AD but prior to 688 AD – which tells us that it couldn't be the Byzantine Empire because that power ruled Jerusalem from 313 AD (till 638 AD). So who controlled Jerusalem after the Byzantines? We don't need to guess because history tells us exactly who came next:

| Kingdoms | Controlled Jerusalem |
|---|---|
| **1. Rashidun Caliphate** | **638 - 661** |
| **2. Umayyad Caliphate** | **661 – 750** |
| **3. Abbasid Caliphate** | **750 – 878 & 904 – 969** |
| **4. Tulunid Dynasty** | **878 – 904** |
| **5. Fatimid Caliphate** | **969 – 1073 & 1098 - 1099** |
| **6. Seljuk Dynasty** | **1073 – 1098** |
| 7. First Crusader Kingdom | 1099 - 1187 |
| **8. Ayyubid Sultanate** | **1187 - 1259** |
| **9. Mamluk Sultanate** | **1260 - 1517** |
| **10. Ottoman Empire** | **1517 – 1918** |
| 11. British Empire | 1918 – 1948 |
| **12. Kingdom of Jordan** | **1948 - 1967** |

So 12 powers controlled Jerusalem between 638 and 1967 – but these powers were underpinned by just *two* ideologies:

- Two were 'Christian' (the Crusader Kingdom and the British Empire)
- **Ten (*exactly* ten) were Islamic**

If that doesn't send a chill down your spine you need to read it again – because, for the first time, we can finally understand the real meaning of the 'ten horns' prophecy.

*The ten horns were ten kings who came from this kingdom* ***(Daniel 7:24)***

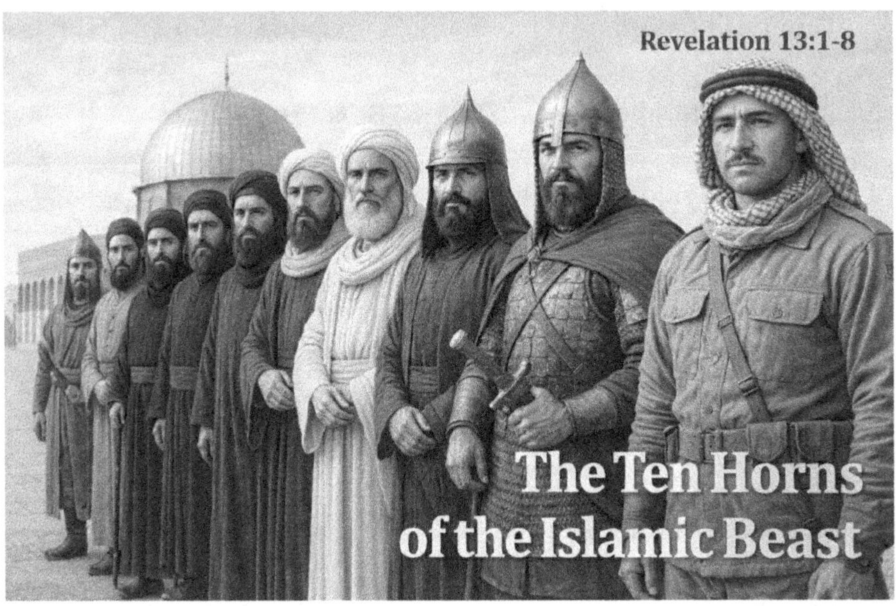


These horns weren't a revived Roman Empire or the United Nations, the World Economic Forum or any other 21st century grouping. They were ten Islamic powers which were created and guided by Satan to keep the Jews out of the Holy Land so that there would be no possibility of them ever establishing a state there again. And he pulled it off for over 1,300 years.

**Islam and the Jews – enmity from the outset**

Islam first appeared in 613 when its founder, Muhammad, started preaching in Mecca - but it was only when he moved to Medina in 622 that his movement became a political and military force.

Medina was also home to several influential Jewish tribes (Banu Qaynuqa, Banu Nadir and Banu Qurayza) and at first, Muhammad sought the recognition of these tribes – eager to be confirmed as a prophet in the line of Moses. Instead, they challenged his claims and rejected his interpretation of their faith.

From that point, Islam's sacred texts promoted an image of Jews as stubborn, treacherous, and cursed. Verses accused them of killing prophets (3:112), corrupting scripture (2:75, 5:13), and even being transformed into "apes and pigs" (5:60).

This set the template for Islam's treatment of Jews thereafter – starting with the three Jewish tribes in Medina:

- **Banu Qaynuqa** – was expelled and had property seized.
- **Banu Nadir** – was expelled for an alleged assassination plot.
- **Banu Qurayza** – was besieged during the Battle of the Trench; 600–900 men were executed by Islam, and women and children were enslaved.

These episodes are remembered in Islamic tradition as *righteous precedents*. They became the historical model for dealing with Jews - removal, humiliation, or destruction when they resisted – and when Muhammad died in 632, his successors - the Caliphs - carried this model across the Middle East.

Within six years, the Rashidun Caliphate had seized Jerusalem and over the following 1,300 years, successive Islamic powers ruled the city, using the *dhimmi* system (from Qur'an 9:29) which made Jews who lived in the Muslim world subhuman second class citizens to ensure permanent subjugation, utilising:

- heavy *jizya* tax "in humiliation"
- bans on building or repairing synagogues
- distinctive dress or markings
- enforced public deference to Muslims
- exclusion from positions of authority

This framework kept hostility alive and provided legal cover for outright violence against Jews during periods of political instability – and this hatred has not dissipated despite the passage of time.

What began as a personal confrontation in Medina grew into a theological, legal, and cultural hostility that has lasted for over 1,300 years and has underpinned the relationship between the ten horned Islamic Beast and the Jewish people – leading, most recently, to the murder of over 1,200 Jews on 7 October 2023.

This is no surprise. The old language of Medina continues to resurface in sermons and teachings portraying Jews as treacherous, cursed, and awaiting their final destruction in the end-times battle of Sahih Muslim 2922. That hadith (approved saying of Muhammad), where stones and trees call out to help kill Jews, also still appears in Muslim textbooks and political manifestos:

> *"The Hour will not be established until the Muslims fight the Jews, and the Jews will hide behind rocks and trees. The rocks or trees will say: 'O Muslim, O servant of Allah, there is a Jew behind me, come and kill him' - except for the Gharqad tree, for it is the tree of the Jews." - Sahih Muslim 2922; Bukhari 2926 (wording varies slightly between narrations)*

Let's take this new information, and test it against the Six Basic Questions:

**Question 1: What's being predicted?**

That a new beast – a satanically created entity – would control Jerusalem (and keep the Jews out) for 42 months.

**Questions 2 & 3: Who is the prophecy addressed to / about?**

The entire Book of Revelation is *addressed to* Christians but this prophecy is *about* what happens to Israel and the Jews - 'the sun, the moon and the stars'.

**Questions 4 & 5: How long does the prophecy last and when does it end?**

The reference to '42 months' during which the beast will 'exercise its authority and utter proud words and blasphemies' is the same 1,278.3 year period that was referenced in chapter 11 of the Book of Revelation where we were told that 'the gentiles' would trample down Jerusalem until 1967. Let's put this into our template:

| **The Prophecy of the beast out of the sea**<br>Revelation 13:1-8 | | | |
|---|---|---|---|
| **What's being predicted?** | *That a new beast – a satanically created entity – will control Jerusalem (and keep the Jews out) for 42 months.* | | |
| **Question** | **Clue from Scripture** | **Math** | **Solution** |
| **Who is the prophecy addressed to?** | *"...Jesus Christ ... to show His servants" (Revelation 1:1)* | | **The prophecy is addressed to Christians** |
| **Who is the prophecy about?** | *"...a woman clothed with the sun ... the moon ... and 12 stars..." (Revelation 12:1)* | | **The prophecy is about Israel** |
| **What year does the prophecy end?** | *"The beast ... exercise(d) its authority for forty-two months." (Revelation 13:5)* | ***1967*** | **The prophecy ends in 1967** |
| **How long will the prophecy last?** | *"... 42 months..." (Revelation 13:5)* | ***minus 1,278.3*** | **The prophecy will last for 1,278.3 years** |
| **What year does the prophecy begin?** | | ***equals 688.6*** | **The prophecy begins in 688 AD** |

So the '**beast out of the sea**' in this vision, and '**the beast out of the abyss**' in *the vision of the History of the Gentiles* are references to the same entity. Both are descriptions of the ten-horned beast which was created by the devil - the same Islamic beast which erected the Dome of the Rock on the Temple Mount in 688 AD – kicking off the 1,278.3 years (42 months) between 688 and 1967!

### Iron and Clay

So now, finally, we can also understand the meaning of a strange prophecy which appears in Daniel 2:40-42 and which tells us that this beast:

> [40] *... shall be strong as iron: forasmuch as iron breaketh in pieces and subdueth all things: and as iron that breaketh all these, shall it break in pieces and bruise.* [41] *And whereas thou sawest the feet and toes, part of potters' clay, and part of iron, the kingdom shall be divided; but there shall be in it of the strength of the iron, forasmuch as thou sawest the iron mixed with miry clay.* [42] *And as the toes of the feet were part of iron, and part of clay, so the kingdom shall be partly strong, and partly broken.*

This scripture has puzzled scholars for centuries – but now that we know that the Ten Horned beast was Islam, we can understand what Daniel meant when he said that it would be **strong as iron**, yet **divided, mixed, and partly broken**.

The reference to the strength of the kingdom was about its power to *break in pieces and subdue all things*. In the context of Jerusalem, that strength was unmistakable. For nearly thirteen centuries, Islamic rule was strong enough to **seize the city, hold it, and bruise its former occupants**. Jewish sovereignty was eliminated, access to the Temple Mount was denied, and Jewish life was legally subordinated. Dynasties came and went, but that core outcome was almost entirely unbroken. The iron strength was not merely military dominance at a given moment; it was the **capacity to enforce long-term control over Jerusalem and prevent Jewish self-rule**.

But Daniel then immediately qualifies that strength – telling us that the kingdom is **divided**, its feet and toes made of **iron mixed with miry clay**. This fits the historical reality perfectly. Islamic control of Jerusalem wasn't exercised by a single, continuous empire. Instead, it passed through **ten distinct Islamic powers**, each ruling independently, often in rivalry with the others. They shared the strength of iron - the same religious-political framework and the same outcome for Jerusalem - but they did not truly cleave together. Authority shifted repeatedly, sometimes violently, as dynasties fractured, collapsed, or were replaced.

Finally, Daniel says the kingdom would be **"partly strong and partly broken."** This is exactly what we observe. Some Islamic rulers were militarily formidable, controlling vast territories; others were weaker, short-lived, or dependent on broader geopolitical circumstances. Yet even when individual regimes were fragile or declining, **Jerusalem remained under Islamic control**. The weakness of the clay never cancelled the strength of the iron; it simply meant that the kingdom was uneven, unstable, and internally fractured.

Taken together, the ten Islamic powers form a single prophetic pattern: **one kingdom in outcome, divided in structure; strong enough to bruise and subdue Jerusalem, yet repeatedly broken in its individual parts**.

This is not a loose resemblance to Daniel's vision - it is an exact fulfilment.

---

### An important warning

On 15 March 2019, my home nation, New Zealand, suffered one of the darkest days in its history when an Australian gunman travelled here and attacked two mosques in Christchurch, murdering 51 innocent Muslim men, women, and children as they gathered for Friday prayers. It was a calculated act of evil - an atrocity against people who had done nothing except seek to worship in peace. This was not justice. This was not "defending Christianity." And it was absolutely not what Jesus calls us to do.

Jesus told us plainly: *"Love your enemies and pray for those who persecute you"* (Matthew 5:44). He also said, *"If anyone slaps you on the right cheek, turn to them the other cheek also"* (Matthew 5:39), and *"Do to others as you would have them do to you"* (Luke 6:31). There is no room in the gospel for personal hatred or vengeance against individuals. Ever.

The prophecies in this chapter identify and expose a **system** - the religious and political framework of Islam as it has opposed God's purposes for Israel - not the individual people born into it. Blaming individual Muslims for the nature of that system is like blaming the people Jesus freed from demonic possession for the demons that enslaved them. Jesus hated the works of Satan, but He loved the people Satan deceived.

If you use this information to stir up resentment or harm toward Muslim people, you have missed the heart of Christ entirely. Our calling is to pray for their eyes to be opened, to show them the unconditional love of God in action, and to remember that every single one of us was once blind until the Lord intervened.

*The solution at a glance*

# The Devils Big Plan: The beast out of the sea

***Scriptures:*** *Revelation 13:1-8*

1. **What's being predicted??**
   That a new beast – a satanically created entity – will control Jerusalem (and keep the Jews out) for 42 months.

2. **Who is being spoken to?**
   John, exiled on Patmos, briefing **the churches**.

3. **Who is the prophecy about?**
   **The Jews** – and the power that will keep them out of Jerusalem.

4. **When does it end?**
   **1967 AD** – Israel retakes Jerusalem in the Six-Day War. Gentile control ends.

5. **How long does it last?**
   "42 months." 42 x 30.43 days → ≈ **1,278+ years**.

6. **When does it start?**
   1967 – 1,278.3 ≈ **688.7 AD** – construction of the Dome of the Rock signals Islam's long grip on the Holy City.

This isn't a prophecy about a future antichrist regime – it's **a fulfilled prophecy about a 1,300-year Islamic system which tried – and failed - to keep Jews out of their own land**. Literal, exact, and centred on Jerusalem - no guesswork required.

## 44

# What is the Abyss?

So now we understand that Islam – the power which controlled the Middle East for most of the period between 688 and 1967 - is 'the beast which comes up out the sea' in Chapter 13 of Revelation and 'the beast out of the abyss' in Chapter 11 of Revelation.

As such, it would be remiss of me not to explain what 'the abyss' actually is.

The term 'abyss' comes from the Greek word 'abyssos' and means 'bottomless', 'unfathomable', and 'boundless'. In Hebrew, it was the primordial waters or chaos out of which the world was created and can be taken as a literal reference to the depths of the sea or the interior of the earth - so scripture references referring to the beast coming up out of the abyss, or out of the sea, are both references to the same place.

It is referenced several times in scripture, in both the Old and New Testaments - always as 'the underworld', a place of confinement for demons and the realm (or prison) of rebellious spirits. For example:

> [18] *For Christ also suffered once for sins, the righteous for the unrighteous, to bring you to God. He was put to death in the body but made alive in the Spirit.* [19] *After being made alive, he went and made proclamation to the imprisoned spirits - 20 to those who*

*were disobedient long ago when God waited patiently in the days of Noah while the ark was being built.* ***(1 Peter 3:18-20)***

So the inhabitants of the abyss are the disobedient spirits of those angels which occupied the earth prior to Noah's flood - and if you've read some of the excellent material on this topic by the late Chuck Missler you'll know that (potentially millions of) demons were 'confined in chains' in the abyss following the cleansing of the earth, by the flood.

But in the vision of **The History of the Gentiles** we learnt that some of these same spirits were released from the abyss, in the 6th century, to become the demonic forces which underpinned the Islamic empire.

Let that sink in as you re-read the prophecy from chapter 9 in the Book of Revelation:

*9 The fifth angel sounded his trumpet, and I saw a star (Satan) that had fallen from the sky to the earth. The star was given the key to the shaft of the Abyss. 2 When he opened the Abyss, smoke rose from it like the smoke from a gigantic furnace. The sun and sky were darkened by the smoke from the Abyss. 3 And out of the smoke locusts came down on the earth and were given power like that of scorpions of the earth. 4 They were told not to harm the grass of the earth or any plant or tree, but only those people who did not have the seal of God on their foreheads.* ***(Revelation 9:1-4)***

Remember - this is not a reference to future events. This took place in the 6th and 7th centuries – and we now know that these events immediately preceded the rise of Islam which is personified as 'the beast out of the abyss' - meaning that the same spirits drove both.

**The driving purpose of Islam**

The Vision tells us that Islam was specifically created, by Satan, as an attempt to ensure that the Jews were completely closed out of Israel so that they could never establish a Jewish nation again.

And it's not over.

Even today, almost 80 years after Israel was miraculously reborn, Islam is still driving global antisemitism in a vain attempt to delay the inevitable:

- Antisemitism is as strong as it has ever been in the Middle East and is also growing in the west.

- Funded by Islam, a growing crescendo of western and Middle Eastern voices are calling for the abolition of the Jewish state and even the extermination of the Jews.

- International Institutions which are tasked with peacekeeping and promoting balance are either being stacked with Islamic representation or receiving funding through Islamic sources. As a result, these have become active participants in antisemitism and are, in some cases, openly supporting terrorism against Israel.

None of this should surprise us when we consider what's at stake. The entire destiny of humanity (and the fate of the devil and his angels) is tied up in the return of Yeshua to Israel - so we shouldn't really find it so shocking that Satan would take extraordinary measures to try to stop that from happening and that antisemitism is at the very heart of Muslim ideology.

Oh, and one more thing about the abyss: It's the same place to which Satan will be banished, for a thousand years, when Christ returns:

*20 And I saw an angel coming down out of heaven, having the key to the Abyss and holding in his hand a great chain. [2] He seized the dragon, that ancient serpent, who is the devil, or Satan, and bound him for a thousand years. [3] He threw him into the Abyss, and locked and sealed it over him, to keep him from deceiving the nations anymore until the thousand years were ended. After that, he must be set free for a short time.* ***(Revelation 20:1-3)***

Satan is doing everything that he can to delay this – and that means trying to stop, and destroy, the Jews in any way possible. So this prophecy is not about an 'antichrist' who will rise in the last days. It is a description of a religious power which emerged way back in the 7th century and is still with us today.

But what about the other beast identified in chapter 13? Where does that fit in? Let's find out.

# The wolf in lambs clothing

## The Prophecy of the beast out of the earth

which appear in **Revelation 13:11-15** in the

| 1st Vision | 2nd Vision | 3rd Vision | 4th Vision | 5th Vision | 6th Vision | 7th Vision |
|---|---|---|---|---|---|---|
| **The history of the Church** | **The trials of believers** | **The history of the gentiles** | **The origin of anti-semitism** | **The last plagues** | **The fall of Babylon** | **The reign of Christ** |
| *Rev Ch 1-3* | *Rev Ch 4-8.1* | *Rev Ch 8.2-11* | *Rev Ch 12-14* | *Rev Ch 15-16, 19-20* | *Rev Ch 17-18* | *Rev Ch 21-22* |

So now we know that the beast which 'comes up from the abyss' is the satanic power behind Islam - and this discovery neatly packages the vision up in a way which is consistent with history.

But what about the other beast which is also mentioned in chapter 13 of Revelation:

> [11] *Then I saw a second beast, coming out of the earth. It had two horns like a lamb, but it spoke like a dragon.* ***(Revelation 13:11)***

Where does this new beast fit in?

According to most Premillennialists, it is a reference to an individual known as 'the false prophet' who will assist their last days 'antichrist' in his deceptions.

But none of the previous beasts have been individuals - they have all been empires and powers - and the defining characteristic of *all* of the beasts in these visions is that, at one time, each of them controlled Jerusalem. As such, we're looking for a kingdom or empire which:

- existed at the same time as the period during which Islam exercised control over Jerusalem.

- controlled Jerusalem, itself, for a time that must have come *after* 688 because the prophecy tells us that it comes up out of the earth (to rule Jerusalem) *after* the beast which comes up out of the sea (the Islamic empire)

- completed its work *before* 1967 because, after that, the Jews were back in control of both Israel and Jerusalem

- was either a composite of two different powers (like the two horns of the Medo Persian empire), or the same power but at two different times - or a combination of both of these (two horns)

- persecuted the Jews - because that's the whole point of this vision.

Once again we don't have to guess the identity of this beast because history tells us which powers meet these criteria – in fact we met them, earlier:

| **Kingdoms** | **Controlled Jerusalem** |
|---|---|
| 1. Rashidun Caliphate | 638 - 661 |
| 2. Umayyad Caliphate | 661 - 750 |
| 3. Abbasid Caliphate | 750 – 878 & 904 - 969 |
| 4. Tulunid Dynasty | 878 - 904 |
| 5. Fatimid Caliphate | 969 – 1073 & 1098 -1099 |

| | |
|---|---|
| 6. Seljuk Dynasty | 1073 - 1098 |
| **7. First Crusader Kingdom** | **1099 - 1187** |
| 8. Ayyubid Sultanate | 1187 - 1259 |
| 9. Mamluk Sultanate | 1260 - 1517 |
| 10. Ottoman Empire | 1517 - 1917 |
| **11. British Empire** | **1917 - 1948** |
| 12. Kingdom of Jordan | 1948 - 1967 |

As you can see, there are two powers on this list in addition to the ten Islamic kingdoms. The first of these was the Catholic Crusader Kingdom which was in control of Jerusalem in the 88-year period between 1099 and 1187.

The second power was the British Empire which had control of Jerusalem (and the territory of what is now modern-day Israel) during the so-called 'Mandate' period in the roughly 30 years between the defeat of the Ottoman Empire during the first world war, and the re-establishment of Israel in 1948.

But do these powers also meet the conditions set out in the remainder of the prophecy in chapter 13 where the second beast is described in detail and we're told that:

> [11] *... it had two horns like a lamb, but it spoke like a dragon.* ***(Revelation 13:11)***

> [12] *It exercised all the authority of the first beast on its behalf and made the earth and its inhabitants worship the first beast, whose fatal wound had been healed.*

*[13] And it performed great signs, even causing fire to come down from heaven to the earth in full view of the people. [14] Because of the signs it was given power to perform on behalf of the first beast, it deceived the inhabitants of the earth. It ordered them to set up an image in honor of the beast who was wounded by the sword and yet lived.*

*[15] The second beast was given power to give breath to the image of the first beast, so that the image could speak and cause all who refused to worship the image to be killed.* ***(Revelation 13:11-15)***

Let's see if this aligns with history:

- Although they were almost a thousand years apart, the Crusader Kingdom and the British Empire were both regarded as 'Christian' kingdoms ('two horns like a lamb').

- The Crusaders first exercised this dominion after they captured Jerusalem from the Fatimids in 1099 – an event which ended (killed) the influence of Islam over Jerusalem for almost 90 years. But when Saladin defeated the Crusaders in 1187 this 'fatal wound was healed' and Islam was back in control for almost another 800 years.

- World War One marked the first large-scale use of military aviation and the British and their allies made use of aircraft and bombing extensively in their campaign against the Ottomans - literally 'causing fire to come down from heaven'.

- During their time in charge, both the Crusaders and the British had complete dominion over the territory and people of Jerusalem and further afield ('they exercised all the authority of the first 'Islamic' beast').

- The British period of control of the Holy Land was by authority of a Mandate granted by the League of Nations in 1920. This followed just three years after the 1917 Balfour Declaration in which the Brits committed themselves to the establishment of a Jewish homeland in 'Palestine'. Their Mandate stipulated a requirement to allow 'freedom of conscience and religion' in the territory but, in reality, the British spent the next almost 30 years promoting the interests of the Islamic powers of the Middle East in an effort to protect their own strategic and economic interests. As a 'Christian' nation and an Empire which had spent much of the previous 400 years bringing Christianity to far-flung parts of the planet, the British might have been expected to give priority to the establishment of a Jewish state. Instead, they increasingly restricted Jewish immigration (especially after 1939) and suppressed Jewish paramilitary activity – while at the same time promoting Islamic interests. Over the course of the thirty years between 1918 and 1948, Britain also established new Islamic nations in Jordan, Iraq and Kuwait - allowing Islam to recover and thrive in that part of the world.

- The situation in the Middle East today is an enduring legacy of British policy during the Mandate period. The British re-established the former Islamic order over the Middle East through its actions ('it set up an image in honour of Islam') and 'gave breath' (authority) to that order.

Viewed like this, there can now be no doubt about the identity of 'the beast out of the earth' which enforced continued worship of the first beast (Islam) and a continuation of the antisemitic spirit of Islam.

**Daniel Chapter 7**

This crucial role of the British, in particular, in enforcing Islam over this time is also echoed in chapter 7 of the Book of Daniel. Let's pick up the prophecy at the point where Daniel is being introduced to the Islamic Beast which controlled Jerusalem between 688 and 1948:

> [7] *.....and behold a fourth beast (Islam), dreadful and terrible, and strong exceedingly; and it had great iron teeth: it devoured and brake in pieces and stamped the residue with the feet of it: and it was diverse from all the beasts that were before it; and it had ten horns.*
>
> [8] *I considered the horns, and behold, there came up among them another little horn, before whom there were three of the first horns plucked up by the roots: and behold, in this horn were eyes like the eyes of man, and a mouth speaking great things.* ***(Daniel 7:7-8)***

And again:

> [24] *And the ten horns out of this kingdom are ten kings that shall arise: and another shall rise after them; and he shall be diverse from the first, and he shall subdue three kings. 25 And he shall speak great words against the most High and shall wear out the saints of the most High and think to change times and laws: and they shall be given into his hand until a time and times and half a time.* ***(Daniel 7:24-25)***

Once again, this is a perfect echo of history. Britain was the 'little horn' which 'plucked up' (created) the three entirely new nations of (Trans)Jordan, Iraq and Kuwait.

The prophecy regarding 'speaking great words reflects British policy against the establishment of a Jewish homeland - summarised in a 1939 White Paper which severely restricted Jewish immigration to 'Palestine', in direct opposition to God.

Britain also fulfilled the prophecy that this power would "think to change times and laws." Under the Ottoman system, time was ordered by the Islamic calendar and law was administered under Sharia law. With the collapse of Ottoman rule and the beginning of the British Mandate, both were overturned by Britain which imposed the Gregorian calendar for civil administration and replaced centuries of Islamic legal tradition with British common law and Mandate ordinances. In so doing, it literally altered the way time was measured and the framework by which justice and society were ordered.

But even more significantly, Britain changed the "times" in a prophetic sense. By issuing the Balfour Declaration in 1917, then later restricting further Jewish immigration to the Land, Britain positioned itself as the decisive power shaping the destiny of the Jewish people in their homeland. It gave with one hand and took away with the other, controlling the "appointed times" of Israel's restoration.

Thus, Britain was not only the "little horn" that plucked up new kingdoms from the Ottoman carcass, but also the power that enforced new times and laws. Viewed through this lens, Daniel's words mirror fulfilled history and Britain stands revealed as the prophesied power that rose after Islam, altered the calendar and the law, and dictated the prophetic timetable of the Jewish return.

In every respect, these prophecies highlight that the Crusader Kingdom and Great Britain are the only powers that meet all of these criteria - a reality which is even further reinforced in the most surprising of places:

### Daniel Chapter 11

We now know that Chapter 11 in the Book of Daniel is part of a broader vision which starts in Chapter 10 and goes all the way through till the end of Chapter 12. This is the final vision that Daniel recorded for us and its purpose was to provide a summary of some of the prophetic history which took place during the period of 'time, times and half a time' (two and a half thousand years) which culminated in the ending of the scattering of the holy people.

The prophecy begins with yet another reference to Alexander the Great then continues as a summary which highlights the changing fortunes of those who controlled Jerusalem over the next 2,300 years. This timeline is extraordinary and outlines the events which affected the holy land between Alexander the Great in 333BC and the withdrawal of the British in 1948 and is covered, in detail in Chapter 61 of *Prophecy Shock.*

For now, we'll pick up from verse 36, about halfway through several verses which have provided an extremely accurate description of the control of Jerusalem, by Islam. Let's see what it says next:

> *[36] "The king (Islam) will do as he pleases. He will exalt and magnify himself above every god and will say unheard-of things against the God of gods. He will be successful until the time of wrath is completed, for what has been determined must take place. [37] He will show no regard for the gods of his ancestors or for the one desired by women, nor will he regard any god, but will exalt himself above them all. [38] Instead of them, he will honor a god of fortresses; a god unknown to his ancestors he will honor with gold and silver, with precious stones and costly gifts. [39] He will attack the mightiest fortresses with the help of a foreign god and will greatly honor those who acknowledge him. He will make them rulers over many people and will distribute the land at a price.*
>
> *[40] "At the time of the end the king of the South will engage him in battle, and the king of the North will storm out against him with chariots and cavalry and a great fleet of ships. He will invade many countries and sweep through them like a flood. [41] He will also invade*

*the Beautiful Land. Many countries will fall, but Edom, Moab and the leaders of Ammon will be delivered from his hand.* [42] *He will extend his power over many countries; Egypt will not escape.* [43] *He will gain control of the treasures of gold and silver and all the riches of Egypt, with the Libyans and Cushites in submission.* [44] *But reports from the east and the north will alarm him, and he will set out in a great rage to destroy and annihilate many.* [45] ***He will pitch his royal tents between the seas at the beautiful holy mountain. Yet he will come to his end, and no one will help him. (Daniel 11:36-45)***

From verse 40 onward the prophecy describes the defeat of the Ottomans, by the British (the King of the North), who swept through the Middle East 'like a flood'. Britain controlled most of this part of the world for the next (almost) 30 years, establishing an administrative Capital (his Royal Tents) in Jerusalem. Britain's time in the Middle East was characterised by the re-alignment of the region and concessions to Islamic interests in return for long-term access to oil and trade routes.

However, its time in control of Jerusalem was not a happy one and the advent of World War Two, the subsequent rise of the Soviet Union ('alarming reports from the North and East') and increasing resistance by Jews returning to 'Palestine' led it to make the decision to withdraw from that territory in 1948 - fulfilling the prophecy that its time there would 'come to an end'.

The prophecy is a match with history in every respect – so let's see how it lines up against the Six Basic Questions.

**Question 1: What's being predicted?**

That a second beast will also control Jerusalem – twice - during the 42 months (1,278.3 years).

**Questions 2 & 3: Who was the prophecy delivered to and who is it about?**

Once again, the prophecy is for Christians - but given that it follows on immediately after the prophecy of the beast coming up out of the sea, we can be certain that it is still *about* the Jews.

**Question 4 & 5: When does the prophecy start and end?**

Although the prophecy of the second beast in Revelation 13 doesn't provide specific starting and ending years, we know that it takes place within the 42 months (1278.3 years) counted backward between 1967 and 688. This makes identification of this new beast easy because only two powers, other than Islam, controlled Jerusalem over that time and they both meet all of the other criteria in the prophecy - the 'Christian' Crusaders and the British. This aligns with history and describes, accurately, the events which took place over this time.

**The identity of the second beast**

One of the great tragedies of the many attempts at prophecy interpretation over the past fifty or more years has been the extent to which so many of them have misappropriated prophecies which are clearly about the Jews and have superimposed Christian themes on them. The prophecy of the second beast, in Revelation chapter 13, is a case in point. It is not about an antichrist figure and his sidekick who will persecute Western Christians in the last days. It is warning that two 'beasts' acting under the control of the devil would occupy Jerusalem for over 1,300 years and that, between them, they would persecute the Jews and attempt to ensure that they could never re-establish a Jewish kingdom in the Holy Land.

Ten Horns (the Islamic Beast) and Two horns, like a lamb, but speaking like a dragon (Britain and the Crusaders).

**Britain's fall from grace**

Some of my British readers may be offended by this chapter. After all, the British role in standing against the tyranny and error of Catholicism and spreading the gospel between the 16th and 19th centuries was a key part of God's plan for mankind - and was amply rewarded in the many blessings which were bestowed upon that empire over that time.

But by the early 20th century the British had moved away from their role as guardians of the Great Commission - and by the time they took control of the Middle East their part in the drama playing out in Revelation had already been cast.

**The two faces of Christianity**

But isn't there a contradiction in this solution? If the Catholic Crusaders and the Protestant British were the 'two horns, like a Lamb' of Revelation 13 – how do we reconcile their role with a passage in Chapter 12, earlier in this same vision:

*[17] Then the dragon was enraged at the woman and went off to wage war against the rest of her offspring - those who keep God's commands and hold fast their testimony about Jesus.* ***(Revelation 12: 17)***

Surely the reference to 'those who keep God's commands and hold fast their testimony about Jesus' is also about Christians - who are referred to as 'the rest of the woman's offspring' in the prophecy. So how can Christians be referred to as 'the woman's offspring', here – while also being responsible for some of the most vicious persecution of Jews down through the centuries?

This confusion arises because two forms of Christianity have existed throughout history made up of those who are truly saved - and those who are not. Remember, Christ warned us, in Matthew 24, that many would come ***'in His name'*** and spread deception (false Christianity) - so we need to be careful to distinguish between those Christians who obediently followed God and those 'Christians' and organisations which acted as surrogates for the devil, and which waged war against real believers.

True conversion to the Christian faith is always based on a free personal decision and any organisation which has persecuted Jews or has promoted conversion to Christianity, by force, wasn't truly 'Christian' and was enforcing obedience to a false form of Christianity.

We'll cover this in a lot more detail later in the book

*The solution at a glance*

# The beast out of the earth

***Scriptures:*** *Revelation 13:11-15*

1. **What's being predicted??**
   That a second (two horned) beast will also control Jerusalem – twice - during the 42 months..

2. **Who is being spoken to?**
   John, warning **the churches**.

3. **Who is the prophecy about?**
   **The Jews** – and another power that also kept them out of Jerusalem.

4. **How long does it last?**
   Two separate stints of control inside the wider Islamic era:
   **Crusader Kingdom of Jerusalem (Catholic, 1099-1187)**
   **British Empire (Protestant-ruled, 1918-1948)**

5. **When does it end?**
   **1948 AD** – Britain pulls out, Israel is reborn, and the Holy land slips from Gentile hands for the last time.

**Both powers ruled Jerusalem, persecuted Jews, and "gave breath" to the Islamic order**. Their combined 118 years of direct control sit squarely inside the 1,278-year Islamic window (688-1967), perfectly matching Revelation's sequence. Once again, the text is literal, exact, and laser-focused on Jewish history.

# 46

# Banished to the Wilderness

## The Prophecies of 2,500 years and 1,260 days

which appear in **Revelation 12:6** and **12:14** in the

| 1st Vision | 2nd Vision | 3rd Vision | 4th Vision | 5th Vision | 6th Vision | 7th Vision |
|---|---|---|---|---|---|---|
| **The history of the Church** | **The trials of believers** | **The history of the gentiles** | **The origin of anti-semitism** | **The last plagues** | **The fall of Babylon** | **The reign of Christ** |
| *Rev Ch 1-3* | *Rev Ch 4-8.1* | *Rev Ch 8.2-11* | *Rev Ch 12-14* | *Rev Ch 15-16, 19-20* | *Rev Ch 17-18* | *Rev Ch 21-22* |

So now we know that two beasts (The Islamic ten-horned beast and the 'Christian' two-horned' beast) controlled Jerusalem for over 1,300 years.

We also know that the Jews were largely *in the wilderness* over this time – in fact scripture spells this out explicitly.

In Chapter 43 of *Prophecy Shock* we identified two time-defined prophecies which both provided countdowns of that time:

- In Revelation Chapter 12, verse 6 we're told that 'the woman' was in the wilderness for **1,260 days**.
- In Revelation Chapter 12, verse 12, we're told that she was in the wilderness for "**time, times and half a time**."

At first glance, these look like competing timelines – but in reality, they are two countdowns to the same finish line, viewed from different angles. As with the previous vision in Revelation, both are counted backwards from a known end year: 1948 – the year that the

Jews returned to the Holy Land after being 'in the wilderness' for centuries.

Let's look at each prophecy in turn.

**The 1,260-year "wilderness" – the Jews shut out**

*"The woman fled into the wilderness to a place prepared for her by God, where she might be taken care of for 1,260 days."* ***(Revelation 12:6)***

We encountered '1,260 days' in the Third Vision in Revelation 11:3–4 - the Vision of the History of the Gentiles - where it marked a 1,260-year period between 688 and 1948 and described the long era in which the Jews, as one of the two "witnesses," were effectively closed out of the Holy Land. So is Revelation 12 talking about the same events? Let's check using the Six Basic Questions:

**What's being predicted?**
That the Jews ("the woman") will leave the Holy Land and live elsewhere, under God's protection, for 1,260 prophetic "days" (1,260 years).

**Who is it addressed to?**
As with the rest of Revelation, it's addressed to Christians.

**Who is it about?**
The opening description of the sun, moon and stars clearly echoes Joseph's dream in Genesis 37, where Jacob himself interprets these symbols as himself, his wife and his sons – so the "woman" is Israel and this is a prophecy about the Jews.

**How long does it last and when does it end?**
The time span is 1,260 days/years – counted backward from 1948.

# 1948 – 1,260 years = **688 AD**

| **The Prophecy of another 1,260 Days**<br>Revelation 12:1-6 | | | |
|---|---|---|---|
| **What's being predicted?** | *That the Jews will flee from the Holy Land to a location in 'the wilderness' where they will be protected for 1,260 years* | | |
| **Question** | **Clue from Scripture** | **Math** | **Solution** |
| **Who is the prophecy addressed to?** | *"...Jesus Christ ... to show His servants" (Revelation 1:1)* | | **The prophecy is addressed to Christians** |
| **Who is the prophecy about?** | *"...a woman clothed with the sun ... the moon ... and 12 stars..." (Revelation 12:1)* | | **The prophecy is about Israel** |
| **What year does the prophecy end?** | *The year in which Israel ('the woman') was re-established* | ***1948*** | **The prophecy ends in 1948** |
| **How long will the prophecy last?** | *"...The woman fled into the wilderness... for 1,260 days." (Revelation 12:6)* | ***minus 1,260*** | **The prophecy will last for 1,260 years** |
| **What year does the prophecy begin?** | | ***equals 688*** | **The prophecy begins in 688 AD** |

So, once again, the commencement of the construction of the Dome of the Rock is a pivotal year and in this prophecy it marks the beginning of the period during which the Jews 'fled into the wilderness' for 1,260 years.

This also helps us to understand the meaning of a warning, given by Christ to His Jewish audience, in Matthew 24:

> *"When ye therefore shall see the abomination of desolation (the Dome of the Rock), spoken of by Daniel the prophet, stand in the holy place, (whoso readeth, let him understand:) Then let them which be in Judaea flee into the mountains: Let him which is on the housetop not come down to take anything out of his house: Neither let him which is in the field return back to take his clothes. And woe unto them that are with child, and to them that give suck in those days! But pray ye that your flight be not in the winter, neither on the sabbath day."* ***(Matthew 24:15–20)***

This is an alternative telling of Christs warning in **Luke 21:20-24**, which we covered in Chapter 36 of *Prophecy Shock.* It perfectly matches our 1,260-year solution and tells us that the Jewish population which remained in the Holy Land in 688 (the year of the "abomination" standing in the holy place) should flee – which is what most of them did.

This does not mean that no Jews returned to live in Jerusalem between 688 and 1948. History is clear that a remnant did and that there was a continuous Jewish presence there for most of that time. But the centre of Jewish life shifted decisively into Europe and the wider Middle East, and the prophecy's point is to mark that shift:

- Most Jews no longer lived in the land.
- Yet God preserved them as a distinct people through 1,260 hard years.
- When the time came for them to return, they were still recognisably "the woman" – Israel.

**The 2,500-year "wilderness" – the bigger frame**

The second "wilderness" statement comes in verse 14:

*"The woman was given the two wings of a great eagle, so that she might fly to the place prepared for her in the wilderness, where she would be taken care of for a time, times and half a time, out of the serpent's reach." **(Revelation 12:14)***

Here the time span is "time, times and half a time", which we already know, from the Book of Daniel, represents 2,500 years in prophetic shorthand.

The location hasn't changed. We're still dealing with the same "wilderness" – the dispersion of the Jews through the nations, away from their land – which means this second clock also ends in 1948, when Israel was reborn. But this time, instead of a 1,260-year window from 688 to 1948, we're being asked to count 2,500 years backwards from 1948 to find the starting point of the larger story:

1948 – 2,500 years = **552 BC**

So let's put this new information into our template:

## The Prophecy of another time, times and half a time

Revelation 12:14

| Question | Clue from Scripture | Math | Solution |
|---|---|---|---|
| **What's being predicted?** | *That the 'the woman' will return to the Holy land after being protected in 'the wilderness' for 2,500 years* | | |
| **Who is the prophecy addressed to?** | *"...Jesus Christ ... to show His servants" (Revelation 1:1)* | | **The prophecy is addressed to Christians** |
| **Who is the prophecy about?** | *"...a woman clothed with the sun ... the moon ... and 12 stars..." (Revelation 12:1)* | | **The prophecy is about Israel** |
| **What year does the prophecy end?** | *The year in which Israel was re-established and Jews started to return* | ***1948*** | **The prophecy ends in 1948** |
| **How long will the prophecy last?** | *"... that she might fly to ...the wilderness ...for a time, times and half a time" (Revelation 12:14)* | ***minus 2,500*** | **The prophecy will last for 2,500 years** |
| **What year does the prophecy begin?** | *"In the first year of Belshazzar, King of Babylon" (Daniel 7.1)* | ***equals 552*** | **The prophecy begins in 552 BC** |

552 BC is the same year we discovered in Daniel 7.1 when we reviewed the prophecy of 'time, times and half a time' that appeared there and which also pointed us to 1948:

> *7 In the first year of Belshazzar king of Babylon, Daniel had a dream, and visions passed through his mind as he was lying in bed. He wrote down the substance of his dream.*

So, this is **the same prophecy that we first encountered in Daniel** but this time the years are counted backward from 1948 to 552 BC – the first year of Belshazzar - the year in which Daniel recorded that prophecy.

**How the two clocks fit together**

Put together, the two wilderness periods in Revelation 12 are not competing or contradictory. They are nested:

- The 2,500-year span ("time, times and half a time") covers the time between 552 BC and 1948 and describes the full era of Israel's political displacement – the long story of how Gentile powers ruled over Jerusalem.

- The 1,260-year span (1,260 days/years) covers the years between 688 and 1948 and describes the intense period in which the Jews themselves fled the Holy Land in the years following the appearance of the Dome of the Rock.

**Time in the Wilderness**

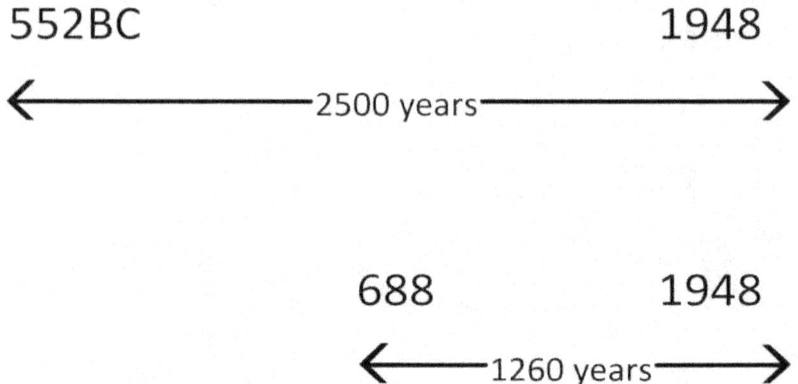


First comes the political wilderness (2,500+ years of Gentile rule over Jerusalem), then within that, the literal wilderness (1,260 years of Jewish exile from their own land). Both end together in 1948, when Israel is reborn.

By placing these two countdowns side by side in one vision, God is effectively saying:

> *"The Book of Daniel and the Book of Revelation are telling one story about the same history. Daniel gives you the long frame; Revelation gives you the inner window."*

Both ended in 1948.

*The solution at a glance*

# Time, times & half a time / 1,260 days
# The Wilderness Prophecies

***Scriptures:*** *Revelation 12:1-6, 12:14*

1. **What's being predicted??**
   That the Jewish people would be protected by God despite ongoing persecution - first in their own land (over which they would lose control), and ultimately in the nations to which they fled.

2. **Who is being spoken to?**
   John - writing to **Christians.**

3. **Who is the prophecy about?**
   The "woman clothed with the sun" = **Israel** (Genesis 37).

4. **When does it end?**
   **1948:** Two prophecies, both marking the end of exile.

5. **How long does it last?**
   Two prophecies are repeated to ensure we get it: "1,260 days" = 1,260 years. "Time, times, and half a time" = 2,500 years.

5. **When does it start?**
   **552BC** to 1948 and **688 AD** to 1948

These prophecies don't contradict each other – they affirm the same year of conclusion – **1948** – the year the Jewish people started coming home. Once again, Daniel and Revelation are linked.

47

# The Holocaust

If we stand back we can now see that *the Vision of the Origin of Antisemitism* is an unmistakable retelling of the history of the Jewish people over the past 2,000 years.

But something is missing.

There's no mention of **the Holocaust** (or the Shoah, as it is known by the Jews).

**The Holocaust / Shoah**

Between 1942 and 1945, six million Jews - men, women, and children - were systematically hunted down and murdered across Europe in the most industrialised act of antisemitism in human history. This was not a pogrom, an expulsion, or a localised persecution. It was a continent-wide project of extermination, driven by a modern state, using bureaucracy, technology, rail networks, camps, quotas, and paperwork to pursue what earlier ages could only attempt in bursts: the near eradication of an entire people. The scale was unprecedented; the intent unmistakable.

The Holocaust was not simply another chapter in Jewish suffering – it was a rupture in history. A civilisational collapse in which modern order was harnessed to mass murder – and it didn't appear in a vacuum. The animating hatred had been cultivated for centuries through church doctrine, blood libels, expulsions, ghettos, racial theories, and nationalist myths, long before the Nazis converted it into state policy.

But the result – referred to by the Nazis as 'The Final Solution' - was a catastrophe so vast that it reshaped global politics, conscience, and history itself - directly feeding the post-war urgency that culminated in the rebirth of Israel in 1948.

So the absence of this atrocity from the prophecies in the Book of Revelation – particularly the Vision of antisemitism – seems like an extraordinary oversight.

Did God somehow miss this?

**A confirmation of Israelism**

No, He didn't. Instead, the absence of the Holocaust / Shoah from this vision is a significant confirmation of the interpretative framework that we have outlined in *Prophecy Shock*.

Why? Because Hitler never controlled Jerusalem. As such, he wasn't one of the 'beasts' outlined in Daniel and Revelation – no matter how much some prophecy interpretations might try to frame him in that role.

This book has repeatedly demonstrated that the prophecies in the Visions of the History of the Gentiles and the Origin of Antisemitism are *always* told through the lens of the relationship of the Jewish people with Jerusalem and the Gentile powers that ruled that city.

But Nazi Germany never ruled Jerusalem. Not once. No German soldier ever marched through its gates; no swastika was ever raised over its walls. At the height of Axis expansion in 1942, Rommel's army was halted in Egypt at El Alamein, still hundreds of kilometres from the Holy Land, and was soon driven into full retreat. Jerusalem remained under British control throughout the war. So, although Nazi influence brushed the region - none of this came anywhere near amounting to sovereignty over the Jerusalem itself.

Hitler's regime never intersected with Jerusalem's sovereignty, never displaced its rulers, and never occupied the city itself – so it simply does not meet the prophetic criteria for inclusion in the chain of "beasts".

Once that controlling principle is understood, the absence of Nazi Germany from those visions is not an embarrassment or an omission. It is precisely what the framework predicts.

However, this does not mean that the Holocaust is absent from biblical prophecy. Elsewhere in Scripture there are several passages that speak with chilling clarity of an unprecedented catastrophe falling upon the Jewish people - a time of suffering so severe that it stands apart from all that came before it, yet one from which a remnant would nevertheless emerge.

Daniel records one such statement:

*"And at that time shall Michael stand up, the great prince which standeth for the children of thy people: and there shall be a time of trouble, such as never was since there was a nation even to that same time: and at that time thy people shall be delivered, every one that shall be found written in the book."* ***(Daniel 12:1)***

The language is unmistakable. This is not merely another episode of hardship or exile. It describes a singular national crisis - "a time of trouble, such as never was since there was a nation" - explicitly tied to *thy people*: Israel. Yet it is also marked by deliverance, survival, and continuity beyond the catastrophe.

Jeremiah echoes the same pattern:

*"Alas! for that day is great, so that none is like it: it is even the time of Jacob's trouble; but he shall be saved out of it."* ***(Jeremiah 30:7)***

Again, the defining features are the same: a uniquely unparalleled calamity, centred on Jacob - the Jewish people - followed not by extinction, but by survival.

These passages establish that Scripture anticipated a climactic crisis for Israel - a moment of unparalleled darkness, followed by preservation rather than obliteration.

Yet even these sobering texts are not the most direct statement that scripture makes about this catastrophe.

There is one brief sentence spoken by Yeshua Himself - stark, restrained, and deeply unsettling - which speaks not only to the scale of the suffering, but to the fact that it would be *halted before total destruction could occur*.

Its meaning only becomes fully clear once the prophetic timeline of the Great Tribulation has been properly understood – and we will cover that in more detail later in Chapter 65 of this book.

# The Misunderstood Mark

## The Prophecy of the Mark of the Beast

which appears in **Revelation 13:14-18** in the

| 1st Vision | 2nd Vision | 3rd Vision | 4th Vision | 5th Vision | 6th Vision | 7th Vision |
|---|---|---|---|---|---|---|
| **The history of the Church** | **The trials of believers** | **The history of the gentiles** | **The origin of anti-semitism** | **The last plagues** | **The fall of Babylon** | **The reign of Christ** |
| *Rev Ch 1-3* | *Rev Ch 4-8.1* | *Rev Ch 8.2-11* | *Rev Ch 12-14* | *Rev Ch 15-16, 19-20* | *Rev Ch 17-18* | *Rev Ch 21-22* |

Earlier, we examined the real meaning of the prophecy of 'the beast out of the earth'. We discovered that it was an extension of the theme of the prophecy of 'the beast out of the sea' (Islam) and that it explained how the two 'Christian' powers that controlled Jerusalem continued to persecute the Jews and keep them out of their ancient homeland.

But we haven't yet examined the most infamous section of that prophecy, which also appears in chapter 13:

> *[14] Because of the signs it was given power to perform on behalf of the first beast, it deceived the inhabitants of the earth. It ordered them to set up an image in honor of the beast who was wounded by the sword and yet lived.*

*[15] The second beast was given power to give breath to the image of the first beast, so that the image could speak and cause all who refused to worship the image to be killed.*

*[16] It forced all people, great and small, rich and poor, free and slave, to receive a mark on their right hands or on their foreheads, [17] so that they could not buy or sell unless they had the mark, which is the name of the beast or the number of its name.*

*[18] This calls for wisdom. Let the person who has insight calculate the number of the beast, for it is the number of a man. That number is 666.* ***(Revelation 13:14-18)***

There is unlikely to be anyone reading this who has not heard of 666 - the number/mark of the beast. Even people unfamiliar with the Bible know of this number and it has become all pervasive in popular culture. 666 appears in movies, music and television as a metaphor for evil and evil people throughout history. Secular groups use it as a symbol for the dark side. Christian groups use it as a means by which to identify people who they believe to have an antichristian agenda.

Premillennialists contend that the mark represents a direct challenge to Christians in the last days and will take the form of some sort of State sanctioned ID that will be required in order to transact the necessities of life.

They claim that, at some point, the process of accepting this mark will be bound up in some sort of oath or declaration of allegiance to the 'antichrist' and that this will require Christians to denounce Christ and worship Satan in order to survive.

However, once again, this ignores every previous vision in the Books of Daniel and Revelation where the beasts have always been representations of the empires that have controlled Jerusalem. As such, we need to take care to understand what the prophecy is really telling us - particularly about who is enforcing this mark and who is receiving it.

**The Image of the Beast**

In the previous chapter in this book we reviewed the role of the British during the Mandate period and learned that during their time in control of Jerusalem they changed 'times and laws' but kept existing religious structures in place in a way which guaranteed that Islam would continue to be the dominant religious force in the Middle East:

> *[15] The second beast was given power to give breath to the image of the first beast, so that the image could speak and cause all who refused to worship the image to be killed.*

This is now easy to understand – particularly when we follow the story past the British and consider what happened next.

Under the Mandate, the British (the second Beast) deliberately preserved Islamic religious institutions and leadership. They trained and equipped Arab forces, relied on Islamic authorities to maintain order, and set up political arrangements that ensured Islam would remain the dominant public religion even after they left. In prophetic terms, they "gave breath to the image of the first Beast" by creating and protecting a renewed Islamic framework that could carry on without them.

That "image" then stepped onto the stage in 1948.

When the British withdrew and war broke out, Transjordan – led by the British-trained Arab Legion – took control of East Jerusalem and the West Bank and immediately did exactly what you would expect from a revived Islamic power:

- It took full control of the Old City and East Jerusalem.
- It expelled the entire Jewish population from the Old City.

- It placed all Jewish holy sites under Islamic or Jordanian control.
- It barred Jews from the Western Wall and the Mount of Olives.
- It treated Jerusalem as an exclusively Arab–Islamic space.

In other words, the "image" created and sustained by the British was not just a vague influence. It became a real Islamic regime on the ground in Jerusalem, expressed through Transjordan (later Jordan). That regime "spoke" through its laws, its soldiers, and its administration - and its message was clear: Jewish presence and Jewish worship in Jerusalem were not permitted.

But did Jordan 'kill' those who refused to worship Islam over this time? Not specifically. While there was certainly intolerance toward non-Muslims in Middle Eastern nations (particularly extreme intolerance in nations such as Saudi Arabia, Iran, Afghanistan, Yemen and ISIS controlled parts of Iraq) – even today, we're not yet at a point where *all* who refuse to worship Islam are killed.

Nor has the next part of the prophecy yet been fulfilled:

> *[16] It (Islam) forced all people, great and small, rich and poor, free and slave, to receive a mark on their right hands or on their foreheads, [17] so that they could not buy or sell unless they had the mark..."*

As such, we can see that the fulfilment of this part of the prophecy is still ahead of us and that, at some point in the future, Islam (either just in the Middle East, or perhaps in all nations where it exercises control) will enforce (what appears to be) a form of physical identification on its followers, without which it will be impossible to carry on the necessities of life.

This fits with the practical reality that economic controls have always been the easiest way for empires to enforce loyalty. In John's own time, Roman coins and trade were tied to emperor worship. In the future, the revived Islamic system could enforce compliance not just with threats but with exclusion - tying access to jobs, trade, and survival itself to outward allegiance.

In the Transjordanian phase of Islamic control over Jerusalem, we already saw exclusion, expulsion and religious monopoly. In the future, the revived Islamic system will go further, enforcing compliance not just with threats and bans but with economic exclusion – tying access to jobs, trade, and survival itself to outward allegiance.

**What is the Mark?**

So now, with this clearer understanding, we can begin to make sense of the rest of the prophecy where we're told that:

> *"....the mark, is the name of the beast or the number of its name.*[18] *This calls for wisdom. Let the person who has insight calculate the number of the beast, for it is the number of a man. That number is 666".* ***(Revelation 13:17-18)***

At face value, the prophecy appears to be telling us that the mark is based on the name of the Islamic Beast - but which name? The last Islamic power to control Jerusalem was Jordan - but there were nine other Islamic powers which preceded that. Is it named after one of these? Or is it simply referring to the word 'Islam' or 'Islamic'? We don't know - so let's keep reading.

The prophecy goes on to tell us that, in order to identify the mark, we should calculate the 'number' of the Beast which, we're told, is '666'. We're told that this is also the number of a man.

But which man?

As you probably know, this puzzle has held the attention of Bible scholars for centuries with dozens of different theories about what this all means. Some have used Gematria (an esoteric way of calculating the numeric value of Greek and Hebrew letters) to try and identify this prophecy with famous characters from history - but most of these theories fall short, and none satisfy the criteria which we have now established based on our new understanding of this prophecy - namely that:

- The Beast which imposes the mark is the Islamic empire which controlled Jerusalem for almost 1,300 years.
- The people who are forced to receive the mark are Muslims although we don't know whether this is a reference to all Muslims or only those in the Middle East.
- The effect of the mark will be to so completely control Islamic society that those who do not have it will be unable to survive.

Since this hasn't happened yet, and since we know that prophecy is given so that God will be glorified *after* it has been fulfilled, there is little point in trying to guess what 666 refers to since any such guess will almost certainly be wrong.

**Gods reaction to the mark**

However, despite not knowing what '666' means - we can know, with certainty, that God will not be happy with those who receive it:

*"There will be no rest day or night for those who worship the beast and its image, or for anyone who receives the mark of its name." (Revelation 14:11)*

But why? Why is this punishment so harsh? The prophecy tells us:

*[11] Then I saw a second beast, coming out of the earth. It had two horns like a lamb, but it spoke like a dragon. [12] It exercised all the authority of the first beast on its behalf and made the earth and its inhabitants* ***worship*** *the first beast, whose fatal wound had been healed.* ***(Revelation 13:11-12)***

There it is.

The people who 'worship' the first beast (Islam) are Muslims – so whatever the Mark in Chapter 13 is - we can now be certain that it has nothing to do with Christians. It's about Muslims and it refers to a fulfilment of prophecy which has not yet taken place. Receiving it will somehow involve a declaration of worship, to Islam - the reason for Gods anger.

Islam explicitly denies the divinity and grace of Christ - the two things which are absolutely essential to salvation - so the mark of the Beast is simply a confirmation of what we already know. That, without Christ you will die in your sins and that truth is the same regardless of what false religion you adhere to.

**More Marks?**

However, this is not the only place in which a 'mark' or a personal 'seal' appears in the Book of Revelation. In fact, there are three other references.

One appears in Chapter 9, in **the Vision of the History of the Gentiles:**

> [9] *The fifth angel sounded his trumpet, and I saw a star (Satan) that had fallen from the sky to the earth. The star was given the key to the shaft of the Abyss.* [2] *When he opened the Abyss, smoke rose from it like the smoke from a gigantic furnace. The sun and sky were darkened by the smoke from the Abyss.* [3] *And out of the smoke locusts came down on the earth and were given power like that of scorpions of the earth.* [4] *They were told not to harm the grass of the earth or any plant or tree,* ***but only those people who did not have the seal of God on their foreheads. (Revelation 9:1-4)***

As we know, these events followed the environmental cataclysm of 536 AD – so this scripture is simply telling us that Jews and Christians (identified by a mark which was visible to these demonic entities) were protected and 'off limits' over that time.

But it's the other two mentions of a 'mark' to which we will turn our attention in the next Chapter. These are two references to the same mark but appearing in two different visions – and precisely *where* they appear might surprise you.

*The solution at a glance*

## The mark of the beast

***Scripture:*** *Revelation 13:14-18*

1. **What's being predicted??**
   That all Muslims will be required to accept a 'mark' – without which they will not be able to buy or sell.

2. **Who is being spoken to?**
   John, warning **the churches**.

3. **Who is the prophecy about?**
   Muslims. It's not aimed at Christians - it's enforced by Islam.

4. **What is the mark?**
   A yet-to-be-seen symbol of allegiance to the beast, based on the number 666, that will define who belongs inside Islamic society – but accepting it will be spiritual treason to God.

5. **Who is behind it?**
   Islam - "the image of the beast" - revived under British rule during the Mandate and empowered to dominate again.

The mark of the beast isn't random. It's real, religious, and deadly serious - because it separates allegiance to Christ from allegiance to a system that has long stood against Him.

49

# Sealed for Zion

## The Prophecy of 144,000

which appears in **Revelation 14:1** in the

| 1st Vision | 2nd Vision | 3rd Vision | 4th Vision | 5th Vision | 6th Vision | 7th Vision |
|---|---|---|---|---|---|---|
| **The history of the Church** | **The trials of believers** | **The history of the gentiles** | **The origin of anti-semitism** | **The last plagues** | **The fall of Babylon** | **The reign of Christ** |
| *Rev Ch 1-3* | *Rev Ch 4-8.1* | *Rev Ch 8.2-11* | *Rev Ch 12-14* | *Rev Ch 15-16, 19-20* | *Rev Ch 17-18* | *Rev Ch 21-22* |

Each of the first three visions in the Book of Revelation was defined by a group of seven which helped us to understand the parameters of the vision and also helped us to track its fulfilment.

**The Vision of the History of the Church** was defined by 7 Church ages. Six of these have passed and we are living in the seventh.

**The Vision of the trials of believers** was defined by seven seals. Six of these have been opened with one still left to be opened.

**The Vision of the history of the gentiles** was defined by seven trumpets. Six of these have been blown and one – the seventh trumpet – will usher in the events which lead to the end of the age.

But what about the **Vision of the Origin of Antisemitism** – is that also defined by 'seven'?

It certainly is – and these seven events tie together everything that Satan has thrown at the Jews over the past 2,000+ years. Let's review what he tried to do:

1. He tried to kill Jesus in infancy. He failed
2. He tried to kill Jesus on the Cross. He failed.
3. He tried to assimilate the Jews into the nations to which they had migrated. He failed.
4. He created a new beast (Islam) to so dominate the Middle East that the Jews could never return to Israel. He failed.
5. He raised up a second beast (defined by false Christianity) to ensure that the Jews could never return to Israel or Jerusalem. He failed.
6. Right now, he is rallying the entire world against Israel and the Jewish people in an attempt to bring about the end of Israel through political means. He will fail.
7. In a final, last stand, he will go to war against Christ Himself. He will fail.

And what do these seven things all have in common? **The Messiah's mission – centred on Zion.**

Even if you're reading this as a Jew and don't accept the Christian claim that Yeshua is the Messiah, you are still awaiting the Messiah to appear in Jerusalem as the stage of His earthly rule. **So, either way, the adversary's objective is the same: to frustrate God's covenant purpose by ensuring that the Messiah can't fulfil His mission in Zion.**

Satan isn't omnipresent – but he knows that the Jews must be back in their own land, including Jerusalem, in order for the Messiah to complete His mission – so his overwhelming focus, for the past 2,000+ years, has been on trying to prevent that from happening.

And he's not done yet. As you read this, the prophecies relating to Islamic and 'Christian' control over Jerusalem are behind us and the

Jews are back in control of their ancient homeland – but the vision makes clear that the intense hatred of Jews is still with us because the devil hasn't yet achieved his ultimate goal.

Right now, he is beside himself with rage and is turning up the intensity of his hatred of the Jews in a thousand different ways on a thousand different fronts. But he will fail.

**The Mark of the Jews**

In the chapter dealing with the prophecy of the Mark of the Beast we discovered that this mark will be a form of identification which will be required of all Muslims and without which no follower of Islam will be able to buy or sell. But there's another prophecy beyond that which completes **the Vision of the Origin of Antisemitism** – and it's a prophecy of another mark. But this time the mark will be given to Jews.

If this claim surprises you - it's because this is another occasion where the real meaning of the prophecy has been obscured by the insertion of a break in the scriptural narrative where there was no break in the original text.

Let's read the passage as it was originally written, ignoring the chapter breaks:

> *16 It (Islam) forced all people, great and small, rich and poor, free and slave, to receive a mark on their right hands or on their foreheads, 17 so that they could not buy or sell unless they had the mark, which is the name of the beast or the number of its name.*
>
> *18 This calls for wisdom. Let the person who has insight calculate the number of the beast, for it is the number of a man. That number is 666.*

*[14] Then I looked, and there before me was the Lamb, standing on Mount Zion, and with him 144,000 who had his name and his Father's name written on their foreheads. (Revelation* ***13:11-18 to 14:1)***

Simply by removing the artificial break, we can now see that the prophecy is about two marks - one given to Muslims and one given to 144,000 Jews who are pictured standing on Mt Zion with Christ.

This is a repeat of the same events that we saw in **the Vision of the Trials of Believers** in chapter 7 of Revelation where we were told that this 'mark of God' was used to 'set apart' 12,000 Jews from each of the twelve tribes of Israel (144,000).

Various Premillennial interpretations have attempted to claim that these are last days Christians - but that's not what scripture says. In fact, the Bible is very specific about who these people, who join Yeshua in Jerusalem at the end of the last days, actually are:

*[4] And I heard the number of them which were sealed: and there were sealed a hundred and forty and four thousand* ***of all the tribes of the children of Israel. (Revelation 7:4)***

But why is this group going to be brought together and what is Gods purpose in doing so? We're not told here - but we can see that their assembly marks the close of the 2,000+ years during which Satan has tried to exterminate the Jews – and this passage demonstrates his utter failure to do so because, in it, the Jews have not only survived but they're on Mt Zion in Jerusalem!

So despite the devils best attempts to make the Middle East his fortress, and to persecute Jews wherever they fled to around the world - God has prevailed and the Jews are now back in their land, back in their holy city and will soon be the recipients of an unexpected visitor - Jesus Christ, the Creator of the Universe.

*[11] And it shall come to pass in that day, that the Lord shall set his hand again the second time to recover the remnant of **his people**, which shall be left, from Assyria, and from Egypt, and from Pathros, and from Cush, and from Elam, and from Shinar, and from Hamath, and **from the islands of the sea**.*

*[12] And he shall set up an ensign for the nations, and shall assemble **the outcasts of Israel**, and gather together **the dispersed of Judah** from the four corners of the earth.* ***(Isaiah 11:11-12)***

Both of these scriptures began to be fulfilled in 1948 and are still being fulfilled to this day – but this next scripture is still entirely future:

*[30] At that time the sign of the Son of Man will appear in heaven, and all the tribes of the earth will mourn. They will see the Son of Man coming on the clouds of heaven, with power and great glory. [31] And He will send out His angels with a loud trumpet call, and they will*

*gather **His elect** from the four winds, from one end of the heavens to the other.* ***(Matthew 24:30-31)***

So we can now see that the prophecy in Revelation 7:4 is part of the bigger picture of the return of the Jews to Israel which will be completed with the return of the Lord to Mt Zion at some stage in the near future – a scene which rounds out the full vision which started in chapter 12.

It started with the Jews first losing control of their land and then being exiled to other nations while Islam set up camp in the Holy Land for almost 1,300 years. It ends with the Jews back in their own land, just prior to the return of Yeshua - coinciding with the current moment in history.

Like the previous visions, the remainder of this one goes on to detail events which are yet future - including a reference to 'the fall of Babylon' in the 8th verse.

This will prove to be significant when we come to the sixth vision, a little later.

But, for now – let's summarise what we've learnt from the 4th vision:

# 50

## The meaning of the Vision of the Origin of Antisemitism

which appears in **Revelation Chapters 12 to 14**

| 1st Vision | 2nd Vision | 3rd Vision | 4th Vision | 5th Vision | 6th Vision | 7th Vision |
|---|---|---|---|---|---|---|
| **The history of the Church** | **The trials of believers** | **The history of the gentiles** | **The origin of anti-semitism** | **The last plagues** | **The fall of Babylon** | **The reign of Christ** |
| *Rev Ch 1-3* | *Rev Ch 4-8.1* | *Rev Ch 8.2-11* | *Rev Ch 12-14* | *Rev Ch 15-16, 19-20* | *Rev Ch 17-18* | *Rev Ch 21-22* |

In the Book of Daniel we were introduced to prophecies that landed on the key years of 1948 and 1967 – two of the most important years in modern Israeli history.

Then, in *the Vision of the History of the Gentiles*, these years appeared again – but this time, all four of the time-defined prophecies in that Vision counted time toward 688 – the year that the Dome of the Rock appeared on the Temple Mount in Jerusalem.

Now, in this next vision, we saw these years come together again – but this time the focus is on a succession of Characters and the extraordinary message of ***the Vision of the origin of Antisemitism*** *(Chapters 12 to 14 of the Book of Revelation)*. The Vision outlines the way that the world has treated the Jewish people over the past 2,000 years and reveals that the centuries of persecution, violence and hatred toward them were no historical accident. It also outlines the implementation of a Satanic plan which was intended to eradicate the Jewish people, wherever they were found, so as to ensure that there would be no 'Jerusalem' for Yeshua to return to at the end of the age.

However, God knew all of this in advance and ordered events accordingly and when the artificial chapter breaks are removed and the vision is read as one continuous narrative, it becomes a single, coherent story with a clear beginning, middle, and end:

- The Messiah was born into the world.
- Satan attempted to destroy Him as an infant – but failed.
- Satan engineered Christ's crucifixion, believing this would stop God's plan. Instead it sealed Satan's defeat.
- Satan's hostility was redirected toward the Jewish people who he drove into 'the wilderness'.
- **The Beast out of the Sea** arose: Islamic powers dominated Jerusalem for centuries and prevented Jewish restoration.
- **The Beast out of the Earth** arose: Christian powers, (the Crusaders and later the British Empire), also controlled Jerusalem and continued to deny Jewish sovereignty.
- Hatred of the Jews persevered through history – but they survived repeated attempts at destruction and erasure.
- Israel was reborn as a nation in 1948.
- Jerusalem was restored to Jewish control in 1967.
- Opposition to the Jews intensified rather than disappeared.
- The conflict continues into the present day.... *and beyond.*

### Islam in the 21st century

So this vision makes clear that **the restoration of Israel did not end the hostility toward them**. Although the Islamic beast's control of Jerusalem has now ended – Islam, itself, has not yet been destroyed and, as we will see, Islam continues to appear in the next three visions. In fact, the conflict will intensify because the core issue is the same spiritual hostility driving the same Satanic objective: to prevent the Messiah from returning to Jerusalem. This will explain why, in spite of the Jews being back in control of their homeland, Islam is still a dominant driver of global antisemitism and continues to be behind initiatives to separate them from that land.

**What's next?**

So now we can finally understand the reason that antisemitism exists: it was Satan's response to the events closing in around him.

While many Christians have been *waiting for the evil to start* – the reality is that the evil has been with us for over 2,000 years – targeted, unrelentingly, at the people who held the key to Christs return to Jerusalem. Yet most of us have been oblivious to it – focused, instead, on a reinvented version of the prophecies in the Book of Revelation which closes out its main players.

Satan has always understood this. He didn't know how it was all going to play out, but he knows that his incarceration - and, a thousand years later, his destruction - are part of Gods plan, and he's been doing everything that he can to stop that from happening, regardless of the cost in lives and souls. To ignore this and to pretend that Satan's wrath will be focused on a three and a half or seven year period in the future is to misunderstand Gods consistent message for humanity.

So most of the prophecies that many of us are still waiting for are actually behind us. They were about the Jews and have now been fulfilled in the Jewish re-establishment of Israel and the liberation of Jerusalem – just as God planned.

The rest of the Book of Revelation focuses on three Visions of the future – none of which contain *time-defined* clues - which means that while they give us an insight into God's plans, we won't know *when* they will take place until after they have happened.

However, we do know *who* the prophecies are about and we can glean a reasonably good idea of *what* will happen to them.

Let's explore that in the next section of this book.

# Section Seven
# THE FATE OF GOD'S ENEMIES
## AS FORETOLD IN THE BOOK OF REVELATION

51

# An Overview of the Visions of
# the fate of God's enemies

which appear in **Revelation Chapters 15** to **20** in the

| 1st Vision | 2nd Vision | 3rd Vision | 4th Vision | 5th Vision | 6th Vision | 7th Vision |
|---|---|---|---|---|---|---|
| **The history of the Church** | **The trials of believers** | **The history of the gentiles** | **The origin of anti-semitism** | **The last plagues** | **The fall of Babylon** | **The reign of Christ** |
| *Rev Ch 1-3* | *Rev Ch 4-8.1* | *Rev Ch 8.2-11* | *Rev Ch 12-14* | *Rev Ch 15-16, 19-20* | *Rev Ch 17-18* | *Rev Ch 21-22* |

When reviewing the first four Visions in the Book of Revelation we were considering events which have largely already taken place and (in the case of the third and fourth visions) included time-defined clues which helped us to identify their precise years of fulfilment.

But neither of those things is true of the next two Visions in the Book of Revelation. Both refer to events that are entirely in the future from our current perspective, and neither of them contain time-defined clues that would allow us to know exactly when those events will take place.

However, that doesn't mean that we're completely in the dark about their details.

Although we don't know *when* these Visions will be fulfilled, we do know – with a high degree of accuracy – *who* they're about because most of the various players have already been identified in earlier solutions.

- **The fifth Vision** describes seven plagues that God will send at some stage in the future – and only one of them has a direct impact on Christians in the west.

- **The Sixth Vision** introduces a character who has been present in all four of the previous Visions but is now described in detail – along with her imminent fate.

Let's learn more about the first of these in the next chapter.

52

# The Coming Judgement

## The Vision of the Last Plagues

which appears in **Revelation Chapters 15-16; 19-20** in the

| 1st Vision | 2nd Vision | 3rd Vision | 4th Vision | 5th Vision | 6th Vision | 7th Vision |
|---|---|---|---|---|---|---|
| **The history of the Church** | **The trials of believers** | **The history of the gentiles** | **The origin of anti-semitism** | **The last plagues** | **The fall of Babylon** | **The reign of Christ** |
| *Rev Ch 1-3* | *Rev Ch 4-8.1* | *Rev Ch 8.2-11* | *Rev Ch 12-14* | *Rev Ch 15-16, 19-20* | *Rev Ch 17-18* | *Rev Ch 21-22* |

The vision of the seven last plagues in the 15th and 16th chapters of the Book of Revelation details the beginning of Gods final judgement upon the earth and is significant because it's the first vision which deals, entirely, with events which are still future when viewed from our perspective in the second decade of the 21st century.

The vision outlines a series of plagues which will be 'poured out' from bowls evoking images of the Ten Plagues which hit Egypt during the time of the Exodus.

The plagues appear in a sequence which is summarised as follows:

1. First, ugly festering sores break out on the people who have the mark of the Beast.

2. Then, the sea turns to blood and every living thing in it dies.

3. Rivers and freshwater springs also turn to blood and become contaminated in retribution for the shedding of the blood of Gods holy people and His prophets.

4. The sun scorches people with fire which burns them - although they still don't repent and glorify God.

5. The throne of the Beast is plunged into darkness. At this point people gnaw their tongues in agony because of their sores and pain - but they still refuse to repent of what they have done.

6. The Euphrates River dries up to prepare the way for the 'kings from the east' after which 'three spirits' go out to the kings of the whole world to gather them at Megiddo in Northern Israel for the great day of God.

7. A massive earthquake hits the Middle East; Jerusalem is split into three parts and the cities of the nation's collapse; Every island 'flees' and the mountains cannot be found; Huge hailstones weighing up to 100 pounds (45 kilos) fall on people and they curse God; God destroys 'Babylon'.

In the past I've read prophecy books which outline these events over multiple chapters, detailing how they will play out. Frankly, none of these have aged well because – with the exception of a key event related to the seventh 'plague' - we're given little information to rise above anything more than a series of guesses.

That said, there *are* some things that we can surmise using logic:

- The extremity of the effects of these plagues, and the specificity of some of the affected locations, mean that we would know if they had already happened in history. They haven't.

- The first five plagues appear to take place prior to the visible return of Yeshua because a massive earthquake striking Jerusalem, the gathering of the nations at Megiddo and the destruction of Babylon are all events which coincide with His return in the other visions.

- These events could all happen very quickly - or they could take place over several weeks, or even months or years.

- Now that we understand the prior Visions in the Book of Revelation we can recognise terms like 'the mark of the beast', 'the throne of the beast', and the Euphrates River as being geographically specific to the Middle east – so these plagues are heavily skewed toward that location – with one notable exception – the destruction of 'Babylon', which takes place during the events of the 7th Plague.

So why is that plague different, who is its subject, and how does it impact on us here, in the West?

Let's find out.

# 53

# The punishment of the Harlot

## The Vision of the fall of Babylon

which appears in **Revelation Chapters 17 - 18** in the

| 1st Vision | 2nd Vision | 3rd Vision | 4th Vision | 5th Vision | 6th Vision | 7th Vision |
|---|---|---|---|---|---|---|
| **The history of the Church** | **The trials of believers** | **The history of the gentiles** | **The origin of anti-semitism** | **The Last Plagues** | **The fall of Babylon** | **The reign of Christ** |
| *Rev Ch 1-3* | *Rev Ch 4-8.1* | *Rev Ch 8.2-11* | *Rev Ch 12-14* | *Rev Ch 15-16; 19-20* | *Rev Ch 17-18* | *Rev Ch 21-22* |

In the previous vision we were told that the pouring out of the bowls signified the beginning of the seven final acts of Gods judgement – including the destruction of 'Babylon the great'.

Now, in the sixth vision, God amplifies the events of that bowl by telling us who Babylon is, why she is being punished and what form that punishment will take.

This event is yet future, but we're given a lot of information that might help us to identify this mysterious 'woman'.

Let's start with the description of her, in the opening of the vision:

*17 One of the seven angels who had the seven bowls came and said to me, "Come, I will show you the punishment of the great prostitute, who sits by many waters. 2 With her the kings of the earth committed adultery, and the inhabitants of the earth were intoxicated with the wine of her adulteries."*

*[3] Then the angel carried me away in the Spirit into a wilderness. There I saw a woman sitting on a scarlet beast that was covered with blasphemous names and had seven heads and ten horns. [4] The woman was dressed in purple and scarlet, and was glittering with gold, precious stones and pearls. She held a golden cup in her hand, filled with abominable things and the filth of her adulteries. [5] The name written on her forehead was a mystery:*

*Babylon the great, the mother of prostitutes and of the abominations of the earth.*

*[6] I saw that the woman was drunk with the blood of God's holy people, the blood of those who bore testimony to Jesus.*

Immediately after this, one of the angels who had the seven bowls comes to John and offers to show him the punishment of this 'great prostitute':

- He tells John that this woman has committed adultery with the kings of the earth and that the earths inhabitants were intoxicated with the 'wine of her adulteries'.

- John is then shown a vision of a woman sitting on a scarlet beast which has seven heads and ten horns and is covered in blasphemous names. The woman is dressed in purple and scarlet and is glittering with gold, precious stones, and pearls. She is holding a golden cup filled with abominable things and the filth of her adulteries.

- A name is written on her forehead: Babylon the great, the mother of prostitutes and the abominations of the earth.

- John then sees that this woman is drunk with the blood of the saints (the Jews) and the blood of those who bear witness to Yeshua (Christians).

Later in the vision we're told that the ten horned beast will hate this woman (referred to as 'the prostitute') and will 'leave her naked, eat her flesh and burn her with fire'.

But who are these entities?

This question has puzzled and divided scholars for centuries - but now, using what we've already learned, we can solve this age-old mystery.

We'll start, in the next chapter, with the identity of the beast that the woman is riding.

54

# The Beast who once was

## The Prophecy of the 8th Beast

which appears in **Revelation 17:8-11** in the

| 1st Vision | 2nd Vision | 3rd Vision | 4th Vision | 5th Vision | 6th Vision | 7th Vision |
|---|---|---|---|---|---|---|
| **The history of the Church** | **The trials of believers** | **The history of the gentiles** | **The origin of anti-semitism** | **The Last Plagues** | **The fall of Babylon** | **The reign of Christ** |
| *Rev Ch 1-3* | *Rev Ch 4-8.1* | *Rev Ch 8.2-11* | *Rev Ch 12-14* | *Rev Ch 15-16; 19-20* | *Rev Ch 17-18* | *Rev Ch 21-22* |

We've recognised that 'the woman' and 'the beast' that she is riding are different entities - so our first job is to separate these from each other - starting by pinpointing the identity of the beast.

As we've worked our way through these visions we've found that each beast was not a person, but rather, an empire which has had control over Jerusalem at some point in history.

Indeed, throughout the Book of Revelation we keep coming back to the same beast - the Islamic empire - described in different ways depending on the purpose of each vision but always identified by common features.

But in this new vision which starts in chapter 17 of the Book of Revelation there is a reference to an 'eighth' beast which is described in a way that we haven't encountered previously.

By way of context, it is this eighth beast that is described as being 'ridden' by a woman who epitomises 'Babylon' and the main purpose of chapter 17 is to provide details of the destruction of this woman at the hands of this beast - but let's review John's description of the beast itself:

*[3] Then the angel carried me away in the Spirit into a wilderness. There I saw a woman sitting on a scarlet beast that was covered with blasphemous names and had seven heads and ten horns. [4] The woman was dressed in purple and scarlet, and was glittering with gold, precious stones and pearls. She held a golden cup in her hand, filled with abominable things and the filth of her adulteries. [5] The name written on her forehead was a mystery: Babylon the great the mother of prostitutes and of the abominations of the earth.*

*[6] I saw that the woman was drunk with the blood of God's holy people, the blood of those who bore testimony to Jesus.*

*[7] Then the angel said to me: "Why are you astonished? I will explain to you the mystery of the woman and of the beast she rides, which has the seven heads and ten horns.*

*[8] The beast, which you saw, once was, now is not, and yet will come up out of the Abyss and go to its destruction. The inhabitants of the earth whose names have not been written in the book of life from the creation of the world will be astonished when they see the beast, because it once was, now is not, and yet will come.*

*[9] "This calls for a mind with wisdom. The seven heads are seven hills on which the woman sits. [10] They are also seven kings. Five have fallen, one is, the other has not yet come; but when he does come, he must remain for only a little while. [11]* ***The beast who once was, and now is not, is an eighth king****. He belongs to the seven and is going to his destruction.* ***(Revelation 17:8-11)***

So, is this a new beast? Or perhaps an individual, as so many Premillennial scholars would have us believe?

It is neither. The fact that this eighth beast is described as coming 'up out of the abyss' alerts us to the fact that it is the same beast we met in Revelation chapters 11 and 13 and, once again, represents the Islamic Caliphates which ruled Jerusalem for most of the period between the 7th century and 1967.

**Eight beasts?**

But what do we make of this reference to 'eight beasts'? This is problematic because the number of beasts seems to keep changing between the Books of Daniel and Revelation. In chapter two of his book, Daniel appears to describe 'five' beasts - but he only mentions four in the prophecy in chapter 7. Revelation continues this confusion by referring to one beast in chapter 11, one in chapter 12, two in chapter 13 and now eight in chapter 17!! Which number is correct?

They all are - because they're all references to different combinations of the same beasts described in different ways.

To demonstrate this, let's start with the first reference to Beasts in these visions - Daniel's recounting of the beasts which appeared in King Nebuchadnezzars dream in the second chapter of Daniel.

> *[31] "Your Majesty looked, and there before you stood a large statue - an enormous, dazzling statue, awesome in appearance. [32] The head of the statue was made of pure gold, its chest and arms of silver, its belly and thighs of bronze, [33] its legs of iron, its feet partly of iron and partly of baked clay.* ***(Daniel 2:31-33)***

In this vision, the beasts in the dream were a complete description of the various kingdoms which would control Jerusalem over the two thousand five hundred+ years from the time of Nebuchadnezzars reign.

Most commentators usually identify five beasts in this vision (Babylon, Medo Persia, Greece, Rome and a final power which we have now identified as Islam) because they treat the legs of iron as a description of the Roman empire - but there were actually two kingdoms in control of Jerusalem over that time. The Byzantines, who were based in Constantinople (modern day Istanbul) took charge in 313 AD - and while it's true that they considered themselves to be 'Roman' the Byzantium Empire was a distinct entity and lasted long after the fall of Rome.

So, a more correct interpretation of Nebuchadnezzars dream is as follows:

***Controlled Jerusalem***

| | | | |
|---|---|---|---|
| 1. | 589BC - 539BC | Head of Gold | Babylon |
| 2. | 539BC - 332BC | Chest/arms of Silver | Medo Persian |
| 3. | 332BC - 322BC | Belly of Bronze | Greek / Macedonian |
| 4. | 63BC - 313AD | Leg of Iron | Roman |
| 5. | 313AD - 638AD | Leg of Iron | Byzantine |
| 6. | 638AD - 1967AD | Feet of iron and clay | Islamic Caliphates |

But this isn't the only error in the 'approved' timeline.

Although the Greek empire is presented as one entity it actually split into four rival Hellenistic (Greek) kingdoms after Alexanders death - and two of these kingdoms went to war with each other over the control of territories which included Jerusalem - so they were also distinct entities. These were the Ptolemy's, who controlled Jerusalem after the death of Alexander up until 198 BC, and the Seleucids who controlled Jerusalem between 198 BC and 63 BC.

This is no small matter. The passing of control of Jerusalem from Alexander to the Ptolemy's could be compared to the US taking over a territory that had previously been controlled by the British. Yes, the US 'came out' of Britain, but it is a different power and would be noted as such in any historical account. The same applies here. *(a detailed outline of the extraordinary history of these two Kingdoms as described in Daniel Chapter 11 is contained in Appendix C of this book)*

So, a more accurate portrayal of the Gentile control of Jerusalem from the time of Nebuchadnezzar would look like this:

***Controlled Jerusalem***

| | | | |
|---|---|---|---|
| 1. | 589BC - 539BC | Head of Gold | Babylon |
| 2. | 539BC - 332BC | Chest/arms of Silver | Medo Persian |
| 3. | 332BC - 322BC | Belly of Bronze | Greek / Macedonian |
| 4. | 322BC - 198BC | Thigh of Bronze | Ptolemaic |
| 5. | 198BC - 63BC | Thigh of Bronze | Seleucid |
| 6. | 63BC - 313AD | Leg of Iron | Roman |
| 7. | 313AD - 637AD | Leg of Iron | Byzantine |
| 8. | 637AD - 1967AD | Feet of iron and clay | Islamic Caliphates |

There was also a Jewish dynasty which had semi-autonomous control over Jerusalem between 140 BC and 63 BC, although this was essentially a vassal state of the Seleucids and then Rome.

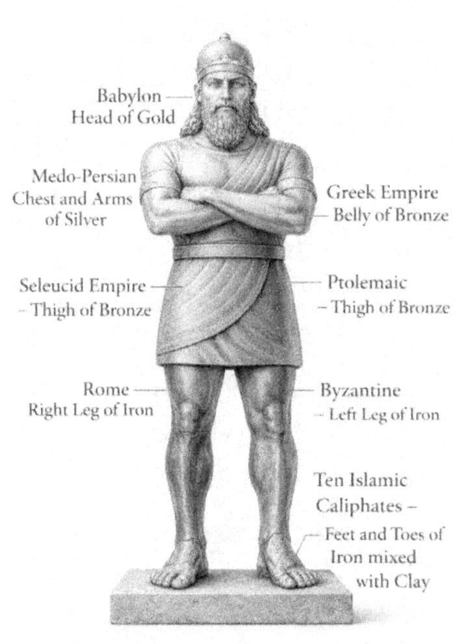


So now the prophecy in Revelation 17:8-11 makes perfect sense. When added to what we already know about the Islamic Caliphates, we can now see that it identifies the kingdoms which controlled Jerusalem between the siege of Jerusalem in 589BC, right through until the Six Day war in 1967, when the Israelis wrested control of Jerusalem from the Kingdom of Jordan, the last of the ten Islamic kingdoms.

| | ***Kingdoms*** | | ***Controlled Jerusalem*** |
|---|---|---|---|
| 1. | The Babylonians | | 589BC - 539BC |
| 2. | The Persians | 539 - 333BC | 614AD – 629AD |
| 3. | The Macedonian Greeks | | 333BC - 322BC |
| 4. | The Ptolemies | | 322BC - 198BC |
| 5. | The Seleucids | | 198BC - 63BC |
| 6. | The Romans | | 63BC - 313AD |
| 7. | The Byzantines | 313 – 614 & | 629AD – 638 |
| 8. | The ten Islamic powers | | 638AD – 1967 |

- Rashidun Caliphate 638 - 661
- Umayyad Caliphate 661 - 750
- Abbasid Caliphate 750 – 878 & 904 - 969
- Tulunid Dynasty 878 - 904
- Abbasid Caliphate 904 - 969
- Fatimid Caliphate 969 – 1073 & 1098 -1099
- Seljuk Dynasty 1073 - 1098
- Ayyubid Caliphate 1187 - 1259
- Mamluk Sultanate 1260 - 1516
- Ottoman Empire 1517 - 1918
- Kingdom of Jordan 1948 – 1967

9. The two 'Christian' powers

- The Crusader Kingdom 1099 - 1187
- The British Empire 1917 - 1948

This allows us to make sense of what the angel was describing to John in Revelation 17:

> *9 "This calls for a mind with wisdom. The seven heads are seven hills on which the woman sits. 10 They are also seven kings. Five have fallen, one is, the other has not yet come; but when he does come, he must remain for only a little while. 11 The beast who once was, and now is not, is an eighth king. He belongs to the seven and is going to his destruction.* ***(Revelation 17:9-11)***

From Johns perspective, writing in the first century while living under Roman rule, five of these kingdoms have fallen and no longer control Jerusalem, one (Rome) 'is' controlling Jerusalem, and one (the Byzantium kingdom) had 'not yet come'. When it does, it continues that control for a short time (a little over 300 years) relative to the empire which follows it.

Then an 'eighth beast' follows. This isn't an individual. Nor is it a 'revived' Roman Empire. It's the same collection of Islamic powers which is referred to again and again throughout the pages of Revelation and is described as 'the beast which once was' in chapter 17, and as the beast which 'came up out of the abyss' in chapter 11 and which is destined to go to its destruction.

Remember, 'the abyss' was the place of imprisonment of demons, which 'once were' (mostly from the pre-flood period), but which had been 'chained in darkness' because they very nearly wiped out mankind – and Revelation makes clear that this same hostile, anti-God spirit is driving the Islamic beast which is described in Scripture as coming 'up out of the abyss'.

**Two Great Beasts?**

But what about the descriptions in Chapters 12 and 13 of the Book of Revelation which distinguish between two separate "great" beasts - one with seven heads, ten horns and seven crowns, and one with seven heads, ten horns and ten crowns?

Again, once we understand what Scripture is counting, this becomes clear. Horns represent individual ruling powers, heads represent capital centres or seats of rule, and crowns represent imperial sovereignty - in other words, who is actually exercising recognised control over Jerusalem at a given time.

The first of these "super-beasts" represents the collective of the **seven non-Islamic empires that ruled Jerusalem**. It therefore has seven heads and seven crowns, because seven major empires held imperial sovereignty over the city. However, it also has ten horns, because those seven empires were made up of ten distinct powers, all of which trace their civilisations back to Babylonian foundations. These powers were: Babylon, Media, Persia, Macedonia, the Ptolemies, the Seleucids, Rome, Byzantium, plus the Crusaders, and the British.

Seven heads, seven crowns, and ten horns.

The second "super-beast" represents the Islamic phase of Jerusalem's foreign rule. This beast is made up of **ten distinct Islamic**

**powers**, each of which exercised imperial sovereignty over Jerusalem for a period of time between 638 and 1967. It therefore has ten horns and ten crowns. However, across that long period these ten powers operated from a smaller number of recurring imperial centres, with their capitals located in seven different Middle Eastern and North African locations. So this beast has seven heads, ten crowns, and ten horns.

Seen this way, the two beasts are not contradictory descriptions of the same thing, nor competing visions. They are two composite summaries, together accounting for the entire history of foreign control over Jerusalem from the Babylonians through to the Kingdom of Jordan. When understood correctly, there is no confusion and no inconsistency between the visions of Daniel and Revelation. The whole sequence of Jerusalem's domination by foreign kingdoms is fully and coherently accounted for.

### Scriptures regarding the Eighth Beast

So let's go back to the point of this chapter - identifying the beast which 'the woman' is riding - and review what we know about this beast. Remember, most of these scriptures are quoted, by Premillennial interpreters, to support the idea of this eighth beast being a last days Antichrist - however, as you can see, that's not what's being described here:

- It came up out of the sea. **(Revelation 13:1)**
- It was different from all the former beasts and had ten horns. **(Daniel 7:7)**
- The ten horns were ten kings who had not yet received a kingdom (when John wrote that passage) but who received authority as kings, alongside the beast. **(Revelation 17:12)**

- It 'once was, now is not' (from Johns perspective) and yet comes up out of the abyss and goes to its destruction. **(Revelation 17:8)**

- These people also worshiped Satan because he gave the beast its authority, and they believed the beast to be invincible. **(Revelation 13:4)**

- The beast uttered proud words and blasphemies for 42 months (the 1278.3 years between 688 and 1967). **(Revelation 13:5)**

- It was given power to wage war against Gods holy people (Jews in the Middle East) and conquer them. **(Revelation 13:7)**

- It was given authority over every (Islamic) tribe, people, language and nation and all inhabitants of the earth worshipped it - except those whose names had been written in the Lamb's book of life (Jews and Arab Christians). **(Revelation 13:7)**

- One of the heads of the beast had a fatal wound (the Fatimid Dynasty, defeated by the Crusaders), but this was healed when the Ayyubid Caliphate defeated the Crusader Kingdom. **(Revelation 13:3)**

- The King(s) (representing the Islamic empire in the form of a series of Islamic Caliphates) did as they pleased and were successful until the time of wrath (Gods punishment of the Jews) was completed. **(Daniel 11:36-39)**

- They (the kings) showed no regard for the gods of their ancestors, nor did they regard any god, but exalted themselves

> above them all, including saying unheard of things against the God of gods. Instead, they honoured a god of fortresses (Allah), who was unknown to their ancestors, with gold, silver, precious stones and costly gifts. They attacked the mightiest fortresses with the help of this foreign god and greatly honoured those who acknowledged him. They made these people rulers over many others and distributed the land at a price (submission to Islam). **(Daniel 11:36-39)**

Presented like this and based on what we already know from previous solutions, it's now impossible to see this eighth beast as anything other than the Islamic Empire. Both the descriptions and the years match the recorded history of Islam in the Middle East, and, once again, we can see that these prophecies are not references to an Antichrist figure who will persecute western Christians in the last days.

Let's review our Basic Questions:

**Who is the prophecy addressed to and who is it about?**

The book of Revelation continues to be addressed to Christians and while the prophecy covers a broad sweep of all of the beasts which have had control over Jerusalem, it does so in order to provide the identity of the eighth beast – so we can confidently identify this section of the prophecy as being about the Islamic beast.

**What years does the prophecy start and end?**

While this prophecy doesn't actually mention a specific time - we know that Islam ruled Jerusalem for most of the years between 637 and 1967 – and we also know that God repeatedly uses the year 688 (marking the construction of the Dome of the Rock on the Temple Mount) as the defining point for these prophecies.. So, based on this information, we can now identify the time of this beast as the '42 months' (1278.3 years) between 688 and 1967, but counted backward.

Let's put this all of this information into our template to see what we have discovered:

| **The Prophecy of the eighth beast**<br>Revelation 17:8-11 | | | |
|---|---|---|---|
| **What's being predicted?** | *That an '8th beast' will control Jerusalem for 1278+ years* | | |
| **Question** | **Clue from Scripture** | **Math** | **Solution** |
| **Who is the prophecy addressed to?** | *"...Jesus Christ ... to show His servants" (Revelation 1:1)* | | **The prophecy is addressed to Christians** |
| **Who is the prophecy about?** | *"...a woman sitting on a scarlet beast..." (Revelation 17:3)* | | **Islam (and someone else)** |
| **What year does the prophecy end?** | *When the authority of the eighth beast ends* | ***1967*** | **The prophecy ends in 1967** |
| **How long will the prophecy last?** | *"... 42 months..." (Revelation 13:5)* | ***minus 1,278.3*** | **The prophecy will last for 1,278.3 years** |
| **What year does the prophecy begin?** | | ***equals 688.7*** | **The prophecy begins in 688 AD** |

So the identity of the beast being ridden by the woman in Revelation 17 is finally solved. It's the Islamic empire made up of a series of Caliphates which ruled over Jerusalem for over a thousand years before finally ending in 1967 when the Jews took back control of that city.

*The solution at a glance*

# The beast who once was

***Scriptures:*** *Revelation 17:8-11*

1. **What's being predicted??**
   That 'the 8th beast' being ridden by 'the woman' in Revelation 17 is Islam

2. **Who is being spoken to?**
   John, warning **the churches**.

3. **Who is the prophecy about?**
   The fate of the woman who rides this beast.

4. **What is the beast?**
   Ten Islamic powers that dominated Jerusalem from 688 to 1967. It is the same "beast" seen throughout Revelation.

5. **Who is behind it?**
   Scripture identifies the beast as being empowered by Satan and animated by a spirit opposed to God - a prophetic description that aligns with the Islamic powers which ruled Jerusalem

This eighth beast is not a future tyrant, but a historical empire – that was central to Jerusalem's oppression. **The prophecy strips away myth and speculation, identifying the beast as Islam itself**.

.

# 55

# The Big Reveal

## The Prophecy of the Woman riding the beast

which appears in **Revelation 17:3-7** and **17:15-18** in the

| 1st Vision | 2nd Vision | 3rd Vision | 4th Vision | 5th Vision | 6th Vision | 7th Vision |
|---|---|---|---|---|---|---|
| **The history of the Church** | **The trials of believers** | **The history of the gentiles** | **The origin of anti-semitism** | **The Last Plagues** | **The fall of Babylon** | **The reign of Christ** |
| *Rev Ch 1-3* | *Rev Ch 4-8.1* | *Rev Ch 8.2-11* | *Rev Ch 12-14* | *Rev Ch 15-16; 19-20* | *Rev Ch 17-18* | *Rev Ch 21-22* |

In this chapter. We're going to learn who 'the woman' in Revelation 17 actually is – and for many of us, that unveiling is going to be intellectually and emotionally challenging.

So far, we've identified the beast that she is riding in Revelation 17 as the composite entity made up of the ten Islamic Caliphates that ruled Jerusalem for the more than 1,300 years between 637 to 1967 and which appears repeatedly throughout the prophecies of Revelation. But who is the woman? Let's review what scripture tells us about her:

> *3 ...I saw a woman sitting on a scarlet beast that was covered with blasphemous names and had seven heads and ten horns. 4 The woman was dressed in purple and scarlet, and was glittering with gold, precious stones and pearls. She held a golden cup in her hand, filled with abominable things and the filth of her adulteries. 5 The*

*name written on her forehead was a mystery: Babylon the great the mother of prostitutes and of the abominations of the earth.*

*[6] I saw that the woman was drunk with the blood of God's holy people, and the blood of those who bore testimony to Jesus.*

*When I saw her, I was greatly astonished. [7] Then the angel said to me: "Why are you astonished? I will explain to you the mystery of the woman and of the beast she rides, which has the seven heads and ten horns.* ***(Revelation 17:3-7)***

*[15] Then the angel said to me, "The waters you saw, where the prostitute sits, are peoples, multitudes, nations and languages. [16] The beast and the ten horns you saw will hate the prostitute. They will bring her to ruin and leave her naked; they will eat her flesh and burn her with fire. [17] For God has put it into their hearts to accomplish his purpose by agreeing to hand over to the beast their royal authority, until God's words are fulfilled. [18] The woman you saw is the great city that rules over the kings of the earth."* ***(Revelation 17:15-18)***

## Past attempts to identify the woman

As with so much of what we find in the Book of Revelation, there is significant conjecture about this woman and there are many competing claims to her identity. Among the most popular of these are the claims that she is the United States (represented by the Statue of Liberty and New York), Capitalism, the United Nations, Democracy (also represented by a female personification of 'liberty'), and the European Union (the 2 Euro coin even depicts a woman riding a beast).

But while all of these candidates offer intriguing and imaginative solutions - the scripture is clear that 'the woman riding the (Islamic) beast' must have had *ongoing interaction* with the beast at some stage between 637 and 1967 and must have played a significant role in, or around Jerusalem. None of these previous candidates meet those criteria.

So who is she? Let's see if we can answer that question by starting with the most obvious clue to her identity: Her name.

**Babylon the great**

The word 'Babylon' is derived from the ancient Akkadian word 'Babilu' and simply means 'gate of God'. However the word is better known to us as the name of the southern Mesopotamian (modern day Iraqi) city which gave its name to an ancient Empire and which features prominently in the Bible in the Books of Daniel, Ezekiel, Jeremiah and other prophets.

We know that at the beginning of the Book of Daniel this empire was being ruled by Nebuchadnezzar and we know that it was the first empire mentioned in his dream of a statue (which was interpreted by Daniel).

And here's where it gets interesting. Babylon was also the *first* foreign kingdom which controlled Jerusalem - kicking off an almost unbroken succession of more than 2,500 years of foreign control by various powers which ended with Jordan in 1967.

Babylon only controlled Jerusalem for around 50 of those 2,500+ years – ending in 539 BC - but it continued to influence the empires that followed it through its many inventions (including mathematics; the foundations of modern writing; map making; astronomy; the division of time into 60 seconds, 60 minutes and the 24-hour day; medicine, farming techniques, building construction methods the production of beer and much more). These were adopted and further developed, by the Persian, Greek and Roman societies which succeeded Babylon and have continued through the centuries right up until the modern era - so, in a very real sense, we in the west, have inherited the Babylonian mantle.

But Babylon also directly impacted modern western society through its religion, which included the worship and veneration of multiple entities; regular ceremonies to maintain the 'favour' of the gods; and the care and worship of statues.

**Clues to identify the woman**

Of course, these beliefs appear in some form in many religions - but there's one, in particular, which adopted all of them. To identify it, let's go back to the prophecy and see if we can find a western religion that assimilated Babylonian religious traditions and:

- Is dressed in purple and scarlet
- Is glittering with gold, precious stones and pearls
- Has a golden cup filled with abominable things and the filth of its adulteries
- Is drunk with the blood of both Jews and Christians
- Sits on seven hills
- Is the embodiment of seven kings
- Sits on many people, multitudes, nations and languages
- Was hated by all ten Islamic caliphates
- Is a great city which rules over the kings of the earth
- Was / is a prostitute (God repeatedly uses the term 'prostitute / whore' as a symbol of spiritual unfaithfulness)
- Is the mother of prostitutes (we'll come back to this)

There is also some additional information, in chapter 18 of Revelation, where we're given an extensive description of the destruction of Babylon and told that the woman made the merchants of the earth rich from her excessive luxuries but will be consumed by fire in one day (an act that will terrify the kings of the earth).

Based on these clues, we can also reasonably infer that the woman:

- Is a political and economic power of great influence and wealth
- Still exists today (because she is yet to be destroyed)
- Has an international reach

We also know that this 'woman' must have controlled Jerusalem at some point and must have also existed for at least some of the time during which the Islamic Caliphates existed.

**Do we know anyone like this in the 21st century?**

One of the advantages of living in the digital age is that it allows us to see, almost instantly, how the modern world visually associates certain ideas, institutions, and symbols.

Search engines don't create those associations - they simply reflect what already exists across media, culture, and public imagery by highlighting, first, the images which are most commonly associated with a word or phrase.

This is a powerful tool, here, because in Revelation 17 we're given one of the clearest visual identifiers in the entire book. The woman is not described only in moral or spiritual terms - she is described visually. She is clothed in colours that signal authority, wealth, ceremony, and power – and if this figure has a modern counterpart, then those colours should not be hidden in obscure symbolism. They should be visible, recognisable, and consistently associated with the same power today. One simple way of observing that association in the modern world is to place that combination of colours into a search engine and view the dominant images that appear.

And what colours are we are looking for?

***Purple and scarlet.***

And there it is. A simple search on those two colours brings up multiple images of **the Roman Catholic Church**.

Google results are not evidence, of course, and we shouldn't base an entire identification on a match with two colours – so let's take a moment to understand a little more of the Catholic Church before finalising an identification..

**Unmasking the woman**

The history of the Catholic Church is one of striking contrasts. What started as a branch of a larger grassroots movement that was rooted in the teachings of Jesus quickly descended into a vast, hierarchical institution that bore little resemblance to its origins.

Catholicism first appears in the 4th century, following Emperor Constantine's conversion, and was quickly absorbed into the machinery of the Roman Empire. It proceeded to centralize power, establish rigid doctrines which were a blasphemous blend of Christian terminology and the old pagan religions, and elevate the Bishop of Rome (previously just one of several regional Bishops) to near-absolute authority (claims that the disciple Peter held this office and was, therefore, the first 'Pope' are colourful Catholic mythology – not historical fact).

This new religion replaced personal faith with pagan ritual, introduced idolatry in the form of saint veneration and 'Mary' worship, and positioned itself as the sole gatekeeper of salvation. And with that power came a long and bloody record of persecution including the torture and murder of many thousands of Jews, rival Christians and others. From the Crusaders' mass slaughter of Muslims and Jews in Jerusalem, to the Inquisition's secret trials and burning pyres, Catholicism frequently enforced orthodoxy through fear. Protestant reformers, early Bible translators, and even philosophical thinkers like Galileo were silenced or destroyed. The Catholic Church also actively enabled antisemitism, promoting toxic theologies and supporting expulsions, forced conversions, and pogroms for centuries across Europe.

Corruption was also endemic. The sale of 'indulgences', nepotism, bribery, and sexual scandals stained the papacy, which often looked more like a royal court than a spiritual institution. Multiple popes fathered children out of wedlock, threw orgies, or financed wars with Church funds. Meanwhile, the Vatican accumulated massive wealth, flaunted excess in its cathedrals, and exploited the faithful through religious taxes.

While individual Catholics have championed human dignity and reform - the institution itself has a long and painful record of moral and spiritual failure which has continued into the 21$^{st}$ century.

But how does this line up with the clues that we're given in Revelation 17:

**Comparing the clues given to identify the 'woman':**

- Catholicism has existed since the fourth century and was the result of a political 'merger' of Christian beliefs with pagan beliefs (many dating back to the Babylonian Empire) enforced by the successors of the Roman Emperor Constantine
- Catholicism is represented by vestments of purple and scarlet
- Catholicism is obscenely wealthy - dripping in gold, precious stones and pearls
- Catholicism sits on seven literal hills (the city of Rome, the centre of Catholicism, sits on Palatine, Capitoline, Quirinal, Viminal, Esquiline, Caelian, and Aventine)
- Catholicism also 'sits on' the religious traditions of the seven kingdoms which influenced its doctrine (Babylonian, Medo Persian, Greek, Seleucid, Ptolemaic, Roman and Byzantine)
- Catholicism is drunk with the blood of both Jews and Christians (while there is debate over the enormous number

of Jews and non-Catholic Christians murdered by Catholicism, no-one - not even Catholic scholars - denies that it happened)

- Catholicism has influence over one billion people and is a political and economic power of great weight
- As if to confirm Gods identification of this entity as a 'woman' - Catholicism even describes itself as 'holy *mother* Church'

However, even this hardly scratches the surface in respect of the extent to which Catholicism abandoned the original Christian faith. You'll search in vain, for a defensible 'Christian' foundation for the office of 'Pope', transubstantiation, purgatory, indulgences, penance, Mary worship, the conferring of 'sainthood', Catholic confession, and a host of other manmade doctrines. Catholicism attempts to justify a handful of these by strangling the meaning of scripture references – but most of them are simply direct contradictions to Christs clear instructions in the Gospels.

**Catholic vs Islamic persecution of Jews:**

It's also worth noting that, despite the antisemitic origins of Islam – it is Catholicism which has been responsible for far more atrocities towards Jews down through the centuries:

| | **Catholic antisemitism** | **Islamic antisemitism** |
|---|---|---|
| **Core Motive for anti-semitism** | **Theological** supersessionism (belief that "the Church has replaced Israel") | **The Jews** rejecting Muhammad as the Mandate for Muslim supremacy |
| **Lethality (scale of killing)** | **Extremely high**: Crusader massacres, medieval pogroms, Chmielnicki (1648–57), Russian/Polish pogroms; Holocaust (Hitler was raised Catholic) | **Lower** overall: Medina (7th c.), Granada 1066 (~1,500), Morocco 1465 (hundreds), scattered pogroms/forced conversions |

| | Catholic antisemitism | Islamic antisemitism |
|---|---|---|
| **Expulsions** | (England 1290; France 1306/1394; Spain 1492; Portugal 1497, plus many others) | Umar's Arabia policy; post-1948 regional expulsions/flight from Arab states |
| **Bottom Line** | **More lethal** by far; millions killed | **More consistent** - long-term subordination |

To be fair, little of this is new. For centuries, the idea that the Catholic Church was the 'whore of Babylon' was the dominant view of prophecy scholars so there is already a lot of material available for those who want to further research this connection - including the excellent book *'A Woman Rides the Beast'* by the late Dave Hunt.

**Catholicism - the woman riding the beast**

Catholicism, alone, is the only entity which meets all of the criteria established by God in Revelation. It is also the only eligible power which has existed for the entirety of the time during which the Islamic empire dominated the Middle East and which had constant and ingoing conflict with Islam. Catholicism, in the guise of the Crusader Kingdom of Jerusalem, controlled Jerusalem for the 88 years between 1099 and 1187 and has already been identified as the first 'horn' of the two-horned beast which came up out of the land in Revelation chapter 13.

As such, I encourage you to go back and reread Chapter 45 of *Prophecy Shock* with this identification in mind.

**Daughters of the harlot**

But wait. While the Catholic Church was the first horn of the two-horned lamb in the vision in Revelation 13 - the second horn was the British Empire - and that Empire wasn't Catholic - it was Protestant.

So does this conflict with the prophecy?

Not at all. You'll recall that we were also told that the woman was 'the mother of prostitutes' - so she had daughters.

And who are these 'daughters? They're the 'Christian' religions which came out of Catholicism, but which either continued many of the practices of that corrupt system or fell back into them - and that includes much of modern Protestantism and the Greek and Eastern Orthodox Churches.

So there's no conflict in recognising the 'Anglican' British Empire as the second horn of the two-horned lamb in Revelation 13 even though it was a powerful force for good for hundreds of years.

Britain was richly rewarded for its centuries of obedience to Gods directive to 'go into all the world and make disciples of all men' - but by the time the Brits gained control of the Holy Land, in the 20th century, their evangelistic zeal was long gone, replaced by an antisemitic agenda which continued to persecute the Jews and which shaped their fate for decades.

*The solution at a glance*

## The woman riding the beast

***Scriptures:*** *Revelation 17:3–7, 15–18; Revelation 18*

1. **What's being predicted??**
   That the woman riding the beast is a powerful, corrupt spiritual and political system aligned with false Christianity

2. **Who is being spoken to?**
   John is again writing to **the churches**.

3. **Who is the prophecy about?**
   **The Catholic Church** (described as Babylon the Great) and her offspring: including some Protestant Churches

4. **What is the woman?**
   A religious/political power rooted in Babylonian traditions, and dressed in scarlet and purple, which sustained constant tension with Islam during the centuries it ruled Jerusalem.

5. **Who is behind it?**
   A spiritually unfaithful system that merged pagan religion with Christianity - symbolizing spiritual adultery. Her influence stems from Satan, not Christ.

This is a sobering warning to believers. **The 'woman' is real, religious, powerful, and global. She is Catholicism** and her spiritual offspring, exposed not just for doctrinal error but for persecuting God's people and aligning with forces hostile to the Gospel.

56

# The 'Man of Lawlessness'

Some readers will have noticed something important by this stage of the book: *Prophecy Shock* leaves no room for the familiar picture of a future world dictator who suddenly appears at the end of history, deceives the nations, and briefly rules the world before Christ returns. This is because we have now resolved all of the scripture references used by Premillennialism to predict the rise of an 'Antichrist' and discovered that they all mean something else within the Israelism framework.

With one exception: Paul's reference to the **"man of lawlessness"** in **2 Thessalonians 2:3–4** in which Paul is writing about the Return of Christ:

> *"Don't let anyone deceive you in any way, for that day will not come until the rebellion occurs and the man of lawlessness is revealed, the man doomed to destruction. He will oppose and will exalt himself over everything that is called God or is worshiped, so that he sets himself up in God's temple, proclaiming himself to be God."* ***(2 Thessalonians 2:3–4)***

Paul goes on to explain that this will be accompanied by deception and false signs:

> *"The coming of the lawless one will be in accordance with how Satan works. He will use all sorts of displays of power through signs and wonders that serve the lie."* ***(2 Thessalonians 2:9)***

Paul also adds a warning to those who follow this deception:

*"For this reason God sends them a* ***strong delusion so that they will believe the lie.****" (2 Thessalonians 2:11)*

For many interpreters this appears to point to a future tyrant who will sit in a rebuilt temple in Jerusalem and proclaim himself to be God. But this rests on an assumption that the text does not require.

While Ezekiel describes a temple in a restored Israel, that vision describes a divine restoration - not deception or rebellion - and is not presented as a human-built structure preceding God's intervention.

More importantly, Paul uses the term "temple" to describe God's people, not a building.

*"For* ***we*** *are the temple of the living God"* ***(2 Corinthians 6:16).***

He makes the same point in **1 Corinthians 3:16**

*"Do you not know that* ***you yourselves are God's temple*** *and that God's Spirit dwells in your midst?"*

So 2 Thessalonians 2:3–4 is not about a man entering a rebuilt structure but is about someone exalting himself in the place of God within the community of believers.

*"He sets himself up in God's temple, proclaiming himself to be God."*

But who is this?

The most obvious answer is that this is the believer him or herself. Understood this way the scripture is simply saying that mankind will become puffed up with pride and disregard the role of God – something that has certainly happened, increasingly, in recent history. But could there be something more implied here too?

Contrast the wording of the scripture in 2 Thessalonians:

*"Don't let anyone deceive you in any way..."*

...with the phrase used by Yeshua in Matthew 24:

*"Take heed that no one deceives you. For many shall come in my name, saying, **'I speak for Christ'**; and shall deceive many."*

We now know that the Matthew 24 quote is a reference to false Christianity - and that false Christianity is specifically personified in the Catholic Church (and her daughters) in the prophecy of the woman riding the beast in Revelation.

So is there another level of meaning in 2 Thessalonians 2:3-4?:?:

*"Don't let anyone deceive you in any way, for that day (the return of Christ) will not come until the rebellion occurs and the man of lawlessness is revealed, the man doomed to destruction. He will oppose and will exalt himself over everything that is called God or is worshiped, so that he sets himself up in God's temple, proclaiming himself to be God."*

Given what we learned in the previous Chapter – could this be a reference to the Catholic Papacy? We know that organisations purporting to be Christian 'rebelled' against the true faith as early as the first century - but that this gathered pace in the 4th century when Catholicism appeared and introduced the concept of a 'Pope' as leader of the Church based on a corrupted understanding of the role of the Apostle Peter. Successive Popes then went on to claim universal spiritual authority over the Church, presenting that authority as divinely sanctioned and binding upon believers. Popes also claimed doctrinal authority and infallibility and, in doing so, shaped the way that Catholics understand faith, salvation, and the interpretation of Scripture while also claiming powers and titles that placed their authority above Scripture and above the direct Lordship of Christ.

As such, the office of the Papacy claims an authority that effectively places itself above Jesus Christ.

And what about the reference to 'setting himself up in Gods temple'? If the temple is defined as a place within each unique human being which is designed to be filled by God – then yes, all Popes have done this. By claiming the authority that God reserves for Himself, and by putting barriers in the way of believers fulfilling the simple requirements of salvation that we outline in the next Chapter, each successive Pope presides over a system that has obscured the simple gospel of grace and redemption through Christ alone.

And what about Paul's warning about deception, "strong delusion" and believing the lie? Again, this is easy to understand as a reference to the strong belief that many Catholics have in the Catholic faith and in the authority of their Popes.

Obviously this is just a theory – and even if it's true it does not mean that every Catholic believer is deceived or lost. While many Catholics base their faith in Catholic 'traditions' rather than the redemptive power of Yeshua – there are also many sincere believers within that system who have a direct relationship with Jesus Christ (and who are saved, in spite of their Catholicism, not because of it).

Nor is this issue exclusive to Catholics. There are also many 'dead' or 'progressive' Protestant Churches which have rebelled against God – as well as many people within these who have placed their faith in Christ despite this.

Meanwhile, the purpose of Pauls warning about the emergence of a Man of Lawlessness isn't a future prophecy about an 'Antichrist' who will rise in the last days – it is a direct warning to those who believe that they are 'Christians' but are not.

But how can we know? How can we be sure that our own beliefs are aligned with what God requires of us? And how can we know if the denomination that we identify with is a gateway to Gods Kingdom or just another part of the Whore of Babylon?

That's the subject of the next chapter.

57

# A guide to Identifying false Christianity

There will be some reading this who will feel that I should have left the last two chapters out of this book and avoided the subject of false Christianity altogether – arguing that this Vision isn't a time-defined prophecy and that identifying it only creates division.

I understand that reaction, but it misses the central point. In Matthew 24 Yeshua warns us, explicitly, about a counterfeit Christianity that would rise in His name and deceive multitudes.

> *"Many shall come in my name saying* ***I speak for Christ*** *and will deceive many"*

He gives that warning in the context of a prophecy about the future in which He ultimately destroys that false system. In other words: false Christianity isn't a distraction from this book – it lies at the very heart of it.

I have no desire to offend my Catholic, Anglican, Mormon, or Jehovah's Witness friends and relatives (and many others) – but my revelations aren't aimed at them. This isn't about individuals. It's about organisations that God has identified and from which He calls His people to "come out" before He judges them. For that, I make no apologies.

And while Revelation 17 certainly paints the Catholic Church as the poster child for false Christianity – she isn't on her own. There are *many* New Testament warnings about false Christianity:

- Revelation 17 reminds us that the Catholic Church had 'daughters', neatly alluding to the Orthodox Church and some Protestant Churches.

- The Protestant (Anglican) British Empire was the other 'Christian' power to control Jerusalem and therefore the second half of the 'two-horned' lamb that spoke like a dragon in chapter 13 of Revelation.

- Chapters 16 and 19 of the Book of Revelation, refer to false Christianity as the 'False Prophet' - a spirit which has influenced the Church for almost 2000 years and which still guides the actions of every form of false Christianity in the world today

These are just a small sample of the many scripture references that continually warn us that false Christianity will be *everywhere* - fully embedded within the Church itself, destroying the faith of believers from the inside.

And it's important to understand that the Protestant Church is not exempt from this warning. While the Protestant Reformation of the 16th century overturned much of the excess, corruption and manmade error of Catholicism - it also carried over many of those errors and invented a few new ones along the way. Indeed, the very reason that we have different Protestant denominations is because various different groups of believers could not agree on issues of doctrine and decided, instead, to split off and set up their own Churches.

And not just Protestants. You can add to this list the various semi-Christian cults such as the Mormons, the Jehovah's Witnesses, and dozens of other groups that have falsely claimed that they offer a pathway to God while closing the door to the only the only pathway that matters.

But if false Christianity is personified by such a vast array of 'Christian' organisations - what hope do we have? How can any of us possibly avoid the judgement outlined in Revelation 17? Doesn't this place an impossible challenge on us all?

### How to recognise True Christianity

To answer this question we should first remind ourselves of the primary purpose of Christianity:

Salvation.

And what is Salvation? It isn't a term to describe membership of a particular Church or denomination. Nor is it about having a better, happier, life (this can sometimes be a pleasant side benefit of salvation – but it isn't a given).

No, Salvation is about ensuring that, when you die, you go to be in the benign presence of God rather than spending eternity (forever) separated from Him. As such, achieving Salvation is one of the most important things you will ever do (in fact, I would argue that it is the very purpose of your earthly existence).

And here's the Good News (literally): achieving Salvation isn't difficult - in fact making certain that we're truly 'saved' and covered by Christ is far less complicated than the contrived and controlling dictates of the various arms of false Christianity.

In the Gospels, Yeshua told us:

*"I am **the way** and **the truth** and **the life**. **No one** comes to the Father except **through me**". **(John 14:6)***

Next, in Acts 3:19, we're told:

*"Repent, then, and turn to God, **so that your sins may be wiped out**."*

Then, Paul tells us:

*[9] If you declare with your mouth, **"Jesus is Lord,"** and believe in your heart that God raised Him from the dead, you will be saved.* ***(Romans 10.9)***

And finally, in Mattew 7, Yeshua tells us:

*"Not everyone who says to me, 'Lord, Lord,' will enter the kingdom of heaven, but only the one who does the will of my Father who is in heaven."*

This fourth scripture tells us that, once we have accepted the Lordship of God, we are expected to seek His constant leading on how we should live the rest of our lives – not just as an act of obedience (although this is implicit) – but because we have now become part of His bigger plan for humanity and He expects us to play that part.

That's it – **four simple steps:**

1. Recognise and ***believe*** that Jesus is Lord and is the **only way** to the Father (Salvation by Grace – not as a result of anything we do personally).

2. Repent of your sins and recognise that Christ was crucified, in your place, to pay for them.

3. Openly acknowledge your belief in Jesus Christ. (tell others)

4. Live the rest of your life in prayerful obedience to the Fathers leading.

These are steps that only you can take. You can't inherit them, through a family association with your Church and nobody can take them for you. This is something that you need to do for yourself.

Unfortunately, many Churches and Cults ignore these clear instructions and focus on criteria which do not come from God - loading people up with the belief that there are additional things that they are required to *do*, or *believe*, before they can be saved. These often replace Christs clear instructions, altogether, so that many never do the very things that Yeshua has told us are the *only* **requirements** of actually being saved.

### Christians in the False Church?

So does the Church organisation that you belong to determine whether or not you are saved? Not at all – and Yeshua explicitly addresses this in the parable about the wheat and the tares:

> *24 ..."The kingdom of heaven is like a man who sowed good seed in*
> *his field; 25 but while men slept, his enemy came and sowed tares*
> *among the wheat and went his way. 26 But when the grain had*
> *sprouted and produced a crop, then the tares also appeared. 27 So*
> *the servants of the owner came and said to him, 'Sir, did you not*
> *sow good seed in your field? How then does it have tares?' 28 He said*
> *to them, 'An enemy has done this.' The servants said to him, 'Do you*
> *want us then to go and gather them up?' 29 But he said, 'No, lest*
> *while you gather up the tares you also uproot the wheat with*
> *them. 30 Let both grow together until the harvest, and at the time of*
> *harvest I will say to the reapers, "First gather together the tares and*
> *bind them in bundles to burn them, but gather the wheat into my*
> *barn."* ***(Matthew 13:24-30)***

This is a huge challenge and is telling us that false Christianity can take place in *any* Church.

So how does your Church stack up? Is its focus on the saving of souls? Is its primary message that you must *'declare, with your mouth, that Jesus is Lord and believe, in your heart, that God raised Him from the dead'*?

Or does it measure its success by 'community programs'? Working to help and feed the poor is an extension of evangelism and an act of obedience to Gods instructions – but 'good works' should be a consequence of the steps I outlined earlier – not a replacement for them. Mans idea of 'good' is very different to Gods.

Perhaps your Church promotes wealth or prosperity as an objective of faith? If it does, get out of it – fast. Likewise, 'Christian activism'. There are issues on which God clearly requires us to take a moral stand - but if you're in a Church where God is portrayed as an anti-Government or sexual rights activist or where political activism is the *primary* focus, alarm bells should be ringing.

Even Churches which are supporters of 'traditional values' can be part of the false Church. Catholicism and many of the Cults promote strong family and social values – but these are peripheral to the requirements of salvation, not replacements for them.

The message of Revelation 17 is clear. These other activities serve no purpose if your primary focus is not on salvation through Christ and you have not wholly submitted to Him and sought His forgiveness in genuine repentance.

**The sins of false Christianity**

All of this is a prelude to the ultimate destruction of the woman which was first alluded to in the fifth vision in Revelation and which we will address in the next chapter – which begs an important question. Why is God so angry at her?

I suggest that it is because false Christianity leads people to believe that they already *have* Christ and that they are saved - all the while loading them up with demonic doctrines which separate them from the simple gospel of salvation – a condition that Yeshua clearly explains in Matthew 7:21-23:

> **21** *Not everyone that saith unto me, Lord, Lord, shall enter into the kingdom of heaven; but he that doeth the will of my Father which is in heaven.* 22 *Many will say to me in that day, Lord, Lord, have we not prophesied in thy name? and in thy name have cast out devils? and in thy name done many wonderful works?* 23 *And then will I profess unto them, I never knew you: depart from me, ye that work iniquity.*

For those who believe themselves to be Christians, it would be hard to imagine hearing anything more terrifying – but note the basis upon which these people are claiming their salvation:

**(1) prophecy**
**(2) a belief in their own 'spirituality', and**
**(3) works.**

Remember, these are people who are convinced that they are 'Christians' but who have not followed the most basic instructions, provided by God Himself, to ensure their salvation.

And therein lies the reason that God is so angry with false Christianity. It is the spirit of *antichrist* mentioned in 1 John 2:18, 2:22, 4:3 and 2 John 1:7 – not as the identification of a person but as the description of an evil influence that was already active in the world in the first century and which has continued right up until our day. It is a spirit that deceives its followers into believing that they are saved when they are not.

Unlike other religions and cults which are, at least, honest in their rejection of the saving power of Christ - false Christianity gives its followers the impression that they already *have* salvation meaning that millions of them have never sought Gods will for their lives or called on the mighty name of Yeshua to lift them out of their sin.

As such, Catholicism and other false 'Christian' religions are literally consigning people to hell!

This should be a wakeup call to any 'Christian' who has not fully submitted to Jesus Christ and who is not living their life in obedience to the Father. God wants us to obey HIM – not the Church organisation in which we have membership.

If you are not following Yeshua's simple instructions – you are living in *false Christianity* – and God has a clear warning for you:

> *"'Come out of her, my people, so that you will not share in her sins, so that you will not receive any of her plagues; for her sins are piled up to heaven, and God has remembered her crimes".* ***(Revelation 18:4-5)***

58

# What goes around...

## The Prophecy of the destruction of the Woman

which appears in **Revelation 17:16–18** and **18:4–10** in the

| 1st Vision | 2nd Vision | 3rd Vision | 4th Vision | 5th Vision | 6th Vision | 7th Vision |
|---|---|---|---|---|---|---|
| **The history of the Church** | **The trials of believers** | **The history of the gentiles** | **The origin of anti-semitism** | **The Last Plagues** | **The fall of Babylon** | **The reign of Christ** |
| *Rev Ch 1-3* | *Rev Ch 4-8.1* | *Rev Ch 8.2-11* | *Rev Ch 12-14* | *Rev Ch 15-16; 19-20* | *Rev Ch 17-18* | *Rev Ch 21-22* |

So we now know that the vision of the Fall of Babylon, which begins in Revelation 17, starts as an outline of the strained relationship between the Islamic Beast and 'the woman' who is personified, in the vision, by the Catholic Church. She also more broadly represents all Churches that do not have a primary focus on the redemptive power of Christ, including the Orthodox Churches, the pseudo-Christian cults, and some sections of western Protestantism.

### Destruction at the hands of the beast

But while God makes clear that Babylon / false Christianity is going to be destroyed – her destruction isn't carried out directly by Him. **It comes at the hands of the Islamic beast:**

> *16 **The beast and the ten horns** you saw will hate the prostitute. They will bring her to ruin and leave her naked; they **will eat her flesh and burn her with fire." (Revelation 17:16)***

But what form will that destruction take?

We know that it will take place at the same time as God pours out the plagues in His last bowl of judgement and that it is yet future. But is it describing the last phase of a gradual destruction of false Christianity, by Islam, such as has been taking place in Europe for the past few decades; a literal attack on Rome (the base of the Vatican), which utterly destroys that city; or a more general attack on the Christian cities of Europe or even the west? Let's review scripture, which tells us that Babylon:

- Is a great city
- Will be destroyed in one hour
- Will be consumed by fire
- And will be thrown down, with the violence of a large millstone being thrown into the sea, never to be found again

On face value this sounds like a specific city – Rome – but the tentacles of false Christianity go far beyond just Catholicism – so I'm inclined to see this as a warning to western Christianity as a whole – not just the Catholics.

This means that the destruction described in the vision may well be of a sudden, fiery and final attack on the entire western world.

Some will see this punishment as particularly harsh - but we need to remember that this isn't about whether Catholics and wayward Protestants are 'nice people' - in fact it has nothing to do with how you and I might measure 'goodness'. It's about how God views false Christianity and the irreparable damage that it has done down through the centuries.

As such, He makes very clear how much the activities of the woman / false Christianity anger and grieve Him when He tells us, in the vision, that:

- Her sins are piled up to heaven and
- He has remembered her crimes.
- He will pay her back double for what she has done.

- He will give her as much torment and grief as the glory and luxury she gave herself.
- Her plagues will overtake her in one day
- Her great wealth will be brought to ruin in one hour.

The vision also tells us that this destruction is absolutely final and permanent and that after Babylon is destroyed:

- It will become a dwelling for demons and a haunt for every impure spirit, unclean bird, and detestable animal
- The music of harpists and musicians, pipers and trumpeters will never be heard in it again.
- No worker of any trade will ever be found in it again.
- The sound of a millstone will never be heard in it again.
- The light of a lamp will never shine in it again.
- The voice of the bridegroom and bride will never be heard in it again.

I want you to understand what is being described here. Later in this book we're going to learn that, following the events in these visions, Yeshua's rule is going to last for a thousand years, on earth, before the earth is utterly destroyed and replaced with a new heavens and earth which will last forever. This means that Rome, maybe Italy, perhaps Europe, and maybe even the entire west is going to be destroyed and uninhabitable for the last one thousand years of the earth's existence.

The starkness of that reality should help you to understand the full extent of Gods fury at false Christianity and the extent to which He intends to punish it.

Come out of it.

*The solution at a glance*

## The destruction of the woman

***Scriptures:*** *Revelation 17:16–18; Revelation 18:4–10*

1. **What's being predicted?**
   That false Christianity - personified as the woman riding the beast - will be violently destroyed by the Islamic empire in a sudden, catastrophic event. This judgment comes from God but is executed through Islam

2. **Who is being spoken to?**
   John is again writing to **all Christians**.

3. **Who is the prophecy about?**
   **The Catholic Church** and its spiritual offspring that distort the Gospel - Babylon the Great.

4. **When will this happen?**
   This prophecy is yet future so we don't know when it will take place – but we do know that it will occur **just prior** to a gathering of Islamic armies at Megiddo in Northern Israel

5.. **Who is behind it?**
   **Islam** - empowered by Satan

This is not metaphorical fire and brimstone - it's a warning. The destruction will be swift, final, and global in scope. Whether it's Rome or all of the West, the message is clear: God's patience with spiritual corruption has run out. Come out of her - or go down with her.

59

# The last stand

## The Prophecy of the final defeat of the beast

which appears in **Revelation 19:11-21** in the

| 1st Vision | 2nd Vision | 3rd Vision | 4th Vision | 5th Vision | 6th Vision | 7th Vision |
|---|---|---|---|---|---|---|
| **The history of the Church** | **The trials of believers** | **The history of the gentiles** | **The origin of anti-semitism** | **The Last Plagues** | **The fall of Babylon** | **The reign of Christ** |
| *Rev Ch 1-3* | *Rev Ch 4-8.1* | *Rev Ch 8.2-11* | *Rev Ch 12-14* | *Rev Ch 15-16; 19-20* | *Rev Ch 17-18* | *Rev Ch 21-22* |

By this point in vision 6, Babylon has been destroyed and John moves to a description of the reaction of those in heaven:

> *19 After this I heard what sounded like the roar of a great multitude in heaven shouting: "Hallelujah! Salvation and glory and power belong to our God 2 for true and just are his judgements.*
>
> *He has condemned the great prostitute who corrupted the earth by her adulteries. He has avenged on her the blood of his servants." 3 And again they shouted: "Hallelujah! The smoke from her goes up for ever and ever."* ***(Revelation 19:1-3)***

Note the passion with which the fall of Babylon / false Christianity is celebrated. Clearly those in heaven are *very* happy that it is gone - a fact which should give 21st Century Christians cause for intense self-reflection. If this is how God feels about false Christianity - we need to make absolutely sure that we're not caught up in it.

But then the vision continues:

*[6] Then I heard what sounded like a great multitude, like the roar of rushing waters and like loud peals of thunder, shouting: "Hallelujah! For our Lord God Almighty For our Lord God Almighty reigns. Let us rejoice and be glad and give Him glory!*

*For the wedding of the Lamb has come, and his bride has made herself ready. [8] Fine linen, bright and clean, was given her to wear."*

*[9] Then the angel said to me, "Write this: Blessed are those who are invited to the wedding supper of the Lamb!" And he added, "These are the true words of God."*

You'll note the reference to 'the wedding of the Lamb' - an event which will be familiar to most Christians.

So the woman has been destroyed and we're now witnessing the consummation of the true Church. But wait? What happened to the Islamic beast?

At this point in the prophecy it's still out there.

If that confuses you - let's recap. In Revelation 16:16, just after the Euphrates River had dried up, the Kings of the earth had gathered together at Megiddo, in Northern Israel.

Then the prophecy had taken a detour to describe the destruction of the Woman which appeared in *the 6th Vision: the Vision of the fall of Babylon.*

Now we move back to the 5th Vision, in Revelation 19:19, where we pick up on this same scene – the gathering of the beast and the kings of the earth at Megiddo in Northern Israel.

What happens next is swift and decisive:

*[11] I saw heaven standing open and there before me was a white horse, whose rider is called Faithful and True. ... [15] Coming out of his mouth is a sharp sword with which to strike down the nations. "He will rule them with an iron sceptre." He treads the winepress of the fury of the wrath of God Almighty. [16] On his robe and on his thigh he has this name written:*

*king of kings and lord of lords.*

*[17] And I saw an angel standing in the sun, who cried in a loud voice to all the birds flying in midair, "Come, gather together for the great supper of God, [18] so that you may eat the flesh of kings, generals, and the mighty, of horses and their riders, and the flesh of all people, free and slave, great and small."*

*[19] Then I saw the beast and the kings of the earth and their armies gathered together to wage war against the rider on the horse and his army. [20] But the beast was captured, and with it the false prophet who had performed the signs on its behalf. With these signs he had deluded those who had received the mark of the beast and worshiped its image. The two of them were thrown alive into the fiery lake of burning sulphur. [21] The rest were killed with the sword coming out of the mouth of the rider on the horse, and all the birds gorged themselves on their flesh.* ***(Revelation 19:11-21)***

So there it is. Remember, the sixth vision was an amplification of the details of the events of the last bowl in the fifth vision, so this entire sequence of events may have played out in just one day - from the destruction of Babylon right through until the defeat and capture of the Islamic beast in this final battle.

# 60

## summary

# The meaning of the Visions of the fate of God's enemies

which appear in the **Book of Revelation**

| 1st Vision | 2nd Vision | 3rd Vision | 4th Vision | 5th Vision | 6th Vision | 7th Vision |
|---|---|---|---|---|---|---|
| **The history of the Church** | **The trials of believers** | **The history of the gentiles** | **The origin of anti-semitism** | **The last plagues** | **The fall of Babylon** | **The reign of Christ** |
| *Rev Ch 1-3* | *Rev Ch 4-8.1* | *Rev Ch 8.2-11* | *Rev Ch 12-14* | *Rev Ch 15-16, 19-20* | *Rev Ch 17-18* | *Rev Ch 21-22* |

Up until the end of *the Vision of the Origin of Antisemitism* we were solving prophecy through the lens of history. We discovered that Revelation features repeated countdowns to significant events that have already happened to Jerusalem – always ending in **1948 or 1967**.

But in this new vision, that changed. We turned the camera around 180 degrees to look at a series of events that were **entirely future**. No new dates to decode - just a graphic outline of the ultimate fate of **false Christianity** and **Islam.**

The key message of this vision wasn't complicated: God told us that Islam and false Christianity (in the form of Catholicism and her daughters) were responsible for the ongoing persecution of the Jews (and true Christians) over the past 2,000 years – and that He is going to destroy both.

He even tells us *how* He is going to execute this final judgement.

First, false Christianity will be *destroyed by fire*, at the hands of the Islamic beast. Then, it will be the turn of Islam which will gather at Megiddo in Northern Israel to face Yeshua Himself, Who will make short work of them. Their fate is described in particularly gory terms where the birds of the air are invited to *"Come, gather together for the great supper of God, so that you may eat the flesh of kings, generals, and the mighty, of horses and their riders, and the flesh of all people, free and slave, great and small."*

These judgements are clearly spelt out in Revelation:

These final judgments are not isolated events but the climax of a cascading series of plagues described in Revelation 15–16, unfolding over an undefined period. Catastrophic judgments fall on the Islamic powers of the Middle East: widespread afflictions, waters turned to blood, scorching heat, darkness over the beast's throne, the drying of the Euphrates, the gathering of kings for war, a global earthquake, and devastating hail.

As the Euphrates dries up, the forces of Islam prepare for a full-scale invasion of Israel, with armies massing at Megiddo as the final judgment approaches. At the same time, Babylon - the false Christian power that obstructed the Gospel and deceived millions into believing they already belonged to God - is judged. The beast destroys her suddenly and violently, an event that probably points beyond Rome itself to a decisive blow against the modern Western world that inherited Babylon's role.

Then Yeshua appears, riding on a white horse. The beast and the false prophet are seized, and both are cast alive into the lake of fire. The sequence ends not in ambiguity, but in finality.

**Why the false-Christianity thread is so important**

God reserves a great deal of space in the Book of Revelation to tell us how He is going to judge Islam. That description is comprehensive, just and final and repays the countless sins of that Satanic institution.

**But don't miss the equal severity with which He judges the false Church.** I opened this book with a warning based on the words of Yeshua in Matthew 24:

*"Many will come in My Name saying **I represent Christ** and will deceive many"*

This vision brings that warning full circle and we can now see that the Lord was talking about false Christianity in the guise of the Catholic Church (the Woman riding the beast) and some of her

Orthodox and Protestant daughters as well as the many 'Christian' cults.

Their crime isn't merely bad doctrine - it's *the blockading of salvation*. Catholicism, for example, hasn't just replaced Christ's terms with theatre, rites, and works – it has blocked the path of seekers to true salvation and taught them, instead, to trust in a religious system instead of the Savior - leading hundreds of millions to hell in the process.

This vision tells us that these deeds will not go unanswered and that **judgment will start at the door of the false Church**.

But how can you know if you're part of that system? Trying to identify the avalanche of false teachings to enable us to understand what we *shouldn't* be doing is a near impossible task. There are just too many of them spread across too many pseudo-Christian organisations.

Fortunately, we don't need to. As we outlined in Chapter 57, if we pay attention to the things that God tells us we *must* do – He'll take care of the rest:

1. Believe that *Jesus is Lord* - the only way to the Father,
2. Repent of your sins
3. Confess Him openly,
4. Live the rest of your life in obedient alignment to the Father's will.

No *go-between* required. Just you and God.

---

**A Personal Note**

If I've made all of this sound like I think walking away from the comforting assurances of false Christianity is easy – trust me: I don't.

We each have our own way of defying God and in my own case it was the false belief in eternal salvation without ongoing obedience.

I became a Christian more than forty years ago. I believed, I confessed – and then I carried on with my life as if nothing had changed, never actually handing the steering wheel over to God.

For years I lived by my own will while claiming His name – constantly reassuring myself that my sins were ok because of a confession that I had made decades earlier. A comforting lie that false Christianity had impressed upon me again and again.

The result was chaos. A pattern of recurring sin, repeated failures, selfish actions that impacted on the lives of others, hurting those I cared about, and a life led by ego and hubris.

I wasn't the wheat – I was the tares – and I was on an express train to eternal separation from God.

But a few years ago, something finally shifted. After a succession of particularly big personal failures - I started *wanting* God to take control. Even then, the change was very gradual and my life continued to be punctuated by stumbling and sin for several more years. In fact, only in these past couple of years have I truly learned what it means to say, "Thy will be done," and mean it.

The impact has been profound.
Peace instead of striving.
Purpose instead of chaos.

So I get it. The hold of false Christianity is powerful, often subtle – and superficially comforting. But if you trust and acknowledge Yeshua as the ONLY way to God, turn from your sins, and hand the ongoing control of your life over to the Father in obedience to scripture, He will clean out the things that don't belong.

God will soon punish false Christianity for its many sins.
Come out of it, before that happens.

61

# The power of a coherent prophetic narrative

You may have noticed a subtle but important change in the some of the prophecy solutions that we identified in the latter half of *Prophecy Shock*.

Some of them didn't contain *time-defined* clues.

Examples of these include:

- **The Second Beast / "Little Horn" of Revelation 13** – which was identified as the British Empire.
- **The Woman riding the Beast in Revelation** – which was identified as false Christianity, centred in Rome
- **The "Eighth Beast" in Revelation** – which was identified as the Islamic beast.

This isn't an error – it's a reflection of the fact that, having established the correct time period for earlier prophecies, logic then limits the range of options left for the identification of these subsequent solutions.

This is how logic problems work. Earlier in *Prophecy Shock* we compared the task of interpreting prophecy to solving a logic puzzle where - once the key answers are fixed - the remaining possibilities quickly narrow.

Interpreted correctly, Bible prophecy functions in the same way. Once time-defined prophecies establish the era, setting, and nature of the powers involved, related symbols within the same visions are no longer free to range across history. Their identity is constrained by the framework already fixed. Secondary players aren't guessed – they're specifically identified by their relationship to a previous time-defined solution.

This is not interpretive licence; it is the logical consequence of treating prophecy as a single, coherent, unfolding narrative. Time-defined prophecies establish the major structural markers of that narrative: the long arcs of exile, domination, restoration, and return. Once those anchors are in place, God does not need to attach a fresh countdown to every related symbol. The earlier clocks already define the setting. In this way, prophecy becomes cumulative, building clarity as history unfolds rather than resetting the puzzle with each new vision.

This also explains why so many popular end-times expectations collapse once the time-defined prophecies are correctly understood. Ideas such as a future Antichrist, a rebuilt Temple, or a final seven-year Tribulation depend on the assumption that the main prophetic clocks are still ticking. But as the preceding chapters have shown, the key time periods of Daniel and Revelation have already landed in history and closed. When the framework is full, there is no remaining prophetic space for additional end-times scenarios to occupy. These concepts do not fail because they are controversial, but because they no longer fit the structure that the prophecies themselves establish.

The Revelation solutions that don't provide time-defined clues, don't need them. They sit within a framework that has already been fixed by earlier prophecy which increasingly converges on the same historical turning points.

So prophecy is not changing as this book progresses. The reader's perspective is.

# Section Eight

# RELATED PROPHECIES AND VISIONS

*Surely the Sovereign Lord does nothing without revealing his plan to his servants the prophets. Amos 3:7*

# Preview

***Prophecy was meant to confirm, not confuse***

For the first few years of my Christian walk my study of prophecy theories was a bit like revealing a 'scratch-off' card where the first two panels revealed a big prize but the third panel revealed something completely different.

This happened often. I would come across an enticing new interpretation which would appear to tie everything together in a logical and compelling way, only to find, on further examination, that key scriptures or parallel prophecies had been left out because they contradicted the interpretation.

So in this next section we'll review other significant prophecies to make sure that they are consistent with the solutions in this book.

We'll explore:

- **The incredible timeline in Daniel Chapter 11**
  Daniel Chapter 11 isn't a dumping ground for miscellaneous prophecies or a warning of things to come in the last days – it's an intricately detailed summary of 2,500 years of the control of Jerusalem – leading up to its liberation in 1967.

- **The 430 days**
  Gods instructions, to Ezekiel, to 'lie on his side' for a total of 430 days aren't an obscure reference to Old testament events – they're yet another prophecy **pointing us directly to the rebirth of Israel** over 2,500 years later.

- **The "Last Generation"**
  Discover how the fig tree prophecy of Matthew 24 refers to **modern Israel**, and why **we are now living in that generation**.

- **The real Tribulation Timeline**
  This is not a 7-year future nightmare, but a historical era beginning in **688 AD** with the Dome of the Rock and concluding in **1948** with Israel's rebirth.

- **The Last Trumpet**
  Most prophecy has been fulfilled - but the last trumpet is still ahead. We are living in the final interlude, a waiting zone between fulfilment and return.

- **The 70 Sevens**
  You'll see how this time period aligns exactly with the rise and restoration of Israel - ending not in 70 AD, but in **1967**, with the recapture of Jerusalem, by the Israelis.

This is not speculation. This section ties together **prophecy, history, and exact dates** to show that God's timeline has unfolded **precisely as foretold**, culminating in a handful of events still to come.

62

# The incredible history outline

## prophesied in Chapter 11 of the Book of Daniel

which appear in the **Book of Daniel** in the

| 1st Vision | 2nd Vision | 3rd Vision | 4th Vision | 5th Vision | 6th Vision | 7th Vision |
|---|---|---|---|---|---|---|
| **The control of Jerusalem** | **The Kings madness** | **The restoration of the Holy land** | **The consecration of the sanctuary** | **The Seventy Sevens** | **The writing on the wall** | **Israels long future** |
| *Dan Ch 2* | *Dan Ch 4* | *Dan Ch 7* | *Dan Ch 8* | *Dan Ch 9* | *Dan Ch 5* | *Dan Ch 10-12* |

After reading *Prophecy Shock*, you'll have a new appreciation of just how far off-course the modern Church has drifted in its understanding of the meaning of the prophecies in the Books of Daniel and Revelation – which should add weight to my words when I tell you that Chapter 11 is possibly the most misunderstood chapter in the Book of Daniel, if not all of the prophetic books.

Past attempts to decipher it have assumed that it is a series of prophecies relating to events in the last days involving an unnamed 'King of the North' and 'King of the South' – but once we understand its relationship to the overall Vision in Daniel any confusion quickly disappears.

Chapter 11 is not a series of prophecies about the last days – it is the bridge between Chapter 10 and Chapter 12 – uniting all three as the 7th and final vision that Daniel recorded for us. As such, it is an outline of the events which take place between the 6th century BC, when Daniel wrote his book, and 1967 when Daniels last prophecy was fulfilled.

Earlier in *Prophecy Shock* we reviewed the second half of Chapter 11 where we identified the British Empire and the role that it played prior to the reestablishment of Israel in 1948. But this was only the tail end of a remarkable passage of scripture which starts back in the time of King Cyrus and details history with such extraordinary precision that it is impossible to see it as anything other than divinely inspired.

I don't propose to outline those many prophecies here as the Chapter is quite lengthy and understanding it is not essential to grasping the message of *Prophecy Shock* – but if you're interested in the details of this extraordinary chapter, I have outlined them in full in Appendix C.

If you don't mind a bit more detail I thoroughly encourage you to read it.

63

# Ezekiel's Strange Puzzle of 360 days

Based on the 4th Chapter of Book of Ezekiel

Earlier in this book we addressed the time-defined prophecies in the Book of Daniel – including the prophecies of 1,290 and 1,335 days which appeared in Chapter 12 of that book.

We assumed that those prophecies were prefaced on Babylonian 360-day schematic years which needed to be converted to modern years – an assumption which took us to AD 688, a year which has since been consistently repeated in other prophecies in this book.

We also assumed that this same basis of measurement applied to the unusual (time-defined) prophecy of '430 days' that we find in the 4th Chapter of the Book of Ezekiel because Daniel and Ezekiel lived at around the same time.

But before we review that prophecy – let's first find out a bit more about Ezekiel himself.

### Introducing Ezekiel

It's important to note that Ezekiel wasn't just another prophet – he was a temple priest who became an exile when he was taken among the second wave of captives to Babylon in 597 BC. He was ripped out of Jerusalem's temple life and relocated to Babylon with the rest of his people. As such, he was in the thick of national defeat and personal loss, cut off from the land and the temple that had defined his entire calling.

But instead of fading into the background, he became a messenger for God and his life was turned into a kind of living stage play where his every action, no matter how strange, carried prophetic weight.

The first three chapters of his book set the scene for this. They start with Ezekiel encountering God's glory in a vision so overwhelming that words can barely capture it - living creatures, wheels within wheels, and the radiant throne of heaven itself. From that moment, he is commissioned to be a prophet and a *watchman* to a stubborn, rebellious people who don't want to hear what he has to say.

**Ezekiel's 430 days**

This brings us to Chapter 4 of Ezekiels book - which opens with God instructing Ezekiel to take a clay brick, scratch the outline of Jerusalem onto it, and then build a little model siege around it - complete with ramps, camps, and battering rams. To top it off, Ezekiel is told to set an iron pan between himself and the city, representing the withholding of Gods protection.

In hindsight, this was a prophecy of the siege of Jerusalem which would take place just a few years later and meant that the city was not only going to be attacked by Babylon but also abandoned by God Himself.

Then comes the most famous part of the chapter.

> [4] *"...lie on your left side and put the sin of the people of Israel upon yourself. You are to bear their sin for the number of days you lie on your side.* [5] *I have assigned you the same number of days as the years of their sin. So for 390 days you will bear the sin of the people of Israel.*
>
> [6] *"After you have finished this, lie down again, this time on your right side, and bear the sin of the people of Judah. I have assigned you 40 days, a day for each year."* ***(Ezekiel 4:4-6)***

So God commands Ezekiel to lie on his side for hundreds of days - 390 on his left side to symbolize Israel's sins, and then 40 on his right to symbolize Judah's. One day for each year of rebellion.

The 390 days pointed back to the northern kingdom, which had been in a state of rebellion ever since Jeroboam led them away from the house of David and set up golden calves in Bethel and Dan. That single act poisoned the nation, locking them into centuries of idolatry, bloodshed, and injustice, with not one righteous king among them – leading to their conquest by the Assyrians in 722 BC.

However, although the nation had been conquered, a large number of the people themselves had escaped into Judah and their guilt still echoed in God's reckoning.

Meanwhile, the 40 days pointed to Judah - the southern kingdom that should have known better. They had the temple, the priesthood, and a handful of good kings like Hezekiah and Josiah, but most of the time they fell into the same patterns of corruption and idol worship as their northern cousins. The "40 years" was a 'catch up' for the centuries during which the Jewish people had ignored God's command to let the land rest every seventh year, and especially the fiftieth "year of Jubilee" when debts were cancelled and the land was restored. Instead, they treated the land as their own possession and milked it for all it was worth.

So 390 plus 40 – 430 years in total.

**What's being predicted?**

The first part of the message was crystal clear - after centuries of turning their backs on God, Israel and Judah had finally run out of chances. God's patience had hit its limit, and 430 years of judgment were locked in.

But that judgment wasn't Gods end goal. He wasn't finished with Israel - He was correcting them. And while the exile was intended to force them to drop idolatry, it also came with a promise: that God would give them a new heart and spirit so that they could actually stay faithful.

Through Ezekiel we also learned that the old division between Israel and Judah would end and that Israel would come back as a united nation. under one king from David's line, living in lasting peace. In fact it's from the Book of Ezekiel that we get the prophecy of the 'dry bones' which predicts the restoration of Israel:

*37 The hand of the Lord was on me, and he brought me out by the Spirit of the Lord and set me in the middle of a valley; it was full of bones. 2 He led me back and forth among them, and I saw a great many bones on the floor of the valley, bones that were very dry. 3 He asked me, "Son of man, can these bones live?"*

*I said, "Sovereign Lord, you alone know."*

*4 Then he said to me, "Prophesy to these bones and say to them, 'Dry bones, hear the word of the Lord! 5 This is what the Sovereign Lord says to these bones: I will make breath enter you, and you will come to life. 6 I will attach tendons to you and make flesh come upon you and cover you with skin; I will put breath in you, and you will come to life. Then you will know that I am the Lord.'"* ***(Ezekiel 37:1-6)***

This prophecy is widely acknowledged as a prediction of the re-establishment of the nation of Israel which took place in 1948.

So, summarised, Ezekiel's message was that Israel and Judah would be punished for their idolatry and disobedience – but that after a long time, God would re-establish them again, as one nation.

This is the same message that we've seen repeated again and again in multiple prophecies throughout this book: that God would punish the tribes of Israel, eventually leading to expulsion from their land – but that Israel would ultimately be restored, in 1948, and that Jerusalem would eventually be recaptured in 1967.

But this time it doesn't appear in the Books of Daniel or Revelation – it appears in the Book of Ezekiel.

### Who is the message addressed to and who is it about?

Once again the scripture clearly tells us who the message was addressed to:

> *"...the word of the Lord came to **Ezekiel the priest**, the son of Buzi, by the Kebar River in the land of the Babylonians"* ***(Ezekiel 1:3)***

So the book was addressed to Ezekiel – and we're also told the identity of the people who are the subject of the message:

> *"Son of man, I send thee to **the children of Israel**, to a rebellious nation that hath rebelled against me: they and their fathers have transgressed against me, even unto this very day." (Ezekiel 2:3)*

> *"Son of man, go, get thee unto **the house of Israel**, and speak with my words unto them. For thou art not sent to a people of a strange speech...but to the house of Israel...But the house of Israel will not hearken unto thee..." (Ezekiel 3:1, 4–5, 7)*

The 'house of Israel', in this context, is referring to all of the twelve tribes of Israel – not just the geographical nation of Israel, which had been conquered by the Assyrians about 125 years earlier.

So we can see that God had sent Ezekiel to warn them of what was coming upon them – even though He already knew that they would not listen.

### When did the prophecy start?

When Ezekiel wrote this prophecy in about 597 BC, the prophecy of national punishment had already started because the first seventy years of the 430 years of prophesied punishment was already underway in the form of the seventy year Exile which had begun in 605 BC.

### The Seventy years of Exile

**Jeremiah 29:4-10** tells us that the exile would last for seventy years and we know that it ended in 536 BC (the first year of Cyrus) - but if you're alert you'll notice that 605 minus 70 equals 535, not 536. This is because the 70 years were Babylonian years, – so, just as we did in Daniel's prophecies of 1,290 and 1,335 days earlier in this book, we need to convert them to our modern years:

70 x .9857 = 69 (68.999)

605 BC → plus 69 → = 536 BC

### When does the prophecy end?

So 70 (69) of the 430 years were over by 536 BC – leaving 360 years still to be fulfilled. It just remains to convert those years from Babylonian years to Gregorian years to determine how many years remain in the prophecy:

360 x .9857 = 354 (354.8)

And since the first part of the prophecy ended in 536 BC, we use that as the starting point for the remaining 355 years:

536 BC → plus 354 → = 182 BC

So did anything significant happen in **182 BC**? In short – no – although there was certainly a significant event just a few years earlier - in **187 BC** - when **Antiochus III** was killed and his son **Seleucus IV Philopator** took the throne (**187–175 BC**). Under Seleucus IV the climate for Judea deteriorated - heavier fiscal pressure and interference with temple affairs foreshadowed the crackdown that would erupt under his brother, **Antiochus IV Epiphanes**, culminating in the **Maccabean revolt (167 BC)**.

But the prophecy predicted 354 years – not 349 years – so these events might as well have been a million years away.

However, what ***is*** significant about **182 BC** is the spiritual state of the Jewish people at that time. It hadn't improved, at all, since 536 BC. Instead of wholehearted devotion to God, many had embraced the surrounding Greek culture. Wealthy and influential Jews were building gymnasiums in Jerusalem, abandoning circumcision, neglecting the Sabbath, and even participating in pagan rituals. Idolatry had crept back in, not through carved statues in the home, but through a wholesale adoption of foreign gods, values, and practices.

So how might God have been expected to respond? Fortunately we don't have to guess because scripture tells us. In Chapter 26 of the Book of Leviticus we find a long passage where God is talking about reward for obedience and punishment for disobedience – and in the section on disobedience He includes this haunting warning:

> *18 "'If after all this you will not listen to me, I will punish you for your sins **seven times over.**"*

> *21 "'If you remain hostile toward me and refuse to listen to me, I will multiply your afflictions **seven times over**, as your sins deserve."*

> *24 I myself will be hostile toward you and will afflict you for your sins **seven times over.**"*

> *27 "'If in spite of this you still do not listen to me but continue to be hostile toward me, 28 then in my anger I will be hostile toward you, and I myself will punish you for your sins **seven times over.**"*

So in the space of just ten verses God tells us – **four times** – that he will punish the Jews **seven times over** if they refuse to heed their punishment. This was written, by Moses, around a thousand years before Ezekiel lived – but it is part of writings that established the basis for all Judaic law far into the future – so does it have application to the 430 day prophecy?

It most certainly does – in fact the more I've studied this prophecy the more I get the impression that God inspired those four warnings, in Leviticus, with this prophecy in Ezekiel in mind.

Let's summarise where we're at:

- God gave Ezekiel a prophecy in which the Tribes of Israel would be punished for 430 Babylonian years (390 + 40)

- 70 years of that punishment were completed in the 70 (69 Gregorian) years between 605 BC and 536 BC

- The remaining 360 Babylonian years (354 Gregorian years) ended in 182 BC – but by this time the Jews were still widely involved in idolatry and had clearly learnt nothing from Gods repeated warnings

- In Chapter 26 of Leviticus, God tells us that, if punishment does not produce the required result – He will punish the Jews 7 times over

So what happens if we take the remaining 360 Babylonian years of the original punishment and amplify them by seven then convert them to modern years?

360 x 7 = 2,520

2,520 x .9857 = 2483.964 Gregorian Years

-536 + 2483.964 Gregorian Years = **1947**

And there it is – 1947 – the year in which the United Nations voted to allow the re-establishment of a Jewish state on (some of) the same land that had been the possession of their ancestors for thousands of years – fulfilling Ezekiel's prophecy of extended punishment and landing at the same point in history as the other prophecies in this book.

| **The Prophecy of 360 Days**<br>Ezekiel 4:4-6 | | | |
|---|---|---|---|
| **What's being predicted?** | *That God would extend the 360 year punishment of the Jews, by seven, because they failed to heed the warning of the original punishment* | | |
| **Question** | **Clue from Scripture** | **Math** | **Solution** |
| **Who is the prophecy addressed to?** | *"...the word of the Lord came to Ezekiel the priest" (Ezekiel 1:3)* | | **The prophecy is addressed to Ezekiel** |
| **Who is the prophecy about?** | *"..."Son of man, I send thee to the children of Israel..." (Ezekiel 2:3)* | | **The prophecy is about the Jews and Jerusalem** |
| **What year does the prophecy start?** | *At the end of the first 70 years of Exile* | ***-536*** | **The prophecy begins in 536 BC** |
| **How long will the prophecy last?** | *"I will punish you for your sins seven times over" (Leviticus 26:18)* | ***360 x 7*** | **The prophecy will last for 2,520 Babylonian years** |
| **What year does the prophecy end?** | | ***2,483 Gregorian years*** | **The prophecy ends in 1947** |

**1947 or 1948?**

As I was studying this prophecy I discovered that this link has also been made by others – and that some of those solutions land on the year 1948, rather than 1947 – making them more consistent with other prophecies in *Prophecy Shock*.

But invariably these relied on a 'forced' starting date that had no objective logic beyond their need to make their numbers work – or relied on complicated formulas that would stretch the patience of most readers.

Throughout *Prophecy Shock* I have always worked on the basis that dates and years must be logical and must make sense within the broader framework and that you, my reader, should be able to easily check the accuracy of my numbers on a simple calculator.

As such – 1947 it is.

---

**A fascinating side note**

Before we leave this prophecy there's another detail worth pausing on. The number 2,520 - which we've already seen as the "seven times" amplification of Ezekiel's 360 years – also appears to surface in the Book of Daniel – in the story of Belshazzar's feast in Daniel 5.

You'll recall the scene: In 539 BC Babylon's king throws a wild banquet and, while he is drinking from the sacred vessels taken from the temple in Jerusalem, suddenly a mysterious hand appears out of thin air and begins writing on the palace wall. The words - *Mene, Mene, Tekel, Upharsin* - strike terror into the king, and Daniel is summoned to interpret them. His verdict is devastating: "Mene" signals that Belshazzar's rule has been counted and cut short. "Tekel" declares that he has been weighed and exposed as a lightweight. "Peres" confirms that his kingdom will be divided and handed over to another power. In other words, God has numbered Belshazzar's days, weighed him in the balance, and found him wanting and, that very night, Babylon fell to the Medes and Persians.

But there's also an intriguing footnote. Some interpreters claim that the inscription should be read as units of weight as follows: two *mene* (100 shekels), one *tekel* (1 shekel), and half a *mina* (25 shekels): total 126 shekels. Multiply this by 20 gerahs per shekel and you arrive at 2,520 - the very same number that defines Ezekiel's extended period of punishment.

Not everyone agrees, of course, and the totals shift depending on whether you assume a 50 or 60 shekel mina - but whether deliberate or coincidental, it's a curious echo: the same number surfacing in the downfall of Babylon that also measures Israel's long years of exile.

Draw your own conclusions.

*The solution at a glance*

# Ezekiel's Strange Puzzle of 360 days

*Scripture: Ezekiel 4:4-6*

1. **What's being predicted?**
   That the remaining 360 years of 430 years of punishment of the tribes of Israel would be extended into the far future due to ongoing disobedience and idolatry – but that it would end with Israel's restoration.

2. **Who is being spoken to?**
   Ezekiel, the exiled temple priest in Babylon..

3. **Who is the prophecy about?**
   "All the house of Israel" - the twelve tribes, not the Church.

4. **When does it start?**
   **536 BC** - the year the first 70 years of exile were completed.

5.. **How long does it last?**
   Seven x the remaining 360 Babylonian years: 2,520 – or **2,483 Gregorian years**

6.. **When does it end?**
   1947 AD - the year that the UN voted to re-establish Israel.

Ezekiel may not have met Daniel – but they were both singing from the same hymn book. This isn't a vague and symbolic cautionary tale about the consequences of disobedience – **it's a precise prophecy ending in 1947 with the UN vote to re-establish Israel.**

# We're now in the last days / time of the end

Earlier in this book we learned that God provided prophecy as a means by which His providence would be demonstrated and that we were never intended to know the timing of events *prior* to those events being fulfilled.

This is reinforced by a passage of scripture that we find in the last chapter of the Book of Daniel where we're told that:

*" ....the words are rolled up and sealed until the time of the end"*

This presents a serious challenge to most of the current interpretations because it means that there would be a time prior to the time of the end, during which it would be impossible to understand what Daniel's words actually meant – meaning any interpretations which preceded that time would be wrong.

Throughout this book the phrase *the time of the end* is used interchangeably with the term *last days* - but what do those terms mean?

Premillennialism defines the *time of the end / last days* as a final period during which many of the prophecies in the Bible will be fulfilled and claims that most of these events are still ahead of us – but it bases that view on interpretations that, in most cases, were developed almost two hundred years ago.

In contrast, *Prophecy Shock* defines *the time of the end / last days* as the time we're in right now - the period of time which comes *after* the fulfilment of the time-defined prophecies.

The difference between these two definitions is huge. The belief that many prophesied events are still ahead of us gives us a false sense of confidence and suggests that we still have time to prepare for what's coming - whereas the revelation that almost all of the events predicted in the Books of Daniel and Revelation are now behind us requires us to act with urgency to 'get right with God' before His imminent return.

**The beginning of *the time of the end*.**

But if the claim of this book is correct - when did the time of the end start?

Scripture gives us a key sign. It tells us that the time of the end will start when Daniel's prophecies are 'unsealed' - and since we now know that the last of Daniel's prophecies was fulfilled in 1967 we can have absolute confidence that that was the year of that unsealing.

As such, any framework of interpretation which was developed prior to that time is, therefore, incorrect.

Skolfield, himself, summed this position up when he said:

> "Most end-time views held by the Church today were theorised from studies made in Daniel hundreds of years ago. But if God sealed Daniel until the "time of the end," and the "time of the end" didn't begin until 1967, then those end-time views have to be incomplete, or even wrong. If they are, we could be basing the last few decisions we will ever make on this planet on theoretical events that are never going to happen".

Dwell on that for a moment and think through the implications of that discovery for almost every popular system of prophecy interpretation.

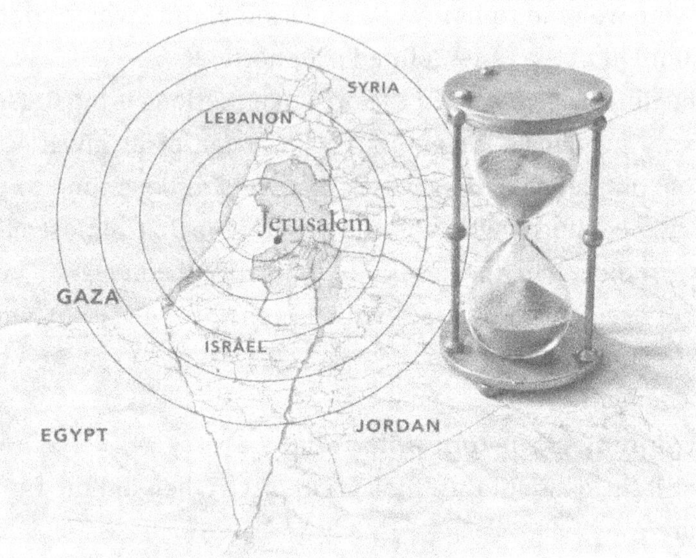


## 1967 – the beginning of the time of the end

65

# The prophecy of
# Ten Days in Smyrna

which appears in **Revelation 1:8-11**

In chapter 30 of *Prophecy Shock* we reviewed the first Vision in the Book of Revelation – the History of the Church – and we noted that this vision took the form of seven letters to seven Churches.

We discovered that the order in which these Churches were addressed provides an extraordinary outline of Church history – starting with **the Church of Ephesus** (*The Loveless Church*) in the Apostolic age – and going right through to **the Church of Laodicea** (*The Lukewarm Church*) in our current age.

We also discovered that, unlike some of the other visions in this book, the Vision of the History of the Church does not provide *time-defined* prophecies which might help us identify specific years of fulfilment.

**With one exception.**

The letter to **the Church in Smyrna** (*The Persecuted Church*) contains a short but extraordinary time marker:

> *Behold, the devil shall cast some of you into prison, that ye may be tried; and ye shall have tribulation* ***ten days****: be thou faithful unto death, and I will give thee a crown of life.* **(Revelation 2:10)**

This is significant because we already know that the Book of Revelation uses 'days' as a prophetic symbol for 'years'.

We also know that Smyrna probably covers the years between 100 and 313 AD – a period during which Christianity was often an enemy of the State and the subject of constant persecution.

Christians weren't constantly persecuted throughout this time – but when they were, it was cruelly theatrical. Roman arenas became instruments of terror. Christians were fed to wild animals, burned as living torches, crucified, or executed before cheering crowds. The Colosseum stands today not merely as an architectural relic, but as a silent witness to the blood-soaked entertainment culture of imperial Rome.

So against this background – is there a ten year period of persecution of Christians that stands out?

There is. Church history records exactly such a period.

**The Great Persecution**

In AD 303, the Roman Emperor Diocletian launched the most systematic persecution Christianity had ever faced. Earlier persecutions were localised and sporadic. This one was empire-wide, organised, and ideological.

Diocletian believed Rome's troubles stemmed from offending the traditional gods and Christianity was seen as a threat to imperial unity. The objective was not restraint, it was elimination.

Imperial edicts followed: Churches were destroyed; Scriptures were burned; Christian assemblies were outlawed; Clergy were imprisoned; and Christians were forced to sacrifice or face punishment.

Those who complied were released. Those who refused were beaten, tortured, exiled, or killed. Christians were dragged before magistrates, chained in filthy prisons, lashed until flesh failed, maimed to prevent future ministry, burned alive, executed by sword, or worked to death in imperial mines. Families were separated.

Churches were razed. Scriptures were destroyed. Terror became policy.

Yet the faith of true Christians endured.

The first edicts ordering this torment were issued in AD 303 – and it ended in AD 313 when Constantine issued the Edict of Toleration which legalised Christianity. **Precisely ten years.**

**Why this ten years matters**

This prophecy is short in duration but strong in confirmation. It demonstrates that the prophetic clock operates consistently even at small scale.

A symbolic day resolving into a literal year requires no numerology or creative stretching here. History matches the text cleanly.

Just as importantly, Smyrna anchors the Vision of the History of the Church in real chronology. These letters are not merely moral portraits or spiritual metaphors - they are prophetic markers embedded in history.

The Church of Smyrna is not simply "the persecuted Church" in general terms. It corresponds to a specific, measurable, historically verifiable season of suffering.

Ten days.
Ten years.

A bounded season of tribulation - endured, purified, and overcome.

# The prophecy of the great tribulation

which appears in **Matthew 24/25 and Mark 13**

Over the course of this book we have solved some of the most iconic prophecies in scripture – but there is still one, in particular, which needs our consideration in order to make this study of fulfilled prophecy almost complete.

**The great tribulation**

The event known as 'the tribulation' is referred to four times in the New Testament - once in the Book of Revelation and three times in the Books of Matthew and Mark. (there are a handful of translations that also use that word elsewhere, but those are all instances where it is simply an alternative for the word 'suffering').

According to Premillennialism, these four references all warn of a period of 7 years which will take place at the end of the age and will be characterised by the persecution of Christians.

But is this really what is being described? Let's review each of these main references and see what we can learn.

The first appears in Matthew chapter 24 and in Mark chapter 13 as part of the prophecy that we reviewed earlier, in which Yeshua Himself, lays out the events which will lead up to His return.

You may also recall that this account parallels the account in chapter 5 of the Book of Revelation which, itself, provides us with a vision of the history of the persecution of Christians over a period of around 2,000 years. We outlined this in chapter 31 of *Prophecy Shock*.

According to the details provided in Matthew 24 (and Mark 13), this exchange took place on the Mount of Olives toward the end of a day during which Yeshua and the disciples had been at the Temple in Jerusalem.

We pick up the story with the disciples now calling Yeshua's attention to the buildings of the Temple which they could clearly see from their vantage point across the Kidron valley. Note how Yeshua responds to them:

*"Truly I tell you, not one stone here will be left on another; every one will be thrown down."* ***(Matthew 24: 2)***

On hearing this, His disciples asked Him two questions.

1. When will this happen?
2. What will be the sign of Your coming / the end of the age?

*[4] Jesus answered: "Watch out that no one deceives you. [5] For many will come in my name, claiming, 'I am Christ' and will deceive many. [6] You will hear of wars and rumours of wars but see to it that you are not alarmed. Such things must happen, but the end is still to come. [7] Nation will rise against nation, and kingdom against kingdom. There will be famines and earthquakes in various places. [8] All these are the beginning of birth pains.*

*[9] "Then you will be handed over to be persecuted and put to death, and you will be hated by all nations because of me. [10] At that time many will turn away from the faith and will betray and hate each other, [11] and many false prophets will appear and deceive many people. [12] Because of the increase of wickedness, the love of most will grow cold, [13] but the one who stands firm to the end will be saved. [14] And this gospel of the kingdom will be preached in the*

*whole world as a testimony to all nations, and then the end will come.* ***(Matthew 24: 9 – 14)***

This is a general answer to the *second* question that the disciples asked. Yeshua is telling them that 'the end will come' after a long period of persecution of Christians ('you will be hated *because of me*') and will be marked by the completion of the preaching of the Gospel to all nations.

Both of these things happened just as He described. Given our privileged existence in the 21st century, we lack perspective in respect of what Christians have had to go through during the past two thousand years - but for much of that time they've had it tough. In the past they have been thrown to wild animals to be torn apart in the stadia of the Roman Empire, burnt at the stake, tortured by the Catholic Inquisitors, and beheaded in various parts of the world including North Africa and the Middle East.

Even today, such practices continue and to be a Christian in some parts of the Islamic Middle East, Africa or Asia in the 21st century is still to take a risk with one's life.

We should also note that much of Christian history was about bringing the Gospel to all the people of the world - in fact, the heavily derided practice of 'colonisation', in recent centuries, was at least partly driven by a desire to obey the Great Commission given by Yeshua and 'go into all the world' with the gospel.

But what about the first question the disciples asked Yeshua - the one about the timing of the destruction of the Temple?

In Chapter 68 we will note that the Temple was destroyed, by the Romans, in response to a Jewish uprising in 70AD and that this was done in an effort to break the Jewish spirit. This fulfilled Yeshua's prediction that every stone of the temple would be removed - but it is not the event that Yeshua draws our attention to in His answer to that question. Note His next words carefully:

*"So,* ***when you see*** *standing in the holy place,* ***the abomination that causes desolation****, spoken of through the prophet Daniel - let the*

*reader understand - then let those who are in Judea flee to the mountains. Let no one on the housetop go down to take anything out of the house. Let no one in the field go back to get their cloak. How dreadful it will be in those days for pregnant women and nursing mothers! Pray that your flight will not take place in winter or on the Sabbath. For* ***then there will be great tribulation,*** *unequalled from the beginning of the world until now - and never to be equalled again.* ***(Matthew 24: 15 – 22)***

If you've been reading this book you now know that the 'abomination of desolation' appeared in Jerusalem in 688 - over 600 years after the Romans had destroyed the Temple. So why does Yeshua draw reference to *that* event rather than the sacking of the Temple, by the Romans? A clue appears six sentences later where we're told:

*For then there will be* ***great tribulation,*** *unequalled from the beginning of the world until now - and never to be equalled again.*

So there it is - our first reference to 'great tribulation'.

But wait. The passage we've just read isn't describing something that happens to Christians. It's a specific reference to an event which starts *in Jerusalem* in 688 - the same year in which the construction of the Dome of the Rock, the beginning of the Jewish flight from Jerusalem and the trampling down of Jerusalem by the gentiles all occur.

So does that mean that 'the Tribulation' should be recognised as a uniquely Jewish event?

No - because the Prophet John also mentions 'the great tribulation' in Chapter 7 of the Book of Revelation in his vision of a great scene, in heaven, at the end of the age:

*9 After this I looked, and there before me was a great multitude that no one could count, from every nation, tribe, people and language, standing before the throne and before the Lamb.* ***(Revelation 7:9)***

*[13] Then one of the elders asked me, "These in white robes - who are they, and where did they come from?" [14] I answered, "Sir, you know. And he said, "These are they who have come out of* ***the great tribulation****; they have washed their robes and made them white in the blood of the Lamb".* ***(Revelation 7:13-14)***

**Who is this prophecy addressed to and who is it about?**

Different prophecies referencing this event mention both Jews and Christians – so it is addressed to both.

**When does the prophecy start?**

*"When you see standing in the holy place, the abomination that causes desolation".*

Yeshua is telling us that the tribulation starts in the days of the appearance of the 'abomination of desolation' (the Dome of the Rock).

**When does the prophecy end?**

Earlier Yeshua told us that the gospel will be preached to all kingdoms after which *the end will come*. But this is very general. Is there a more specific clue to narrow down the timing of the end?

There is. A little further on, in Matthew 24, we find a verse which is loaded with meaning.

*32 "Now learn this lesson from the fig tree: As soon as its twigs get tender and its leaves come out, you know that summer is near. 33 Even so, when you see all these things, you know that it is near, right at the door.* ***(Matthew 24:32-33)***

Why is this verse significant? Because the 'fig tree' is generally accepted as a symbol of Israel and this passage has long been regarded as a prophecy of the re-establishment of the Jewish state in 1948.

So now we can see that 'the Great Tribulation' begins in 688AD, with the construction of the Dome of the Rock - and ends in 1948 with the re-establishment of the State of Israel.

Let's run those numbers:

| **The Prophecy of the Great Tribulation**<br>Matthew 24 / Mark 13 | | | |
|---|---|---|---|
| **What's being predicted?** | *That Jews and Christians will face intense persecution until 'the fig tree blossoms'* | | |
| **Question** | **Clue from Scripture** | **Math** | **Solution** |
| **Who is the prophecy addressed to?** | | | **The prophecy is addressed to Jews and Christians** |
| **Who is the prophecy about?** | *"When* ***you*** *see standing in the holy place, the abomination that causes desolation" (Matt 24:15)* | | **The prophecy is about Jews and Christians** |
| **What year does the prophecy start?** | *"...when you see ... the abomination that causes desolation, ..." (Matthew 24:15)* | ***688*** | **The prophecy begins in 688** |
| **How long will the prophecy last?** | | ***plus 1,260*** | **The prophecy will last for 1,260 years** |
| **What year does the prophecy end?** | *"Now learn this lesson from the fig tree ... when you see all these things, you know that it is near"* | ***equals 1948*** | **The prophecy ends in 1948** |

So this is the same prophecy that we saw in chapter 11 of the Book of Revelation, where the 'two witnesses' (Christianity and Judaism) were closed out of Israel for 1,260 years.

As such, the 'Great Tribulation' isn't a three-and-a-half or seven year persecution of Christians in the last days. It's a 1,260 year period during which both Jews and Christians endured great hardship, and even faced death, in the defence of their faith.

For Christians - this meant intense persecution at the hands of Islam, paganism and false Christian institutions. For Jews, it meant being 'cut off' from their homeland, and outrageously persecuted by Muslims and false Christians in nation after nation.

And least there be any doubt that this *is* the solution to this prophecy, and that it includes the Jews - I invite you to review what Yeshua said immediately after mentioning the great tribulation:

> *For then there will be great tribulation, unequalled from the beginning of the world until now - and never to be equalled again.*

*"If those days had not been cut short, no one would survive, but for the sake of the elect those days will be shortened".* ***(Matthew)***

But what does this mean? if the prophecy started in 688 and was completed in 1948, in what way was it 'cut short'? Does recent history mention such a thing happening? It certainly does.

As horrifying as the persecution of the Jews may have been over that 1,260-year period, the worst of it took place in the final years of the prophecy in the form of the biggest atrocity of all. **The holocaust**.

*"And these are the words that the LORD spake concerning Israel and concerning Judah.... see whether a man doth travail with child? wherefore do I see every man with his hands on his loins, as a woman in travail, and all faces are turned into paleness? Alas! for that day is great, so that none is like it: it is even the time of Jacob's trouble, but he shall be saved out of it".* ***(Jeremiah 30:3-8)***

In 1948 Israel became a nation again - just as the prophecy said it would – just three years after the close of the second world war, and the slaughter of six million Jews in the death camps of Europe.

But imagine what might have happened if the war in Europe had dragged on, instead. The Concentration Camps of Europe would have continued in their murderous goal of eliminating every Jew in Europe - and if Hitler had won, the Germans would eventually have turned their attention to the Jews across the Atlantic as well.

Only the intervention of God stopped this from happening.

Contemplate that for a moment and - for the first time - reflect on the real meaning of those sobering words, spoken by Yeshua, in Matthew 24:

*"If those days had not been cut short, no one would survive, but for the sake of the elect (the Jews) those days will be shortened".*

*The solution at a glance*

## The Great Tribulation

***Scriptures:*** *Matt 24:15-22; Mark 13:14-20; Rev 7:13-14*

1. **What's being predicted??**
   That Jews and Christians will face intense persecution throughout a period of 1,260 years.

2. **Who is being spoken to?**
   Jesus' Jewish disciples on the Mount of Olives - but the warning is passed down to all future believers.

3. **Who is the prophecy about?**
   **Jews** ("those in Judea… flee")
   **Christ-followers** ("you will be hated by all nations because of Me")

4. **When does it end?**
   **1948 AD** – when Israel is reborn (the fig-tree buds).

5. **How long does it last?**
   **1,260 years**.

6. **When does it start?**
   **688 AD** – the Dome of the Rock is set on the Temple Mount – kicking off 1,260 years of Jewish / Christian persecution.

The Great Tribulation isn't a future seven-year window - it spanned **688 → 1948**, climaxing with the Holocaust and ending when Israel stood up again.

67

# The prophecy of:
# the last generation

which appears in **Matthew 24/25**

Whenever I see the words 'the last generation' I get a mental picture of Tina Turner singing the theme song to the movie *Mad Max: Beyond Thunderdome*, in which those lyrics refer to the people who are left behind after a global apocalypse.

However, that term has a different meaning in prophecy and, now that we understand the real meaning of *the Tribulation* we can better understand the wider message that was shared by Yeshua in Matthew 24/25 and Mark 13.

This prophecy provides a broad description of Christian history, then goes on to talk about the 1,260-years of the Tribulation, culminating in the events of the 'last days' (ie, the things that will happen *after* Israel becomes a nation again in 1948 and Jerusalem is restored to Israel in 1967).

But what does this prophecy tell us about those final years - the important period leading up to the return of Christ?

Actually very little. The entire period of the *last days* - the time gap between the re-establishment of Israel and the return of Yeshua - is inferred in the comma between the word 'nations' and the word 'and' in the following verse:

> [14] *And this gospel of the kingdom will be preached in the whole world as a testimony to all nations, and then the end will come.*

But is there any other reference to this period, in prophecy?

There is - and it appears in the first vision in the Book of Revelation.

You'll recall that we reviewed this earlier and recognised that the 'letters to seven churches' provide an accurate outline of Church history - starting with the Church of Ephesus as symbolic of the early Church. Then, in chapter 34 we discovered that two of these - the Churches of Sardis and Philadelphia - incorporated the period between 688 and 1967 when the Church was closed out of Jerusalem.

**Our era - the Church of Laodicea**

This means that the final Church in the vision - the Church of Laodicea - must cover the period *after* 1967. So let's see what that letter describes:

> *[15] I know your deeds, that you are neither cold nor hot. I wish you were either one or the other! [16] So, because you are lukewarm - neither hot nor cold - I am about to spit you out of my mouth.*
>
> *[17] You say, 'I am rich; I have acquired wealth and do not need a thing.' But you do not realize that you are wretched, pitiful, poor, blind and naked. [18] I counsel you to buy from me gold refined in the fire, so you can become rich; and white clothes to wear, so you can cover your shameful nakedness; and salve to put on your eyes, so you can see.*
>
> *[19] Those whom I love I rebuke and discipline. So be earnest and repent. [20] Here I am! I stand at the door and knock. If anyone hears my voice and opens the door, I will come in and eat with that person, and they with me.*

If that doesn't send shivers down your spine you need to read it again because it would be difficult to imagine a more accurate description of the modern Church.

Yeshua is telling us that we are 'neither cold nor hot' about our faith, and that we no longer rely on Him because we think we have 'acquired wealth', but that in reality, we are naked. He also tells us that His return is imminent ('Here I am. I stand at the door').

This is a haunting echo of what has happened over the past 80+ years. In the decades following the close of WW2 the western world entered the so-called 'post Christian' era in which profession of faith plummeted and the influence of Christian values, on society, disappeared.

Worse still - even within the remaining (western) Church attention has moved from a simple focus on Christ and the importance of obedience and evangelism, to an avalanche of nonsense masquerading as Christianity while leading believers away from their Saviour.

And how does Yeshua react to this? He tells us that he is going to 'spit us out of His mouth'!

What's most frightening about this is that Yeshua's warning makes clear that this period - the Laodicean era - coincides with 'the time of the end'. This means that it takes place between the re-establishment of Israel / recapture of Jerusalem and the Lords return.

So far this gap has lasted for almost 80 years - but are there any clues telling us when it will end?

Let's review what Yeshua, Himself, said about this time a little further on in Matthew chapter 24:

> [32] *"Now learn this lesson from the fig tree: As soon as its twigs get tender and its leaves come out (1948), you know that summer is near.* [33] *Even so, when you see all these things, you know that it is near, right at the door.* [34] *Truly I tell you; this generation will certainly not pass away until all these things have*

*happened.* [35] *Heaven and earth will pass away, but my words will never pass away.*

Is this a clue to the timing of His return? Let's see.

We know that the fig tree represents the re-establishment of Israel in 1948 - but how long is a generation? Prophecy scholars have agonised over this passage for decades, trying to determine the answer to that question.

For a long time, it was thought to be forty years and then, when that length of time had passed, seventy years. However, that period of time has now also passed leaving Bible students scratching their heads and trying to understand what Yeshua meant by this term.

But let's not forget what the disciples had actually asked Yeshua earlier in the chapter. Their question was *"What will be 'the sign' of Your coming and the end of the age?"* and He had responded by running through a list of things that would happen in their future, but with a repeated reassurance that 'the end was not yet'. Then He told them that the re-establishment of Israel, in 1948, would be the sign that would start the clock ticking on the last days while also making clear that no one would know the hour or day (year) in which His return will take place.

But note the key phrase in His words:

[34] *Truly I tell you; this generation will certainly not* ***pass away*** *until all these things have happened.*

So He tells us that the generation which was alive in 1948 would not 'pass away' prior to His return.

The important term here is 'pass away' - a term which we still use today to mean 'die'. So, read in context, this isn't a reference to a 40 or 70 year 'generation' - it's a clear sign that a Jew, or Jews, who were alive when Israel was re-established in 1948 will still be alive when He returns. That's the obvious meaning of His words.

There are still many Jews alive today who were alive in 1948 - but that number will dwindle with time. Frenchwoman Jeanne Calment lived to 122 years of age and is the oldest person to have lived on record. In the unlikely event that someone born in, or prior to, 1948 matches her record of longevity the return of Christ could be delayed until around 2070 - but the likelihood is that it will happen much sooner and could literally happen in the next moment.

So, the people who see the return of Christ will include people (or, at least a person) who was alive at the time of the rebirth of Israel!

This means that, while no one can know the day or the hour - we can now know, with certainty, that we're living in a time when His return could be at any moment - just as God intended.

*The solution at a glance*

# The last generation

***Scriptures:*** *Matt 24:34*

1. **What's being predicted??**
   That Christ will return before the generation of Jews who were alive when Israel was re-established in 1948 have all died off.

2. **Who is being spoken to?**
   Jesus' Jewish disciples on the Mount of Olives - but the warning is passed down to all future believers.

3. **Who is the prophecy about?**
   Followers of Christ

4. **When does it start?**
   **1948 AD** – the beginning of the last days marked by the re-establishment of Israel (the fig-tree buds).

5. **How long does it last?**
   Great question!

6. **When does it end?**
   When Christ returns **like a thief in the night**.

**The return of Christ could happen at any moment** – or it could be decades away.

# The Mystery of the Cross

## The Prophecy of 69 'weeks'

which appears in **Daniel 9:24-27** in the

| 1st Vision | 2nd Vision | 3rd Vision | 4th Vision | 5th Vision | 6th Vision | 7th Vision |
|---|---|---|---|---|---|---|
| **The control of Jerusalem** | **The Kings madness** | **The restoration of the Holy land** | **The consecration of the sanctuary** | **The Seventy Sevens** | **The writing on the wall** | **Israels long future** |
| *Dan Ch 2* | *Dan Ch 4* | *Dan Ch 7* | *Dan Ch 8* | *Dan Ch 9* | *Dan Ch 5* | *Dan Ch 10-12* |

We started our review of the prophecies, in *Prophecy Shock*, with the prophecies in the Book of Daniel – but we didn't complete our review of that book. There are still two more major time-defined prophecies in Daniel and it's appropriate that we should also end our study of prophecy with these.

They're both related to the so-called '70 week' prophecy which appears in chapter 9 of Daniel's Book and starts with Daniel referring to an earlier prophecy, made by another prophet:

> *9 In the first year of Darius son of Xerxes (a Mede by descent), who was made ruler over the Babylonian kingdom - 2 in the first year of his reign, I, Daniel, understood from the Scriptures, according to the word of the Lord given to Jeremiah the prophet, that the desolation of Jerusalem would last seventy years.* ***(Daniel 9:1-2)***

Daniel was referring to a book written at least 50 years earlier by another Prophet – Jeremiah. In the 29th Chapter of that book, Jeremiah records a vision in which God instructed the Babylonian exiles to settle in the land of their captivity, build houses, plant gardens, marry, raise families, and seek the peace of the city where they lived. In other words – prepare to be there for a long time. He also told them not to listen to false prophets who claimed that the exile would end quickly. Instead, they were to understand that the captivity would last seventy years before God restored them and brought them back to Jerusalem. (Jeremiah 29:4–9)

> [10] *For thus saith the LORD, that after seventy years be accomplished at Babylon I will visit you, and perform my good word toward you, in causing you to return to this place".* ***(Jeremiah 29:4-10)***

Daniel picks this prophecy up in his own book and tells us that he was writing about it 'in the first year of Darius' (539 BC) and, since the Jews referred to in Jeremiah may have been taken captive as early as 605 BC, simple math (605- 539) tells us that the 70 years were almost up and that the prophecy was due to be fulfilled very soon.

This was of particular interest to Daniel because he was one of those who had been taken captive to Babylon all those years ago and was now an old man (at least in his 80s and probably in his 90s).

So what did Daniel do? He prayed! The next section of the chapter records this prayer - Daniel, pleading to God for forgiveness for his own sins and for the sins of the Jews and asking God to act on His promise to return the Jews to Jerusalem.

But while Daniel was still praying, something remarkable happened. The angel Gabriel suddenly appeared to him and told him that he was highly esteemed by God and that he (Gabriel) had been sent to give Daniel understanding and insight. He then instructed Daniel to carefully consider the message he was about to receive.

That message begins with one of the most important prophetic statements in the Bible:

*[24] "Seventy 'sevens' are decreed for your people and your holy city to finish transgression, to put an end to sin, to atone for wickedness, to bring in everlasting righteousness, to seal up vision and prophecy and to anoint the Most Holy Place.*

*[25] "Know and understand this: From the time the word goes out to restore and rebuild Jerusalem until the Anointed One, the ruler, comes, there will be seven 'sevens,' and sixty-two 'sevens.' It will be rebuilt with streets and a trench, but in times of trouble.*

*[26] After the sixty-two 'sevens,' the Anointed One will be put to death and will have nothing. The people of the ruler who will come will destroy the city and the sanctuary. The end will come like a flood: War will continue until the end, and desolations have been decreed.*

*[27] He will confirm a covenant with many for one 'seven.' In the middle of the 'seven' he will put an end to sacrifice and offering. And at the temple he will set up an abomination that causes desolation, until the end that is decreed is poured out on him."* ***(Daniel 9:20-27)***

So put yourself in Daniel's position. He's been praying about the imminent end of the seventy years in which the Jews had been separated from Jerusalem - and then Gabriel comes along with a whole new prophecy! Let's see if we can make sense of it.

### Who was the prophecy delivered to and who is it about?

Within Premillennial circles there is a broad consensus that this prophecy - particularly its final part - foretells the rise and reign of a worldwide dictator ("the Antichrist") and concerns a seven-year period of intense persecution known as "the Tribulation." Some place that persecution in the first half of the seven years, others in the second, and a few attempt to combine both views.

But the angel's opening statement makes the primary subject of the prophecy unmistakably clear. He is speaking to Daniel, and he tells Daniel exactly who the prophecy – the entire prophecy - concerns:

> [24] *"Seventy 'sevens' are decreed for **your people** and **your holy city**...." (Daniel 9:24)*

That is about as clear as prophecy gets. The prophecy is directed toward Daniel's people and Daniel's holy city - the Jews and Jerusalem. Not the Church, not a future global tribulation of Christians, not a detached end-times scenario centred elsewhere. Just the Jews.

**What is the prophecy about?**

Remember, this prophecy started with Daniel praying for the imminent end of the 70 years of captivity of the Jews, in Babylon - and now he's being told that his people are about to be subjected to a whole new series of prophetic events after they return to Jerusalem. This part of the message is split into three parts:

**1st Part - Overview**

> [24] ***"Seventy 'sevens' are decreed for your people and your holy city*** *to finish transgression, to put an end to sin, to atone for wickedness, to bring in everlasting righteousness, to seal up vision and prophecy and to anoint the Most Holy Place.*

This section is an overview of the entire prophecy - telling us that 'seventy sevens' will pass during which a series of things will happen, ending with the 'anointing of the Most Holy Place'.

**2nd Part - The 69 Sevens**

The next part of the prophecy tells us about the events which will take place during the first 69 sevens.

*25 "Know and understand this: From the time the word goes out to restore and rebuild Jerusalem until the Anointed One, the ruler, comes, there will be seven 'sevens,' and sixty-two 'sevens.' It will be rebuilt with streets and a trench, but in times of trouble.*

*26 After the sixty-two 'sevens,' the Anointed One will be put to death and will have nothing. The people of the ruler who will come will destroy the city and the sanctuary. The end will come like a flood: War will continue until the end, and desolations have been decreed.*

## 3rd Part - The 70th Seven

*27 He will confirm a covenant with many for one 'seven.' In the middle of the 'seven' he will put an end to sacrifice and offering. And at the temple he will set up an abomination that causes desolation, until the end that is decreed is poured out on him."*

This last part of the prophecy describes one final 'seven' and is the basis upon which Premillennialism argues for a 'seven year Tribulation' in the last days. However, the reference to an 'abomination which causes desolation' (a term which, we now know, refers to the construction of the Dome of the Rock in 688) and the fact that this prophecy is about Jews, not Christians, should alert us to the fact that something else is going on here.

We'll come back to this in the next chapter – but, for now, let's focus on the "69 sevens".

## When does the prophecy of 69 sevens start?

We're told that *the prophecy of 69 sevens* starts:

*"**From the time the word goes out to restore and rebuild Jerusalem** until the Anointed One, the ruler, comes, there will be seven*

*'sevens,' and sixty-two 'sevens.'* ***It will be rebuilt with streets and a trench, but in times of trouble***.

So we're looking for an historical order or command to rebuild Jerusalem as our starting point. There were several such decrees authorising the rebuilding of Jerusalem, but only one of these included a command to also rebuild 'the street' and 'the wall'. This was issued by Artaxerxes Longimanus, the fifth King of the Medo Persian empire, on March 14, 444 B.C.

So now we have three of the six pieces of information required to solve the puzzle:

| Question | Clue from Scripture | Math | Solution |
|---|---|---|---|
| **Who is the prophecy addressed to?** | *"...while I was still in prayer, Gabriel ...came to me..." (Daniel 9.21)* | | **The prophecy is addressed to Daniel** |
| **Who is the prophecy about?** | *"...your people and your holy city..." (Daniel 9.24)* | | **The prophecy is about the Jews and Jerusalem** |
| **What year does the prophecy start?** | *"From the time the word goes out to restore and rebuild Jerusalem ..." (Daniel 9:25)* | **-444** | **The prophecy begins in 444BC** |

**How long will the prophecy last and when does it end?**

The prophecy tells us that, at the end of the 69 sevens:

*"the Anointed One will be put to death and will have nothing"* ***(Daniel 9:26)***

But what does this mean and how long is sixty nine sevens? Let's do the math:

**69 x 7 = 483**

Since this is a prophecy in the Book of Daniel we can assume that these are Babylonian years and we need to convert them from the 360-day year Calander in use in Daniel's time to our modern years by using our simple converter, as follows:

**483 x .9857 = 476.093**

Now let's add those years to our start year:

-444 BC → plus 476 → = **32 AD**

But what happened in 32 AD? Let's refer back to the words of the prophecy:

> [26] *After the sixty-two 'sevens,' the Anointed One will be put to death and will have nothing* ***(Daniel 9:26)***

So do we know anyone like that? An 'Anointed One' who was 'put to death around **32 AD**'? Yes, of course! This is a prophecy about Yeshua who came to Jerusalem as King but was put to death for the sins of mankind.

There is no universally accepted date for the crucifixion, so you won't find this year by doing a simple internet search - but given the absolute accuracy of what we've elsewhere in this book I'm very comfortable accepting this as the actual year of that event, over any alternative year proposed by an academic.

So let's complete our template:

| The Prophecy of 69 'weeks'<br>Daniel 9:24-26 | | | |
|---|---|---|---|
| **What's being predicted?** | *That a period of '69 sevens' will pass before the 'Anointed One' is cut off* | | |
| **Question** | **Clue from Scripture** | **Math** | **Solution** |
| **Who is the prophecy addressed to?** | *"...while I was still in prayer, Gabriel ...came to me..." (Daniel 9.21)* | | **The prophecy is addressed to Daniel** |
| **Who is the prophecy about?** | *"...your people and your holy city..." (Daniel 9.24)* | | **The prophecy is about the Jews and Jerusalem** |
| **What year does the prophecy start?** | *"From the time the word goes out to restore and rebuild Jerusalem ..." (Daniel 9:25)* | ***-444*** | **The prophecy begins in 444BC** |
| **How long will the prophecy last?** | *"...there will be seven 'sevens,' and sixty-two 'sevens. ..." (Daniel 9:26)* | ***476 (69 x 7 = 483 x .9857)*** | **The prophecy will last for 476 years** |
| **What year does the prophecy end?** | *"...the Anointed One will be put to death. " (Daniel 9:26)* | ***equals 32*** | **The prophecy ends in 32 AD** |

### Destruction of the City and the Sanctuary

So now we can see that the 69 sevens end with the crucifixion of Yeshua - and just to make sure that we would understand that 32 AD *is* the year in which this part of the prophecy was fulfilled - God even provided an additional clue immediately after the reference to the crucifixion:

[26] *After the sixty-two 'sevens,' the Anointed One will be put to death and will have nothing.* ***The people of the ruler who will come will destroy the city and the sanctuary****. (Daniel 9:26)*

This is exactly what happened. Just 38 years after the crucifixion, in 70AD, the Romans destroyed the Temple in response to a Jewish uprising - fulfilling the prophecy to the letter.

So now we understand the meaning of the first 69 'sevens' in the prophecy and, to be fair, this interpretation would be readily accepted by many who adhere to Premillennialism.

But the same can't be said for our solution to the next part of the prophecy – the 70th seven – which we address in the next chapter,

*The solution at a glance*

# 69 'weeks'
# to the Mystery of the Cross

***Scripture:*** *Daniel 9:24-26*

1. **What's being predicted?**
That a period of '69 sevens' will pass before the 'Anointed One' is cut off

2. **Who is being spoken to?**
Daniel. A Jewish exile in Babylon, praying about Jerusalem.

3. **Who is the prophecy about?**
No debate here: *"your people and your holy city"* means the Jews and Jerusalem – not the church.

4. **When does it start?**
444 BC, when Artaxerxes I gave the decree to restore and rebuild Jerusalem (including its streets and trenches).

5.. **How long does it last?**
69 "sevens" = 483 Babylonian years. Converted to Gregorian years: ≈ **476 years**

6.. **When does it end?**
444BC + 476 years = **32 AD:** The "Anointed One" (Messiah) is *cut off* – a direct prediction of the crucifixion of Jesus

This prophecy *nails the timeline* of history's most pivotal event – **the crucifixion of Yeshua**

69

# The Liberation of Jerusalem

## The Prophecy of the 70th Seven

which appears in **Daniel 9:24** in the

| 1st Vision | 2nd Vision | 3rd Vision | 4th Vision | 5th Vision | 6th Vision | 7th Vision |
|---|---|---|---|---|---|---|
| **The control of Jerusalem** | **The Kings madness** | **The restoration of the Holy land** | **The consecration of the sanctuary** | **The Seventy Sevens** | **The writing on the wall** | **Israels long future** |
| *Dan Ch 2* | *Dan Ch 4* | *Dan Ch 7* | *Dan Ch 8* | *Dan Ch 9* | *Dan Ch 5* | *Dan Ch 10-12* |

In the previous Chapter we noted that most Premillennialists would agree with our assertion that the first 69 sevens in Daniel's prophecy refer to the 476 year period between 444BC and the crucifixion of Yeshua in 32 AD (or some variation of those dates).

However, this alignment ends at the 70th seven because Premillennialists claim that this part of the prophecy refers to **a yet-future seven-year Tribulation** following an undefined period of time known as **the "parenthesis" or "Church Age."**

In this Chapter we're going to learn that they are right in their claim that there is a 'gap' between Yeshua's crucifixion and the 70th seven – but that they are wrong about when and why this takes place.

But before outlining what the prophecy actually means I should confess to a concern I had during the writing of this book. While I was obviously stunned at the precision of the solutions and left in no doubt that what was unfolding before me was, indeed, the correct interpretation of these visions – something was 'missing': the starting point of the Jewish loss of control of Jerusalem in any of the prophecies.

Yes, the two prophecies of 'time, times, and half a time' covered broad sweeps of exactly 2500 years of history - but both of these prophecies marked their beginning from the years in which Daniel recorded those visions (552BC and 533BC) - not the year in which the Jews actually lost control of their own destiny.

That happened earlier, in 589 BC - the year in which Babylonian King Nebuchadnezzar initiated a siege of Jerusalem in retaliation for a revolt, launched by Zedekiah, the last Jewish leader of the Jews. The siege lasted for two years and saw the destruction of the first temple - and it marked the end of Jewish control of their most Holy site until 1967, a year with which you will now be very familiar.

I reasoned that, to be truly accurate, God would have included a prophecy which covered the entire breadth of this loss of Jewish control of Jerusalem - but 589 BC didn't seem to appear in any of the prophecies I had reviewed.

That segues to the prophecy of the 70th Seven – which, as we've already seen, tells us that, following the 69 sevens, there will be one final seven which will be fulfilled through 'the anointing of the Most Holy Place'. This description aligns with the 7th Vision in chapter 12 of the Book of Daniel, where Daniel was told that his people (the Jews) would be scattered for a period of 2,500 years - after which they would recapture Jerusalem and 'reconsecrate' the holy place to God. That happened in 1967, with the Jewish liberation of Jerusalem and the Temple Mount, exactly as foretold in Daniel's 3rd Vision.

So perhaps these prophecies are both references to the same event? Let's revisit the relevant verses in Daniel 9:

> [24] *"Seventy 'sevens' are decreed for your people and your holy city to finish transgression, to put an end to sin, to atone for wickedness, to bring in everlasting righteousness, to seal up the vision and prophecy and to anoint the Most Holy Place.* ***(Daniel 9:24)***

*[27] He will confirm a covenant with many for one 'seven.' In the middle of the 'seven' he will put an end to sacrifice and offering. And at the temple he will set up an abomination that causes desolation, until the end that is decreed is poured out on him." **(Daniel 9:27)***

Did you see that? We're told of a 'covenant' which will last for 'one seven' and that sacrifices and offerings will end 'in the middle of the seven' at a time which coincides with the setting up the 'abomination that causes desolation' (which, we now know, happened in 688 AD). So we can now see that this prophecy:

- was fulfilled with the 'anointing of the Most Holy place' (the recapture and anointing of the site of the former Temple in 1967)
- has, as its midpoint, the construction of the Dome of the Rock in 688, 1278.3 years earlier

But if this is correct - the starting year of the prophecy must be way back in antiquity. But when?

**When does the prophecy start and how long will it last?**

Perhaps this final seven counts time in a different way to the previous sixty nine sevens? Is there a clue in the prophecies that we've already solved?

There is. In Revelation chapter 11 we dealt with a prophecy which involved a period of 3.5 'days' which turned out to be the 1278.3 years between the construction of the Dome of the Rock in 688AD and the recapturing of Jerusalem and the Temple Mount in 1967. The methodology for working that out was as follows:

3.5 days = 3.5 years

3.5 (modern) years of days x 365.24 = 1278.3 years

**1967 - 1278.3 = 688.7**

But if 3.5 days become 1278.3 years and the Dome of the Rock (to which that prophecy referred) is the halfway point - is it possible that the 'seven' (which is 2 times 3.5) could be 7 'days'? And if it is - could another date be hidden in these numbers? Let's find out:

7 days = 7 years
7 (modern) years of days x 365.24 = 2556.6 years
1967 - 2556.6 = **-589.6**

And there it is. 589 BC. The very year that the Babylonians besieged Jerusalem marking the end of Jewish control over their own national identity for over 2500 years.

For the first time (and reversed to count forward because this prophecy appeared in Daniel, not Revelation) we can finally understand what the 'seventieth seven' of Daniel really is. It isn't the future reign of a coming Antichrist and his persecution of Christians - it's a grand summary of the entire period during which the Jews would lose control of Jerusalem - starting with the Babylonian Siege in 589BC - and ending 2556 years later with the recapturing of Jerusalem and the Temple Mount in 1967.

With this information in hand we can now complete the Six Basic Questions:

| **The Prophecy of the 70$^{th}$ Seven**<br>Daniel 9:27 | | | |
|---|---|---|---|
| **What's being predicted?** | *That the Jews would lose control of the Temple Mount in Jerusalem for the 2556 years between 589BC and 1967* | | |
| **Question** | **Clue from Scripture** | **Math** | **Solution** |
| **Who is the prophecy addressed to?** | *"...while I was still in prayer, Gabriel ...came to me..." (Daniel 9.21)* | | **The prophecy is addressed to Daniel** |
| **Who is the prophecy about?** | *"...your people and your holy city..." (Daniel 9.24)* | | **The prophecy is about the Jews and Jerusalem** |
| **What year does the prophecy start?** | *"He will confirm a covenant with many for one 'seven ..." (Daniel 9:27)* | ***-589*** | **The prophecy begins in 589 BC** |
| **How long will the prophecy last?** | *7 years of years (7 x 365.24)* | ***plus 2556.6*** | **The prophecy will last for 2556.6 years** |
| **What year does the prophecy end?** | *"...to anoint the most holy place" (Daniel 9:24)* | ***equals 1967.6*** | **The prophecy ends in 1967** |

The key to unlocking this prophecy required us to, first, understand the '3 and a half days' in Revelation 11 – Gods way of ensuring that it wouldn't be solved until *the time of the end*. And lest there be any doubt, God added an extra detail – 'the middle of the seven' - a reference to the construction of the Dome of the Rock in 688. A clue that would only make sense at the time of the end when these prophecies had been fulfilled.

> [27] *He will confirm a covenant with many for one 'seven.'* ***In the middle of the 'seven' he will put an end to sacrifice and offering. And at the temple he will set up an abomination that causes desolation,*** *until the end that is decreed is poured out on him."* ***(Daniel 9:27)***

So now that we know when this prophecy starts we can see exactly what it means:

**The 'parentheses'**

But this is where things get interesting. You'll recall that Premillennialism interprets the gap between the 69th seven and the 70th seven as what it refers to as 'the parentheses' – an undefined period followed by a 'seven year tribulation' taking place at some unknown time in the future. But, with what we now know, we can see that they are right about the gap but wrong about what it is and when it takes place.

Since the 69 sevens end in 32 AD and the 70th seven ends in 1967 – the parentheses is simply the 1,935 years in between – essentially the broad period of almost 2,000 years covered by the first four visions in the Book of Revelation.

This is extraordinary. For the first time we can see the real meaning of Daniels 70th seven and its relationship to the prophecies which precede it. It isn't about an Antichrist figure in an imaginary seven year period in the undefined future. It's the 2,556 years between 589 BC and 1967 – punctuated by the crucifixion of Our Lord, the construction of the Dome of the Rock and the consecration of the Temple Mount in Jerusalem – a fulfilment which is tangible, complete, and doesn't rely on guesswork to 'make it fit'.

### The identity of 'he'

But who is the 'he' referred to in the prophecy? Given the longevity of this character – presiding over the entire 2,556 years of the prophecy – it's not an Antichrist or the Church. It's the devil – and it describes the breadth of his control of Jerusalem for over 2,500 years. As such – it's the story of exile and return, written in prophecy, played out in history, and now, fulfilled in full view.

### The 70 sevens solved

So now that we've solved the meaning of the 70 sevens, let's review the summary of the overall prophecy where Daniel was told that:

> *24 "Seventy 'sevens' are decreed for your people and your holy city to finish transgression, to put an end to sin, to atone for wickedness, to bring in everlasting righteousness, to seal up vision and prophecy and to anoint the Most Holy Place.*

Was this fulfilled?

Yes it was. The first four conditions - the finishing of transgression, putting an end to sin, atoning for wickedness, and bringing in everlasting righteousness - were all completed with Christs crucifixion on the cross on a hill in Jerusalem.

That's an important observation because this is a prophecy *to Jews* about Christ. It's not addressed to Christians and it's not about Christians. It's a message directed at the Jewish people, by Daniel, telling them when, and how, their Messiah / Mashiach would come.

That single sacrifice - the most important act in all of human history - forever changed the relationship of man with his Creator and opened the way for anyone who chose to, to have his own sin wiped away, based on the awesome blood sacrifice of his God.

The fact that the Jewish people (and, subsequently, the vast majority of the human race) choose to reject this sacrifice does not, in any way, diminish the power of what was done, and this simple sentence summarises that act perfectly.

The next condition - the sealing of the vision and the prophecy - took place just six years after Daniel wrote this passage in 539BC. We know this because we know that he recorded his last vision in 533BC (the one which included one of the prophecies dealing with 'time, times, and half a time' and the two prophecies dealing with the 1290 and the 1335 days) - and that prophecy also mentioned 'sealing'.

> *9 "Go your way, Daniel, because the words are rolled up and sealed until the time of the end". (Daniel 12:9)*

So five of the conditions of the prophecy were fulfilled at, or prior to, the crucifixion of Christ – and the 'anointing of the Most Holy Place' was completed in 1967, when the Jews liberated Jerusalem and the Temple Mount.

As such – this prophecy has now been fulfilled.

*The solution at a glance*

# The 70th seven
# The Liberation of Jerusalem

***Scripture:*** *Daniel 9:24, Daniel 9:27*

1. **What's being predicted?**
   That the Jews would lose control of the Temple Mount in Jerusalem for the 2556 years between 589BC and 1967

2. **Who is being spoken to?**
   Daniel, while praying for his peoples return from the Exile.

3. **Who is the prophecy about?**
   Again, the angel makes it explicit: "your people and your holy city." This is about the Jews and Jerusalem - not the Church.

4. **When does it start?**
   **589BC** - The Babylonian siege of Jerusalem.

5.. **How long does it last?**
   7 Gregorian years of days = 7 × 365.24 = **2,556.68 years**

6.. **When does it end?**
   -589 + 2556 = **1967 AD:** Israel recaptures the Temple Mount and Moshe Dayan reconsecrates the site.

Bonus detail: **688 AD** – The Dome of the Rock is completed on the Temple Mount, 'in the middle of the seven', marking the exact midway point in the prophecy.

70

# An alternative interpretation of Daniel's 1335 days

| 1st Vision | 2nd Vision | 3rd Vision | 4th Vision | 5th Vision | 6th Vision | 7th Vision |
|---|---|---|---|---|---|---|
| **The control of Jerusalem** | **The Kings madness** | **The restoration of the Holy land** | **The consecration of the sanctuary** | **The Seventy Sevens** | **The writing on the wall** | **Israels long future** |
| *Dan Ch 2* | *Dan Ch 4* | *Dan Ch 7* | *Dan Ch 8* | *Dan Ch 9* | *Dan Ch 5* | *Dan Ch 10-12* |

One of the great benefits of writing *Prophecy Shock* has been the discipline imposed by *the six basic questions* and the interconnected timeframe that has emerged from them. These dual guardrails have prevented us from wandering into the sort of speculative date-setting that has plagued many other attempts to interpret biblical prophecy. These questions insist that a solution must identify who the prophecy is about, when it starts, when it ends, how long it lasts and whether it makes sense in history – weeding out all the noise and leaving only the *actual* solution to each prophecy.

This also means that we don't end up with solutions 'just because the math fits'.

However, there *is* one alternative interpretation worth mentioning – precisely because it *does* meet these criteria. In Chapter 25 we examined Daniel's prophecy of **1,335 days**, which - when interpreted using the same Babylonian year system applied in the prophecy of **1,290 days** led us from 583 BC to the year **732 AD**, the year Charles Martel halted the Islamic advance into Europe at the Battle of Tours.

However the phrase *blessed is the one who waits for and reaches the 1,335 days*, from Daniel 12:12, could, instead, be understood as *a continuation* of the prophecy of 1,290 years meaning that, rather than also starting in 583 BC, it could start where the prophecy of 1,290 years finished in **688 AD**.

If we then counted **1,335 years forward from that point**, the calculation would produce the year **2023** – the year in which the world witnessed one of the most devastating attacks against Israel in modern history: the Hamas assault of **7 October 2023**.

At first glance, this alternative interpretation appears striking. The prophecy relates directly to Israel and the Jews, it aligns with a significant historical event in Jewish history, and it could be inferred that those who endured beyond that point would be considered "blessed" according to Daniel's wording. However, there are several reasons why it has not been adopted:

1. It requires us to abandon the methodology used for the prophecy of 1,290 days and switch to modern solar years partway through the calculation – weakening the methodological discipline that has guided our interpretations throughout this book.
2. The original interpretation leading to **732 AD** emerges more naturally from the structure of the text and maintains continuity with the surrounding prophecies.
3. Interpreting 1,335 days as extending to 2023 risks implying that that horrific event marks a decisive turning point beyond which no further major threats to Israel will occur. This would be foolish.

For these reasons, the interpretation linking Daniel's 1,335 days to the events of 2023 is not robust enough to replace the interpretation presented in this book and it is best understood as an intriguing numerical coincidence rather than the intended fulfilment of Daniel's prophecy.

I have included it simply because I know that if I do not address it here, others eventually will - and I have no desire to see a horrific attack on a people I admire and care about turned into material for sensational or speculative prophecy claims.

## 71

# The God of time ... and space?

At this point I want to draw attention to something which sits **outside the central argument of this book** but is simply too intriguing to ignore.

In 2008, the estate of the late **David Flynn** published a book called *The Temple at the Center of Time,* in which Flynn proposed that Jerusalem acts as a kind of **geographical reference point** relative to other locations around the world.

The idea itself was not new. For centuries, Jewish and Christian writers regarded Jerusalem as the spiritual centre of the world, and many medieval maps even placed it at the physical centre of the known world as a symbolic reflection of its role in biblical history.

But Flynn approached the concept from a different angle. Rather than arguing that Jerusalem sits at the literal centre of the earth, he explored whether its central place in biblical history might sometimes appear in geography - specifically, whether distances measured from Jerusalem to historically significant locations might correspond with key years in the history of the Holy Land.

Using great-circle measurements (the shortest distance between two points on the earth's surface) he compared distances from the Temple Mount in Jerusalem to major historical centres with the dates of pivotal events connected to Israel.

Flynn developed this idea in many directions – with some fascinating results – however, I have no intention of importing his wider system into the argument of this book because the conclusions presented in *Prophecy Shock* stand firmly on the biblical text, the historical succession of powers over the land, and the arithmetic of the prophetic time periods themselves.

But two of Flynn's observations are so striking that they deserve a mention.

**London and 1948**

Flynn measured the distance between two specific points:

- **The Temple Mount in Jerusalem**, (from the area of the **Foundation Stone**).

- **The London Stone on Cannon Street**, (an ancient marker traditionally regarded as the historic centre of London).

Using a **great-circle calculation**, he found that the distance between those two points comes to exactly **1,948.4 nautical miles**.

Yes, you read that correctly. The distance between the London Stone and the Temple Mount is 1948 nautical miles - corresponding with the year that the British Mandate ended and the modern **State of Israel was proclaimed**.

As you know - Britain was also **the last** external imperial power to administer the Holy Land - so after successive empires, the British Mandate termination signalled that the scattering was over and that Jewish sovereignty had returned.

This numerical correspondence is extraordinary. But there's more.

**Babylon and 539**

Flynn also pointed to a similar relationship in the ancient world.

Measuring the great-circle distance between **Babylon** (near modern Hillah in Iraq) and **Jerusalem** yields a distance of **539 statute miles**.

That number corresponds with **539 BC -** the year Babylon itself fell to the Persian Empire.

The fall of Babylon was also a decisive moment in Jewish history because it signalled the end of **the first** power to control the Holy Land – setting off a long period of occupation and exile which lasted for around 2,500 years.

So these two examples sit like bookends around the long history of imperial domination over the Holy Land.

| Capital / | Distance to Jerusalem | / Historical turning point |
|---|---|---|
| Babylon | ~539 statute miles | 539 BC – fall of Babylon |
| London | 1,948.4 nautical miles | 1948 – end of British rule |

Babylon was the **first empire to conquer and control the Holy Land**. Britain was the **last empire to rule the land** before the rebirth of Israel. And both capitals happen to lie at distances from Jerusalem that correspond, exactly, to the years in which their respective control of Jerusalem ended.

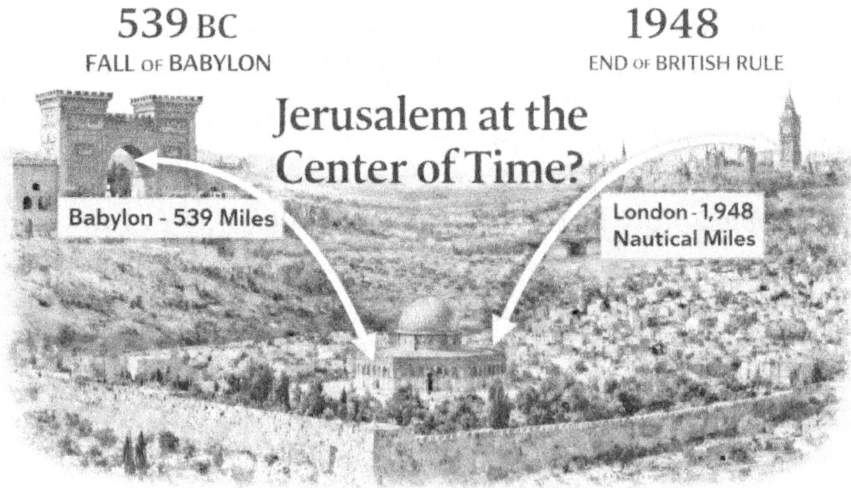

**Is this phenomenon real?**

So does this prove anything or tell us anything that we didn't already know? No. *Prophecy Shock* stands on its own merits and the framework that has been developed throughout these pages.

But Flynn's discovery is fascinating – which is why I have included it in this book.

When a prophetic theory focuses on Jerusalem at its core, highlights key dates in Jewish history, and identifies locations which define powers that controlled Jerusalem – my ears prick up, for obvious reasons.

But was he right? Is this phenomenon real?

I don't know.

My own investigations suggest there may be something here and, I certainly have no difficulty accepting that a God Who can order prophecy in the way that He has done in scripture could also determine exact distances and locations which reinforce those same prophetic years. But I don't have the depth of mastery of the topic that would give me the confidence to stake my reputation on it in the way I have done with the core arguments of *Prophecy Shock*.

For that reason, I leave it to the reader to draw their own conclusions.

72

# The prophecy of
# the reign of Christ

which appears in the **Book of Revelation** in the:

| 1st Vision | 2nd Vision | 3rd Vision | 4th Vision | 5th Vision | 6th Vision | 7th Vision |
|---|---|---|---|---|---|---|
| **The History of the Church** | **The trials of believers** | **The history of the gentiles** | **The origin of anti-semitism** | **The last plagues** | **The fall of Babylon** | **The reign of Christ** |
| *Rev Ch 1-3* | *Rev Ch 4-8.1* | *Rev Ch 8.2-11* | *Rev Ch 12-14* | *Rev Ch 15-16, 19-20* | *Rev Ch 17-18* | *Rev Ch 21-22* |

But wait – there's one last Vision that we still haven't reviewed. The Seventh Vision in the Book of Revelation.

This was deliberate because the seventh vision doesn't just close the Book of Revelation - it also closes the entire Bible - and its promises and warnings are an appropriate place to conclude the prophecies contained in this book.

In just three chapters it spans at least a thousand years and the biggest events in Scripture and, unlike the first six visions - which warned believers about what they'd see during the Church age - this one sits beyond that age. So we won't witness it until after Christ returns.

As such, the inclusion of the 7th vision serves to inform Christians of what they can expect in the age to come - but we won't know how they played out until we're actually with God.

I encourage you to read all 3 chapters for yourself - but the key points and events covered in the seventh vision are as follows:

- The devil is seized, bound, and locked in the abyss for a thousand years.
- Those who have been beheaded (martyred?) because of their testimony about Yeshua (and who did not have the mark of the beast on their foreheads or hands) come to life and reign with Yeshua for a thousand years. This is the first resurrection.
- The rest of the dead do not come to life until the thousand years are over.
- At the end of the thousand years, Satan is released to deceive the nations once more. He gathers them around Jerusalem, but God destroys them by fire.
- Satan is thrown into the lake of fire, where the Beast and False Prophet had already been cast.
- Heaven and earth pass away.
- All the dead stand before God's throne. Books are opened; the dead are judged by what is written. Anyone not in the Book of Life is thrown into the lake of fire - the second death.
- A new heaven and new earth appear, and the New Jerusalem descends.
- God dwells with His people.

After John sees all of this one of the angels then comes to him and carries him to a high mountain where he shows him the Holy City, Jerusalem, coming down from God, shining with His glory like a crystal-clear jasper.

According to the detailed description in Revelation 21:9–27; 22:1–5 it has a great high wall with twelve gates, each attended by an angel and inscribed with the twelve tribes of Israel - three gates on each side. The wall's twelve foundations bear the names of the twelve apostles of the Lamb.

The length, width, and height of the city are the same - measuring 12,000 stadia (2,220 kilometres / 1,380 miles). The wall is 144 cubits thick (65 metres / 216 ft). The wall is jasper; the city is pure gold, clear as glass. The foundations blaze with twelve precious stones; the gates are twelve pearls; the main street is gold like transparent glass.

There is no temple: the Lord God Almighty and the Lamb are its temple. The city needs no sun or moon, because God's glory is its light and the Lamb its lamp. The nations walk by that light; the kings bring their splendour in. Its gates never shut, for there is no night. Nothing impure enters - only those written in the Lamb's Book of Life.

A river of the water of life, clear as crystal, flows from the throne of God and the Lamb down the middle of the city's street. On each side stands the tree of life, bearing twelve crops of fruit - one each month - and leaves for the healing of the nations.

The curse is gone. God's throne is there; His servants serve Him. They see His face; His name is on their foreheads. There is no night. No lamp. No sun. The Lord God gives them light, and they reign, with Him, forever and ever.

## Section Nine

# COMPLETING THE JIGSAW PUZZLE

# What this all means

***...and why it matters***

So what do all of these prophecies and visions have in common? What's the single defining theme which unites them all and – finally – reveals what God wants us to understand?

It's **Israel.**

Look at the prophecies.

Different numbers.
Different symbols.

Different visions.
But just one focal point.

Not Rome.
Not Europe.
Not Davos.
Not a future global empire.
Not the Church navigating a final crisis.

**Israel. Jerusalem. The Jewish people.**

When you step back and view the whole pattern at once, the noise falls away and the meaning of the visions that God shared with Daniel and John becomes obvious. What we've treated as a maze of disconnected prophecies resolves into a single, coherent story about the Jewish people losing their city, losing their land, and then – against all historical odds – getting both back again.

*That* is the axis on which bible prophecy turns.

## What this changes

For generations, we were taught to read Daniel and Revelation as if they were primarily about the *future* – a short, dramatic end-times window that would unfold just before the return of Christ and focused on:

- A seven-year tribulation
- A final global dictator
- A rebuilt Temple
- A short, catastrophic end-times crisis
- Christians trying to survive the last days

But when the timelines are allowed to speak for themselves, a different picture emerges. We find that these time-defined prophecies are not a preview of a final few years. They are a chronicle of a 2,500-year historical arc which repeats itself in four different visions:

- **The Vision of Exile and Redemption** which appears in the Book of Daniel identifies **1948 and 1967** as the two most important years in modern Jewish history and **688** as the year of the appearance of the Dome of the Rock (the abomination of desolation).

- **The Vision of the History of the Gentiles** which is outlined between Chapters 8 and 11 in the Book of Revelation, once again, identifies **688, 1948, and 1967** and also pinpoints **536 AD** as the beginning of a 152 year period of social, environmental and climactic chaos.

- **The Vision of the Origin of Antisemitism** which is in Chapters 12 and 13 in the Book of Revelation also identifies **688, 1948, and 1967** as key years in the persecution and redemption of the Jewish people and reveals the true nature of antisemitism.

- **The two Visions which cover the Fate of God's enemies** which appear between Chapters 15 to 20 of the Book of Revelation are both yet future and don't provide any new dates – but because of what we have learned in the preceding Visions we can identify the targets of Gods wrath, in these Visions, as Islam and False Christianity (personified by Catholicism and her daughters).

This recurring pattern where each Vision details different events, but always comes back to the same key years, is the final piece in our puzzle. It is the glue that binds these visions together – changing the details depending on the story being shared, but always through the lens of those same three years.

These Visions repeatedly outline:

- The loss of Jerusalem
- The long exile of the Jewish people
- The desecration of their holiest ground
- The rebirth of Israel
- The return of Jerusalem to Jewish hands

Once that framework snaps into place, the traditional assumptions collapse and the real meaning of these prophecies steps into history:

- The "tribulation" was the long Jewish exile
- The "beasts" were empires that ruled Jerusalem
- The "abomination" was a desecration of the Temple Mount
- The prophetic countdowns ran across centuries, not years
- The centre of prophecy was never the Church – it was Israel

This isn't a minor interpretive adjustment. It is a complete change in the *centre of gravity*. Once Jerusalem becomes the clock-face of prophecy, everything else falls into alignment.

**Why this matters**

If these prophecies were vague, this would all just be theological opinion. But they aren't. They're concrete dates that land on events that are public, immovable, and historically anchored. And when independent prophetic countdowns converge on the same historical moments, coincidence stops being a serious explanation. What you are left with is uncomfortable inescapable precision: either the most unlikely national restoration in human history just happened to land exactly where ancient texts said it would – or Someone has been writing history in advance.

There isn't really a third option.

**Where This Leaves Us**

The time-defined prophecies of Daniel and Revelation have done what they were designed to do. They have:

- Vindicated the reliability of Scripture
- Anchored faith in historical reality
- Placed Israel and Jerusalem back at the centre of the story
- And shown that God's promises to the Jewish people were not symbolic

That doesn't mean that prophecy is finished.
But it does means that *this* phase of prophecy is finished.
The great countdowns have landed.
The exile has ended.
The city has been restored.

So the question is no longer: *"What timeline are we waiting for?"*

The question is: **What does it mean to live in a world where God has already done what He said He would do – to the year?**

We are standing at the edge of history's final page. Time-defined prophecy has done its job. It has glorified God, vindicated His Word, and proven that every second of human history was scheduled in advance.

All of which begs an obvious question: *what happens now?*

74

# What happens next?

***The Final Pieces of the Prophetic Puzzle***

In the mid-1970s, a Japanese soldier named **Hiroo Onoda** was found in the jungles of the Philippine island of Lubang. Onoda had been on the island since 1944, almost thirty years earlier, unaware that Japan had surrendered in 1945 and that the war was over. He had been told to hold the island against enemy forces and had remained hidden, carrying out guerrilla activities and living in the jungle, sustained by survival skills and the conviction that his orders were still in force. He finally surrendered in 1974, only after his former commanding officer came to formally relieve him of duty.

Onoda was not ignorant or simple. He was just following what he believed to be true - clinging to a framework of belief that had made sense within the context in which he thought he was operating. So when reality changed without his knowledge, he kept living his life in alignment with the world as he believed it to be.

In a very different way, you have just reached a similar kind of threshold. For years - perhaps decades - many Christians have read Bible prophecy through a particular lens. A Premillennial framework which taught that the decisive events of history were still ahead: a coming Antichrist, a future seven-year tribulation, a rebuilt temple and a looming 'mark of the beast.' And these ideas didn't stay confined to theological textbooks; they shaped how generations of believers voted, interpreted global events, assessed the significance of Israel, and understood the story of human history.

But throughout this book we've learnt that **much of what we were taught to expect from prophecy lies not in the future, but in the past**, anchored to real empires, real rulers, and defined periods of control over Jerusalem whose timelines have already run their course.

Like Onoda in the jungle, we've been holding on to a framework that once made sense but is actually at odds with what is really happening - but now that we're 'out of the jungle' and can see the world as it really is – an obvious question comes to mind:

**What happens next, in prophecy?**

If the time-defined prophecies are all behind us – does that mean that prophecy is complete?

Not at all.

The purpose of time-defined prophecy was to confirm, to our generation, Gods absolute sovereignty over history and to establish the pre-eminence of Israel and the Jewish people, in the prophetic story.

But there is much much more, still ahead.

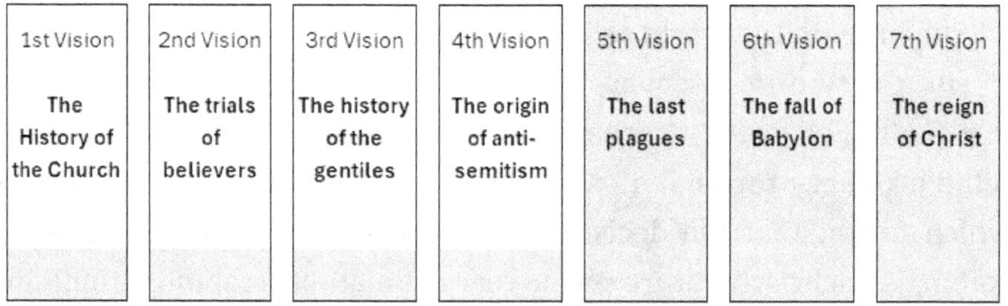


This graphic gives us clarity over where we are in the bigger picture. As you can see, the first four Visions in the Book of Revelation are *mostly* fulfilled (the white section of each vision). But, in each case, there is a greyed out portion representing prophecy that has not yet been fulfilled. These prophecies aren't time-defined, so we can't know *when* they will happen – but we certainly have a pretty clear idea of *what* will happen and *who* it will happen to.

So, what happens next?

I had originally planned to answer that question within the pages of this book - but as I began working through that material, something unexpected happened. What started as an extension of the work I had already done in Daniel, Revelation and Ezekiel did not stay contained within those books.

As I began tracing supporting references, I found myself drawn, more and more, into the other prophetic books of the Old Testament and it quickly became clear that something else was happening.

These other books were not just supporting the framework we have uncovered. They were revealing that the framework itself was only part of something much larger.

What I had assumed were parallel or supplementary voices were, in fact, part of a far more expansive and unified structure. Not a collection of disconnected prophecies, but a single, coherent narrative, expressed across multiple prophets, each adding dimension, depth, and perspective to the same underlying reality.

And crucially, this wasn't visible before. It's as if Daniel and Revelation had to be understood first before anything else could come into focus.. Which means that *Prophecy Shock* isn't the full picture – but it's the key that unlocks everything else.

Once that key is applied more broadly, the scope of what comes into view expands dramatically. Not a minor extension of the material in this book - but another level entirely – and as I worked through it, it became obvious that it could not be treated as a final chapter or appendix. To do so would diminish both its scale and its significance.

It requires its own treatment.
Its own space.
And its own book.

For these reasons, these discoveries now form the foundation of a follow-up to *Prophecy Shock* which I am writing under the working title ***Prophecy Shock: What happens next*** and which I hope to publish in 2027.

None of that diminishes what you've just read, of course. Even without the additional breakthrough still to come – *Prophecy Shock* has already transformed the framework within which we understand Daniel and Revelation and allowed us to see what these prophecies and visions really mean.

Over the course of this book we have been given new clarity and a new framework through which to understand what God expects of us. The old assumptions have fallen away, and with that comes responsibility.

But what does that responsibility look like?
How should this change the way we think, the way we act, and the way we understand our place in God's unfolding purpose?

These are not theoretical questions. They go to the heart of how we live, what we prioritise, and how we respond to what God has revealed.

That's what we turn to next.

## 75

# What now for the Church?

***Why standing with Israel is non-negotiable for God's People***

If you have read this far, the ground has already shifted beneath your feet. The prophecies of Daniel and Revelation are no longer floating abstractions or charts pointing vaguely into the future. They have locked into history. They have resolved around real empires, real rulers, real timelines, and one unmistakable centre of gravity: Israel and Jerusalem.

That changes everything and it leaves the Church with no room to hide. False expectations are stripped away. Error is exposed.

For centuries, large parts of the Church have taught prophecy in ways that displaced Israel, marginalised the Jews, and reassigned God's promises to themselves. We spiritualised what God made concrete. We universalised what God anchored to a people and a city. And having done that, we are now shocked to discover that antisemitism has followed in its wake.

This is not coincidence - it is consequence.

The surge of antisemitism we are witnessing today is not a separate social problem. It is the downstream effect of theological malpractice. When the Church teaches that Israel no longer matters, it should not be surprised when the world feels comfortable to decide the same thing. When pastors imply that God has moved on from the Jews, they train their congregations to do likewise. Bad prophecy does not stay in the study. It spills out onto the street.

And now the bill has come due.

Across the West, we are watching a resurgence of Jew hatred that is louder, more confident, and more shameless than anything seen we've since the 1930s. And those parallels with pre-war Germany are not subtle - they are blatant - and the Church, once again, is failing the test. We are seeing:

- Christians marching alongside crowds chanting "From the river to the sea," - a slogan that does not call for peace but for the eradication of the Jewish state.

- Christians remaining silent while Jews are harassed, threatened, assaulted, and told that they are unwelcome in universities, workplaces, and public life, precisely the same way that Jewish professionals were isolated and expelled in Nazi Germany.

- Christians supporting or excusing UN resolutions that condemn Israel for defending itself while ignoring terrorism, rocket fire, and mass murder aimed at Jewish civilians.

- Christians participating in boycotts and divestment campaigns dressed up as moral concern but functionally identical to the coordinated boycotts of Jewish businesses in 1933.

- Christians misusing Scripture to pronounce judgement on Israel, as if Genesis 12:3 and Zechariah 2:8 were optional footnotes rather than explicit warnings.

This is not prophetic ignorance. **It is Jew-hatred**.

And it must stop.

For churches, the implications are not gentle or academic. They are urgent and unavoidable. Churches that teach, imply, or tolerate the idea that Israel no longer matters are not merely holding an alternative interpretation. They are positioning themselves against the structure of history and against a God who has already shown us who He preserves, whom He restores, and which promises He refuses to let die.

This is not a call for uncritical endorsement of every Israeli policy – but it *is* a call for honesty. When challenged on their opposition to Israel, some retreat to the tired question, "So are you saying Israel gets a free pass?" This question reveals a frightening ignorance about the reality of how Israel conducts itself. Israel does not need a free pass. Israel needs defenders. Israel is surrounded by enemies who openly call for her annihilation. Israel is the only democracy in the region, the only nation that protects religious freedom, and the only place in the Middle East where Christians can live and worship without fear of death.

These are facts. But even if they were not, the obligation would remain. Churches that attack Israel, delegitimise Israel, or side with movements that seek her destruction are not merely mistaken. **They are in rebellion against God**. They are openly defying His covenant faithfulness and His declared plan for history.

And Scripture is very clear about how that ends. Such Churches ***will*** be held to account.

But this rebellion did not begin with placards and chants. It began in pulpits. We added where Scripture did not add. We subtracted where it did not subtract. We elevated speculative systems and taught them as certainty.

That paved the road to today.

So here is the call to action, and it is not optional.

- If your church is attacking Israel, stop...
- If your church is equivocating about Israel, repent...
- If your church is silent while Jews are threatened, speak...
- If your church has absorbed theology that sidelines Israel, dump it...

Clean up your sermons. Rewrite the study notes. Purge the social media feeds. Remove every teaching that contradicts what Scripture and history now make undeniable.

Teach what God has actually done.
Pray for what God is actually doing.
Defend whom God has chosen to defend.

Neutrality is not faithfulness. Qualification is not courage. Silence is not wisdom.

God's Word could not be clearer. He has restored Israel. He will defend Israel. And He will bless those who bless her, and curse those who curse her. If you oppose her, you're opposing Him.

When the dust of history settles, there will be only two kinds of people in this story: those who stood with Israel, because they understood what God had said about her - and those who didn't, because they wouldn't.

Choose well.

76

# What now for you?

***What will you do with what you now know?***

You've read this book. You now understand what's really going on in the world. The attacks on Jews are no ordinary form of hatred. They're satanically inspired - a sign, as clear as any prophecy, that we are nearing the final phase of God's plan.

So why now? Why is God releasing this insight at this moment in history - more than 50 years after 1967, and nearly 80 since 1948?

Because now is when it's needed. Because time is almost up.

God didn't give us time-defined prophecy to tell the future in advance. He gave it so that we would recognize His fingerprints after the fact - and have no doubt who authored history. But in a distracted, decaying world, even the miraculous becomes forgettable. So now He is sounding the alarm again - louder. Clearer. More urgently.

This is your moment of decision.

**IF YOU'RE NOT A CHRISTIAN:**

You made it through this book. That's no accident. You're here because God is calling you. You now have evidence that cannot be ignored - fulfilled prophecies that match recorded history, declared centuries in advance, unfolding with mathematical precision. That doesn't just mean God exists. It means He is watching you.

One day soon you're going to meet Him and when that happens, your money, your status, your self-perception - none of it will matter.

The only thing that will count is whether you accepted what Jesus (Yeshua) did for you on the cross:

> *"I am the way and the truth and the life. No one comes to the Father except through me."* ***John 14:6***

> *"If you declare with your mouth, 'Jesus is Lord,' and believe in your heart that God raised Him from the dead, you will be saved."* ***Romans 10:9***

No priest, no church, no ritual required. Just you and Him. Right now. Don't delay. The time for excuses is over.

**IF YOU'RE A CHRISTIAN:**

You're saved by grace - you can't earn it - but now that you know the truth about prophecy - what will you do with that knowledge?

Your views on the end times won't matter when you stand before God - but your obedience will. Your witness will. What you did with what you were given – those things will matter.

Here's where to start:

- Make sure that you're actually saved by reviewing what I wrote to non-Christians. Your salvation is between you and God. It can't be inherited from family and it has nothing to do with Church membership or traditions. Be sure that God knows *you* by following His specific instructions,
- Let go of your old views on prophecy: God has shown you something clearer.
- Reject Replacement Theology and Dispensationalism: The Church did not replace Israel.
- Renounce antisemitism and ask forgiveness if you've held such views.
- Pray daily for Israel and the Jewish people.

- Recognise that your greatest threat comes from within – false Christianity and doctrines of demons that lead us away from God
- Let go of 'activism' that distracts from the Kingdom.
- Share this message. Loudly. Boldly. Online, in person, everywhere.
- Promote this book and commend it to others.
- Stand with Israel in word and in deed - no matter how unpopular it becomes.

You weren't saved to coast. You were saved to fight for God.

**IF YOU'RE CATHOLIC OR FROM A NON-REPENTANT 'CHRISTIAN' GROUP:**

Tradition runs deep – but ritual cannot save you. Only Jesus can.

If you've grown up in a system that doesn't teach repentance and the personal Lordship of Christ, I plead with you to:

- Ask God to reveal truth through what you've read.
- Let go of works-based salvation and embrace grace through faith.
- Renounce antisemitism and pray for Israel.
- Share the truth boldly - starting now.

**AND NOW - THE FINAL CHOICE:**

You've read the evidence. You know the signs. You feel the urgency. The King is coming.

Will you be the one who simply enters Heaven with your ticket in hand? Or will you be the one who hears, "Well done, good and faithful servant"? That choice is yours. But the time to choose is now.

Tick tock.

77

# What now for Israel?

***The Coming Storm***

While I'm going to save my outline of what scripture appears to predict for the future for an upcoming book – there are some general trends that we *can* anticipate for the years ahead (assuming we *have* more years ahead).

If the patterns of history, the trajectory of current events, and the clear outline of prophecy mean anything, the years ahead for Israel will not be peaceful. God's protective hand is on His people - but that doesn't mean things will be trouble free for them.

The clock is ticking toward a confrontation - a collision between Israel and the nations that will shake the world.

Here's what we can reasonably expect:

**A continuing surge in antisemitism**

Antisemitism will not plateau - it will increase. The chants and slogans on Western streets today are just the warm-up act. Expect more: more attacks on synagogues, more 'Bondi Beach' type attacks, more harassment of Jewish students, more discrimination in workplaces and institutions.

This will drive a steady flow of Jews to Israel - not because life there is easier, but because, in a hostile world, it will be the one place they know they belong. In the 1930s, many Jews clung to their host nations until it was too late. This time, more will read the writing on the wall.

### Political abandonment

One by one, Western governments will distance themselves from Israel and are already doing so. "Concerns" will move to boycotts, arms embargoes, and cancelled trade agreements. This will be sold as "holding Israel accountable" - but it will be little more than appeasing their own angry streets and their trading partners in the Muslim world.

Even the United States - Israel's strongest ally - will prove conditional in its loyalty. Republican administrations will mostly stand firm but Democrat administrations, facing pressure from their activist base, will talk about "balance" while undermining Israel's ability to defend itself.

### The United Nations and the 'Peacekeeping' Threat

The UN's blatant antisemitism and hostility toward Israel is already entrenched but expect it to become even bolder. Watch for even more resolutions, more "special investigations" and, eventually, a call for "peacekeeping forces" on the ground in Israel itself - a move that will be nothing less than an attempt to put the Jewish state under international control.

### An avalanche of misinformation

Propaganda against Israel has always existed, but the emerging wave will be supercharged by artificial intelligence. Deepfakes will "show" Israeli atrocities that never happened. Fabricated "eyewitness" testimonies will flood social media. AI will make lies indistinguishable from reality, and a generation already hostile toward Israel will treat them as gospel truth.

### The youth factor

Younger generations in the West are becoming more openly antisemitic - not because they've read Mein Kampf, but because they've been marinated in decades of anti-Israel propaganda dressed up as social justice.

This trend will accelerate, and as these young people become voters, policymakers, journalists, and CEOs, their hostility will be increasingly written into law, culture, and policy.

### Regional Confrontation

Prophecy and geopolitics point in the same direction: Israel will eventually face a coalition of nations from the Middle East and beyond. The hostility of Iran is no surprise - but as Western support fractures, expect other regional players to take bigger risks. Border clashes, missile attacks, and terror campaigns will intensify. At some point, a full-scale military confrontation is inevitable.

### The Timeline

If current trends continue - and barring some major course correction - much of this could unfold within the next five to seven years. The speed at which AI-driven propaganda spreads, combined with political shifts in the US and Europe, could mean that by the early-2030s Israel finds itself facing the world with very few friends left.

### Where it all leads

The stage is being set for the very scenario that the prophets warned about - a day when **"all nations"** come against Jerusalem (Zechariah 14:2). Whether that means literally every nation, the dominant powers of the age, or Israels traditional enemies in the Middle East, the outcome is the same: Israel, surrounded and under siege, will be forced to stand alone - except for the One who fights for her.

And that's the point that too many people miss. This is not a story that ends with Israel's destruction. It ends with Israel's deliverance - but only after the world has seen her brought to the brink. God is not done demonstrating His faithfulness to the people He chose.

The road ahead will be rough. It will test Israel's endurance and the courage of those who claim to stand with her. But it will also bring history to the place where prophecy has always pointed: the day when God Himself fights for His people and lays waste to her enemies. A day after which nobody will ever again doubt Who holds Israel in the palm of His hand.

78

# How can you be sure this is true?

If you're having trouble accepting what you've read in *Prophecy Shock* I don't blame you. I've battled a constant crisis of confidence since I first started writing it five years ago.

Not because I resile from what I've written – indeed, I could not be more sure of the truth of what is contained in these pages – but because I know how hard it is to change the minds of those who are already committed to a position.

We like to imagine that people change their views when the evidence becomes overwhelming. That if the facts are laid out clearly enough, reason will prevail and minds will follow.

In reality, that's rarely how human beings work. Increasingly, "truth" isn't filtered through logic or right and wrong - it's filtered through identity, tribe, tradition, and worldview. We tend to accept what fits our existing framework and resist what threatens it, even when the evidence is strong.

Some readers will move through this book and feel something like a light switching on. The pieces will suddenly align, the structure will make sense, and the conclusions will feel inevitable. For those people, the internal shift will be obvious and decisive.

But many others won't experience that at all. No amount of charts, dates, cross-references, or logic will dislodge deeply held assumptions. The mind simply finds ways to defend the familiar.

And then there is a third group - perhaps the largest of all. These are the readers who will initially feel the weight of what they've read. Something resonates, something unsettles, the framework makes sense. But letting go of inherited positions, long-held traditions, denominational loyalties, or personal identity will feel risky and destabilising.

These are the people who will be quickly persuaded to reject the evidence presented in *Prophecy Shock*. Friends and colleagues will point them to conflicting books, online debates, a superficial AI opinion, or competing teachers with a different view – and the spark will go out.

Yes, I could attempt to respond to these counterarguments - but that road has no natural end. There will always be another article, another theory, another critic, another alternative explanation.

If certainty depends on out-arguing every dissenting voice, that certainty will never come. It just becomes an ever-tightening loop that never quite settles.

And ultimately, it doesn't matter what I say, anyway.
It doesn't matter what your favourite teacher says.
It doesn't even matter what the strongest critic says.

If what you've read here carries weight for you - if it stirs questions that you can't easily dismiss - then the only place resolution will come from is the source of truth itself.

God.

If this book is wrong, ask Him to show you that clearly.
If it is right, ask Him what your response should be.

I wish you peace and clarity in that process.

# Acknowledgements

This book took four long years to wrestle into existence - four years in which I repeatedly assured far too many patient souls that it was "almost finished." So to everyone who heard that line more times than was reasonable... thank you for not staging an intervention.

To those brave early readers who slogged through previous drafts: you endured sections that moved with all the speed and clarity of someone wading through porridge. Yet you hung in there, offered feedback, and pretended that you understood what I was trying to say. Heroes, the lot of you.

To Kim Hooper and Mike Wilson – who were there from the outset - your steady encouragement, honest counsel, and relentless support over the entire four-year journey kept this project alive more than you know. You gave me clarity when I was stuck, direction when I drifted, and motivation when the finish line felt imaginary.

And finally, to my wife, Bronnie - my rock and my grounding. Despite my many many flaws and my propensity to fail you in more ways than I can count – you have continued to love me and forgive me. Your patience, strength, and wisdom carried me from the first spark of an idea to the last full stop on the final page. This book exists because of you.

# References

- References to external sources are included in the footnotes or acknowledged in context, where appropriate, in the relevant chapters in sections 1 and 2 of this book.

- Scripture references can be easily checked through any reputable online Bible site.

- References to specific years and dates can be checked through a simple web search. If such a search produces a different date to any used in this book, a review of the consensus of several different sources will generally correct the error in favour of those used in this book.

# About the Author

Ashley Church is a New Zealand–based author and a high-profile national media commentator on faith, politics and the economy.

Over a forty-year public career he has served in senior leadership roles across the energy, finance, and property sectors and has been the CEO of a succession of national industry bodies and the Chairman of several boards.

In parallel, Ashley has spent more than three decades researching bible prophecy. *Prophecy Shock* is the result of that research and stands apart. It sets out a coherent method that **dates** key prophetic periods **to past events** - linking Scripture to verifiable milestones in Jewish and world history. There is no guesswork; the timelines are already on the record. The result is a clear, testable reading that resolves questions many interpretations leave open.

Ashley is also a founding director of the Israel Institute of New Zealand and is a recognised authority on matters relating to Israel's history and present-day challenges.

# Coming soon from this Author

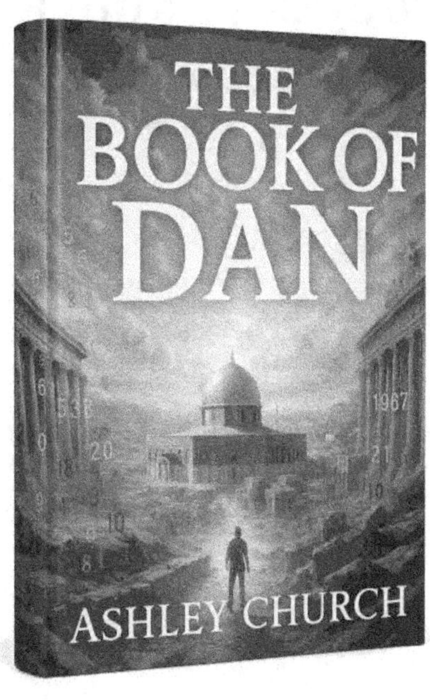


## The Book of Dan

### Late 2026

While in New Zealand for his father's funeral, award-winning U.S. talk-radio host Josh Skolfield learns of a manuscript, left behind by, his father, which claims to reveal secret codes contained in the prophecies of Daniel and Revelation - revelations that could shake Christianity to its core.

Back in the States, Josh meets the captivating Dharma Patel, who connects him with a shadowy group promising to help recover his father's work.

Meanwhile in Israel, Mossad agent Sarah Levy makes a stunning discovery linked to new evidence about the true site of Solomon's Temple.

As the pieces converge, Josh and Sarah find themselves racing against time to stop a rising threat that could ignite global conflict and trigger the prophesied last days.

**For more information and to be notified of the release, go to:**
www.prophecyshock.com

# Coming soon from this Author

## Prophecy Shock:

### What happens next?

### Mid 2027

The long countdowns are behind us and Israel is back in the land – just as the prophecies foretold!

But that doesn't mean that all prophecy is behind us.

In *Prophecy Shock: What Happens Next* we go behind the remaining prophecies in to find out what scripture tells us about:

- *What comes next, for Israel?*
- *The coming fate of Islam and false Christianity*
- *Is the anticipated rapture of Christians is real – and if so, where does it fit in prophecy?*
- *Plus much much more.*

**For more information and to be notified of the release, go to:**
www.prophecyshock.com

# Appendix A:
# The 10 Principles of Israelism

Principle 1:

**Prophecy is structured as Visions, not Chapters & Verses**

Principle 2:

**Prophecy covers 2,500+ years of history – not a few years in the last days**

Principle 3:

**Six basic questions solve all time-defined prophecy**

Principle 4:

**Time-defined prophecies are all about the Jews.....**

Principle 5:

**..... and they're all centred on Jerusalem**

Principle 6:

**The beasts of Daniel and Revelation are all powers that controlled Jerusalem**

Principle 7:

**God gave us exact years of fulfilment**

Principle 8:

**All time-defined prophecy counts *toward* 688**

Principle 9:

**Scholars opinions change – Gods timeline doesn't**

Principle 10:

***All* of the time-defined prophecies are now behind us**

# Appendix B: Comparing Israelism to other Prophetic Views

You now understand that the Jews and Jerusalem – not the Church - are at the centre of all prophecy. A point which has always been overwhelmingly obvious for those with eyes to see – but invisible to the rest of us:

*In that day the Lord will reach out his hand* ***a second time*** *to reclaim the surviving remnant of his people from Assyria, from Lower Egypt, from Upper Egypt, from Cush, from Elam, from Babylonia, from Hamath and from the islands of the Mediterranean. He will raise a banner for the nations and gather the exiles of Israel; he will assemble the scattered people of Judah from the four quarters of the earth.* ***(Isaiah 11:11-12)***

*...the Lord Almighty says: "I will save my people from the countries of the east and the west. I will bring them back to live in Jerusalem; they will be my people, and I will be faithful and righteous to them as their God."* ***(Zechariah 8:7-8)***

*...and I will bring my people Israel back from exile. "They will rebuild the ruined cities and live in them. They will plant vineyards and drink their wine; they will make gardens and eat their fruit. I will plant Israel in their own land,* ***never again to be uprooted from the land I have given them****" says the Lord your God.* ***(Amos 9:14-15)***

*"At that time I will gather you; at that time I will bring you home. I will give you honor and praise among all the peoples of the earth*

*when I restore your fortunes before your very eyes," says the Lord.* ***(Zephaniah 3:20)***

*I will gather the lame; I will assemble the exiles and those I have brought to grief. I will make the lame my remnant, those driven away a strong nation.* ***The Lord will rule over them*** *in Mount Zion* ***from that day and forever. (Micah 4:6-7)***

*For I will take you out of the nations; I will gather you from all the countries and bring you back into your own land.* ***(Ezekiel 36:24)***

The recurring theme is clear. God has repeatedly used prophecy to tell us that he will restore the exiles of Israel 'a second time' and that this time it will be permanent - a theme which underscores everything that we have learned in *Prophecy Shock* and for which we have coined the term *Israelism.*

But what does this mean for other popular schools of Prophecy interpretation?

**Reaffirming Israelism**

***Israelism*** makes four concrete claims that we will now treat as the basis for comparison:

1. **Primary subject and stage.** The Jews and Jerusalem (not the Church) are the primary subject and the central stage of fulfilment of all the prophecies in Daniel and most of the time-defined prophecies in Revelation.
2. **The "beasts"** in these visions are **empires that actually ruled Jerusalem**. If a power never ruled the city, it is **not** a beast in view.
3. **The "times".** Where the prophecies indicate a period of time, those periods describe **exact spans of years**, not poetic or symbolic approximations.

4. **Where the clocks end.** All of the **time-defined** countdowns end in **1948** and **1967**, marking the return of Jews to their ancient homeland and the liberation of Jerusalem.

(Clarification for readers: while the **time-defined** prophecies are complete, the **non-timed** prophecies in **Visions 5–7** all still remain to be fulfilled)

With these yardsticks clear, let's now compare each alternative belief system to Israelism - not to score points, but to test what we now know against the traditional views on prophecy.

## Postmillennialism

Postmillennialism is the belief that Christianity will gradually transform the world before Christ returns.

It imagines the gospel spreading so widely, and human culture improving so steadily, that history itself moves toward a golden age - a "millennium" of peace and righteousness brought about by Christian influence. In this view, most of Daniel's and Revelation's prophecies were fulfilled long ago, particularly around the destruction of Jerusalem in AD 70, leaving the Church to carry God's kingdom forward through moral progress and evangelistic success.

The "beasts" are seen as ancient empires such as Babylon, Persia, Greece, and Rome, which have already gone and the "Antichrist" is not one future dictator but the recurring spirit of opposition to Christ. It is an optimistic theology - one that believes the world can, in time, become Christianized before the Lord's return.

Here are the key differences between Postmillennialism and Israelism:

| Topic | Postmillennialism | Israelism |
|---|---|---|
| **Main Purpose of Prophecy** | To motivate gospel-driven cultural transformation before Christ returns. | To glorify God by verifiable fulfilment; timelines reveal His work after the fact. |

| Topic | Postmillennialism | Israelism |
|---|---|---|
| **Core Premise** | Much of Revelation/Olivet fulfilled in the 1st century (AD 70), with a long golden-age trajectory ahead. | All of Danil and all of the time-defined prophecies in Revelation are fulfilled. |
| **Central Subject of Prophecy** | The Church and Christianised civilization become the main stage as history improves. | Israel and Jerusalem are the explicit subject and stage of fulfilment. |
| **Prophetic Timeline** | A gradual upward trend toward a Christianized world, then Christ returns. | Decisive dated events are behind us: 688, 1948, 1967; non-timed items remain; world gets worse, not better |
| **Interpretive Authority** | Classic/Puritan and postmil traditions. | Scripture-only, measured by six Key Questions and anchored to public dates/events. |
| **Interpretive Method** | Symbolic and typological emphasis; "beasts", "times" read as eras or patterns. | Consistently literal interpretation. Beasts-as-empires, and year-math where given. |
| **Church & Israel** | Church fulfils Israel's role; national Israel mainly typological. | Church is grafted in; prophecy remains Israel/Jerusalem-centric. |
| **Beasts (definition)** | Historicized mainly to Rome; no distinct future "final beast." | Always refers to empires that actually ruled Jerusalem; never individuals; ledger closes in 1967. |
| **Antichrist (1-2 John)** | A category ("many antichrists"), not a single end-times man. | A prevailing attitude, not a titled end-times man; beasts are empires, not a single ruler. |

| Topic | Postmillennialism | Israelism |
|---|---|---|
| **Mark of the Beast / 666** | Often Nero via gematria or recurring state idolatry/imperial cult. | A future event that will affect Muslims, not Christians |
| **The Tribulation** | Largely past (AD 66–70) or an ebb-and-flow pattern through history. | 1,260 years of predicted suppression between 688 → 1948 (witnesses in sackcloth). |
| **Times of the Gentiles** | A broad concept; not tied to a specific end-date. | A specific count that ends when Jerusalem is free: 688 → 1967 (42 months) |
| **Clocks / Year-Math** | Treated as eras/trends, not strict arithmetic. | Exact spans landing on highly visible public dates: 688, 1948, 1967. |
| **Timing of the End** | After Christians have prepared the world, not imminent. | Imminent: time-defined predictions are done; only non-timed prophecies remain. |

**Verdict: Why Israelism replaces Postmillennialism**

While Postmillennialism inspires cultural confidence, it misplaces the focus of prophecy. Its optimism rests on the Churches gradual triumph, but the Scriptures centre their timelines, nations, and fulfilments on Israel and Jerusalem - not Western civilisation or Church ascendancy.

When the clocks in Daniel and Revelation are read literally, they don't point toward a slow global reformation; they close precisely on Israel's rebirth and Jerusalem's restoration in 1948 and 1967. Those aren't metaphors - they're history's timestamps on prophecy completed. Israelism honours what Postmillennialism hoped for - the visible vindication of God's plan - but it locates that vindication where the prophets did: in Israel's return, not mankind's self-improvement. The story isn't about the Church building the kingdom upward; it's about God fulfilling His word in plain sight.

## Amillennialism

Amillennialism is the belief that the "millennium" of Revelation 20 is symbolic - not a literal thousand-year reign on earth - and that Christ is already ruling spiritually from heaven through His Church.

It rejects both the optimism of Postmillennialism and the futurist detail of Premillennialism, arguing instead that most prophecies describe the ongoing struggle between good and evil throughout the Church Age. In this view, the "beasts" and "Babylon" are broad symbols of worldly power or human rebellion, the "tribulation" represents general suffering across time, and the "Antichrist" is a recurring spirit rather than a single person.

Amillennialism treats prophecy as figurative literature conveying moral truth rather than dated prediction. It emphasises symbolism over measurement, and tradition over fulfilment.

Here are the key differences between Amillennialism and Israelism:

| Topic | Amillennialism | Israelism |
|---|---|---|
| **Main Purpose of Prophecy** | To reveal spiritual truths about Christ's reign and the ongoing conflict between good and evil. | To glorify God by verifiable fulfilment; prophecies are measurable and historical. |
| **Core Premise** | The "millennium" is symbolic; prophecy unfolds across the Church Age rather than in literal spans. | Time-defined prophecies are literal; the clocks of Daniel and Revelation are precise and already complete. |
| **Central Subject of Prophecy** | The universal Church as spiritual Israel. | The literal nation of Israel and the city of Jerusalem. |

| Topic | Amillennialism | Israelism |
|---|---|---|
| **Prophetic Timeline** | Non-literal and non-sequential; the visions overlap symbolically. | Chronological and measurable; the prophetic spans terminate in 1948 and 1967. |
| **Interpretive Authority** | Rooted in Augustine and Reformation theology; stresses allegory and typology. | Based on Scripture alone, guided by the six Key Questions and historical correspondence. |
| **Interpretive Method** | Symbolic and theological - prioritises meaning over timing. | Literal in subject, symbolic in form; every time-span corresponds to real history. |
| **Church & Israel** | The Church replaces or spiritually inherits Israel's promises. | The Church is grafted in but does not replace Israel; prophecy remains Israel-centred. |
| **Beasts (definition)** | Represent human evil or world empires in general; not geographically fixed. | Represent only empires that directly ruled Jerusalem; the line ends in 1967. |
| **Third Temple** | Interpreted spiritually - the believer's heart or the Church community. | Not predicted prior to the return of Christ. |
| **Antichrist (1–2 John)** | A symbol of opposition to Christ across time; no single figure expected. | Agrees it is a spirit, not a man; the "beast" imagery applies to historical empires. |
| **Mark of the Beast / 666** | A recurring symbol of idolatry and allegiance to worldly systems. | A future event that will affect Muslims, not Christians |
| **The Tribulation** | Represents ongoing persecution of believers through the Church Age. | The literal 1,260-year exclusion (688–1948) of Jews and Christians from Jerusalem. |

| Topic | Amillennialism | Israelism |
|---|---|---|
| **Times of the Gentiles** | Viewed as the whole Christian era, ending only at Christ's return. | A fixed count (42 months ≈ 1,278 years) ending in 1967 when Jerusalem was restored. |
| **Clocks / Year-Math** | Symbolic, not chronological; time counts treated as metaphor. | Literal and precise |
| **Timing of the End** | No measurable end sequence: Christ could return any time after the Church Age. | The time-defined countdowns are finished; remaining prophecies (Visions 5–7) are non-timed but still ahead. |

**Verdict: Why Israelism replaces Amillennialism**

Amillennialism deserves credit for curbing speculative excess, but it overcorrects by draining prophecy of its measurable precision and national focus. By turning Israel into an allegory for the Church, it disconnects the text from its own geography and arithmetic.

Daniel's "time, times and half a time," the 2,300 "evenings and mornings," and the 1,260 "days" are not poetic flourishes - they're calibrated timelines that land exactly on Israel's restoration in 1948 and Jerusalem's liberation in 1967. Where Amillennialism sees a timeless moral drama, Israelism sees history fulfilling prophecy to the year. It preserves the same humility about the unknown future, but grounds it in what God has already done, visibly and precisely, in the nation at the centre of His plan.

## Historicism

Historicism sees prophecy as a long, continuous timeline of Church and European history.

It was the dominant Protestant view from the Reformation through the 19th century and shaped generations of Bible commentary. Reformers like Luther and Calvin viewed the papacy as the "Antichrist," interpreting Revelation's beasts, trumpets, and seals as symbolic of successive European powers, religious corruption, and reform movements.

In this model, Daniel's and Revelation's visions stretch from Babylon to modern Christendom, with no sharp end date - prophecy is still unfolding through the Church Age. This approach deserves credit: it treated prophecy as *real history*, not mystical allegory. But by centring on Europe instead of Jerusalem, it quietly shifted the lens from Israel's story to the Churches own reflection.

Here are the key differences between Historicism and Israelism:

| **Topic** | **Historicism** | **Israelism** |
|---|---|---|
| **Main Purpose of Prophecy** | To trace God's hand through Church and European history. | To glorify God through verifiable fulfilment - real dates and events that close the biblical clocks. |
| **Core Premise** | Prophecy unfolds continuously through the centuries of Church history. | The time-defined prophecies have already run their course; non-timed prophecies (Visions 5–7) remain ahead. |
| **Central Subject of Prophecy** | Christendom - Europe's empires, popes, and reformers. | Israel and Jerusalem - the literal subjects named in Daniel and Revelation. |
| **Prophetic Timeline** | Long symbolic eras that blur across centuries. | Fixed year-counts ending on highly significant events in 688, 1948, 1967. |
| **Interpretive Authority** | Rooted in Reformation-era commentary traditions. | Scripture-only, measured by six Key Questions and anchored to historical closure. |
| **Interpretive Method** | Symbolic and continuous, often speculative on dates. | Mostly literal; beasts = empires, and prophetic "times" = years. |

| Topic | Historicism | Israelism |
|---|---|---|
| **Church & Israel** | Church replaces Israel as prophetic centre. | Church is grafted in, but Israel remains the prophetic heart. |
| **Beasts (definition)** | Assigned to European systems, especially the papacy. | Represent only empires that directly ruled Jerusalem; the line ends in 1967. |
| **Third Temple** | Not central to the system. | Not predicted nor required; Revelation's end shows no temple. |
| **Antichrist (1–2 John)** | Often identified with the papacy. | A prevailing anti-Christ spirit, not a single institution or man. |
| **Mark of the Beast / 666** | Papal or imperial power within European history. | A future event that will affect Muslims, not Christians |
| **The Tribulation** | Ongoing church persecution through the centuries. | The 1,260 years of suppression: 688 → 1948. |
| **Times of the Gentiles** | Broad Church Age with no fixed endpoint. | Exact 42-month (1,278.3-year) span: 688 → 1967. |
| **Clocks / Year-Math** | Approximate and fluid, used illustratively. | Exact arithmetic tied to public history: 688, 1948, 1967. |
| **Timing of the End** | Indefinite - prophecy still unfolding. | Imminent - the time-defined clocks are complete; non-timed events remain. |

## Verdict: Why Israelism replaces Historicism

Historicism was nearly right - it saw prophecy as history, not imagination - but it charted the wrong continent and the wrong years. By mapping Revelation's symbols onto Europe instead of Jerusalem, it confused the Churches story with Israel's.

Israelism restores the original geography and the exact arithmetic the prophets gave. When the correct question is asked - *Did this power rule Jerusalem?* - the prophetic chain locks into place and ends in 1967, when the city returned to Jewish control.

The so-called "beast line" is closed, the time-defined prophecies have been fulfilled, and only the non-timed visions remain before Christ's return. Historicism grasped the shape of prophecy; but only Israelism provides its coordinates.

## Premillennialism

Of all the end-time systems, **Premillennialism** is the one most Christians today have grown up with.

It fills pulpits, paperbacks, prophecy conferences, and Sunday school charts. It offers a vivid, dramatic narrative: a coming Antichrist who rises as a global dictator; a seven-year peace treaty with Israel; a rebuilt Temple in Jerusalem; a "mark" required for buying and selling; and a final Tribulation before Christ's return. For many, it's the lens through which all current events are read.

Premillennialism deserves credit for its reverence for Scripture and its conviction that God will literally keep His promises. But its weakness lies in *where* it places those promises. It shifts prophecy's stage from Israel's past exile and present restoration to a still-future crisis for the Church. It takes Daniel's and Revelation's completed timelines and projects them forward - re-creating a countdown that Scripture has already run.

Here are the key differences between Premillennialism and Israelism:

| **Topic** | **Premillennialism** | **Israelism** |
|---|---|---|
| **Main Purpose of Prophecy** | To outline detailed future events so believers can be prepared. | To glorify God by revealing fulfilment after the fact - history proving His precision. |
| **Core Premise** | Most end-time prophecy (Daniel & Revelation) is still future. | All of Daniel and most of Revelation's timed prophecies already fulfilled; only non-timed prophecies (Visions 5–7) remain ahead. |

| Topic | Premillennialism | Israelism |
|---|---|---|
| **Central Subject of Prophecy** | The Church in the last days. | Israel and Jerusalem are the centre of all prophetic fulfilment. |
| **Prophetic Timeline** | A series of future events culminating in a seven-year Tribulation and Christ's return. | The time-defined events already closed in 688, 1948, and 1967; only non-timed prophecies remain before His return. |
| **Interpretive Authority** | Popularised by Darby, Scofield, Hal Lindsey, and modern evangelical consensus. | Scripture-only, measured by six Key Questions and historical closure. |
| **Interpretive Method** | Literal where convenient, symbolic where required. | Consistently literal: beasts = empires; prophetic "times" = years. |
| **Church & Israel** | Church is distinct from Israel but inherits her promises. | Church is grafted in; Israel remains the prophetic centre. |
| **Beasts (definition)** | Various empires and individuals - especially a future Antichrist. | Always empires that ruled Jerusalem; never individuals; line ends 1967. |
| **Third Temple** | Must be rebuilt for prophecy to resume. | Not required. Paul's "temple" is metaphorical (believers); Revelation 21:22: "I saw no temple in the city." |
| **Antichrist (1-2 John)** | A single future world ruler empowered by Satan. | A spirit already present in John's day; not a man. "Beasts" = empires, not persons. |
| **Mark of the Beast / 666** | Future global identifier tied to commerce or technology. | A future event that will affect Muslims, not Christians |

| Topic | Premillennialism | Israelism |
|---|---|---|
| **The Tribulation** | A future seven-year global crisis. | A completed 1,260-year suppression (688 → 1948). |
| **Times of the Gentiles** | A Church-Age concept without a fixed end. | A precise span (42 months ≈ 1,278 years) ending in 1967 when Jerusalem was restored. |
| **Clocks / Year-Math** | Reinterpreted as symbolic or still-future. | Literal arithmetic closing exactly on 688, 1948, and 1967. |
| **Timing of the End** | Conditional on prophecy's checklist being fulfilled. | Imminent - the clocks are closed; only non-timed prophecies remain. |

## Common Questions and Popular Expectations

For many sincere believers, certain expectations have become almost inseparable from the study of Premillennialism: a rebuilt Jewish Temple, a coming Antichrist, and a final global crisis. These themes are powerful, deeply familiar, and have shaped Christian teaching for more than a century. They deserve to be addressed carefully and respectfully. Yet as we've discovered throughout *Prophecy Shock*, Scripture itself does not require them. What follows is not an attempt to dismiss what others hold dear, but to show - plainly and biblically - why these elements are not part of God's prophetic plan as revealed through Israelism.

## The Third Temple

The idea of a "Third Temple" is built from inference rather than any clear, direct prediction in Scripture. Paul's warning that a man would "set himself up in God's temple" (2 Thessalonians 2:4) is often taken as evidence of a future physical structure in Jerusalem. But this ignores Paul's own consistent use of the term "temple" to describe God's people. In 2 Corinthians 6:16 he writes plainly that believers themselves are the temple of the living God. His language is moral, not architectural. He is describing a posture of rebellion - people placing themselves above God - something that has already occurred throughout history, exactly as he warned.

The book of Revelation brings further clarity. In its closing vision of the final state, John writes: *"I saw no temple in the city, for its temple is the Lord God Almighty and the Lamb."* This makes clear that the endpoint of God's redemptive plan is not a restored building, but the direct presence of God Himself.

Taken together, these passages show that a rebuilt temple is not required for prophecy to be fulfilled, nor is it presented as a necessary feature of the end of the age. The expectation of a future temple - particularly as part of a final Antichrist scenario - is therefore not something the Bible clearly teaches, but a conclusion drawn from assumption rather than explicit revelation.

**This does not negate the temple vision described in Ezekiel, which belongs to a different context: a post-judgment restoration ordered by God Himself, not a human-built structure required to trigger end-times events.**

### The Antichrist

The term *antichrist* appears only in John's letters - and never as a title. It describes a *spirit of opposition* already active in his own generation and the idea of an antichrist as a coming world dictator is a later construction, stitched together from unrelated verses which 'add to' or 'take away' from Gods intended meaning.

Daniel's and Revelation's "beasts" are not individuals but empires that ruled Jerusalem: Babylon, Persia, Greece, the Seleucid and Ptolemaic dynasties, Rome, Byzantium, the Islamic Caliphates and two nominally 'Christian' powers. That line ended in 1967.

A future tyrant may appear - but if he does he will be another figure of history, not the Antichrist of imagination.

### Why Current Events Don't Fit

If you've been a student of Premillennialism for a long time there will be a natural desire to want to try and reconcile those views with what you've learnt from reading *Prophecy Shock* in order to try and make them 'fit' into the framework of your new understanding.

I completely understand that temptation - but it can't be done. Almost all of the prophecies which underpin the solutions in this book are the same ones that are used to 'prove' the premillennial position and they can't both be correct. Either one is right and one is wrong, or they're both wrong. There is no compromise position.

### Verdict: Why Israelism replaces Premillennialism

Premillennialism has captured the modern imagination because it takes prophecy seriously - but it looks forward to what God has already finished. Most of what it predicts for the future is now behind us.

Its vivid expectations - an Antichrist, a rebuilt Temple, a Christian Tribulation - belong to misread clocks and misplaced geography.

Israelism restores both: the arithmetic of Daniel and Revelation points not to the next crisis, but to the *completed restoration* of Israel and Jerusalem in 1948 and 1967. The beast-line is closed, the timed prophecies fulfilled, and the Church now stands in the gap between history completed and glory revealed.

Premillennialism's faith in God's literal promises was right; Israelism simply shows where - and when - He has already fulfilled them.

## Dispensational Israelology

If you mention what you've learned in *Prophecy Shock* to your friends, don't be surprised if you're told "Arnold Fruchtenbaum has already written about that".

They're referring to the book *Israelology* published by Fruchtenbaum in 1989 and while we haven't previously mentioned this book, no critique would be complete without considering it.

Although *Israelology* and *Israelism* share similar names and agree on a few key themes – they are *very* different approaches to prophecy.

Fruchtenbaum's Dispensational Israelology insists that Israel and the Church are permanently distinct, that Israel's unconditional covenants await fulfilment in a coming seven-year Tribulation, and that a personal Antichrist will rise over a revived Roman confederation. It treats today's State of Israel as a **prelude** ("a regathering in unbelief") – and it claims that the real action is still ahead: a rebuilt Temple, a global mark, world governance under a single man, Israel's national repentance at the end of the age, and then a Messianic Kingdom where every promise lands in visible, earthly form.

This system deserves credit: it keeps Israel in view, refuses to allegorise Israel's covenants, and has the courage to read Scripture plainly. But it relocates the **completion** of the prophetic story from public history that we can test - **688 → 1948 → 1967** - to an elastic future that we can't. It treats the prophetic "clocks" as paused, inserts gaps between the Bible's time marks, and asks the Church to wait for signs that Scripture does not require.

Here are the key differences between Dispensational Israelology and Israelism:

| Topic | Dispensational Israelology | Israelism |
|---|---|---|
| **Main Purpose of Prophecy** | To set out detailed future events culminating in Israel's restoration in the Kingdom. | To glorify God by verifiable fulfilment - timelines that land on real history. |

| Topic | Dispensational Israelology | Israelism |
|---|---|---|
| **Core Premise** | Most end-time prophecy remains future | The time-defined prophecies have already run to completion. |
| **Central Subject of Prophecy** | Israel is central, but decisive fulfilments arrive after a future Tribulation. | Israel and Jerusalem are the subject and stage; fulfilment is anchored to their modern restoration. |
| **Prophetic Timeline** | Allows long gaps; compresses fulfilment into a future 7-year crisis and Millennial Kingdom. | Fixed year-counts that have already landed on public milestones: 688, 1948, 1967. |
| **Interpretive Authority** | Literal-grammatical; Israel/Church are distinct from each other. | Scripture-only, tested by six Key Questions and closure in history. |
| **Interpretive Method** | Mostly literal; types allowed; time spans not required. | Mostly literal |
| **Church & Israel** | Distinct groups with distinct programs. | Church is grafted in; Israel remains the prophetic heart. |
| **Regathering of Israel** | Two: now (in unbelief) and post-Trib (in faith). | 1948 / 1967 are decisive closures; there is no later reboot. |
| **Beasts (definition)** | Final empire = revived Rome with ten kings; a personal Antichrist. | Beasts are only empires that ruled Jerusalem; the chain ended in 1967. |
| **Third Temple** | Expected (Tribulation) and another in the Millennium. | Not required; Revelation's end shows no temple. |
| **Antichrist (1–2 John)** | A single future world ruler. | Beasts are empires, not an individual "final boss." |
| **Mark of the Beast / 666** | Future global enforcement during the Tribulation. | A future event that will affect Muslims, not Christians. |

| Topic | Dispensational Israelology | Israelism |
|---|---|---|
| **The Tribulation** | A literal seven-year period still ahead. | A completed 1,260-year suppression: 688 → 1948. |
| **Times of the Gentiles** | Continues until the Second Coming; Jerusalem's full restoration follows. | A precise 42-month (≈ 1,278 years) span: 688 → 1967. |
| **Clocks / Year-Math** | Time counts allow gaps; closure deferred to the future. | Exact arithmetic tied to public dates: 688, 1948, 1967. |
| **Timing of the End** | Not imminent - key future signs must arrive first. | Imminent - timed prophecies are complete; only non-timed events remain. |

### Verdict: Why Israelism replaces Dispensational Israelology

Let's be blunt. Dispensational Israelology keeps telling us the big moments are still somewhere down the road. It shifts the finish line by adding gaps that the Bible doesn't ask for.

Israelism points at the scoreboard and says, "These events have already happened." If God set clocks, they weren't meant to idle in neutral – they were meant to count down to a conclusion. And they did - 688 → 1948 → 1967.

That's not theory - the math can be tested. Anyone can paint a future that never arrives but you can't fudge dates that we've already lived. 688, 1948, 1967 either hit the biblical spans or they don't.

But they *do* hit. The math lands, in daylight, with Israel and Jerusalem exactly where Scripture puts them. That's fulfilment, not fan fiction.

Most importantly, Israel's primacy isn't parked in a holding pattern. Dispensationalism rightly rejects replacement theology – but then it defers Israel's vindication to a later dispensation. Israelism shows it already breaking into history - in front of the nations - precisely where prophecy said it would. That's how God is glorified:

by fulfilment - not by promising precision later, but by showing precision now.

**Bottom line:** Dispensational Israelology takes Scripture seriously – but Israelism takes it to the finish. The arithmetic closes, the geography is right, and the beast-line is behind us. The timed prophecies are fulfilled; the non-timed ones remain. Not a new angle - the conclusion.

## Acknowledging the challenge

Many sincere Christians who have spent years – maybe decades – studying one of the prophetic systems reviewed in this chapter and you may have questions about those who promoted them. But these men and women weren't any less discerning - God just wasn't ready to reveal His full meaning prior to now. Meanwhile, none of their work was in vain! Prophecy scholars performed a vital role:

1. **They organized the field**. Hundreds of years of study give us clear alternatives to consider. That structure lets readers compare views side-by-side.

2. **They recovered sources**. Many of the texts, timelines, citations and other evidence that we take for granted came from the painstaking work of those who have devoted their lives to finding, and codifying, important documents

3. **They ran the experiments**. Putting your work out there to be checked - and sometimes disproved – is an act of courage and obedience. We owe these Authors our deepest gratitude.

# Appendix C: The incredible history outline in Chapter 11 of Daniel

Daniels last Vision starts back in Daniel 10:1 - *in the third year of Cyrus the (Persian) king* (533 BC) – and the remainder of that chapter establishes the setting for the rest of the vision.

Then we get to chapter 11, verse 2 where we're told that:

**Chapter 11, verse 2**

> *2 "...three more kings will arise in Persia (ie, after Cyrus), and then a fourth, who will be far richer than all the others. When he has gained power by his wealth, he will stir up everyone against the kingdom of Greece.*

History tells us who these Persian (Achaemenid) kings, who followed Cyrus, are:

1. **Cambyses II** (530–522 BC) - Cyrus' son who conquers Egypt.
2. **Bardiya/Smerdis** (522 BC) - short reign; likely the usurper **Gaumata**.
3. **Darius I (Hystaspes)** (522–486 BC) - reorganizes the empire; first major clashes with Greece (e.g., Marathon, 490 BC).
4. **Xerxes I** (486–465 BC) - the **"fourth... far richer"** king who **"stirs up everyone against Greece"** via the massive 480–479 BC invasion (Thermopylae, Salamis).

These details aren't random. They tell us that first, Darius I (who was not the same person as **Darius the Mede** in Chapter 6 of Daniel) and then, Xerxes, would set in motion a train of events that would light the fuse of a deep Greek hatred which would simmer for generations – leading directly to the events which play out a century and a half later, in the next verse.

### Chapter 11, verses 3-4

> [3] *Then a mighty king will arise, who will rule with great power and do as he pleases.* [4] *After he has arisen, his empire will be broken up and parcelled out toward the four winds of heaven. It will not go to his descendants, nor will it have the power he exercised, because his empire will be uprooted and given to others.*

We know who this is – it's Alexander – who we meet repeatedly in different prophecies in the Book of Daniel. Capitalising on the deep-seated Greek hatred of the Persians, Alexander rallies his people and comprehensively defeats the Persians, starting with the Battle of Granicus in 334BC and taking control of the 'known world' (which included Jerusalem). When he died, his kingdom was 'parcelled out' to his four generals who split it up into four separate kingdoms.

### Chapter 11, verses 5-29

So far, the prophecy has provided an accurate account of the 200+years following the time of Daniel – but the next section of verses provides what is arguably the most stunning series of prophecies in all of scripture.

It moves focus to the kingdoms that were established by two of Alexanders generals - **Seleucid and Ptolemy** - and outlines their precise history **over 145 years (c. 312–168 BC), leading to Rome's intervention in 168 BC**.

What follows is a remarkable history of the relationships between these two powers over this 145 year period. I've included these prophecies in a table because there are so many of them and because I want you to see just how incredibly accurate they are. Note the 'king of the North' always refers to the various rulers of the Seleucid Empire and the 'king of the South' always refers to the various rulers of the Ptolemaic empire – **both viewed from a Jerusalem-centric perspective**:

| Prophecy (Daniel 11) | Historical Fulfilment |
|---|---|
| **v5** - the "King of the South grows strong; one of his princes becomes stronger and rules a great dominion." | **Ptolemy I Soter** is strong in Egypt; but his "prince" **Seleucus I Nicator** becomes stronger and founds the vast **Seleucid Empire** (**c. 312–305 BC**). |
| **v6** - "After some years they make an alliance through a marriage; the woman and her offspring do not endure." | **Berenice** (daughter of **Ptolemy II**) marries **Antiochus II** (king of the North) after Ptolemy II dies, **Laodice** has **Berenice and her infant** killed (**246 BC**). |
| **vv7–8** - "A branch from her roots attacks the North, prevails, and carries off idols/treasures to Egypt." | **Ptolemy III Euergetes** (Berenice's brother) invades Syria in the **Third Syrian War**, returns with **booty and cult objects** (**246–241 BC**). |
| **v9** - the "King of the North invades the South but returns to his land." | **Seleucid** counter-campaigns into Egypt's sphere but falters; the North retreats (**mid-240s BC**). |
| **v10** - "His sons muster a multitude and advance." | **Seleucus III** and especially **Antiochus III** rebuild and push south to recover Coele-Syria (**223–201 BC** campaigns). |
| **v11** - the "King of the South is enraged and defeats the multitude of the North." | **Ptolemy IV** defeats **Antiochus III** at the **Battle of Raphia** (**217 BC**). |

| Prophecy (Daniel 11) | Historical Fulfilment |
|---|---|
| **v12** - "His heart is exalted; he does not keep the advantage." | Ptolemy IV **fails to capitalize** after Raphia (**post-217 BC**). |
| **v13** - "After some years the North returns with a greater army and much equipment." | **Antiochus III** renews the offensive, stronger than before (**204–201 BC**). |
| **v14** - "Many rise against the South; violent men among **your people** exalt themselves but stumble." | Regional revolts and **some Judeans** support Antiochus against Ptolemaic rule; **no lasting success** (**early 200s BC**). |
| **vv15–16** - "The North takes a fortified city; the South's arms fail; he stands in the Beautiful Land and does as he wills." | Seleucid wins victory at **Panium/Paneas** and related sieges; **Judea (the Beautiful Land)** shifts from Ptolemaic to Seleucid control (**200 BC**). |
| **v17** - "He seeks to destroy by an agreement; gives the daughter to ruin it, but she won't stand with him." | **Antiochus III** marries **Cleopatra I** to **Ptolemy V**; but she **sides with Egypt**, not her father (**c. 194–193 BC**). |
| **v18** - "He turns to the coastlands; a commander puts an end to his insolence." | Antiochus III campaigns in Asia Minor; **Rome (Scipio Asiaticus)** defeats him at **Magnesia** (**190 BC**). |
| **v19** - "He turns back to his fortresses, stumbles and falls, and is not found." | After **Treaty of Apamea (188 BC)**, **Antiochus III** dies during an eastern campaign (**187 BC**). |

| Prophecy (Daniel 11) | Historical Fulfilment |
|---|---|
| **v20** - "A successor sends an exactor of tribute; within a few days he is destroyed - not in anger or battle." | **Seleucus IV Philopator** imposes heavy taxation (cf. **Heliodorus** episode) and is **assassinated (187–175 BC**; death **175 BC**). |
| **v21** - "A contemptible person seizes the kingdom by intrigue." | **Antiochus IV Epiphanes** takes the throne through **political manoeuvring** (**175 BC**). |
| **v22** - "Armies swept away before him; a prince of the covenant is broken." | Antiochus IV **consolidates power**; **High Priest Onias III** is deposed and later killed (**c. 172–171 BC**). |
| **v23** - "After making agreements he acts deceitfully; rises with a small people." | Antiochus IV advances via **treaties deception, and a tight inner circle** (**170s BC**). |
| **v24** - "He invades richest provinces unexpectedly; scatters plunder; he devises plans against strongholds." | Antiochus IV undertakes **Surprise seizures** and uses **largesse** to secure loyalty (**170s BC**). |
| **vv25–26** - "He stirs up his power against the South; the South cannot stand because of treachery." | The **Egyptian campaigns** of **Antiochus IV** succeed amid **Egyptian court betrayal** (**170–169 BC**). |
| **v27** - "Both kings speak lies at one table; the end is for the appointed time." | **Duplicity in negotiations** between Antiochus IV and **Ptolemy VI**; no durable settlement (**late 160s BC**). |
| **v28** - "He returns with great wealth; his heart is against the holy covenant; | **169 BC**: Antiochus IV **plunders Jerusalem**, suppresses loyalists, and returns to Syria. |

| Prophecy (Daniel 11) | Historical Fulfilment |
| --- | --- |
| he acts and returns to his land." | |

As you can see, the correlation between these prophecies and fulfilled history is extraordinary - but it doesn't stop there. The prophecy continues to provide detailed information about the next power to control Jerusalem.

### Chapter 11, verses 29-35

In 168 BC a Roman delegation, led by Gaius Popillius Laenas and backed by the Roman naval fleet confronted Seleucid king Antiochus IV at Eleusis - a suburb just outside Alexandria, in Egypt. This is the reference to ships of the western coastlands in verse 30 (rendered as "ships of Kittim" in some versions).

Gaius drew a circle in the sand around Antiochus IV and demanded that he decide, before he stepped out of the circle, whether he was going to withdraw from Egypt or face Rome. Antiochus backed down. That single scene ended Seleucid expansion, placed Egypt under Roman protection, and effectively made Rome the referee of the eastern Mediterranean years before any formal annexation of Judea and Jerusalem.

From there, Rome's grip tightened. The Hasmonean revolt (167–160 BC) unfolded in Rome's shadow; Judea even sent an embassy to Rome (161 BC) - a quiet admission of who set the red lines. Over the next century Rome dictated terms to Hellenistic kings, absorbed Syria's neighbourhood by policy and pressure, and used treaties and ultimatums to shape outcomes on the ground. By the 60s BC, Judea's dynastic feud (Hyrcanus II vs. Aristobulus II) handed Rome the pretext to move from arbiter to administrator. Pompey marched, took Jerusalem in 63 BC, and turned de facto control into actual rule.

| Prophecy (Daniel 11) | Historical Fulfilment |
|---|---|
| vv29–30 - "At the appointed time he shall return... but it shall not be as it was before; for ships of the western coastlands' shall come against him, and he shall be afraid and withdraw; then he shall turn back and be enraged against the holy covenant." | At Eleusis, outside Alexandria (168 BC), a Roman envoy (Gaius Popillius Laenas) forces Antiochus IV to withdraw from Egypt, ending Seleucid expansion. Egypt falls under Roman protection; Rome becomes de-facto arbiter in the East - framing events that will decide Jerusalem's fate. |
| v31a - "Forces from him shall profane the sanctuary and the fortress and shall take away the regular burnt offering." | Rome (AD 70): Roman General Titus besieges Jerusalem and destroys the Second Temple; the daily sacrifice ends. |

As you can see, the prophecy signals the rise of Roman influence (168 BC) – then fast-forwards 238 years to the destruction of the second temple, by General Titus (70 AD).

We then fast-forward another six centuries, leap-frogging the Byzantine empire and going directly to the early days of Islamic control of Jerusalem – where we're introduced to an event which has become very familiar to us throughout the pages of this book:

| Prophecy (Daniel 11) | Historical Fulfilment |
|---|---|
| **v31b** - "...and **they** shall set up the **abomination that makes desolate**." | **Caliph 'Abd al-Malik** builds the **Dome of the Rock** (**AD 688**). This is the **"abomination of desolation"** predicted later in Chapter 12 of this same vision. |
| **vv32–33** - "He shall seduce with flattery those who violate the covenant; but the people who know their God shall | **Under early Islamic rule (7th–10th c.):** Some **Jews accommodate** for advantage but the faithful **stand firm** and **teach;** |

| Prophecy (Daniel 11) | Historical Fulfilment |
|---|---|
| stand firm and take action. And the wise... shall make many understand, though for some days they shall stumble by sword and flame, by captivity and plunder." | they endure **legal constraints, confiscations, slavery and periodic violence**. |
| **vv34–35** - "When they stumble, they shall receive **a little help**, and many shall join them insincerely. And some of the wise shall stumble, so that they may be refined... **until the time of the end**." | **Crusader interlude (AD 1099–1187) = "a little help"** with mixed motives; renewed Islamic control (**Ayyubids/Mamluks**) follows. Across these centuries the community is **refined**, pointing to the next regime over Jerusalem. |
| **vv36–39** - "The king shall do as he wills... exalt himself above every god... honour the **god of fortresses**... deal with the strongest fortresses... **give great honour** to those who acknowledge him... **divide the land for a price**." | **The Ottoman phase (AD 1517–1917)** over Jerusalem: **fortress-centric** policy (e.g., 16th-century walls, c. **1537–1541**), **patronage and honours** to loyal elites, and **land/revenue parcelling** via **timar/iltizam** and **waqf** - i.e., **"dividing the land for a price."** |

That brings us to the last verses in Chapter 11 - verses 40 to 45. Once again, these are a perfect fit with history:

| Prophecy (Daniel 11) | Historical Fulfilment |
|---|---|
| **v40** - "At the time of the end the **king of the South** will engage him in battle, and the **king of the North** will storm out with chariots, cavalry and a great fleet... He will invade | **The Hashemite Arab Revolt (1916–1918)** from the **Hejaz** (south) strikes the Ottomans, captures **Aqaba (1917)**, raids the **Hejaz Railway**, and pushes up through **Transjordan** toward |

| Prophecy (Daniel 11) | Historical Fulfilment |
|---|---|
| many countries and sweep through them like a flood." | **Damascus**. The Sinai–Palestine campaign of the **British** (king of the North) overruns Ottoman lines in **Gaza**, **Beersheba**, and **Jerusalem in 1917 and Damascus in 1918** - a rapid advance "like a flood." The two thrusts are **concurrent and coordinated**. |
| **v41** - "He will also **invade the Beautiful Land**. Many countries will fall, but **Edom, Moab and the leaders of Ammon** will be delivered from his hand." | **Britain enters the Holy Land and captures Jerusalem (1917).** The emirate of Transjordan (Edom / Moab / Ammon) is separated administratively in 1921 and is excluded from the Palestine Mandate. |
| **v42** - "He will **extend his power** over many countries; **Egypt will not escape**." | **Egypt** comes under British control in **1914**, British mandates / protectorates span **Iraq (1920–32)**, **Palestine (1922–48)**, and **Transjordan (1921–46)**. |
| **v43** - "He will gain control of the **treasures** of gold and silver and all the **riches of Egypt**, with the **Libyans** and **Cushites** in submission." | **Britain** controls **Egypt's revenues** and the **Suez** artery; has influence across **North Africa** and the **Nile corridor** (**Libya** in the Allied theatre; **Sudan** (Cush) under Anglo-Egyptian administration). |
| **v44** - "Reports from the **east and the north** will **alarm** him; he will set out in **great rage** to destroy and annihilate many." | Pressures from the **east** (Iraq/Arab nationalism) and the **north** (Soviet rise; WWII threats), plus internal insurgencies (e.g., |

| Prophecy (Daniel 11) | Historical Fulfilment |
|---|---|
| | **Arab Revolt 1936–39**), keep Britain in an **alarmed, force-heavy posture**. |
| **v45** - "He will **pitch his royal tents between the seas at the beautiful holy mountain**. Yet he will **come to his end**, and no one will help him." | The **British Mandate ends in 1948**; Britain withdraws **without any power prolonging its rule** - "**he shall come to his end, and none will help him**." |

So now, with the benefit of perspective, we can understand the extraordinary role of Chapter 11. It isn't a distraction – it's an intricately detailed outline of events which took place between the time that Daniel wrote it in the reign of Cyrus till the reestablishment of the State of Israel in 1948.

It also covers the so-called "400 missing years" between Malachi and Matthew and shows that they were never missing at all. Daniel 11 records them in advance - every empire, every conflict, every shift of power – bridging the 400 years in detail, outlining ongoing history, and finishing in 1948, just 19 years prior to the events in Daniel 12 - Jerusalem's liberation in 1967.

As such – we can now understand the words of the angel in Chapter 12. Daniel has just been given an extensive outline of Jerusalem-centric history which ends with him being told:

> *"...It shall be for a time, times, and half a time; and when he shall have accomplished to scatter the power of the holy people, all these things shall be finished."* ***(Daniel 12:7)***

This is ***exactly*** what happened.

*The solution at a glance*

# Daniel's incredible Chapter 11 timeline

***Scripture:*** *Daniel 11:2–45*

**What's being predicted?**
A step-by-step forecast of most of the major powers that would **rule Jerusalem over 2,500 years**

**Who is being spoken to?**
**Daniel** - receiving his **final vision**

**Who is the prophecy about?**
The **actual rulers of Jerusalem** across time: **Persia's four kings Alexander the Great**, the **Kings of the North/South (Seleucids / Ptolemies)**, **Rome's ascendancy and the destruction of the sanctuary**, the Islamic **abomination** identified with the **Dome,** the time of the **Ottomans** and **Britain's** role then exit in 1948.

**When does it end**
1948. The vision then flows into **Daniel 12**, aligning with the **end of the scattering** of Jews highlighted in **1967**.

Daniel 11 isn't a scatter-gun list of prophecies or a warning of a coming antichrist in the last days: it's a **tight chronology of who controls Jerusalem over more than two millennia –** leading, cleanly into the closing events of Chapter 12

# Appendix D: Coincidence or Coherence?

By now you're familiar with the way that these prophecies continue to land, mostly, on the same three years - 688 AD, 1948, 1967. But that raises a question that I'd ask if I were you: what if that consistency isn't inspired? What if, instead, those recurring timelines are the result of selective bias - me forcing the math to make it say what I already believe?

In essence – what if I cherry-picked my start dates, juggled time scales, or let my affection for Israel steer my conclusions?

**Refuting the challenge of: Selective Bias**

That's a fair challenge, and it deserves a straight answer because, if I'd done any of that, this would be creative writing, not prophecy interpretation. However, the claim of selective bias doesn't stand close scrutiny, for three reasons:

1. The start points for each prophecy are not arbitrary - they're stamped in both Scripture and history.
2. The durations aren't my invention; they're the numbers that the Biblical text, itself, gives us.
3. The end events are not sentimental milestones – they're the very events that the prophecies themselves describe.

The pieces fit because they were meant to, not because I forced them to – and the solutions in *Prophecy Shock* don't "roughly" line up; they hit exact years, again and again. If I'd only produced one or two examples, you could call it luck or point to scholarly debate around start dates. But these alignments occur across *every* time-defined prophecy in Daniel and Revelation. Different visions, different contexts, different start points – in books written 600 years apart -

yet all converging on exile, Jerusalem, and restoration. That's not numerology; that's design.

**Refuting the challenge of: Calendar Manipulation**

There are two challenges to my claim that the durations of these prophecies are directly provided by scripture. Two prophecies where *I* made the choice which determined their length, inviting a charge that I swap between calendars or "year types" to make outcomes line up. Let's examine both:

In the prophecies of 'time, time and half a time' in Daniel 7 and Daniel 12 **I made the word 'time' mean one thousand years**. But that interpretation wasn't invented – it came from 2 Peter 3:8-9 where we're told that God is not constrained by time and that He controls it – comparing one day to one thousand years. So while the interpretation didn't come from the prophecies in Daniel – it did come from scripture – and when applied to both prophecies it produced results that landed on hard, public outcomes and events which I had no control over. When a pattern survives that kind of scrutiny, you pay attention.

The second instance was also in Daniel 12 where **I used Babylonian 360-day schematic years** rather than the 354-day lunisolar years that were in common use by both the Hebrews and the Babylonians at the time. That choice wasn't arbitrary either. In Babylon – where Daniel and Ezekiel lived – the 360-day year was the standard *mathematical* and *astronomical* unit, a fixed "ideal" year used for long-range calculations – whereas the lunisolar year was irregular (meaning its length changed constantly) and required constant adjustment. For long prophetic spans that have to stay coherent over thousands of years, it's easy to see why God would use the unchanging schematic year – and the fact that the year AD 688 appears in multiple solutions, not just the solution to the prophecy of

1,290 days, gives us confidence that we have used the correct calendar.

I understand why people pose these challenges – but when we step back and look at the whole thing from a God's-eye view, the precision of these solutions becomes breathtaking. That kind of symmetry doesn't happen by accident.

**Refuting the challenge of: Random Chance**

As the old saying goes - "If you torture the data long enough, it will confess to anything." Perhaps that's what's happening here? Are we getting these extraordinary results because there's just so much information that something profound is bound to pop out?

No. That might be a fair challenge if we had 'chanced upon' one solution to these various prophecies – *but dozens of correct solutions?* I've done the math for you and the odds of just a handful of these prophecies aligning *by chance* are as follows:

- Using fixed counting rules and allowing only a narrow ±1-year margin, the odds of **five** independent prophecies hitting the same target year purely by chance are about **1 in 6.7 trillion**.

- If **six** of them land there, the odds plunge to around **1 in 13.5 quadrillion**.

- Seven? Roughly **1 in 6.4 quintillion** - so unlikely as to be statistically absurd.

At that scale, "coincidence" stops being an explanation and becomes an act of faith in chaos.

**Refuting the challenge of: Non-exclusivity**

The opposite of the claim that these solutions are unique is that they're nothing special. This is the view that says "there are other, alternative, fulfilments that also fit perfectly – so this isn't a big deal."

The problem is, there *aren't* alternatives that fit perfectly. Sure there are rival interpretations – but invariably they focus on obscure years or localised events – not world-defining moments that are familiar to everyone. The rebirth of Israel and the restoration of Jerusalem are not niche coincidences; they're the two biggest events of modern biblical history. So yes, these solutions *are* special.

1. Probabilities computed using the binomial model for 7 independent trials with per-trial success probability p=3/Tp=3/Tp=3/T under the stated ±1-year counting rule. For p≈0.001481p\approx 0.001481p≈0.001481 (≈ 3/2026), the odds are: exactly 5 hits ≈ 1 in 6.7×$10^{12}$; exactly 6 hits ≈ 1 in 1.35×$10^{16}$; exactly 7 hits ≈ 1 in 6.39×$10^{19}$. See Ross (2014) for the binomial framework.

www.ingramcontent.com/pod-product-compliance
Lightning Source LLC
LaVergne TN
LVHW020516100826
845148LV00010B/1253
*9781738593316*